Focus on GRAMMAR 4

FOURTH EDITION

Marjorie Fuchs
Margaret Bonner

D1122517

ALWAYS LEARNING   PEARSON

**FOCUS ON GRAMMAR 4: An Integrated Skills Approach, Fourth Edition
Teacher's Resource Pack**

Pearson Education, 10 Bank Street, White Plains, NY 10606

Staff credits: The people who made up the *Focus on Grammar Teacher's Resource Pack* team, representing editorial, production, design, and manufacturing, are Iris Candelaria, Dave Dickey, Christine Edmonds, Nancy Flaggman, Ann France, Shelley Gazes, Lester Holmes, Stacey Hunter, Pamela Kohn, Theodore Lane, Christopher Leonowicz, Jennifer McAliney, Lise Minovitz, Jennifer Raspiller, Mary Perrotta Rich, Debbie Sistino, Ken Volcjak, Marian Wassner, and Adina Zoltan.

Contributing writers (Level 4): Carol Chapelle, Leslie Grant, Bethany Gray, Elizabeth Henly, Joan Jamieson, Xiangying Jiang, Hsin-Min Liu, Ruth Luman, Kathleen Smith, Raudy Lance Steele, Gabriele Steiner, Silvia Tiberio, BJ Wells, and Kevin Zimmerman.

Cover image: Shutterstock.com
Text composition: ElectraGraphics, Inc.
Text font: New Aster

ISBN 10: 0-13-216972-X
ISBN 13: 978-0-13-216972-1

Printed in the United States of America

1 2 3 4 5 6 7 8 9 10—V001—16 15 14 13 12 11

CONTENTS

INTRODUCTION

ABOUT THE TEACHER'S RESOURCE PACK

This Teacher's Resource Pack offers a multitude of ideas for working with the material for the new edition of *Focus on Grammar 4: An Integrated Skills Approach*. The Teacher's Resource Pack includes:

- a **Teacher's Manual** (including General Teaching Notes, Unit Teaching Notes, Student Book Audioscript, and Student Book Answer Key)
- a **Teacher's Resource Disc** (including interactive PowerPoint® grammar presentations, placement test, reproducible Unit and Part assessments, and test-generating software)

THE TEACHER'S MANUAL

The Teacher's Manual includes the following sections:

- **General Teaching Notes** (pages 1–13) provide general suggestions for teaching and assessing the activities in the Student Book. A Strategies for Teaching Grammar section offers a quick reference for some of the most common and useful grammar teaching techniques. A Frequently Asked Questions section answers some of the most common issues that teachers encounter.
- **Unit Teaching Notes** (pages 15–145) provide step-by-step instructions on how to teach each unit and supplementary "Out of the Box Activities." They also include suggestions on when to use activities and tests from **www.myfocusongrammarlab.com**, assignments from the workbook, and materials from the Teacher's Resource Disc.
- The **Student Book Audioscript** (pages 147–163) includes scripts for the Listening and Pronunciation exercises in the Student Book.
- The **Student Book Answer Key** (pages 164–210) includes answers for the exercises in the Student Book.

THE TEACHER'S RESOURCE DISC

The Teacher's Resource Disc includes additional teaching resources and a complete assessment program:

Teaching Resources

- **PowerPoint® Presentations** of all Grammar Charts for each unit in the Student Book offer an alternative teaching tool for introducing the grammar presentation in the classroom. For select units, animated theme-based grammar presentations provide interactive follow-up practice activities for the contextualized instruction of grammar.
- **Internet Activities** for each unit in the Student Book provide opportunities for students to expand on the content and interact with each other creatively and fluently.

Assessments

- **Placement Test** in PDF format can be printed and used to place students into the appropriate level. Along with this 40-minute test is an audioscript and an answer key in PDF format, and audio as an MP3 file.
- **Part and Unit Tests** in PDF format can be printed and used in class. These include Part Pre-Tests, Part Post-Tests, and Unit Achievement Tests. Also included are assessment audioscripts and answer keys in PDF format, and audio as MP3 files.
- **Test-Generating Software** provides thousands of questions from which teachers can customize class-appropriate tests.

GENERAL TEACHING NOTES

These notes are designed to guide you in teaching and assessing the recurring sections of the Student Book. Experimenting with the various options will enliven your classroom and appeal to students' different learning styles.

In the following section and in the Unit Teaching Notes, the icon ⏱ indicates an optional step you may wish to include if time permits.

PART OVERVIEW

The part overview previews the grammar and themes covered in each unit.

⏱ Part Pre-Tests

Before beginning each part, you may want to have students complete a diagnostic test. There are two options.

1. You can use the provided Part Pre-Tests to help you determine how well students know the material they are about to study in the next part of the Student Book. Since the material is usually new, students often score low on these tests. Each test takes about 50 minutes and includes about 60 items. The test begins with a listening exercise, includes several contextualized grammar exercises, and ends with an editing exercise. The tests are offered in two formats:
   - automatically graded tests at **www.myfocusongrammarlab.com**
   - reproducible tests on the Teacher's Resource Disc in this manual
2. You can use the **Test-Generating Software** on the Teacher's Resource Disc to create customized part diagnostic tests of any length. The test items focus on grammar.

UNIT OVERVIEW

The **Grammar Overview** portion of the Unit Overview (offered in this Teacher's Manual) highlights the most important grammar points of each unit. It also points out common grammar trouble spots for students. You may also find it helpful to review the Grammar Charts and Grammar Notes in the Student Book before teaching each unit. The **Unit Overview** previews the unit theme.

Step 1: Grammar in Context

Each unit opens with a reading selection designed to raise students' interest and expose them to the target grammar in a realistic, natural context. The selections include newspaper and magazine excerpts, websites, newsletters, advertisements, conversations, and other formats that students may encounter in their day-to-day lives. All of the texts are recorded and available on the audio program or at **www.myfocusongrammarlab.com**.

Before You Read (5 minutes)

This prereading activity creates interest, elicits students' knowledge about the topic, and encourages students to make predictions about the reading.

Suggested Procedure
1. Have the class look at the illustrations.
2. Ask students to respond to the questions. Ask these questions in a conversational way, instead of reading them from the book.
3. If you have time, you can ask additional questions to elicit students' personal experiences with or knowledge about the topic.

Option A
- Have the class read the questions in pairs or small groups and discuss their answers.
- Call on pairs to share their ideas with the class.

Option B
- Have students prepare questions about the topic in pairs.
- Call on pairs to share their questions and write them on the board.

Read (15–20 minutes)

Depending on the needs of your class, have students complete the reading in class or at home. Encourage students to read with a purpose and to read the passage once or twice without stopping to look up new words.

Suggested Procedure
1. Write the comprehension questions from the Unit Teaching Notes on the board. Establish a purpose for reading by going over the questions with the class. Have students think about the questions as they read and listen to the passage.

2. Play the audio and have students follow along in their books. Have them underline any new words.
3. Have students read the passage again silently, looking for answers to the questions.
4. ⏱ Have students discuss their answers with a partner or in small groups.
5. ⏱ Put students in pairs or small groups to discuss the reading. Invite them to respond to the reading in a way that is meaningful to them: What was most interesting? What did they learn? Refer to the Discussion Topics in the Unit Teaching Notes to help generate ideas for discussion.

Option A (At Home / In Class)
• Write the comprehension questions on the board for students to copy, or prepare them as a handout for students to take home.
• Go over the questions as a class and clarify as needed.
• Have students read the passage and answer the questions at home.
• ⏱ Have students write a few additional questions about the reading.
• Have students discuss their answers in pairs or small groups.
• ⏱ Have students take turns asking and answering the questions they prepared at home.
• Follow Steps 4–5 in the Suggested Procedure for Reading.

Option B (In Class)
• Have students work in pairs. Divide the reading in half, and have each student in the pair read one half.
• Have students summarize the information in their half of the reading for their partner.
• Follow Steps 3–5 in the previous notes for Suggested Procedure for Reading.

After You Read (10–20 minutes)

A. Vocabulary

Suggested Procedure
1. Have students find and circle the vocabulary words in the opening reading.
2. Elicit or explain the meanings of any new words.
3. Have students complete the vocabulary exercise individually or in pairs.
4. Call on volunteers to read their answers aloud.

B. Comprehension (5 minutes)
These post-reading questions help students focus on the meaning of the opening reading. In some cases, they may also focus on the target grammar without explicitly presenting the grammar point.

Suggested Procedure
1. Have students answer the questions individually.
2. Have students compare answers in pairs.
3. Call on volunteers to read their answers aloud.

Step 2: Grammar Presentation
There are many ways to teach the material in the Grammar Presentation. As a general rule, the more varied and lively the classroom activities, the more engaged students will be— and the more learning will occur. Approaching grammar from different angles and trying out different classroom management options can help increase student motivation.

The Strategies for Teaching Grammar on page 10 provide some guidelines to keep in mind when presenting a new grammar point. In addition to these strategies and the procedures outlined below, you can find specific suggestions for presenting the unit's grammar in the Unit Teaching Notes.

Grammar Charts (5–10 minutes)
The Grammar Charts provide a clear reference of all the forms of the target grammar. Students also become familiar with grammatical terminology. The charts also enable you to preteach some of the Grammar Notes that follow. You may want to use the charts in the PowerPoint® presentations on the Teacher's Resource Disc to help direct all of your students' attention to the same focus point. Select presentations also include colorful graphics, animations, and interactive practice activities that reinforce the grammar point.

Suggested Procedure
1. Using the examples from the charts and/ or the PowerPoint® presentations, draw students' attention to important features by pointing them out or asking questions.
2. Confirm students' understanding by engaging them in some recognition activities. Try one or two activities from Strategies 3, 4, 5, or 6 (page 10).
3. Get students to manipulate the new structures through substitution or transformation drills. See Strategy 7 (page 10) for an example of a transformation drill.
4. Encourage students to make sentences that are personally meaningful using the new grammar.

Option A
• Have students study the Grammar Charts at home.

- In class, follow Step 1 in the suggested procedure above.
- Move directly to the Grammar Notes section. Carry out Steps 2, 3, and 4 in the suggested procedure above using the notes together with the charts.

Option B
- Assign individual students responsibility for presenting a topic to the class by combining the information in the charts and the relevant notes. You may want to give them large pieces of paper and markers to prepare posters.
- ⏰ Meet with students individually. Allow them to practice their presentations and provide any coaching needed.
- Call on students to present their topics to the class. Encourage questions from the class.
- Choose appropriate practice activities from Strategies 4–8 (page 10) OR move directly to the Grammar Notes section.

Grammar Notes (20–30 minutes)
These notes provide helpful information about meaning, use, and form of the grammatical structures that students have encountered in the opening text and Grammar Charts. They include the following features to help students understand and use the forms.
- Where appropriate, timelines illustrate the meaning of verb forms and their relationship to one another.
- *Be Careful!* notes alert students to common errors among English-language learners.
- *Usage Notes* provide guidelines for using and understanding different levels of formality and correctness.
- References to related structures are provided below the notes.

Suggested Procedure
1. Have students read each note at home and/or in class.
2. For each note, write examples on the board and elicit or point out the key features of the form (see Strategy 1, page 10).
3. If possible, demonstrate the meaning of the grammatical form(s) by performing actions (see Strategy 6, page 10).
4. Model the examples and have students repeat after you so that they become comfortable with the appropriate stress, intonation, and rhythm.
5. Engage students with the grammar point by choosing appropriate activities, for example:
   - Elicit examples of the target structure.

- Confirm students' understanding by having them categorize examples or perform actions that illustrate the structure (see Strategies 5 and 6, page 10).
- Provide controlled practice with quick substitution or transformation drills (see Strategy 7, page 10).
- Encourage students to make personally meaningful sentences using the new grammatical forms.
- Use the Focused Practice exercises in the Student Book.
6. You may want to repeat Steps 2–5 for each Grammar Note.

Option
- Photocopy one set of Grammar Notes for each group of three or four students in your class. Cut them up so that the notes and their corresponding examples are not attached.
- Divide the class into groups of three or four students and give a set of cut-up notes to each group.
- Give students their task:
   1. Match the examples with the correct notes.
   2. Attach the notes and corresponding examples to a sheet of newsprint (a large piece of paper).
   3. Create and write more examples for each note.
- Circulate to ensure that students are on the right track and provide help as needed.
- Have students post their results around the room and invite groups to look at each other's work.
- Regroup as a whole class to answer questions.

Identify the Grammar (5–10 minutes)
This optional activity helps students identify the target grammatical structures embedded in the context of the opening text. This helps students learn the form, meaning, and usage of the target grammar point and helps you make a smooth transition from the Grammar Presentation to Discover the Grammar in Focused Practice.

Suggested Procedure
1. Choose an example of the target grammar from the opening text and write it on the board.
2. Point out that the target grammar is presented in boldfaced type in the opening text. Elicit more examples from students and write them on the board.

Ask students to identify the form, meaning, or usage of the grammar in the examples. Have them refer to the Grammar Charts and Grammar Notes if needed.

Step 3: Focused Practice

The exercises in this section provide practice for the structures in the Grammar Presentation. You may want to have students complete the corresponding exercise immediately after you have presented the relevant Grammar Note. Another option is for students to complete one or more of the exercises at home.

If you decide to have students complete the exercises in class, you can keep them motivated by varying the order of the exercises and/or the way you conduct them. Following are various ways of conducting the exercises.

Following the Student Book practice, you may want students to go to **www.myfocusongrammarlab.com** for automatically graded grammar exercises or to the workbook for traditional grammar exercises. You may want to assign these to be completed in class or as homework.

Discover the Grammar (5–10 minutes)

This opening activity gets students to identify the target grammar structures in a realistic context. It also sometimes checks their understanding of meaning. This recognition activity raises awareness of the structures as it builds confidence.

Suggested Procedure

1. Go over the example with the class.
2. Have students complete the exercise individually or in pairs.
3. Elicit the correct answers from the class.

Controlled Practice Exercises (5–10 minutes each)

Following the Discover the Grammar activity are exercises that provide practice in a controlled, but still contextualized, environment. The exercises proceed from simpler to more complex and include a variety of exercise types such as fill in the blanks, matching, and multiple-choice. Exercises are cross-referenced to the appropriate Grammar Notes so that students can review as necessary. Students are exposed to many different written formats, including letters, emails, websites, charts, and graphs. Many exercises are art-based, providing a rich context for meaningful practice.

Options

- Have students complete the exercises in pairs.
- If the exercise is in the form of a conversation, have students practice the completed exercise in pairs and role-play it for the class.
- When going over answers with students, have them explain why each answer is correct. For example, have them point to the appropriate rule in the Grammar Charts or Grammar Notes.
- Whenever possible, relate exercises to students' lives. For example, if an exercise includes a timeline, elicit from students some important events that have happened in their own lives.

Editing (10 minutes)

All units include an editing exercise to build students' awareness of incorrect usage of the target grammar structures. Students identify and correct errors in a contextualized passage such as a student's composition, a journal entry, or an email. The direction line indicates the number of errors in the passage.

Suggested Procedure

1. Have students read the passage quickly to understand its context and meaning.
2. Have students read the passage line by line, circling incorrect structures and writing in the corrections.
3. Have students take turns reading the passage line by line, saying the structures correctly. Alternatively, read the passage aloud to the class and have students interrupt you with their corrections.
4. There are also usually examples of the correct usage of the structures in each editing exercise. After students have identified the errors, point out the correct usages and ask why they are not errors.

Step 4: Communication Practice

These in-class exercises give students the opportunity to use the target structure in communicative activities. These activities help develop listening and speaking fluency and critical thinking skills, as well as provide opportunities for students to "own" the structures. As with the Focused Practice exercises, you may wish to vary the order of these activities to keep student motivation high.

Since there are many different exercise types in the Communication Practice section, specific ideas and guidelines are provided in the Unit Teaching Notes. Following are general suggestions for the main types of exercises. (**Note:** See the FAQs on pages 11–13 for more information about setting up pair work and group work.)

Following the relevant Student Book practice, you may want your students to go to **www.myfocusongrammarlab.com** for automatically graded Listening, Pronunciation, Speaking, and Writing exercises and activities. The Pronunciation exercises provide additional practice with the pronunciation feature from the Student Book; the Listening, Speaking, and Writing exercises and activities are on related topics.

Listening (10 minutes)

The first exercise in each Communication Practice section deals with listening comprehension. Students hear a variety of listening formats, including conversations, phone calls, voicemail messages, news reports, and interviews. After listening, students complete a task that focuses on the form or meaning of the target grammar structure. The recordings for the listening exercises are on the audio program and at **www.myfocusongrammarlab.com**, so students can complete the exercises outside of class.

Suggested Procedure

Before Listening
1. Explain the situation or context of the listening passage. Provide any necessary cultural information and preteach any vocabulary students may need to know. Since some of these words and phrases may appear in the listening, not in the exercise itself, refer to the audioscript at the back of this manual as necessary.
2. Have students read the exercise questions first so that they know what to listen for.

First Listening Task
1. Play the audio. Have students listen with their pencils down.
2. Play the audio again. Have students listen again and complete the task.
3. You may want to let students listen as many times as necessary to complete the task.

Second Listening Task
1. See Steps 1–3 from the first listening task for general instructions.

2. Have students compare their answers in pairs or small groups.

After Listening
1. Elicit answers for the exercise items and write them on the board. Answer any questions the students may have.
2. ⏱ Students listen a final time and review the passage.

Option A
- Rather than play the audio, read the audioscript aloud.
- Speak with a lot of expression and at a natural pace. Change positions and tone of voice to indicate who the speaker is.
- Draw stick figures on the board and label them with the characters' names. Then point to the appropriate character as you change roles.

Option B
- Make photocopies of the audioscript and hand it out to students.
- Play the audio recording and have students read along with it in chorus. Explain that this exercise will help them to hear and practice the rhythms, stresses, and clusters of English sounds.

Option C
Have students listen and complete the exercise at home or in a language lab.

Pronunciation (10 minutes)

The first or second exercise in each Communication Practice section deals with pronunciation. The pronunciation exercise generally focuses on the grammar presented in the unit or a difficult sound that appears in the opening text. It also prepares students for the speaking activities that follow. The recordings for the pronunciation exercises are on the audio program and at **www.myfocusongrammarlab.com**, so students can practice the exercises outside of class.

Suggested Procedure

First Task
1. Go over the instructions and point out the Pronunciation Note.
2. Play the audio.

Second Task
1. Play the audio. Have students close their eyes and notice the pronunciation feature.
2. ⏱ Play the audio again. Have students listen again and follow along in their books.

Third Task
1. Play the audio again.
2. Have students repeat in pairs or small groups. Circulate and monitor their pronunciation.
3. ⏱ Call on students to practice in front of the class.

Role Plays (10–20 minutes)
In these classroom speaking activities, students role-play a real-life encounter, such as a business meeting or an interview.

Advantages of Role Plays
• They are fun and motivating for most students.
• Role-playing characters often allows the more hesitant students to be more outgoing than if they are speaking as themselves.
• By broadening the world of the classroom to the world outside, role playing allows students to use a wider range of language than less open-ended activities.

Suggested Procedure for Role Plays
1. When possible, bring in props or costumes to add drama and fun.
2. Review the task so students understand what is required.
3. Perform a sample role play with a volunteer in front of the class.
4. Divide the class into the suggested groupings and give them a fixed time limit for completing the task.
5. Have students write a script for the role play. Then have them write key words on cards and perform the role play using the cards as prompts. Or have students plan the action without a script and present it extemporaneously.
6. While students are working, circulate among the pairs or groups to answer students' questions and help them with the activity.
7. Have various pairs or groups perform their role plays in front of the class. If possible, record the role plays for students' own listening or viewing.

Information Gaps (10–20 minutes)
Information Gaps are designed to encourage communication among students. In these activities, each student has a different set of information. Students have to talk to their partners to solve a puzzle, draw a picture (describe and draw), put things in the right order (describe and arrange), or find similarities and differences between pictures.

Advantages of Information Gaps
• Like role plays, Information Gaps are motivating and fun.
• There is a real need for communication in order to combine the information to solve a problem and complete the task.
• Information sharing allows students to extend and personalize what they have learned in the unit.

Suggested Procedure
1. Explain how the Student A and Student B pages relate to each other (how they are different or similar).
2. Refer students to the examples and to any language provided.
3. Divide the class into pairs (Student As and Student Bs). Have them position themselves so that they cannot see the contents of each other's books.
4. Tell the Student Bs what page to turn to. Circulate to check that they are looking at the correct page.
5. Have students read their separate instructions. Check comprehension of the task by asking each group, "What are you going to do?"
6. Remind students not to show each other the contents of their pages.
7. As students are working, circulate to answer individual questions and to help students with the activity.

Games (10–20 minutes)
Games are designed to encourage communication among students. In these activities, students compete in pairs or small groups to complete a task such as guessing something or winning points.

Advantages of Games
• They can create a fun and stress-free environment.
• They involve friendly competition and keep students engaged.
• They can improve students' ability to speak in a communicative way.

Suggested Procedure
1. Go over the instructions to make sure students understand the task.
2. Have students model the example or provide one of your own.
3. Have students carry out the instructions. Circulate and help as needed.
4. Go over answers as a class or ask who won.
5. ⏱ Write on the board any sentences you noticed using incorrect grammar. Have the students correct them as a class.

Surveys / Interviews (10–20 minutes)

In these classroom speaking activities, students ask and answer interesting and meaningful questions about their personal preferences, opinions, feelings, and experiences.

Advantages of Surveys / Interviews

- They are fun and motivating for most students.
- By broadening the world of the classroom to the students' real lives, surveys and interviews allow students to use a wider range of language than less open-ended activities.
- Interviews can help students build confidence in their ability to ask and answer extemporaneous questions.
- Interviews provide students with an opportunity to learn about each other.

Suggested Procedure

1. Review the task so students understand what is required.
2. Model the survey or interview with a student in front of the class.
3. Divide the class into the suggested groupings and give them a fixed time limit for completing the task. If you have a mixed-level class, you may want to vary the groupings based on the specific activity. Sometimes you may want groups to have both higher and lower level students. Other times you may want groups to be homogeneous.
4. While students are working, circulate among the pairs or groups to answer students' questions and help them with the activity.
5. Have students share what they have learned about each other with the class.

Discussions (10–20 minutes)

In these classroom speaking activities, students express their ideas about a variety of topics. These activities include Picture Discussions and other types.

Advantages of Discussions

- They help students move from speaking accuracy to speaking fluency.
- They help students develop critical thinking skills as they explore the pros and cons of an issue.
- They help students build confidence in their ability to express their opinions on a variety of topics.

Suggested Procedure

1. Go over the instructions so students understand the task.
2. Elicit or present useful language and write it on the board.
3. Have two or three students model the example discussion.
4. Divide the class into the suggested groupings and give them a fixed time limit for completing the task.
5. Circulate while the students discuss the topic. Help with language or monitor their grammar as needed.
6. Ask volunteers from each group to summarize the discussion or conclusions.
7. ⏱ Write on the board any sentences you noticed using incorrect grammar. Have students correct them as a class.

Writing (15–25 minutes)

These activities give students the opportunity to develop their writing skills and provide additional practice using the target grammatical structures. There is a variety of realistic formats, including paragraphs, essays, letters, and journal entries. The themes are related to material covered in the unit so that students already have some preparation for the writing task.

Suggested Procedure

Prewriting (in class)

1. Go over the instructions with the class.
2. Write some questions on the board, and have students work in pairs or small groups to brainstorm ideas for the writing assignment. The Unit Teaching Notes provide suggestions for questions you might write on the board.
3. Call on volunteers to answer the questions as you write key words and phrases on the board.
4. Brainstorm ideas for the assignment with the class and write them on the board.
5. Encourage students to include grammar and vocabulary from the unit in their assignment.

Writing and Editing (at home)

1. Have students compose a draft of the writing assignment at home.
2. Have students use the Editing Checklist to correct their work.

Wrap-Up (in class)

1. Have students submit the draft to you or share it with a partner in class.
2. You can comment on the following features:
    - Content: Has the student responded appropriately to the task? Are the main points well supported?

- Organization: Is the flow of ideas logical and effective?
- Accuracy: Are there any major errors in the grammar points taught in the unit? (At this stage, you may want to focus your comments on errors related to the target grammar point. Circle the errors, but let students make the corrections. If students are providing feedback to each other, encourage them to focus on content and organization.)
3. ⏱ For longer assignments, have students complete a second draft. When you check these drafts, point out any further areas needing correction, concentrating especially on errors in the target grammar point or grammar points from a previous unit.
4. Have students prepare their final draft at home.

Option A

Have students share their final drafts in class. For example:
- Post students' work on the class bulletin board.
- Publish their work on a website or in a class magazine.
- Have students exchange papers with a partner.
- Have students read their papers aloud in small groups or to the class.

Option B

Have students put the final drafts of their written work in a folder, or portfolio, which you can review at the end of the course. This will allow students and you to see the progress they have made.

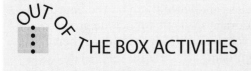
OUT OF THE BOX ACTIVITIES

One or more activities for further practice (in the Teacher's Manual only) can be found at the end of every unit in the Unit Teaching Notes. These activities offer additional communicative practice with the target structure of the unit. Most can be done in class with no before-class preparation. The activities often involve a combination of skills, such as grammar and speaking or grammar and writing.

Unit Review

The last section of each unit of the Student Book is a review feature that can be used as a self-test. These exercises test the form and use of the grammar content presented and practiced in that unit. They give students a chance to check their knowledge and to review any problematic areas before moving on to the next part. An answer key is provided at the back of the Student Book.

Suggested Procedure
1. Have students complete the exercises at home and check their answers in the Answer Key.
2. During the next class, go over any remaining questions students may have.

Option
- Have students complete the exercises in class. Give them a time limit of 10 minutes and circulate as they work.
- Have students use the Answer Key to check and correct their answers in pairs. Or you can go over the answers as a class.

⏱ Unit Achievement Tests

After the Unit Review, you may want to have students complete an achievement test. There are two assessment options.
1. You can use the provided **Unit Achievement Tests** to help you assess students' knowledge of the specific grammatical topics presented in the unit. If students have mastered the material presented in the unit, they should answer most of the questions correctly. Each test takes about 30 minutes and includes about 30 items. The test begins with a listening exercise, includes two or three contextualized grammar exercises, and ends with an editing exercise. The tests are offered in two formats:
   - automatically graded tests at **www.myfocusongrammarlab.com**
   - reproducible tests on the Teacher's Resource Disc in this manual.
2. You can use the **Test-Generating Software** on the Teacher's Resource Disc to create customized unit achievement tests of any length. The test items focus on grammar.

⏱ Part Post-Tests

At the end of each part, you may want to have students complete an achievement test. There are three assessment options.

1. You can have students go to **www.myfocusongrammarlab.com** for an automatically graded review. Students can complete the review on a computer in class, at home, or in a language lab. Each review takes about 25 minutes and includes about 30 items. The test focuses on grammar.

2. You can have students take the provided Part Post-Tests to help you determine how well students have mastered the material they have studied in that part of the Student Book. If students have mastered the material presented in the part, they should answer most of the questions correctly. Each test takes 50 minutes and includes about 60 items. The test begins with a listening exercise, includes several contextualized grammar exercises, and ends with an editing exercise. The tests are offered in two formats:
   - automatically graded tests at **www.myfocusongrammarlab.com**
   - reproducible tests on the Teacher's Resource Disc in this manual.

3. You can also use the **Test-Generating Software** on the Teacher's Resource Disc to create customized part achievement tests of any length. The test items focus on grammar.

From Grammar to Writing

The From Grammar to Writing section at the end of each Part of the Student Book integrates grammar presented in the units. It also goes beyond the grammar in the unit and gives additional information about writing in English. This information may include mechanics (e.g., punctuation, capitalization), cohesion (e.g., compound sentences, time clauses), format (e.g., business letters, reports), and rhetoric (e.g., expressing an opinion). Each section gives students a specific writing task and begins with prewriting strategies. These strategies may include the use of graphic organizers, such as charts, outlines, and Venn diagrams. Students are also given example texts that serve as a model for the writing task. Text types include both formal and informal writing, such as personal letters, business letters, essays, summaries, emails, and descriptive paragraphs. The section concludes with peer review and editing.

Depending on your class's needs, you may want to have students go to an additional From Grammar to Writing exercise at **www.myfocusongrammarlab.com**.

Suggested Procedure

Prewriting

1. Explain the prewriting task. Where appropriate, provide a model for students on the board or on an overhead.

2. Have students complete the prewriting task in pairs or small groups. Circulate and answer any questions.

Composing and Correcting

1. Go over the instructions to make sure students understand the task.

2. Have students complete the writing assignment at home.

3. In class, complete the peer review portion of the task. Circulate while students are working together to make sure they are on task and to provide appropriate feedback.

4. ⏱ Have students revise their writing and turn in the second draft to you. You may wish to correct these drafts and to include the drafts as part of the students' writing portfolios.

STRATEGIES FOR TEACHING GRAMMAR

1. Develop awareness

• Ask questions that help students become aware of the form of the structure. For example, for the contrast between the simple past and past progressive (Student Book, page 17, Grammar Note 3), ask: "What was he doing?" *(He was driving.)* Ask what verb form is used in that question and answer *(past progressive)*. Then ask: "What happened while he was driving?" *(He saw an accident.)* Ask what verb form is used in this question and answer *(past)*. Ask for the difference between the verb forms used for *drive* and *saw. (One happened over a period of time; the second took only an instant.)* When he saw the accident, it interrupted his driving, so the simple past is used with *saw.* How do we decide which verb should be in the past progressive? *(We determine which action is interrupted by the other.)*

• Compare information in the Grammar Charts. For example, the comparison of the past with the present perfect and the present perfect progressive (Student Book, page 28) shows a difference in the use of auxiliary verbs in questions (both *wh-* and *yes / no*) and in the short answer form. Ask: "What do we need to add to the simple past in order to make a *wh-* and *yes / no* question or a short answer?" *(did / didn't)* "What do both present perfect and present perfect progressive take to form a *wh-* and *yes / no* question or short answer?" (has / have *or* hasn't / haven't, *which are already in the verb*)

2. Present meaning

Show the meaning of a grammatical form through a classroom demonstration. For example, to illustrate the use of present perfect progressive, you could show a picture of a person carrying grocery bags full of food *(He / she has been shopping)*.

3. Identify examples

Ask students to go to the Grammar in Context section and label examples in the reading passage with grammatical terms.

4. Generate examples

Find examples that could fit into the Grammar Charts. One way to do this is to photocopy and enlarge the Grammar Chart. White out the targeted structures and draw a blank line for each missing word. Make copies and distribute them to students in pairs or small groups. Have students fill in the blanks, using examples from the reading. Then generate more examples.

5. Show understanding by categorizing

Check comprehension of a grammatical principle by asking students to label multiple examples appropriately. For example, students can label verbs "present" or "future" or they can label examples "correct" or "incorrect."

6. Show understanding by performing actions

Check comprehension of the meaning of a grammatical form by having students follow instructions. Ask students, for example, to think of and perform a set of actions that they could describe using the past progressive and the simple past. (Some grammatical forms lend themselves better than others to this strategy.)

7. Manipulate forms

Have students manipulate the examples in the Grammar Charts to practice the form. Drills such as substitution or transformation help students to build fluency. For example, in Unit 6 (Student Book, pages 82–83), you might have students transform future perfect statements into future perfect questions and then provide short affirmative answers, followed by negative answers:

A: I'll have earned interest by then.
B: Will you have earned interest by then?
A: Yes, I will.
B: No, you won't!

Similar drills can be done with the future perfect progressive on page 83.

8. Personalize

On page 93 in Exercise 9, students are asked about their goals. Have two or three students share a personal goal with the rest of the class:

A: I want to finish my thesis by next June.
B: I want to buy a car by the end of the summer.

Have other students paraphrase these goals, using the target verb form:

C: By next June, [A] will have finished his thesis.
D: By the end of the summer, [B] will have bought a car.

9. Repeat, reinforce

Students need to be exposed to new grammar many times in order to internalize it completely. You can first present a new structure on the board, then point it out in the book, then have students use it in an informal oral exercise, then do a written exercise in pairs, and finally review the same structure in homework. Varying the content and focus of these activities will keep students interested, and the grammar will be reinforced almost automatically.

FREQUENTLY ASKED QUESTIONS (FAQs)

1. When should I have students work in pairs or groups rather than individually or as a class?

Varying your classroom organization to suit particular activity types will result in more effective and more interesting classes. Many students are not accustomed to working in pairs or groups, so it is important to use these groupings only when they are most beneficial.

- **Whole-class teaching** maximizes teacher control and is especially good for:
  - presenting information, giving explanations, and providing instructions
  - showing material in texts and pictures or on audio or video recordings
  - teacher-led drills (such as substitution or transformation) or dictations
  - reviewing answers or sharing ideas after students have completed an activity
  - enabling the whole class to benefit from teacher feedback to individuals
- **Students working individually** allows quiet, concentrated attention and is most effective for:
  - processing information or completing a task at the students' own pace
  - performing writing tasks

For objective exercises such as fill-in-the-blank, matching, multiple-choice, and editing, vary your class organization to keep student motivation high. Students can sometimes complete these exercises individually, and sometimes they can work with a partner.

- **Students working in pairs** maximizes student speaking time, breaks up the routine and "teacher talk," and is ideal for:
  - information-gap activities
  - role plays and interviews
  - writing and/or reading dialogues
  - predicting the content of reading and listening texts
  - comparing notes on what students listen to or see
  - checking answers
  - peer assessment

Pair-work can also be very effective for completing objective exercises such as fill-in-the-blank, matching, multiple-choice, and editing.

- **Students working in groups** creates ideal conditions for students to learn from each other and works well for:
  - generating ideas
  - pooling knowledge
  - writing group stories
  - preparing presentations
  - discussing an issue and reaching a group decision

2. How should I set up pair work and group work?

Here are a few different techniques:

- **Streaming.** Grouping students according to ability or participation has certain advantages.
  - **ability:** Grouping weaker and stronger students together allows more able students to help their less fluent classmates.
  - **participation:** If you see that some students participate less than others, you could make a pair or group of weak participants. By the same token, you can also put especially talkative students together.
- **Chance.** Grouping students by chance has many benefits, especially if it results in students working with varied partners. You can group students by chance according to:
  - **where they sit:** Students sitting next to or near one another work in pairs or groups. This is the easiest option, but if students always sit in the same place, you will want to find other ways of grouping them.
  - **the "wheels" system:** Half the class stands in a circle facing outward, and the other half stands in an outer circle facing inward. The outer circle revolves in a clockwise direction, and the inner circle revolves in a counterclockwise direction. When you tell them to stop, students work with the person facing them. This is a very effective way to have students engage in meaningful repetition, such as asking the same question of many different partners.
  - **assigned letters:** Assign each student a letter from A to E. Then ask all the As to form a group, all the Bs to form a group, and so on.

- **birthdays:** Students stand in a line in the order of their birthdays (with January at one end and December at the other). The first five students form one group, the second five students another group, and so on.
- **native language:** If possible, put students in groups or pairs with others who don't share a native language. This helps create an "English-only" classroom.

3. How can I make activities more successful?
Before the activity:
- **Motivate students and explain the purpose.** Make it clear that something enjoyable or interesting is going to happen. Explain the rationale for the activity. Make sure that students understand that the purpose of the activity is to help them practice what they have learned and encourage them to participate.
- **Provide clear instructions.** Explain what students should do in every step of the activity. Have students paraphrase or demonstrate the task to be sure they understand it.
- **Demonstrate.** Show the class what is supposed to happen in an activity. This might involve asking a student to demonstrate the activity with you or having two students role-play in the front of the room.
- **Provide a time frame.** It is helpful for students to know how much time they have and exactly when they should stop. Approximate times are given for all the activities in this Teacher's Manual.

For open-ended activities, such as the Internet activity or writing exercises, you will also want to:
- **Stimulate thinking.** When there are choices for students to make, it is often helpful to set up small-group and / or whole-class brainstorming sessions to define the focus and / or content of their task.
- **Prepare language.** Review grammar and vocabulary that students may need to complete the task. This can be done as a follow-up to a brainstorming activity where you elicit ideas and write key language on the board.

During the activity:
- **Observe students.** Walk around the room watching and listening to pairs or groups.
- **Provide assistance as needed.** (See FAQ 5 for suggestions on giving feedback and correcting errors.)

After the activity:
- **Elicit student responses.** For some activities, you may ask for volunteers or call on students to share some of their ideas with the class. For other types of activities, a few pairs or groups can be asked to role-play their discussions to demonstrate the language they have been using.
- **Provide feedback.** In many cases, this is most conveniently done in a whole-class setting. It may be preferable, however, for you to meet with individuals, pairs, or groups. While the principal focus in a grammar class is language use, it is also important to acknowledge the value of students' ideas. (See FAQ 5 below for suggestions on feedback and error correction.)

4. What can I do to encourage students to use more English in the classroom?
It is perfectly natural for students to feel the need to use their first language in an English class. There are a number of actions that teachers can take to promote the use of English.
- **Set clear guidelines.** Some teachers in monolingual classes find that activities such as providing vocabulary definitions, presenting a grammar point, checking comprehension, giving instructions, and discussing classroom methodology are best done in the students' native language.
- **Use persuasion.** Walk among the students during speaking activities and say things such as "Please speak English!" or "Try to use English as much as possible." This helps to ensure that students will speak English most of the time.

5. What's the best approach to giving feedback and correcting errors?
Here are two considerations:
- **Be selective in offering correction.** Students can't focus on everything at once, so concentrate first on errors relating to the target grammar point and grammar points from units previously studied, as well as any errors that interfere with communication. Whether you respond to other errors depends on your judgment of students' readiness to take in the information. If you see a teachable moment, seize it. Rather than correct every error individual students make in the course of activities, it is generally preferable to note commonly occurring mistakes and give a short presentation to the class at the end of the activity.

- **Recasting.** If a student makes an error—for example, "I *didn't came* to class yesterday because I was sick"—you can recast it as, "You *didn't come* to class yesterday because you were sick?" The student ideally notices the difference and restates the original sentence: "Right. I didn't come to class yesterday because I was sick." This process can be effective because the student has the opportunity to self-correct an error that is still in short-term memory. As a variation, you can restate but stop, with rising intonation, right before the potential error: "You didn't . . . ?"

6. What can I do to accommodate different learning styles?
Focus on Grammar recognizes different styles of learning and provides a variety of activities to accommodate these different styles. Some learners prefer an analytical, or rule-learning (deductive), approach. Others, especially younger learners, respond best to an inductive approach, or exposure to the language in meaningful contexts. Indeed, the same students may adopt different styles as they learn, or they may use different styles at different times.

As teachers, we want to help the students in our classes who prefer to follow rules become more able to take risks and plunge into communicative activities. We also want to encourage the risk-takers to focus on accuracy. *Focus on Grammar* provides the variety to ensure that students achieve their goal: to learn to use the language confidently and appropriately.

UNIT TEACHING NOTES

PART I OVERVIEW

PRESENT AND PAST: REVIEW AND EXPANSION

UNIT	GRAMMAR FOCUS	THEME
1	Simple Present and Present Progressive	Names
2	Simple Past and Past Progressive	First Meetings
3	Simple Past, Present Perfect, and Present Perfect Progressive	Hobbies and Interests
4	Past Perfect and Past Perfect Progressive	Musicians

Go to **www.myfocusongrammarlab.com** for the Part and Unit Tests.

Note: PowerPoint® grammar presentations, test-generating software, and reproducible Part and Unit Tests are on the *Teacher's Resource Disc.*

UNIT 1 OVERVIEW

Grammar: SIMPLE PRESENT AND PRESENT PROGRESSIVE

Students will learn the meanings and practice the uses of the simple present and present progressive.

- The simple present describes events, situations, or activities not connected to time restrictions; it is also used for general statements of truth or fact.
- The present progressive describes what is happening right now or in the extended present with action verbs.
- In sentences with both simple present and present progressive, the present describes the situation and the present progressive describes the continuing action.

Theme: NAMES

Unit 1 focuses on language that we use to introduce ourselves and talk about our names.

- Nicknames are sometimes a short version of a name (*Liz* for *Elizabeth*). They can also describe a personality trait (*Tiger*) or a physical trait (*Red, Tiny*).
- A *mouthful* is something that is not easy to pronounce.

Step 1: Grammar in Context (pages 2–3)

See the general suggestions for Grammar in Context on page 1.

Before You Read

- Have students look at the chart and circle any last names they have heard before.
- Have students discuss the questions in pairs. For Question 1, encourage students to think about what their name reveals about their identity. For Question 2, ask them to write a short list of common first and last names.
- Call on pairs to share their answers with the class.

Read

- To encourage students to read with a purpose, write these questions on the board:
  1. What is the woman's name? (*Yevdokiya Ivanova*)
  2. Where is she from? (*Russia*)
  3. Where do middle names come from in her country? (*from the father's first name*)
  4. What is the man's name? (*Jorge Santiago García de Gonzalez*)
  5. Where is he from? (*Mexico*)
  6. Where do last names come from in his country? (*from the father's last name and the mother's last name*)
- Have students read the text. (Or play the audio and have students follow along in their books.) Then call on students to share their answers with the class.
- Have students discuss the following questions in small groups:
  1. Does your family have a naming tradition (e.g., naming a child after a grandparent)? Explain.
  2. Why do some people change their names? How do you feel about your name? Do you like your name? Explain.

After You Read

A. Vocabulary

- Have students find and circle the vocabulary in the text. Encourage them to use the surrounding context to figure out the meaning.
- Have students compare answers in pairs. Then go over answers as a class.

- ⏱ To reinforce the vocabulary, ask the following questions and call on students to answer them.
  1. What names are in style at the moment?
  2. Do you know anyone who uses a title? What title does he or she use?
  3. Have you ever learned anything at an institute? If yes, what?
  4. Do you know if either of your parents convinced the other to give you your name? Explain.
  5. Do you actually *like* your name?

B. Comprehension

- Have students complete the exercise individually. Encourage them to underline the information in the text that supports their answers.
- Have students compare answers in pairs. Then call on different students for answers.

Go to **www.myfocusongrammarlab.com** for an additional reading, and for reading and vocabulary practice.

Step 2: Grammar Presentation (pages 4–5)

See the general suggestions for Grammar Presentation on page 2.

Grammar Charts

- Write the following on the board:
  1. I speak Spanish at home.
  2. I'm speaking French now.
  3. He works in the city center.
  4. He's working from home today.
- Ask: "How do we form the simple present?" (*base form of verb or base form of verb* + s) Ask: "How do you form the present progressive?" (*form of* be + -ing *form of verb*)
- Restate Items 1 and 2 from above using negative forms. Say: "I don't speak Spanish at home. I'm not speaking French now." Write the negative statements on the board. Ask: "How do you form the negative simple present?" (*form of* do + not + *base form of verb*) "How do you form the negative present progressive?" (*form of* be + not + -ing *form of verb*)
- Change Items 1 and 2 into questions. Ask: "Do I speak Spanish at home? Am I speaking French now?" Write the questions on the board. Then ask: "How do you form *yes / no* questions in the simple present?" (*form of* do + *subject* + *base form of verb*) "How do you form *yes / no* questions in the present progressive?" (*form of* be + *subject* + -ing *form of verb*)

- To explain *wh-* questions, write on the board:
  Where does he work?
  Where is he working today?
- Ask: "How do you form *wh-* questions in the simple present?" (wh- *word* + *form of* do + *subject* + *base form of verb*) "How do you form *wh-* questions in the present progressive?" (wh- *word* + *form of* be + *subject* + -ing *form of verb*) Point out that questions that ask about the subject do not need auxiliaries (*do* or *does*) or question word order (inversion).

Grammar Notes

Note 1

- Have students find examples of the simple present in Dusya's profile. (*In my country people always call their teachers by a first and a middle name.*) Have students use the simple present in sentences about the use of names, titles, and nicknames in their own country.
- Have students find sentences in the opening reading that express continuing action. (*I'm living and working in Canada. I'm studying English here.*) Have students make up imaginary examples about what Dusya and Jorge are doing these days. Examples: *Dusya is working in a department store. Jorge is studying hard. He's also going out a lot with his new friends.*
- Point out that the simple present expresses things that generally happen and the present progressive expresses things that are happening now. Give an example: *I wear slippers at home, but I'm wearing shoes now.* Ask random students: *What do you wear at home / are you wearing now? What language do you speak at home / are you speaking now?*

Note 2

- Go over the list of non-action verbs in Appendix 2, page A-2. Ask students which verbs they use frequently and write them in a column on the board.
- Write the column heads *Emotions, Mental States, Perceptions, Appearance*, and *Possession* on the board.
- Ask pairs to find three verbs for each heading and make a sentence with each verb. Call on pairs to share their sentences.

Note 3

- Write things that are unchanging on the board (*the Earth, the sun, the moon*). Write an example sentence using a scientific or physical fact on the board:
  The sun rises in the east.
  Then have students work in pairs to write more sentences using the simple present. (*The Earth moves around the sun. / Ice floats on water.*)

- Point out that general statements and specific statements can use simple present and present progressive to show a contrast between what usually happens and what is happening now. (*It doesn't rain much in the desert, but it's raining in Phoenix today.*)

Note 4
- Point out that we can use the simple present to describe books or movies we have read or seen. Give an example: *In the film* Titanic, *a luxury ship hits an iceberg.* Ask students to identify the verb in the simple present tense in the example. (*hits*)
- Have students make one-line statements in the simple present about recent movies they have seen. (*The main actor plays the part of an unusual doctor.*)
- ⏱ Have pairs take turns asking and answering the question "Have you seen any good movies lately? Which one?" Then ask students to comment on books or stories they have read.

Note 5
- Write on the board:
  He's always telling jokes.
- Ask: "What tense does the example use?" (*the present progressive*) Point out that we can use the present progressive with *always* to express a repeated action.
- Have students think of both positive and annoying habits of people they know, and write examples of things "they are always doing." (*Carolina is always smiling. / My brother is always talking in class. / The teacher is always correcting my spelling.*)

⏱ **Identify the Grammar:** Have students identify the grammar in the opening reading on page 2. For example:
  My name **is** . . .
  I'm from Russia . . .
  . . . this year **I'm living** and **working** . . .
  . . . it**'s coming back** into style.
  My classmates **find** it difficult to pronounce . . .

Go to **www.myfocusongrammarlab.com** for grammar charts and notes.

Step 3: Focused Practice (pages 6–7)
See the general suggestions for Focused Practice on page 4.

Exercise 1: Discover the Grammar
- Go over the examples with the class. Ask: "What is the first underlined item an example of?" (*the present continuous*) "And the second?" (*the simple present*)

- Have students complete the exercise individually and compare answers in pairs. Then elicit the correct answers from the class.

Exercise 2: Statements and Questions
- Complete the first item with the class. Ask: "Why is *call* the correct answer?" (*because the simple present is used to describe what people generally do*)
- Have students read the conversations and complete the exercise in pairs. Call on pairs to read the conversations aloud.

Exercise 3: Editing
- Have students read the post. Ask: "What's his name?" (*Peter Holzer*) "Where's he from?" (*Germany*) "Where's he now?" (*in Miami*) "What's he doing there?" (*studying English*) "Why has he posted this message?" (*because his teacher asked students to write a profile*)
- Have students find and correct the mistakes individually and compare answers in pairs.
- Go over answers as a class. Have students explain why the incorrect structures are wrong.
- ⏱ Ask students to point out examples of correct usages of the present progressive and the simple present.

Go to **www.myfocusongrammarlab.com** for additional grammar practice.

Step 4: Communication Practice (pages 8–11)
See the general suggestions for Communication Practice on page 4.

Exercise 4: Listening
A
- Have students discuss the photos in pairs or small groups. Ask: "What do you notice about each person? Which names in the box fit the pictures?" Encourage students to guess the names and write them in pencil.
- Play the audio. Have students listen and check their guesses.

B
- Have students read the sentences silently. Then play the audio. Encourage students to take notes.
- Elicit the answers and have students explain their choices. (*For example, in Item 1, the man / woman says that giving girls names like Alex is the style now.*)
- ⏱ Have students discuss in small groups why people's names fit / don't fit them.

Exercise 5: Pronunciation

A
- Play the audio. Have students read along as they listen to the Pronunciation Note.
- Write on the board:
  I usually work from home, but this week I'm working at the office.
- Ask: "Which words would you stress in the example?" (*usually, home, this week, office*)

B
- Play the audio. Have students listen and mark the stressed words.

C
- Have students listen and repeat the statements. Then have students play both roles as they practice the conversations with a partner.

Exercise 6: Find Someone Who . . .

A
- Go over the example with the class. Explain anything that is unclear.
- Encourage students to use the present progressive to identify the person they were asked about. Give an example: *That's him over there. He's standing by the window. / He's talking with the woman in blue.*

B
- Elicit get-to-know-you questions and write them on the board. Examples: *What kind of movies do you like? Where is your family living now? Are you reading a good book?*
- Encourage students to make notes of their classmates' answers when they ask their questions.

C
- Have students use their notes as a guide to introduce their classmates to the class.

Exercise 7: Writing

A
- Write these questions on the board to help students generate ideas and elicit the necessary vocabulary:
  Where are you from?
  Do you use a title?
  Where does your first name / middle name / last name come from?
  Do you have a nickname? If yes, how did you get it?
  What are your interests?
  What are your plans for the future?

- Have students make notes for each question. Then have them use Exercise 3 on page 7 as a model as they write.

B
- After students write their profile, have them correct their work using the Editing Checklist.

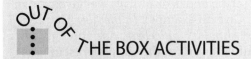

OUT OF THE BOX ACTIVITIES

Writing and Speaking
- Have students work in groups to create a "profile" for a famous person. Encourage them to include information about the person's name, what he / she usually does, and what he / she is doing these days. Circulate and give help as needed.
- Have groups present their profile to the class. Have the class guess the identity of the famous person.

Writing and Speaking
- Have students bring in family (or other) photos.
- Write these questions on the board:
  What is the background for the picture?
  What do you see in the picture?
  What is happening in the picture?
- Have students describe their pictures in small groups.

Go to **www.myfocusongrammarlab.com** for additional listening, pronunciation, speaking, and writing practice.

Note
- See the *Focus on Grammar Workbook* for additional in-class or homework grammar practice.

Unit 1 Review (page 12)

Have students complete the Review and check their answers on Student Book page UR-1. Review or assign additional material as needed.

Go to **www.myfocusongrammarlab.com** for the Unit Achievement Test.

Grammar: SIMPLE PAST AND PAST PROGRESSIVE

Students will learn the meanings and practice the use of the simple past and the past progressive—specifically when these verb forms appear in sentences with two clauses.

- The simple past describes an action that was completed at a specific time in the past.

- The past progressive describes an action that was in progress at a specific time in the past.

- In sentences with both the simple past and the past progressive, the past progressive describes an action that was interrupted by another action; the simple past describes the interrupting action.

Theme: FIRST MEETINGS

Unit 2 focuses on language that we use to talk about important life events, such as meeting people who became influential in our lives.

Step 1: Grammar in Context (pages 13–15)

See the general suggestions for Grammar in Context on page 1.

Before You Read

- Have students look at the photos and discuss the questions in pairs. Ask students to make notes for each answer.
- Call on pairs to share their answers with the class.
- ⏱ Ask students to name other famous couples they know and share information about them.

Read

- To encourage students to read with a purpose, write these questions on the board:
  1. Why are these couples special? *(because they accomplished great things)*
  2. Did they all get married? *(yes)*
  3. Who had to go through very hard times? When? Were they able to recover? *(Maria Sklodowska, when her husband was hit by a horse-drawn carriage and died; Frida Kahlo, when she had a serious bus accident; Steffi Graf, when a fan stabbed her opponent on the court. They all managed to recover.)*
- Have students read the text. (Or play the audio and have students follow along in their books.) Then have students answer the questions. Call on students to share their answers with the class.

- Have students discuss one or both of the following topics in small groups:
  1. All four couples described in the readings overcame great obstacles to find success. Who do you know who has faced difficulties on their way to achieving their goals?
  2. Ask students to talk about their personal or public heroes. Here is an example to use as a model: "Christopher Reeve, who played Superman in the movies, was famous for his strength and grace. One day while riding his horse, Reeve fell and became paralyzed from the neck down. Although he no longer looked like a hero in the physical sense, he became a Superman in a different way: He spoke for paralyzed people everywhere who didn't have a voice. When Christopher Reeve died in 2004, he was mourned by all as a true American hero."

After You Read

A. Vocabulary

- Have students find and circle the vocabulary in the text. Encourage them to use the surrounding context to figure out the meaning.
- Have students compare answers in pairs. Then go over answers as a class.
- ⏱ To reinforce the vocabulary, use the words in the box in questions about the text:
  1. Which couple from the article isn't real? *(Clark Kent and Lois Lane)*
  2. What stories was Lois interested in covering? *(stories about Superman)*
  3. Why are Rivera and Kahlo considered influential artists? *(because they changed people's minds about art in Mexico)*
  4. What happened to one of Steffi Graf's opponents? *(She was stabbed by a fan.)*
  5. Who was able to recover from a serious traffic accident? *(Frida Kahlo)*
  6. Who won a prize for their research? *(Maria Sklodowska and Pierre Curie)*

B. Comprehension

- Have students complete the sentences. Encourage them to underline the information in the text that supports their answers. Then have students compare answers in pairs.
- Call on students to read the answers aloud. Encourage them to support their answers with information from the text.

Go to **www.myfocusongrammarlab.com** for an additional reading, and for reading and vocabulary practice.

Step 2: Grammar Presentation (pages 16–18)

See the general suggestions for Grammar Presentation on page 2.

Grammar Charts

- Write on the board:
  1. Marie left Poland.
  2. She moved to Paris.
  3. She was planning to return to Poland.
  4. Marie and her husband were doing research.
- Have the class name the regular verb. *(moved)* Ask: "How do we form the simple past of regular verbs?" *(base form of verb + -d or -ed)* Have the class name the irregular verb. *(left)* Ask: "How do we form the simple past of irregular verbs?" *(There is no rule. They have to be learned.)*
- Erase the verbs in the examples and replace them with blanks. Have students make example sentences negative. *(Marie didn't leave Poland. She didn't move to Paris. She wasn't planning to return to Poland. Marie and her husband weren't doing research.)* Ask: "How do we form the negative simple past?" *(didn't + base form of verb)* Ask: "How do we form the negative past progressive? (wasn't / weren't + -ing form of verb)*

Grammar Notes

Note 1

- Write on the board:
  Brad met Jenny in London in 2008.
- Have students study the example. Ask: "Does the simple past describe a completed action?" *(yes)* "Do we know when the action happened?" *(yes, in 2008)* Remind students that we use the simple past for completed past actions that happened at a definite past time.
- Have pairs take turns asking and answering *what time* questions about common daily activities. *(What time did you get up yesterday? What time did you leave the house?)* Then have several students write their partner's responses on the board. *(Kim got up at 5:30. Kim left the house at 6:30.)*
- ⏱ To review irregular simple past verbs, drill the class on some of the more common verbs listed in Appendix 1, pages A-1–A-2. Give a base form and have students quickly respond with the past.

Note 2

- Write on the board:
  Brad was working in London in 2008.

- Have students study the example. Ask: "What was Brad doing in London in 2008?" *(He was working.)* "Was the action completed or in progress at the time?" *(It was in progress.)* Remind students that we use the past progressive for actions in progress at a definite past time.
- Ask: "What were you doing last night at 8:30?" Ask students to respond with complete sentences, and have other students stand at the board and write them down. For example:
  At 8:30 last night,
     Ines was eating dinner.
     Carlos was working.
     Jonah and Yuri were watching TV.
     Susan was doing homework.
- Draw attention to the *Remember* note. Ask: "Why is it incorrect to say *Marie was having a degree in physics?* (*because* have *is a non-action verb so it cannot be used in the progressive*)
- Elicit additional examples of non-action verbs not usually used in the progressive *(love, remember, want, see, seem)*. Refer students to Appendix 2, page A-2 for a list of non-action verbs.

Note 3

- Write on the board:
  The guests arrived while Jane was cooking. =
     When the guests arrived, Jane was cooking.
- Have students study the examples. Then ask: "Which action was in progress?" *(Jane was cooking.)* "What interrupted that action?" *(the arrival of the guests)* Remind students that we use the past progressive and the simple past to express an action in progress (past progressive) that was interrupted by another action (simple past).
- Point to the example on the board. Explain that *while* is usually used with the past progressive and *when* is usually used with the simple past.
- Have students work in small groups to think of sentences using the two tenses. Have them act out their sentences for the class. As students share their sentences, write a few of them on the board. *(While Tim was walking in, his cell phone rang.)*

Note 4

- Draw the timeline from the Student Book on the board. Point to the word *now* and say: "Right now I'm talking and you're listening." Then point to the word *past* and say: "A minute ago, you were talking and I was writing on the board."

- Write on the board:

  When | you were talking, I was writing.
  While |

- Have students study the examples. Then ask: "Do *when* and *while* have the same meaning in the examples?" *(yes)* Point out that we can use either *when* or *while* for two past actions in progress.
- Have pairs think up and act out simultaneous actions for the class to describe. *(While Alicia was reading a book, Natasha was polishing her nails.)*

Note 5
- Have students study the *Be Careful!* note.
- Write on the board:

  When my roommate called his parents, I was making breakfast.

- Ask: "Which action happened first?" *(I was making breakfast.)* To indicate the order of the actions, write 1 above the main clause and 2 above the *when* clause:

         2   1

  When my roommate   I was making
  called his parents,   breakfast.

- Point out that in the example, *when* means "at the time."
- Then write a new example on the board:

  When my roommate called his parents, I left the house.

- Ask: "Which action happened first?" *(My roommate called his parents.)* To indicate the order of the actions, write 1 above the *when* clause and 2 above the main clause:

         1   2

  When my roommate   I left the house.
  called his parents,

- Explain that in this example, *when* means "after."
- Ask pairs of students to create additional examples and write them on the board, numbering the clauses to show the order of the actions.

Note 6
- Have students study the *Remember* note.
- Ask: "In writing, what do we need if the time clause comes first?" *(a comma at the end of the time clause)* Point out that when speaking, we pause.

⏱ **Identify the Grammar:** Have students identify the grammar in the opening reading on page 13. For example:
  . . . the two **were working** . . .
  . . . Lane **wasn't** interested in . . .
  . . . she **wanted** to cover stories . . .
  . . . she **changed** her mind.

When Kent **proposed**, Lane **accepted**. What **were** these other super couples **doing** when they **met**?

Go to **www.myfocusongrammarlab.com** for grammar charts and notes.

Step 3: Focused Practice (pages 18–21)
See the general suggestions for Focused Practice on page 4.

Exercise 1: Discover the Grammar
- Have students read what Lucky says and underline the past progressive and past simple verbs. *(was riding, saw)* Then ask: "Why is the statement false?" *(because Lucky was already on his bike when he saw Elena)*
- Have students complete the exercise individually and compare answers in pairs. Then elicit the correct answers from the class.

Exercise 2: Simple Past or Past Progressive
- Go over the example with the class. Ask: "Why is *saw* the correct answer?" *(because it expresses a completed past action)*
- Have students read the conversations for meaning before choosing their answers. Then have them compare answers in pairs.
- To review as a class, call on pairs to read the conversations aloud.

Exercise 3: Simple Past or Past Progressive
- Ask: "Why is *were you looking* the correct answer?" *(because it expresses an action in progress)*
- Have students read the conversations for meaning before choosing their answers. Encourage students to decide whether the verbs express completed actions or actions in progress to help them choose their answers.
- Have students compare answers in pairs. Then call on pairs to role-play the conversations.

Exercise 4: Connecting Clauses: *When* or *While*
- Have students study the timeline and find actions that were in progress for some time. Ask: "What things did Monique do in her life that lasted for some time?" *(living in Australia, studying medicine, working, writing a book)* "When did each action start and finish?" *(She moved to Australia in 1993 and she still lives there, she started medical school in 2000 and got her degree in 2004, and she started a book in 2008 and finished it the following year.)*

- Go over the examples with the class. Ask the class to express the same facts in two ways. *(When she got married, she was studying medicine. While she was studying medicine, she got married.)*
- Have students compare answers in pairs. Then go over answers as a class.

Exercise 5: Editing
- Have students read the email quickly to find out what it is about.
- Ask: "What important things did Monique do in her life?" *(She wrote a book on women's health issues, she got an interview on TV, she got a contract to write a second book, she quit her job and became a full-time writer.)* "Why did she remember her friend Crystal?" *(While she was writing a chapter about rashes, she remembered the time when Crystal fell into a patch of poison ivy and got a terrible rash.)*
- If necessary, explain the meaning of *rash* (a lot of red spots on someone's skin caused by an illness or a reaction to food, plants, or medicine) and *poison ivy* (a bush with an oily substance on its leaves that makes your skin itch after you touch it).
- Review the example. Then have students find and correct the mistakes individually and compare answers in pairs.
- To review as a class, have students explain why the incorrect structures are wrong.
- ⏱ Ask students to point out examples of correct usages of the simple past and the past progressive.

Go to **www.myfocusongrammarlab.com** for additional grammar practice.

Step 4: Communication Practice (pages 22–24)
See the general suggestions for Communication Practice on page 4.

Exercise 6: Listening
A
- Have students describe what is happening in each series of pictures. Then have them list the differences between the pictures. *(Series a starts and ends when it's sunny; series b starts and ends during a storm; series c starts during a storm and ends when it's sunny.)*
- Play the audio. Have students listen and choose the correct series of pictures.

B
- Have students read the statements before listening. Encourage them to take notes while listening to support their answers. Play the audio.

- To review as a class, have students support their answers with information they remember. Example: *They didn't work for a TV news show. They worked for a newspaper.*
- ⏱ Have pairs retell the story as they look at the pictures. Encourage students to use the past progressive and the simple past.

Exercise 7: Pronunciation
A
- Play the audio. Have students read along as they listen to the Pronunciation Note.
- Write on the board:
  While we were sleeping, the phone rang.
- Ask the class: "When saying the sentence on the board, where should we pause?" *(after sleeping)* "Where does the voice rise and fall?" *(in sleeping)* "Where does it fall without rising?" *(in rang)*

B
- Play the audio. Have students listen and complete the exercises.
- Have students practice the conversations with a partner. Then have students play both roles. Remind students to pause after time clauses and use the correct rising and falling intonation.

Exercise 8: What About You?
- Point out the contrast between the simple past and the past progressive in the example. Ask: "What was the person doing?" *(walking to class)* "What happened while she was doing that?" *(a guy came over and asked her for the time)*
- Give or elicit additional examples of short anecdotes using simple past and past progressive. Example: *I was waiting for the elevator last night when a young woman and her little boy came down the hall. She was pushing him in his stroller, and they were singing. When the little boy saw me, he stopped singing and said, "Hi. My name's Toby and this is my mommy, Lauren."*
- Circulate as students work in small groups. Encourage students to make their stories more interesting by varying clause order and sentence length. Then ask a few students to share their stories.

Exercise 9: Ask and Answer
- Elicit examples of important life events *(moving to a new place, getting married, going on a trip)*. Then have students write their timelines. Students may refer to the timeline on page 20 for ideas.

- Encourage students to ask at least three questions about their partner's timeline.
- Call on several students to tell the class what they learned about their partners.

Exercise 10: Writing

A
- Write the following questions on the board to help students generate ideas and elicit vocabulary:
  Who is an important person to you?
  Why is this person important to you?
  Where and when did you meet this person?
  What were you doing when you met him / her? What was he / she doing?
  What were you thinking about when you first met?
- Have students make notes for each question and then use them as a guide as they write their paragraphs.

B
- Have students correct their work using the Editing Checklist.

OUT OF THE BOX ACTIVITIES

Speaking
- Ask students to name famous couples (for example: *Romeo and Juliet, Victoria and Albert, Tristan and Isolde, Antony and Cleopatra, Bonnie and Clyde*).
- Create a role play card for each person named. Write the name of the person and information about that person on the card.
- Distribute one card to each student. Each student takes on the role of the person on the card. They take turns giving clues about themselves to find their partners. The other students guess who they are. For example:
  A: I was working on radioactivity, and you were working with me.
  B: That's right! We won a Nobel Prize.
  C: They're Pierre and Marie Curie.

Writing and Speaking
- Bring in some newspaper or magazine pictures of events that happened in the recent past (for example, a weather disaster, a blackout, a sports event).

- Give pairs of students one picture and ask them to write three sentences about it, combining the simple past and past progressive. Call on students to read their sentences to the class.
- ⏱ Alternatively, have pairs or groups create a news story about their picture and present it to the class. Record "the news" with the class.

Go to **www.myfocusongrammarlab.com** for additional listening, pronunciation, speaking, and writing practice.

Note
- See the *Focus on Grammar Workbook* for additional in-class or homework grammar practice.

Unit 2 Review (page 25)

Have students complete the Review and check their answers on Student Book page UR-1. Review or assign additional material as needed.

Go to **www.myfocusongrammarlab.com** for the Unit Achievement Test.

UNIT 3 OVERVIEW

Grammar: SIMPLE PAST, PRESENT PERFECT, AND PRESENT PERFECT PROGRESSIVE

Students will learn the meanings of and practice the uses of the simple past, present perfect, and present perfect progressive—specifically when more than one of these verb forms appears in a single sentence or situation.

- The simple past describes an action that occurred in the past or was completed at a specific time in the past.
- The present perfect and present perfect progressive describe an action that began in the past and is just ending or might continue into the future.
- Note that these differences in verb forms do not exist in other languages, and therefore students will not find equivalents in their native languages.

Theme: HOBBIES AND INTERESTS

Unit 3 focuses on language that we use to talk about free time activities that we have done or have been doing lately.

Step 1: Grammar in Context (pages 26–27)

See the general suggestions for Grammar in Context on page 1.

Before You Read

- Have students look at the photo and discuss the questions in pairs.
- For Question 2, encourage students who have participated in an adventure sport to tell their partners where and when that was and what they liked / disliked about it. For Question 3, ask students to write a list of the things they do and make notes of the reasons they like them.
- Call on students to share their answers with the class.

Read

- To encourage students to read with a purpose, write these questions on the board:
  1. Who has written this web page? *(Jason Barricelli)*
  2. Where is he from? *(Australia)*
  3. What sport does he do? *(skydiving)*
  4. How did he learn to love adventure sports? *(from his family)*
  5. What kind of person has Jason always been? *(a work-hard, play-hard kind of guy)*
  6. Who is skydiving with him in the photo? *(his girlfriend / fiancée)*
- Have students read the text. (Or play the audio and have students follow along in their books.)
- Have students answer the questions. Call on some students to share their answers with the class.
- In pairs or small groups, have students discuss one or all of the following questions:
  1. What kind of sports do you like? What kind of sports did you like when you were a child? What kind of sports did you like 10 years ago?
  2. Have you ever gone skydiving or sailing? Have you ever been to Australia? Have you traveled anywhere else?
  3. Would you like to go skydiving, bungee-jumping, or motorcycle riding? Why or why not?

After You Read

A. Vocabulary

- Have students find and circle the vocabulary in the text. Encourage them to use the surrounding context to figure out the meaning.

- Have students complete the exercise individually and compare answers in pairs. Then go over answers as a class.
- ⏱ To reinforce the vocabulary, ask students to write down:
  1. A person they know who is engaged.
  2. An example of an extreme sport.
  3. A good place to celebrate an important event.
  4. A fantastic person they know.
  5. A historic event in their life.
- Call on students to share their answers in full sentences, and write some of them on the board.

B. Comprehension

- Have students choose the answers individually. Encourage students to underline the information in the text that supports their answers. Then have them compare answers in pairs.
- Call on individual students to say an answer. Have students support their answers. *(For example, for Item 1, the event is unfinished because Jason says he's almost finished.)*

Go to www.myfocusongrammarlab.com for an additional reading, and for reading and vocabulary practice.

Step 2: Grammar Presentation (pages 28–30)

See the general suggestions for Grammar Presentation on page 2.

Grammar Charts

- Write on the board:
  They celebrated their engagement.
- Have students name the verb in the example. *(celebrated)* Ask: "What tense is it in? *(simple past)*
- Write on the board:
  He has moved to Sydney.
  They have gotten engaged.
- Ask students to name verbs in the examples. *(has moved, have gotten)* Underline them as students say them. Then ask: "How do we form the present perfect?" (have / has + *past participle*)
- Write on the board:
  They have been working hard.
  He has been building a site.
- Ask students to name the verbs in the examples. *(have been working, has been building)* Underline them as students say them. Then ask: "How do we form the present perfect progressive?" (have / has + been + -ing *form of verb*)

Grammar Notes

Note 1

- Write on the board:
  Mike lived in Toronto for one year.
- Have students study the example. Then ask: "Does Mike still live in Toronto?" *(no)* Point out that we use the simple past for completed past actions. To show that the time is finished, draw the following timeline on the board. Leave the timeline on the board to use when reviewing Note 2.

past	2005	now		future

Canada

- Write a new example with two time expressions with the same meaning. **Note:** Change the number of years as necessary to make a time expression with the same meaning as *in 2005*.

[Five] years ago In 2005	Mike lived in Canada. He didn't live here.

- Remind students that we use the simple past with specific past time expressions. Have students call out the time expressions in the example. *(five years ago, in [2005])*
- Ask individual students: "When did you move to this city?" "When did you start learning English?" "Where did you get that [jacket]?"
- ⏱ Do a quick teacher-directed oral review of the principal parts of common irregular verbs such as *choose, wear, drive, read, grow, fly, see, buy, give, shake, speak.* (See Appendix 1, pages A-1–A-2.) You can model this by saying, "drink, drank, drunk" as you count off the three parts on your fingers, then prompting a student with "choose . . . ?" and holding up one and then two and three fingers until the student responds with "choose, chose, chosen."

Note 2

- Write on the board:
  1. Anna has lived in Brazil for two years. = Anna has been living in Brazil for two years.
- Have students study the examples. Then ask: "Does Anna still live in Brazil?" *(yes)* Point out that we use the present perfect for actions that started in the past and are not completed. To show that the time is unfinished, draw the following timeline on the board. **Note:** Change the year 2008 as necessary to include a year that is two years from now. Have students compare it with the timeline in Note 1. **Note:** Leave the example and the timeline on the board.

past	2008	now	future

Brazil

- Point out that both examples have the same meaning. Explain that present perfect and present perfect progressive are connected to the present and can mean the same thing with certain verbs like *live, work,* and *study.* Give new examples: *I have worked here for [six months]. I have been working here [for six months].*
- Remind students that there are two ways to express the information shown on the timeline. Write the following examples on the board. Change the year as necessary.
  2. Anna has lived in Brazil since [2008]. = Anna has been living in Brazil since [2008].
- Have students compare the examples in Items 1 and 2. Point out that they mean the same thing.
- Point out that we use *for* with a length of time and *since* with a point in time.
- Have pairs take turns asking each other: "How long have you lived here? How long has your family lived in their house? How long have you studied English?" Encourage students to answer each question twice, once with *for* and once with *since.*
- ⏱ Be sure that your students understand that the same situation can be described with different verbs and different tenses: *I came here five years ago. I've been here for five years.* To provide practice, have pairs ask each other questions about the same situation, using both tenses:
  A: When did you come here?
  B: I came here three years ago.
  A: So you've been here for three years.

  A: When did you buy that jacket?
  B: I bought it last year.
  A: So you've had it for a year.

Note 3

- Write on the board:
  Joy has bought a car.
- Have students study the example, then ask: "Is the action finished?" *(yes)* "Do we know when it happened?" *(no)* Point out that we use the present perfect for completed past actions when the time is not known or not important. Also point out that the action expressed in the present perfect can affect the present. Say: "From now on, Joy is going to drive to work."

- To explain the difference between the present perfect and the present perfect progressive, write on the board:
  1. Jason has painted a mural.
  2. Jason has been painting a mural.
- Have students study the examples. Then ask: "In Example 1, has Jason finished painting the mural?" *(yes)* "And in Example 2?" *(no)* Point out that the present perfect <u>without</u> *for* or *since* shows that something is finished, either recently or at some unspecified time in the past, while present perfect progressive shows that something is still going on.
- Have pairs practice the following conversation:
  A: What's your favorite book?
  B: My favorite book is _____.
  A: How many times have you read it?
  B: I've read it _____ times.
  A: And what have you been reading lately?
  B: Lately I've been reading _____.

Note 4
- To compare the use of the present perfect and the simple past with finished and unfinished time periods, write on the board:
  a. Finished time period + simple past
  b. Unfinished time period + present perfect (the action might happen again)
  c. Unfinished time period + simple past (the action won't happen again)

  1. He has traveled twice this year.
  2. He traveled twice this year.
  3. He traveled twice last year.
- Have students match the patterns with the examples. *(a–3; b–1; c–2)*
- Point out that the time of day sometimes determines whether simple past tense or present perfect is appropriate. We use the present perfect to ask about breakfast before noon: *Have you eaten breakfast?* After noon (lunchtime), we would ask in the past tense: *Did you eat breakfast this morning?*

🕐 **Identify the Grammar:** Have students identify the grammar in the opening reading on page 26. For example:
  I've been building this website for a while . . .
  I've written this page to introduce myself.
  I've always **been** . . .
  I **grew up** in Perth . . .

Go to **www.myfocusongrammarlab.com** for grammar charts and notes.

Step 3: Focused Practice (pages 30–33)

See the general suggestions for Focused Practice on page 4.

Exercise 1: Discover the Grammar
A
- Go over the examples with the class.
- Have students complete the exercise individually and compare answers in pairs. Elicit the correct answers from the class.

B
- Ask: "Why is the first statement false?" *(because the text says they have always loved the outdoors)*
- Encourage students to underline the information in the text that supports their answers.
- Have students compare answers in pairs. Then go over answers as a class.

Exercise 2: Simple Past, Present Perfect, or Present Perfect Progressive
- Go over the example with the class. Ask: "Why is *has been making* the correct answer?" *(because the action is not finished so the present perfect progressive is needed)*
- Have students read the article for meaning before choosing their answers.
- Have students complete the exercise individually and compare answers in pairs. Then go over answers as a class.

Exercise 3: Simple Past, Present Perfect, or Present Perfect Progressive
- Go over the example with the class. Ask: "Why is *has been taking* the correct answer?" *(because it shows that the activity is unfinished; she's still taking photos)*
- Have students read the paragraphs for meaning before writing their answers.
- Call on students to read the sentences aloud.

Exercise 4: Editing
- Have students read the email message quickly to find out what it is about. Ask: "What does Lise want to know?" *(if Erden will climb Mt. Erciyes again, how he has communicated with people on the different continents he has been to, if he studied other languages before his trip, and if he has received many emails since he started his project)*
- Have students find and correct the mistakes individually and compare answers in pairs.
- To review as a class, have students explain why the incorrect structures are wrong.
- 🕐 Ask students to point out examples of correct usages of the present perfect, present perfect progressive, and simple past.

Go to **www.myfocusongrammarlab.com** for additional grammar practice.

Step 4: Communication Practice (pages 33–36)

See the general suggestions for Communication Practice on page 4.

Exercise 5: Listening

A

• Have students read the statements before listening. Then play the audio.

B

• Go over the meanings of each of the items on the list. Have students expand the phrases into sentences. For example, *renew passport* means "send the passport to the Passport Office with a completed application form, a money order, and new photographs."

• To go over answers, have students say full sentences. *(Jason has picked up the plane tickets.)*

• (!) Have pairs take turns asking and answering questions about the items on the list. Examples: "Have you ever renewed your passport?" "When did you renew your passport?" "How long does it take to renew a passport?" "Have you traveled often?"

Exercise 6: Pronunciation

A

• Play the audio. Have students read along as they listen to the Pronunciation Note.

• Ask: "Are these reductions used in questions or in statements?" *(in questions)*

B

• List the sentence starters on the board:
  has he
  did he
  have you
  did you

• Play the audio. Have students listen and complete the conversations.

C

• Have students play both roles.

Exercise 7: What About You?

• Go over the example with the class. Ask students to underline examples of simple past, present perfect, and present perfect progressive verbs.

• Ask students to name their hobbies and interests. Write a vertical list on the board. After each hobby or interest, write some vocabulary words that will help students in asking and answering questions about them. *(sewing: shirt, skirt, pattern, zipper, thread, sewing machine)*

• Provide some sentence cues on the board: Have you ever _____? I have _____ since I was (age).

• Have students work in small groups. Encourage students to keep the conversation going. Call on students to report to the class on the hobbies they discussed.

• (!) Ask students who have easily portable hobbies (knitting or stamp-collecting, for example) to bring examples of their hobbies to class.

Exercise 8: Ask and Answer

A

• Tell students about your own plans for the week: "Last week I had so many plans. I wanted to clean my desk, to write to my grandmother, to pay my bills, and to go shopping. But I didn't do anything."

• Ask students: "How about you? What plans did you have for last week?"

• Have students write a list of their plans for this week. Be sure students include things they did and things they still haven't done.

B

• Go over the example. Encourage students to use the verb forms they have learned in this unit. Give additional examples: *Last week I wanted to clean my room. I have been cleaning it a little each day this week. Last week I planned to take my coat to the cleaners, but I haven't done it yet.*

• Have students discuss their plans with a partner. Then have students say what they found out about what their partners have / haven't accomplished.

Exercise 9: Writing

A

• Write the following questions on the board to help students generate ideas and elicit the necessary vocabulary:
  Where do you live? How long have you lived there? Where else have you lived?
  What have you done that other people might be interested in?
  What have you been doing recently?
  What are your plans for the next few years?

• Have students make notes for each question. Have them use the notes as a guide as they write their paragraphs.

B

• Have students correct their paragraphs using the Editing Checklist.

OUT OF THE BOX ACTIVITIES

Speaking

- Make a list of time expressions and write them on the board: *last week, since I was born, for 10 years, that long, last month, since last month, for two weeks.*
- Have pairs play a game: Student A makes a sentence using a time expression from the board. *(I have lived in this country since I was born.)* Student B makes a new sentence using the same time expression and true information about himself / herself. *(I have liked music since I was born.)* Then Student B says a new sentence, and so on.
- **Option:** Make a simple board game with the time expressions in numbered boxes on a sheet of paper. You will need a distinctive button for each student and a die. Students throw the die, advance to a box, and make up an original sentence with the time expression specified in that box and appropriate grammar. Give a prize for originality or outrageousness.

Listening and Speaking

- Bring in a DVD cued to a scene. Play the scene. Then ask other students to guess what the history of the character is, up to right before the scene. *(He's only been living in New York for a short time. He just came home from a party. He just got some bad news.)*
- Have students bring in pictures of a famous person who's been in the news lately and give a short report about what the person has done, has been doing, just did, and/or has never done.

Go to **www.myfocusongrammarlab.com** for additional listening, pronunciation, speaking, and writing practice.

Note

- See the *Focus on Grammar Workbook* for additional in-class or homework grammar practice.

Unit 3 Review (page 37)

Have students complete the Review and check their answers on Student Book page UR-1. Review or assign additional material as needed.

Go to **www.myfocusongrammarlab.com** for the Unit Achievement Test.

UNIT 4 OVERVIEW

Grammar: PAST PERFECT AND PAST PERFECT PROGRESSIVE

Students will learn the meanings and practice the uses of the past perfect and the past perfect progressive verb forms in comparison with the simple past; the contractions involved in conversational use; and the uses of *yes / no* questions, *wh-* questions, and positive and negative short answers for both verb forms.

- The past perfect is used in contrast with the simple past; the past perfect action happened before the past action.
- The past perfect progressive is also used in contrast with the simple past, but it describes continuing action before (or by) a specific point of time in the past.

Theme: MUSICIANS

Unit 4 focuses on language that we use to talk about musicians, their careers, and their personal lives.

Step 1: Grammar in Context (pages 38–40)

See the general suggestions for Grammar in Context on page 1.

Before You Read

- Write on the board:
  composer
  classical music
  orchestra
  conductor
- Discuss the meaning of the words as a class. *(composer: a person who writes music; classical music: music written by composers such as Mozart; orchestra: a group of musicians who play different instruments; conductor: a person who directs the musicians of an orchestra)*
- Have students look at the photo and read the title and the first paragraph. Have students discuss the questions in pairs. Encourage them to make notes for each question.
- Call on students to share their answers to the questions with the class.

- Ask: "Why is the article called 'The People's Conductor'?" *(because he's very popular, because people like him, because people around the world show interest in him)*

Read
- To encourage students to read with a purpose, write the following questions on the board:
  1. Who is the man in the photo? Where is he from? *(Gustavo Dudamel. He's from Venezuela.)*
  2. What instrument could he play when he was a child? *(the violin)*
  3. What changed his life? *(participating in El Sistema, a program that teaches music to poor children)*
  4. What happened in the Hollywood Bowl in 2009? *(He conducted the Los Angeles Philharmonic in a free concert that was attended by thousands of people.)*
  5. What did he do to help young people? *(He set up a program in Los Angeles modeled on El Sistema.)*
- Have students read the text. (Or play the audio and have students follow along in their books.) Then call on students to share their answers with the class.
- Have students discuss one or both of the following topics:
  1. Many people have to overcome problems before success. Dudamel's story is one example. Have pairs take turns sharing stories about being successful in spite of health or personal problems. Encourage students to share stories about celebrities or people they know.
  2. Many successful people don't forget their roots and work hard to help others. Dudamel is an example. Have pairs take turns sharing stories they may know about successful people who work hard to help people in need.

After You Read

A. Vocabulary
- Have students find and circle the vocabulary in the text. Encourage them to use the context to figure out the meaning.
- Have students complete the exercise individually and compare answers in pairs. Then go over answers as a class.

- To reinforce the vocabulary, use the vocabulary words in questions about the article. Ask the class: "What does El Sistema do to transform the lives of poor kids?" *(It teaches them music.)* "Do kids have to pay to participate in the program?" *(No, it's free.)* "How old was Dudamel when he signed his first contract as a conductor?" *(28)* "What did people do at the end of the October 3 concert?" *(They applauded enthusiastically.)* "Are Dudamel's fans people of the same age and ethnic background?" *(No, his fans are a mix of ages and ethnic backgrounds.)*

B. Comprehension
- Have students complete the exercise individually. Encourage students to find the events in the text before putting them in order.
- Have students compare answers in pairs. Then go over answers as a class.

Go to **www.myfocusongrammarlab.com** for an additional reading, and for reading and vocabulary practice.

Step 2: Grammar Presentation (pages 40–42)

See the general suggestions for Grammar Presentation on page 2.

Grammar Charts
- Write on the board:
  By 2009, he had signed his first contract.
- Ask students to name the verb form in the example. *(had signed)* Underline it as students say it. Point out that it is the past perfect. Then ask: "How do we form the past perfect?" (had + *past participle*) Point out that *had* can be contracted. Circle *he had* on the board and write *he'd* below the circle. Say: "By 2009, he'd signed his first contract."
- Write on the board:
  They had been waiting for three hours.
- Ask students to name the verb form in the example. *(had been waiting)* Underline it as students say it. Point out that it is the past perfect progressive. Then ask: "How do we form the past perfect progressive?" (had +been + -ing *form of verb*)

Grammar Notes

Note 1
- Write on the board:
  By 2009, I had bought my car.
- Have students study the example. Then ask: "Did I buy my car before or after 2009? *(before)*

- Point out that we use the past perfect to show what happened before a specific time in the past.
- Have students say what they had or hadn't done by 2009. *(By 2009, I had left my hometown. / I had studied English here for four years. / I hadn't found a job. / I had started school here. / I hadn't met you.)*
- ⏱ Write a past month on the board, for example, *June this year.* Ask various students: "How many parties had you been to by June this year? How many exams had you had? Had you taken a vacation? What things had you bought?"

Note 2
- Write on the board:
  When I came here, | I had studied English for five years.
  | I had been studying English for five years.
- Point out that in the first example *(had studied)* the emphasis is on the amount of time *(five years)*, whereas in the second *(had been studying)* the emphasis is on the process.
- Remind students that the past perfect progressive is not usually used with stative verbs. For example: *I had always wanted to succeed.* (NOT: *I had always been wanting to succeed.*)
- Write on the board:
  Her eyes were red. She had been crying.
- Have students study the example, then ask: "Was she crying the moment I saw her?" *(no)* "Had she stopped long before or a short while before?" *(a short while before)* "How do you know?" *(because her eyes were red)*
- Point out that we use the past perfect progressive for finished actions that have just ended. Also point out that we can often see the results of the action (her eyes were red).

Note 3
- Draw a timeline on the board, noting several years. Write an event for each date. For example:

2000	2004	2008	2010
learned to drive	came to this city	bought a pet	got a job

- Write on the board:
  I had learned how to drive when I came to this city.

- Have students study the timeline and the example. Then ask: "What did I do first—learn how to drive or come to this city?" *(learn how to drive)* "What verb form do we use for the action that happened first?" *(the past perfect)* "And for the one that happened next?" *(the simple past)*
- Have students create their own timeline with important dates / years in their lives.
- Then have students work in pairs to create sentences comparing a past and a "more past" event, as shown in the example. Remind them to use the past perfect and the simple past.
- To explain the use of the past perfect progressive with the simple past, write a new example on the board:
  I had been saving for a new computer when I won one in a raffle.
- Point out that we can also use the past perfect progressive with the simple past to show the relationship between two past events.
- To explain sentences with *after, before,* and *as soon as,* write on the board:
  After I had passed my driving test, I bought a car.
  After I passed my driving test, I bought a car.
- Have students study the examples, then ask: "Do both sentences use the same verbs forms?" *(No, one uses the past perfect and the other uses the simple past.)* "Do they have the same meaning?" *(yes)*
- Point out that with the words *after, before,* and *as soon as,* the past perfect is not really necessary because the difference in time between the two events is clear, so the simple past can be used for both events.
- To provide practice, have pairs write sentences with *after, before,* and *as soon as* plus the past perfect. Then have students restate the sentences using the simple past.

Note 4
- Write on the board:
  By + time, + past perfect (progressive)
  By + time clause, + past perfect (progressive)
- Point out that we often use the past perfect and past perfect progressive with *by* plus a time or *by* plus a time clause. Give two examples: *By 2006, I had visited 10 different countries. / By the time I was four, I had been abroad twice.* Have students create their own sentences.
- Point out that we often use the past perfect with *already, yet, ever, never,* and *just.* Give examples: *When he arrived, I had already / just gone to bed. / When you came to this country, had you ever lived away from home? When the bell rang, I hadn't finished yet.*

- Draw attention to the *Be Careful!* note. Ask: "Why is that last example incorrect?"
- Have students create their own examples in pairs.

(!) **Identify the Grammar:** Have students identify the grammar in the opening article on page 38. For example:

> . . . he **had** already **started** taking music lessons by the young age of four.
> . . . young Dudamel **had been hoping** to take up the same instrument.
> Many of these kids **had been getting** into pretty serious trouble . . .
> . . . by the time he was 15, he **had become** the conductor . . .

Go to **www.myfocusongrammarlab.com** for grammar charts and notes.

Step 3: Focused Practice (pages 43–49)

See the general suggestions for Focused Practice on page 4.

Exercise 1: Discover the Grammar
- Go over the examples with the class. Ask: "Why is the description false?" *(because the statement says that he had already won the competition)*
- Have students complete the exercise individually and compare answers in pairs.
- Go over the correct answers as a class.

Exercise 2: Past Perfect: Statements with *Already* and *Yet*
- Have students study the timeline.
- Go over the example with the class. Point out the position of *yet* between *hadn't* and the past participle. Elicit the position of *already*. *(between* had *and the past participle)*
- Have students compare answers in pairs. Then go over answers as a class.
- (!) Have students play a memory game in pairs. Individually, students use the timeline to write three statements about Dudamel using the past perfect. One or two of the statements should be false. Example: *He had won an international prize long before he met his wife.* Students close their books and take turns reading their statements. Their partner should say if the sentences are true or false.

Exercise 3: Past Perfect: Questions and Short Answers
- Go over the diary notes with the class.
- Have students complete the exercise individually or in pairs.
- To review, ask a pair of students to read the conversation aloud.

- (!) Have students write their own diary notes about what they did last Saturday. Encourage them to include four or five items. Form pairs. Have students exchange notes and take turns asking and answering questions starting with *At [time] on Saturday, had you . . . ?*

Exercise 4: Past Perfect Progressive: Statements
- Go over the example with the class. If necessary, review how to form the past perfect progressive. (had + been + -ing *form of verb*)
- Have students read the paragraphs for meaning before choosing their answers.
- Have students compare answers in pairs. Then go over answers as a class.

Exercise 5: Past Perfect Progressive: Questions
- Go over the example with the class. Point out that *before* is also possible. *(What kind of work had she been doing before she quit her job to play full-time?)*
- Remind students that we can use the past perfect progressive with the simple past to show the time relationship between two past events.
- Have students complete the exercise individually and compare answers in pairs. Then go over answers as a class.

Exercise 6: Past Perfect and Past Perfect Progressive
- Go over the example with the class. Ask: "Why is *had received* (past perfect) the correct answer?" *(because the action happened before a specific time in the past [1975] and it's not in progress; it's finished)*
- Have students read the reports for meaning before choosing their answers.
- Have students compare answers in pairs. Then go over answers as a class.

Exercise 7: Time Clauses
- Go over the example with the class. Remind students to use the progressive form when possible.
- Have students read the interview for meaning before choosing their answers.
- To review, call on a pair of students to role-play the interview.

Exercise 8: Editing
- Have students read the article quickly to find out what it is about.
- To check comprehension, ask: "Where was Brueggergosman born?" *(in Canada)* "When did she decide to become a singer?" *(when she was 15)* "What kind of singer is she?" *(a soprano)*

- Review the example.
- Have students find and correct the mistakes individually. Then have students compare answers in pairs.
- Call on students to explain why the incorrect structures are wrong.
- ⏱ Ask students to point out examples of correct usages of the past perfect and the past perfect progressive.

Go to **www.myfocusongrammarlab.com** for additional grammar practice.

Step 4: Communication Practice (pages 50–53)

See the general suggestions for Communication Practice on page 4.

Exercise 9: Listening

A
- Have students read the sentences before listening. Then play the audio.

B
- Have students read the sentences and identify the two past events. Remind students to listen carefully to decide which event happened first.
- Go over the answers as a class.

Exercise 10: Pronunciation

A
- Play the audio. Have students read along as they listen to the Pronunciation Note.
- Ask: "How do we often pronounce *had* after all pronouns except *it*?" *(d)* "How do we pronounce *had* after *it* and nouns?" *(id)*

B
- Have students read the statements and circle the words that they will hear reduced. Then play the audio.

C
- Have students play both roles.

Exercise 11: What About You?
- Go over the example with the class. Have students complete the sentences individually. Remind them to use the past perfect and past perfect progressive.
- Have students exchange papers with a partner. Call on students to tell the class about what their partners did yesterday.
- ⏱ Partners of very busy people can nominate their partners for the "Busy Bee Award." Have nominees read their answers aloud, and then have classmates vote. Another possibility is to nominate the least busy person for the "Couch Potato Award."

Exercise 12: Conversation
- Form small groups. Have students choose a past event or time of the year to talk about what they had / hadn't done / had been doing before then.
- As students share their experiences, encourage them to talk about all the topics on the list (and other topics that they may think of). Encourage the use of high-frequency verbs such as *eaten, seen, tasted, attended, played with, visited, tried,* and *considered.*
- Call on students to share interesting information they found out about their classmates. You may want to have students come to the front and write a few sentences on the board.

Exercise 13: Game: Find the Differences
- Point out that the two pictures show a scene at different times.
- Have students work in pairs to find the differences in the two pictures. Instruct pairs to write 6 sentences describing differences in the scene. Remind students to use *by* + past perfect in their sentences.
- To make the game competitive, set a time limit and see which pair writes the most sentences about the differences.

Exercise 14: Writing

A
- Students can work on Part A individually or in small groups. If students work in groups, ask them to choose a celebrity, find information, and then share their findings with their group before they make their timeline.
- Write the following questions on the board to help students generate ideas and elicit the necessary vocabulary:
Where was he / she born?
When did he / she decide to become a musician / singer?
When did he / she start singing / playing the [instrument]?
When was his / her first public performance?
What are his / her main achievements? When did they happen?
Has he / she ever won a prize? When?
When / Where did he / she meet his / her wife / husband?
When did he / she get married?
Has he / she ever moved to a different city / country? When?

- Have students make notes for each question and then use them as a guide as they write their timeline.

B
- Have students write their paragraphs individually, either in class or for homework. Remind them to use the past perfect and past perfect progressive to describe events in the musician's life.

C
- After students write their paragraphs, have them correct their work using the Editing Checklist.

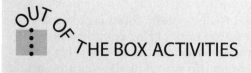
OUT OF THE BOX ACTIVITIES

Speaking
- As a class, brainstorm a list of five to seven questions to use in an interview with a famous sports figure, movie star, writer, composer, or singer about his or her childhood and entrance into the world of fame. Write the questions on the board.
- Form small groups. Have students choose a famous person and write questions for their interview. Encourage them to start with a question about the star's first success and then ask about previous experiences (which led to stardom). Have them use this question form, which you can write on the board:
  Before your big break, what / how / when had you . . . ?
- Call on a volunteer to role-play one of the famous people the groups have chosen. Have the class interview him or her. Point out that he or she can make up the answers, if necessary.

Listening and Writing
- Record a talk-show interview of a famous person.
- Select a five-minute segment during which the famous person is talking about his or her past.
- Play the recording and pause it after each piece of information about the famous person's past. Have the students write a sentence about it, using past perfect or past perfect progressive.
- Have students work in small groups to write paragraphs from their sentences.

Go to **www.myfocusongrammarlab.com** for additional listening, pronunciation, speaking, and writing practice.

Note
- See the *Focus on Grammar Workbook* for additional in-class or homework grammar practice.

Unit 4 Review (page 54)
Have students complete the Review and check their answers on Student Book page UR-1. Review or assign additional material as needed.

Go to **www.myfocusongrammarlab.com** for the Unit Achievement Test.

From Grammar to Writing (pages 55–57)
See the general suggestions for From Grammar to Writing on page 9.

Go to **www.myfocusongrammarlab.com** for an additional From Grammar to Writing Assignment, Part Review, and Part Post-Test.

PART II OVERVIEW

FUTURE: REVIEW AND EXPANSION

UNIT	GRAMMAR FOCUS	THEME
5	Future and Future Progressive	Life in the Future
6	Future Perfect and Future Perfect Progressive	Money and Goals

Go to **www.myfocusongrammarlab.com** for the Part and Unit Tests.

Note: PowerPoint® grammar presentations, test-generating software, and reproducible Part and Unit Tests are on the *Teacher's Resource Disc.*

Grammar: FUTURE AND FUTURE PROGRESSIVE

Students will learn the meanings and practice the uses of the future and the future progressive—specifically how different tenses are used to show future meaning.

- The simple present, the present progressive, the auxiliary *will* + base form, and *be going to* + base form all show future meaning with a future time adverb.
- The future progressive uses either *will* or *be going to* + *be* + *-ing*.

Theme: LIFE IN THE FUTURE

Unit 5 focuses on language that we use to talk about what life in the future will be like and what our plans for the future are.

Step 1: Grammar in Context (pages 60–62)

See the general suggestions for Grammar in Context on page 1.

Before You Read

- Have students look at the pictures. Then discuss Question 1 as a class.
- Read Questions 2 and 3 aloud. Brainstorm topics that could present problems in the future. Make a list on the board:
  housing, population, fresh water, food, transportation, waste disposal, energy sources
- Have students discuss Questions 2 and 3 in pairs. Encourage them to expand on the topics listed on the board. Ask them to make notes of problems and solutions.
- Draw the following diagram on the board and complete it with students' ideas:

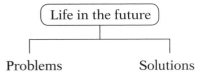

Read

- To encourage students to read with a purpose, write the following questions on the board:
  1. What kind of cities will people live in? What will they be like? *(floating cities; they will use solar, wind, and wave power; homes will be underwater)*
  2. Where will famers grow food? Who will do the difficult work? *(on vertical farms; robots)*

3. What vehicles will people take to work? What other use will these vehicles have? *(airships; they will be used as flying hospitals)*
4. Where will people go on vacation? How will they get there? *(to sky hotels, the moon, Mars, and beyond; on space elevators)*

- Have students read the text. (Or play the audio and have students follow along in their books.) Then call on students to share their answers with the class.
- Have students discuss the following questions in small groups:
  1. Which of the predictions from the article do you think will come true? Give your reasons.
  2. The article suggests solutions to problems the future might bring regarding housing, farmland, fuel, and places to go on vacation. Do you think the solutions are good? Why? / Why not? Can you think of other solutions?

After You Read

A. Vocabulary

- Have students find and circle the vocabulary in the text. Encourage them to use the context to figure out the meaning.
- Have students compare answers in pairs. Then go over answers as a class.
- ⏱ Write the following on the board. Have students complete the paragraph with the words in the box:

challenges	vehicles	creative
vertical	innovative	technologies

We are hopeful that _____ people will find _____ solutions that will help us face the _____ of the future. New _____ will be needed. Futurists believe that farmers will grow food on _____ farms and that people will travel in solar-powered _____.

B. Comprehension

- Have students choose the answers individually. Encourage them to underline the information in the article that supports their answers.
- Have students compare answers in pairs. Then call on individual students to say an answer.

Go to **www.myfocusongrammarlab.com** for an additional reading, and for reading and vocabulary practice.

Step 2: Grammar Presentation (pages 63–65)

See the general suggestions for Grammar Presentation on page 2.

Grammar Charts

- Write the following column heads on the board:

		Present	Simple
Going to	Will	Progressive	Present

- Have students find examples in the reading of the four types. Write the verb phrases on the board under the appropriate column heads.
- Write on the board:
  We will be using robots for hard work.
  We are going to be using robots for hard work.
- Ask: "Do both sentences have the same meaning?" *(yes)* Have students name the verb forms in the examples. *(will be using, are going to be using)* Underline them in the sentences on the board. Then ask: "How do we form the future progressive?" (will + be + -ing *form of verb or form of* be + going to + be + -ing *form of verb*)

Grammar Notes

Note 1

- Write on the board:
  1. We're going to travel into space.
  2. We'll take a space shuttle.
  3. We're taking very little luggage.
  4. The shuttle leaves at four o'clock.
- Have students study the examples. Then have students identify the four ways to talk about the future. Write them next to each example. *(be going to, will, present progressive, simple present)*
- Point out that some of the differences among the four ways are related to the situations. Notes 2–6 cover the different meanings and uses.

Note 2

- Point out that we use *be going to* or *will* for facts that we know will happen in the future. Give examples: *The traffic is going to get heavier at six o'clock. The traffic will get heavier at six o'clock.*
- Ask individual students: "What time will the sun / is the sun going to set today? What time will the sun rise / is the sun going to rise tomorrow?" Encourage students to answer in complete sentences.

Note 3

- Point out that we use *be going to* or *will* for predictions. Give examples: *We're going to use flying cars. We'll use flying cars.*

- Have pairs write their own predictions for the future. Call on students to share some of their predictions with the class.

Note 4

- Point out that we use *be going to* or the present progressive for plans that have been decided. Give examples: *We're going to have a meeting on Thursday. We are having a meeting on Thursday.*
- Have students ask their partners: "What are you going to do this weekend? / What are you doing this weekend?" Emphasize that there is almost no difference between these two forms.

Note 5

- Say: "I've just decided that I'm going to give a test tomorrow. What will you do tonight?" *(We'll study.)* Point out that we use *will* for quick decisions made at the moment of speaking.
- Write on the board:
  There's going to be a party tomorrow night. Ask one student: "You got an invitation a week ago, and you've already bought new shoes just for the party, so . . ." (Student 1: *I'm going to go.* [It's sure.]) Ask another student, "You just heard about the party today, and you're not really busy, so maybe . . ." (Student 2: *Maybe I'll go.*)
- Then write on the board:
  A: I can't find my pen.
  B: I'll lend you one.
- Have students read the example. Point out that we use *will* to make offers and promises.
- Have pairs create two short conversations using *will* for a quick decision and *will* for an offer or promise. Have pairs role-play their conversations for the class. Encourage students to use contractions and reductions: *I'll do it* instead of *I will do it.*

Note 6

- Write on the board:
  a bus / train / plane
  a conference / meeting / party
  a tour / a trip
- Point out that the simple present is used for scheduled events. Give an example: *My train leaves at three.*
- Have students write true or imaginary sentences using the cues on the board. Call on students to share their sentences with the class. (*I'm going on vacation next month. The plane leaves at 8:00 P.M. / I have a meeting tomorrow. It starts at 10 o'clock.*)

Note 7

- Draw a timeline on the board:

today	tomorrow		
		jogging	
	9:00	10:00	11:00

- Say: "At 10 o'clock tomorrow, I'll be jogging in the park."
- Have students look at the timeline. Ask: "Will I be jogging at 9:45 tomorrow?" *(yes)* "Will I be jogging at 10:15?" *(yes)* Point out that we use the future progressive for actions that will be in progress for some time in the future.
- Have pairs ask each other: "What will you be doing at this time tomorrow?" "On Saturday or Sunday at this time?" "Next month?" "In three months?"

Note 8

- Write on the board:

Main Clause	Time Clause
I'll leave / I'm going to leave	when he comes.
I'll be cleaning my house	while he is studying.

- Have students study the examples. Then ask: "What verb forms can we use in the main clause?" (will, be going to, *or the future progressive*) "And in the time clause?" *(the simple present or the present progressive)*
- Draw attention to the *Be Careful!* note.
- Point out that *when* indicates a point in time (simple tense) and *while* denotes a length of time (progressive). In either case, one half of the sentence is some form of present tense even though the idea is future.
- Have students ask their partners: "What will you do when you get home tonight?" "What will you be doing while [teacher's name] is [cleaning his / her house] on Saturday?"

⏱ **Identify the Grammar:** Have students identify the grammar in the opening reading on page 60. For example:
   . . . 10 billion people **will be living** on the
    planet . . .
   . . . the population **is growing** . . .
   . . . land **will be shrinking** . . .
   . . . there **is not going to be** enough fresh
    water . . .
   Where **will** people **live** . . . ?
   . . . as rising oceans **cover** the land . . .

Go to **www.myfocusongrammarlab.com** for grammar charts and notes.

Step 3: Focused Practice (pages 66–71)

See the general suggestions for Focused Practice on page 4.

Exercise 1: Discover the Grammar

A

- Have students name the future forms they have learned. Write them on the board: be going to, will (*present progressive, simple present, future progressive*)
- Go over the example with the class. Ask: "What is *Are you presenting* an example of?" (*present progressive for the future*)
- Have students complete the exercise individually and compare answers in pairs. Then elicit the correct answers from the class.

B

- Go over the example with the class.
- Have students complete the exercise in pairs. Encourage students to refer to the grammar notes if necessary.
- Then go over the answers as a class.

Exercise 2: Forms of the Future

- Go over the example with the class. Ask: "Why is *are you going to report* the correct answer?" (*because Eon is asking about a plan; for plans we can use* be going to *or the present progressive*)
- Have students read the conversations for meaning before choosing their answers. Then have students compare answers in pairs.
- ⏱ Have pairs role-play the conversations.

Exercise 3: Future Progressive

- Go over the example with the class. Review how to form the future progressive. (will *or* be going to + be + -ing *form of verb*)
- Have students read the interview for meaning before writing their answers.
- Have students compare answers in pairs. Then go over answers as a class.
- ⏱ With books closed, have pairs write sentences about what personal robots and the companies that make them will be doing in the future. Students should use the future progressive.

Exercise 4: Future Progressive: Affirmative and Negative Statements

- Go over the examples with the class.
- Have students complete the exercise individually and compare answers in pairs. Then go over answers as a class.

- ⏱ Have students imagine they have a robot and write its schedule for tomorrow. Point out they can include things they think are drudgery (not fun) and would love to have a robot do. Form pairs. Have students take turns describing their robot's schedule using the future progressive.

Exercise 5: Future Progressive Statements and Time Clauses
- Go over the example with the class. Then have students read the ad for meaning.
- Before students write their answers, ask them to find and circle the words that introduce time clauses. *(while, While, before, After, While)*
- Have students compare answers in pairs. Then go over answers as a class.

Exercise 6: Editing
- Have students read the article quickly to find out what it is about.
- Ask: "Have engineers started working on flying cars?" *(yes)* "What will the car described in *Car Trends Magazine* do?" *(unfold its wings and fly)* "What will it need to take off and land?" *(an airport)* "What is a VTOL?" *(a vertical takeoff and landing vehicle that won't need an airport to take off and land)*
- Go over the example with the class.
- Have students find and correct the mistakes individually. Then have students compare answers in pairs.
- To review as a class, have students explain why the incorrect structures are wrong.
- ⏱ Ask students to point out examples of correct usages of the future and future progressive.

Go to **www.myfocusongrammarlab.com** for additional grammar practice.

Step 4: Communication Practice (pages 72–77)
See the general suggestions for Communication Practice on page 4.

Exercise 7: Listening
A
- Explain the concept of *being available*. Say: "I'm available at three o'clock. I can see you then. I'm not available at four; I can't see you then."
- Remind students to take notes as they listen. Then play the audio and have students complete the exercise.

B
- Go over the example in the chart. Play the audio again and stop it when Skyler asks, "What about you, Jarek?" Ask: "Why is the chart marked on the third and fourth week of August? *(because Skyler won't be available; he's taking a vacation with his family the last two weeks of August)*
- Have students answer in full sentences. For example, *Jarek won't be available the second and third weeks of July.*
- ⏱ Have students listen again and take notes of the reasons why each person won't be available in the weeks students marked on the chart. Review as a class.

Exercise 8: Pronunciation
A
- Play the audio. Have students read along as they listen to the Pronunciation Note.
- Write on the board:
  People won't be taking buses. They'll be taking airships.
- Ask: "Which words would you stress in the example?" (buses *and* airships) Underline the words as students say them. "Does the voice go up or down on these words?" *(It goes up.)*

B
- Have students listen and repeat the responses. Be sure they stress the right words and use the correct intonation.

C
- Have students take turns playing both roles.

Exercise 9: Reaching Agreement
- Have students complete the chart individually. Point out that they can include true or imaginary information.
- Go over the example with the class. Brainstorm ways to ask about plans and write them on the board. *(What are you doing on . . . ? And on . . . Any plans? What are your plans for . . . ? What about the rest of the week? Are you doing anything special on . . . ?)*
- Before students interact, remind them to use the present continuous or *be going to* for plans and *will* for quick decisions.
- Ask a few students to share their plans for this week.

Exercise 10: Discussion
- Go over the list of activities with the class.
- Brainstorm other activities robots might do in the future. Write them on the board.

- Go over the example with the class. Ask students to identify words used to express one's opinion or ask about someone's opinion. Have students underline them. *(I don't think . . . I don't agree. Do you think . . . ?)*
- Have students share their views about why they think robots will / won't be doing too much.

Exercise 11: Information Gap: Dr. Eon's Calendar

- Have students study the calendar. Make sure students understand that neither calendar is complete.
- Draw attention to the first arrow. Point out that it indicates that she will be doing the same activity Wednesday through Saturday.
- Go over the example with the class. Point out that students can ask *yes / no* questions to make guesses about what the doctor will be doing. *(Will she be attending a conference then?)*

Exercise 12: Writing

A

- Write *Now* and *10 Years from Now* on the board. Then write the following questions under the headings:

Now
1. What are you doing now?
2. What are your plans for today?
3. What hobbies do you have now?
4. How are you preparing for the future?

10 Years from Now
1. What will you be doing in 10 years?
2. Where will you be living?
3. What are you going to be doing for relaxation?
4. How are you going to be using your education?

- Have students make notes for each question and then use them as a guide as they write their paragraphs.

B

- After students write their paragraphs, have them correct their work using the Editing Checklist.

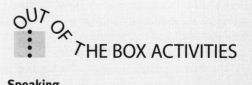

OUT OF THE BOX ACTIVITIES

Speaking

- Have students work with partners to answer one or more of the following questions in the most outrageous way they can. Encourage them to think of something bigger, better, funnier, or more unusual than anyone else.
  1. Your country's ruler is coming to dinner at your house. What are you going to serve?
  2. You have been invited to a costume party. What will you wear?
  3. A television crew is coming to your house to interview you. What are you going to be doing when they arrive?
  4. You have been asked to give a speech on any topic. What do you plan to say?
- Have students share their ideas with the class.

Speaking

- Brainstorm ideas about interviewing people who are not students or teachers. Students will ask about typical days at work. Students can use the following questions to get started:
  — Where do you work? (They might not have to ask this one.)
  — What time do you get to work?
  — By (two hours later), what work will you be doing? What will you still have to do?
  — By the time your workday is half over, what are you probably doing? — An hour before you finish your work for the day, what are you going to be doing?
- Then have students report on what a working person's life is like.
- **Note:** Suggestions of people to ask are: people who work at fast-food restaurants and have to follow strict schedules; people who work in bookstores; office assistants; people who work in supermarkets; and professionals such as nurses, doctors, lawyers, or artists.

Go to **www.myfocusongrammarlab.com** for additional listening, pronunciation, speaking, and writing practice.

Note

• See the *Focus on Grammar Workbook* for additional in-class or homework grammar practice.

Unit 5 Review (page 78)

Have students complete the Review and check their answers on Student Book page UR-2. Review or assign additional material as needed.

Go to **www.myfocusongrammarlab.com** for the Unit Achievement Test.

UNIT 6 OVERVIEW

Grammar: FUTURE PERFECT AND FUTURE PERFECT PROGRESSIVE

Students will learn the meanings and practice the uses of the future perfect and the future perfect progressive.

• The future perfect, like one of the future forms, uses *will*, and like the present perfect, it also uses *have*. It is used for actions that will be completed by a specific time in the future (for example, *by this time next week*).

• The future perfect progressive uses *been* + base verb form + *-ing* in addition to *will* and *have*. Like all progressive forms, this tense is used to talk about actions in progress at a certain time (in the future).

Theme: MONEY AND GOALS

Unit 6 focuses on language that we use to talk about goals for the future.

• Taking a show on the road (traveling to different cities and broadcasting from different cities) increases its popularity because people enjoy watching shows being made and participating in them.

• A good credit history is important for nearly everyone. Most people, for example, need to borrow money in order to buy a car.

Step 1: Grammar in Context (pages 79–81)

See the general suggestions for Grammar in Context on page 1.

Before You Read

• Tell students that they are going to read the transcript of a TV show. Point out that the photos show the people who were interviewed.

• Have students look at the photos and read the information below each photo. Then have students discuss the questions in pairs. Encourage students to write notes for each question.

• Call on pairs to share their answers to the questions with the class. Write students' ideas of what the show is about on the board. Have them confirm their guesses after reading the text.

Read

• To encourage students to read with a purpose, write the following questions on the board:
  1. What do the three panel members have in common? *(They are students at Gibson College in Nebraska. / They are college freshmen.)*
  2. How do college freshmen get credit cards? *(Credit card companies send them offers.)*
  3. What two mistakes do many college students make with their credit cards? *(They use them for things they want, not things they need. They pay only the minimum payment and thus have to pay a great deal of interest later.)*
  4. Why should a college student get at least one credit card and use it? *(to build up a credit history)*

• Have students read the text. (Or play the audio and have students follow along in their books.) Then call on students to share their answers with the class.

• Have students discuss the following questions in small groups:
  1. What are the advantages of using a credit card? What are the disadvantages?
  2. Do people who use cash (and not credit cards) really buy less?

• ⏱ Ask each student how many credit cards they have. Keep a running tally of the numbers on the board as each student answers. When every student has answered, add up the numbers. Then divide the total by the number of students in the class to determine the average number of credit cards. Have the students, in small groups, discuss what they use the credit cards for, and whether they think they have more cards than they need.

After You Read

A. Vocabulary

• Have students find and circle the vocabulary in the text. Encourage them to use the surrounding context to figure out the meaning.

- Have students compare answers in pairs. Then review answers as a class.
- (⏰) To reinforce the vocabulary, write the following sentence halves on the board. Have students match them:

1. If you don't have a credit history,	a. you don't have to pay interest on your purchases.
2. Students' debts increase each month	b. that the average American student has four to five cards.
3. If you use cash,	c. it's hard to get credit.
4. Statistics show	d. because they only pay the minimum.

B. Comprehension
- Have students choose the answers individually. Encourage students to underline the information in the text that supports their answers.
- Have students compare answers in pairs. Then go over answers as a class.

Go to **www.myfocusongrammarlab.com** for an additional reading, and for reading and vocabulary practice.

Step 2: Grammar Presentation (pages 82–85)

See the general suggestions for Grammar Presentation on page 2.

Grammar Charts
- Point out that the future perfect examples focus on a number or an amount (eight cards, twice as much) while the future perfect progressive examples focus on a length of time (for a month, for nine months).
- Write a sentence that can work in either tense on the board, for example (future perfect): By 2013, I'll have lived here for six years.
- Have students change the sentence to future perfect progressive. Remind them that, as with present perfect and present perfect progressive, some verbs (live, work, teach) can be used in either form with little or no difference in meaning.
- Have students work in pairs to find three time expressions for future perfect and future perfect progressive in the reading. Ask them to find differences between the forms. (future perfect: point in time; future perfect progressive: action in progress; also, future perfect is used with yet, already, and amounts or quantities and future perfect progressive with duration of time)

Grammar Notes
Note 1
- To explain the future perfect, draw a timeline on the board:

Past   Now   The end of the year

—X———X—X—————————————

visited four countries

- Point to the timeline and say: "By the end of the year, I'll have visited four different countries."
- Point out that we use the future perfect to explain what will happen (visit four countries) before a time in the future (the end of the year).
- To check comprehension, ask: "By this time next week, what will we have finished in class?" (We will have finished Unit 6. We will have started Unit 7.)
- Have partners ask each other: "What will you have done by this time next week?"

Note 2
- To explain the future perfect progressive, draw a new timeline on the board:

Past   Now   The end of the year

—[▭▭▭▭▭▭▭]—————————

teach English for six years

- Point to the timeline and say: "By the end of the year, I'll have been teaching English for six years."
- Have students think of an activity they started doing in the past, that they do in the present, and that they will continue to do in the future and say how long they will have been doing it by the end of the year. (By the end of the year, I'll have been playing tennis for three years. By the end of the year, I'll have been taking a painting course for five months.)
- Write the following sentence on the board: Mariana and Jim moved into their apartment on December 20, 2009.
- Ask students to create two sentences (one each in future perfect and future perfect progressive) from the information. If necessary, give them the hint that they'll need to use the verb live. (They will have lived in their apartment for [two] years. They will have been living in their apartment for [two] years.)
- Then write on the board: Mariana and Jim were married in December 2009.
- Ask students if both forms are possible here. (no, only future perfect, because no progressive form is possible with be)

Note 3

- Write on the board:
  When my grandfather turns 70, he will have been a sailor for 50 years.
- Have students identify the present simple verb in the time clause *(turns)* and the future perfect form in the main clause *(will have been)*.
- Call on students to say how long they will have been doing something or how many times they will have done something by the time they turn an age of their choice.

Note 4

- Brainstorm with students a list of five personal goals for next year. Write them on the board.
- Then have partners ask each other *yes / no* questions about these goals. For example:
  A: Will you have learned to drive a stick shift car by next year?
  B: Yes, I will. / No, I won't.
- Use the list of goals on the board and establish a particular date (maybe two years from now). Have pairs ask each other future perfect progressive questions with the goals and a length of time. For example:
  A: By _____, how long will you have been volunteering at the hospital?
  B: I'll have been volunteering for five years by then.
- Point out that *yet* plus a negative means we expect the action to happen—soon. *Already* indicates that the action happened before we expected it to happen.

🕐 **Identify the Grammar:** Have students identify the grammar in the opening reading on page 79. For example:
  . . . we**'ll have been traveling** for a month . . .
  . . . we**'ll have been** in 22 cities . . .
  A typical college freshman **will have gotten** eight credit card offers . . .
  . . . the average student in the United States **will have tripled** the number of cards . . .
  . . . you**'ll have doubled** your credit card debt by graduation.

Go to **www.myfocusongrammarlab.com** for grammar charts and notes.

Step 3: Focused Practice (pages 85–90)

See the general suggestions for Focused Practice on page 4.

Exercise 1: Discover the Grammar

- Go over the example with the class.
- Have students complete the exercise individually and compare answers in pairs.
- Go over answers as a class.

Exercise 2: Future Perfect

- Have students look at the timeline and name the things Debbie will do in the future. *(She will go to college, move into an apartment, travel to France, get a job in a bank, buy a car, graduate, get married, move to a new house, and have a baby.)*
- Go over the example.
- Have students complete the exercise individually and compare answers in pairs.
- Go over answers as a class.

Exercise 3: Time Clauses with *Already* and *Yet*

- Go over the example with the class. If necessary, remind students to use *already* between *have* and the participle and *yet* at the end of a clause.
- Have students complete the exercise individually and compare answers in pairs.
- Go over answers as a class.

Exercise 4: Future Perfect or Future Perfect Progressive

- Go over the example with the class.
- Remind students to use the future perfect progressive to ask or answer a question with *how long* and the future perfect to ask or answer a question with *how many* or *how much*.
- Have students complete the exercise individually and compare answers in pairs.
- Call on pairs to read the questions and answers aloud.

Exercise 5: Editing

- Have students read the blog entry quickly to find out what it is about.
- Ask: "What goal would the college student like to achieve?" *(get his debt under control)* "What will he have done by February?" *(recorded his spending for a month)* "What will he have done by March?" *(transferred his balances to just two cards)* "What kind of experience does he hope to have by the time he graduates?" *(experience in managing debt)*
- Go over the example with the class.
- Have students find and correct the mistakes individually and compare answers in pairs.
- Have students explain why the incorrect structures are wrong.

- ⏰ Ask students to point out examples of correct usages of the future perfect and future perfect progressive.

Go to **www.myfocusongrammarlab.com** for additional grammar practice.

Step 4: Communication Practice (pages 91–94)

See the general suggestions for Communication Practice on page 4.

Exercise 6: Listening

A
- Have students read the list of things the family will do to save money. Have students explain the more expensive options for each item. (*Eating out is more expensive than packing a lunch. If you buy only scarves and earrings, you spend less money than if you buy a whole outfit. Clothes from thrift shops are cheaper than brand-new clothes. If you take the commuter van, you spend less money than if you drive your car. Going to the movies is more expensive than watching DVDs at home.*)
- Before students listen, point out that more than one box might be correct in each case.

B
- You may want to stop the audio after each answer is given and have students discuss the correct answers with a partner.

C
- Have students complete the exercise individually.
- ⏰ To personalize, say: "The Caputos will have saved $4,580 by next summer—that means $1,145 per person." Form small groups. Have students discuss where they would go on vacation if they could save $1,145 per person in their family by next summer.

Exercise 7: Pronunciation

A
- Play the audio. Have students read along as they listen to the Pronunciation Note.
- Have students look at the examples. Ask: "Is *have* the main verb in the examples?" (*no, it's an auxiliary*) "Which is the main verb in each example?" (*left, spoken, driving*) Point out that, in the examples, *have* is reduced and is not stressed because it is not a main verb. The main verb carries the stress in each example.

B
- Have students read the conversations before listening and writing their answers.

C
- Have students play both roles.

Exercise 8: Conversation
- To help students prepare for the conversation, draw the following chart (with the example) on the board:

By the end of . . .		
this week	this month	this year
		my brother will have finished high school

- Have students use the chart to write notes of their ideas. Tell students they can write about themselves or people they know. They can change the time periods if necessary.
- As students interact, be sure they use the future perfect.

Exercise 9: What About You?

A
- To help students generate ideas, brainstorm big and small goals and write two lists on the board.

B
- Encourage students to write three goals on their timeline.

C
- To prepare students for the discussion, have them write a few sentences describing the information on their timeline. Point out that they should use the future perfect and future perfect progressive.

Exercise 10: Writing

A
- Help students think of reasonable goals by brainstorming ideas as a class. Write them on the board:
  learn to play tennis, get fit by exercising and improving diet, learn to drive, train a dog to behave well, climb a mountain, redecorate my living space, take the TOEFL
- Go over the questions. Have students interview a partner to find out the information they will need to write about him or her. Encourage them to take notes of their partner's answers.

B
- Go over the example as a class. Point out the use of the future perfect and future perfect progressive.
- Have students use their notes as a guide as they write.

C

- After students write their paragraphs, have them correct their work using the Editing Checklist.

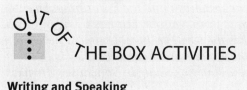

OUT OF THE BOX ACTIVITIES

Writing and Speaking

- Write on the board:
Ten years from now, I will be a successful _____. I will own my own home. This is what I will have done to make it my dream house: _____.
- Have students use their own ideas to complete the sentences on the board. Encourage them to add more sentences in the future perfect about making their houses into dream houses.
- Form pairs. Have students discuss their dream homes.

Speaking and Listening

- Team up students from the same area for this activity. If many of your students are from the same area, have some choose a place that they would like to visit to present to the class.
- Ask students to prepare a one-minute presentation on visiting their home regions (or other area). Encourage the use of future perfect and future perfect progressive tenses: *By the time you get to Phoenix, you will have experienced a five-hour airplane ride. You will probably have been wondering how hot it will be. You will have seen many brown and gray mountains from the plane. By the time you arrive at the hotel, you will have passed . . .*
- Tell students they can bring in maps and pictures (or get them from the Internet) to make their presentation more interesting.
- Have groups come to the front to give their presentation. Allow the class to ask follow-up questions after listening to each presentation.

Go to **www.myfocusongrammarlab.com** for additional listening, pronunciation, speaking, and writing practice.

Note

- See the *Focus on Grammar Workbook* for additional in-class or homework grammar practice.

Unit 6 Review (page 95)

Have students complete the Review and check their answers on Student Book page UR-2. Review or assign additional material as needed.

Go to **www.myfocusongrammarlab.com** for the Unit Achievement Test.

From Grammar to Writing (pages 96–98)

See general suggestions for From Grammar to Writing on page 9.

Go to **www.myfocusongrammarlab.com** for an additional From Grammar to Writing Assignment, Part Review, and Part Post-Test.

PART III OVERVIEW

NEGATIVE QUESTIONS, TAG QUESTIONS, ADDITIONS AND RESPONSES

UNIT	GRAMMAR FOCUS	THEME
7	Negative *Yes / No* Questions and Tag Questions	Places to Live
8	Additions and Responses: *So, Too, Neither, Not either,* and *But*	Similarities and Differences

Go to **www.myfocusongrammarlab.com** for the Part and Unit Tests.

Note: PowerPoint® grammar presentations, test-generating software, and reproducible Part and Unit Tests are on the *Teacher's Resource Disc.*

Grammar: Negative *Yes* / *No* Questions and Tag Questions

Students will learn and practice negative *yes* / *no* questions and tag questions.

- Negative *yes* / *no* questions can begin with a form of *be* (*isn't* / *aren't*) or an auxiliary like *don't* / *doesn't*, *didn't*, *haven't* / *hasn't*, *can't*, or *won't*.

- Tag questions use the appropriate form (number and tense) of *be* or the auxiliary (the appropriate form of *do* or a modal) and the pronoun that matches the subject.

Theme: Places to Live

Unit 7 focuses on language that we use to comment on a situation and check or get information about places where people live.

To help students activate their passive tourism vocabulary, have them gather tourist brochures, travel magazines, and Internet information sites about cities of the world and post them in the classroom.

Step 1: Grammar in Context (pages 100–102)

See the general suggestions for Grammar in Context on page 1.

Before You Read
- Have students write notes about why they would like to live in one of the places in the photos and what they like / don't like about the places where they live.
- Have students discuss the questions in pairs.
- Call on students to share their answers to Question 2. Take a poll to find out the most popular place.
- Write two headings on the board:
  What people like about their town / city
  What people don't like about their town / city.
  Call on students to share their answers to Question 3 and write the answers under the correct heading.

Read
- To encourage students to read with a purpose, write the following questions on the board:
  1. Where are the people from?
  2. Where are they living?
  3. What do they like about it?

(1. Sousa is from Portugal, but she's living in Rio. She likes the bay, the beach, the mountains, the sky, and the places for entertainment. 2. Kada is from Berlin, but he's living in Seoul. He likes the skyscrapers next to ancient structures and the beautiful palaces. 3. Okaya is from Nairobi, but he's living in Cairo. He likes the weather there. It almost never rains and the winters are mild. 4. Bradley is from England, but he's living in Vancouver. He likes the wide-open spaces in Canada.)

- Have students read the text. (Or play the audio and have students follow along in their books.) Then call on students to share their answers with the class.
- Have students discuss the following questions in small groups:
  1. What attracts you most about a big city? Why do you want to visit it?
  2. What kind of tourist are you? Do you like to see the "tourist places," or do you prefer to get to know about the daily lives of the native people? Do you like to visit many places or spend a long time in one or two?

After You Read

A. Vocabulary
- Have students find and circle the vocabulary in the text. Encourage them to use the surrounding context to figure out the meaning.
- Have students compare answers in pairs. Then go over answers as a class.
- To reinforce the vocabulary, call on students to answer the following questions:
  1. Where are your grandparents from originally?
  2. Is there an interesting structure in your area?
  3. What bothers you about the place where you live?
  4. What do you like about where you live? What are you attracted to?
  5. Why might a foreigner have difficulty adjusting in your country?
  6. What are some opportunities a country might provide a foreigner?

B. Comprehension
- Have students choose the answers individually. Then have students compare answers in pairs.
- Call on students to say an answer each.

Go to **www.myfocusongrammarlab.com** for an additional reading, and for reading and vocabulary practice.

Step 2: Grammar Presentation (pages 103–106)

See the general suggestions for Grammar Presentation on page 2.

Grammar Charts

- Write some example sentences with tag questions on the board.
- Have students change the sentences with tag questions into negative *yes / no* questions.
- Try this drill to practice tag questions: Quickly say statements and have students supply the tags. Go in an order of progressive difficulty: "He's Japanese" *(isn't he?)* "She's not French" *(is she?)* "He doesn't speak French" *(does he?)* "She speaks English" *(doesn't she?)* "He was here yesterday" *(wasn't he?)* "She wasn't here Sunday" *(was she?)* (This is easier if you stay away from "I" and "you.")
- You can add a brief review if you work your way up to more complicated verb forms: "By 2013 he will have been studying English for many, many years" *(won't he?)*. This will also show students that even if the question is very long, the tag is still short and simple.

Grammar Notes

Note 1

- Provide examples of the use of negative *yes / no* questions and tag questions to check information. *Our next class in on [Friday], isn't it? There are [15] students in this class, aren't there? Don't you have a test [next week]?*
- Provide more examples of the use of negative *yes / no* questions and tag questions to comment on a situation. *It's a [beautiful] day, isn't it? Isn't it [too hot] in here? This is a [spacious room], isn't it?*
- Call on students to provide examples of their own.

Note 2

- Point out that people who ask negative questions usually expect positive answers.
- Do a quick review by asking students questions to which they know you know the answers. *(Isn't your name Pablo? Don't you usually write with a green pen?)* Then have students ask you similar questions.

Note 3

- Emphasize that positive statements have negative tag questions and negative statements have positive tag questions.
- Write simple information statements on the board:
  It's raining. She has a dog. We always come to school on time. He didn't call. They don't like apples.

- Have students identify the verbs in the statements and underline them. *(It's raining. She has a dog. We always come to school on time. He didn't call. They don't like apples.)*
- Call on students to provide the tag questions. *(It's raining, isn't it? She has a dog, doesn't she? We always come to school on time, don't we? He didn't call, did he? They don't like apples, do they?)*

Notes 4 and 5

- To practice commenting / checking information with question tags, prepare two sets of cards, using a different color for each set. One set has simple statements:
  Today is Tuesday. It rained yesterday. We're having a test tomorrow. You've been working really hard lately.
  Each card in the other set (an equal number of cards, in a different color) says either *Get information* with an arrow that indicates rising intonation or *Check / Comment* with an arrow that indicates falling intonation. Have students work in pairs: One draws a statement card, the other an intonation card. Together they create the tag question with the appropriate intonation.

Note 6

- Rapid oral drill: Ask students simple but fast-paced negative *yes / no* questions and tag questions: "You're from Argentina, aren't you?" "You're not a musician, are you?" and insist on fast, short answers. Many students have difficulty with the negative answer to a negative question. ("Didn't you come here on Sunday?" *No, I didn't.*) This rapid drill can be a good warm-up exercise even after you finish this unit.

⏲ **Identify the Grammar:** Have students identify the grammar in the opening reading on page 100. For example:
  It's a great place to live, **isn't it**?
  Aren't you Paul Logan?
  Doesn't the cold weather bother you?

Go to **www.myfocusongrammarlab.com** for grammar charts and notes.

Step 3: Focused Practice (pages 107–111)

See the general suggestions for Focused Practice on page 4.

Exercise 1: Discover the Grammar

- Go over the example with the class. Ask: "Is the example a tag or a negative question?" *(a tag)*

- Have students complete the exercise individually and compare answers in pairs.
- Elicit the correct answers from the class.

Exercise 2: Affirmative and Negative Tag Questions
- Go over the example with the class. Have students identify the verb phrase in the statement. *(have called)*
- Encourage students to underline the verb in each statement. This will help them choose their answers correctly.
- Have students compare answers in pairs. Then go over answers as a class.

Exercise 3: Affirmative and Negative Tags
- Go over the example with the class. Ask: "Why is the tag negative?" *(because the statement verb is affirmative)*
- Have students read the conversation for meaning before writing their answers.
- Have students complete the exercise individually and compare answers in pairs. Then call on two students to read the conversation aloud.

Exercise 4: Negative *Yes / No* Questions and Short Answers
- Go over the examples with the class. Direct attention to the information following the short answer. *(My name is Anton Kada.)* Point out that the sentences following the short answers provide the information to complete the conversations.
- Have students read the conversations for meaning before writing their answers.
- Have students complete the exercise individually and compare answers in pairs.
- ⏱ Have pairs role-play the conversations.

Exercise 5: Negative *Yes / No* Questions and Tag Questions
- Go over the example with the class. Point out that both answers (negative *yes / no* question or tag question) are possible.
- Have students complete the exercise individually.
- Call on two students to read the conversation.

Exercise 6: Negative *Yes / No* Questions and Tag Questions
- Go over the example with the class.
- Have students complete the exercise individually. Then go over answers as a class.

- ⏱ For further practice, have pairs write five false statements about famous people. Encourage them to include information they expect other students might know. Example: *Julia Roberts is Mexican.* Have pairs join another pair. Students take turns reading their sentences aloud and correcting them using negative *yes / no* questions or tag questions. *(Isn't she American? She is American, isn't she?)*

Exercise 7: Editing
- Have students read the script quickly to find out what it is about.
- Ask: "Who is wanted by the police?" *(Joe)* "What does Joe ask Ben?" *(to stay in his place for one night)* "Does Ben finally agree?" *(yes)*
- Review the example.
- Have students find and correct the mistakes individually and compare answers in pairs.
- To review as a class, have students explain why the incorrect structures are wrong.
- ⏱ Ask students to point out examples of correct usages of negative questions, tag questions, and short answers.

Go to **www.myfocusongrammarlab.com** for additional grammar practice.

Step 4: Communication Practice (pages 112–116)
See the general suggestions for Communication Practice on page 4.

Exercise 8: Pronunciation
A
- Play the audio. Have students read along as they listen to the Pronunciation Note.
- Ask: "When does the voice rise at the end of a tag question?" *(when the speaker is asking for information)* "When does it fall?" *(when the speaker is making a comment and expects the listener to agree)*

B
- Play the audio. Have students listen and draw the arrows.

C
- Play the audio. Have students listen and repeat the questions.

Exercise 9: Listening
A
- Play the audio. Have students listen to the conversation and check the correct column in each case.
- Play the conversations again, stopping after each conversation to review answers.

B

- Have students read the statements before listening.
- Remind students to pay attention to the rising or falling intonation of tag questions. Play the audio.
- Go over answers as a class.

Exercise 10: Information Gap: London and Vancouver

- Form pairs. Have students complete the questions by choosing the information they think is true. Point out that they will confirm their answers by asking their partners questions.
- Have students read the paragraphs.
- Have students take turns asking and answering the questions. Encourage them to use rising intonation to ask for information and falling intonation to check information they believe is correct.

Exercise 11: Conversation

- Go over the examples with the class. Point out that students should answer the questions and provide additional information as shown in the examples.
- Before students write the questions, encourage them to read the tags carefully to decide which verb to use in the statement.
- Have students take turns asking and answering the questions. Encourage them to use falling intonation because they are checking information they believe is correct.

Exercise 12: Writing

A

- Write the following questions on the board to help students generate ideas and elicit the necessary vocabulary:
  Is it a big city / capital city?
  Is it an important tourist attraction / business center?
  Is it near the beach / the mountains?
  Are there a lot of theaters / restaurants / museums?
  Are there any skyscrapers / ancient structures?
  Is it busy / safe / crowded?
  Does it have a port / a zoo / a big park?
- Have students interview a classmate. Remind them to take notes.

B

- Have students use their notes to write up their interviews.

C

- Have students correct their work using the Editing Checklist.

OUT OF THE BOX ACTIVITIES

Speaking

- Tell students they will play a game. Provide the following information: The police are looking for someone who has been stealing bicycles on campus. They know that the bicycle thief always wears black clothes and gloves, that the person uses a black van, that the stealing happens only at night, and that the thief must be aware of the campus police patrol schedule (because the police can never catch the thief). They also know that the thief is very strong (able to cut through bicycle security chains) and can ride any bicycle fast.
- Have students make up questions for suspects.
- To role-play, assign four to six people to be the police. Then secretly select a "thief" by passing (to the rest of the class) a cap with folded pieces of paper, one of which has the word *thief* on it. Only the student who draws the *thief* slip knows that he or she is "guilty."
- Encourage the use of negative questions (*Don't you have a black van?*) or statements with tag questions (*You can ride bicycles well, can't you?*), and then let the interrogation begin.

Speaking

- As a class, brainstorm what is necessary to prepare for a road trip. Write the verb phrases on the board. Examples: *get maps, gather information from the Internet on places to see, make motel reservations, check the tires, fill the gas tank, pack the suitcases, stop mail delivery, arrange for someone to take care of the pets.*
- Tell students they will interview their partners to ask them about what they have done / haven't yet done to prepare for an imaginary road trip.
- Have students form pairs. Give pairs five to eight slips of paper on which to write questions using the negative *yes / no* question form: *Haven't you . . . ? Didn't you . . . ?* These slips can be put into a bag to be chosen by the person who will answer. Then have students change partners and interview their new partners, taking slips out of the bag and alternating *yes* and *no* answers. (*Yes, I already have / did.* OR *No, I haven't done that yet.*)

Go to **www.myfocusongrammarlab.com** for additional listening, pronunciation, speaking, and writing practice.

Note
- See the *Focus on Grammar Workbook* for additional in-class or homework grammar practice.

Unit 7 Review (page 117)

Have students complete the Unit Review and check their answers on Student Book page UR-2. Review or assign additional material as needed.

Go to **www.myfocusongrammarlab.com** for the Unit Achievement Test.

UNIT 8 OVERVIEW

Grammar: ADDITIONS AND RESPONSES: *So, Too, Neither, Not either,* AND *But*

Students will learn and practice the use of *so, too, neither, not either,* and *but* for additions to sentences.

Theme: SIMILARITIES AND DIFFERENCES

Unit 8 focuses on language that we use to talk about differences and similarities between people.

Identical twins look alike and, in fact, are physically identical because they come from the same egg. Fraternal twins come from two eggs; therefore, they do not usually look alike. In fact, one can be female and the other male.

Step 1: Grammar in Context (pages 118–120)

See the general suggestions for Grammar in Context on page 1.

Before You Read
- Have students look at the photos and discuss the questions in pairs. Ask students to make notes for each question.
- Call on pairs to share their answers to the questions with the class.

Read
- To encourage students to read with a purpose, write the following questions on the board:
  1. What do the three pairs of twins have in common? *(They were separated at birth and grew up in different families and places.)*
  2. Why are scientists interested in identical twins? *(because they share the same genes, so they offer the chance to study the effect of genetic heredity on health and personality)*

3. Why do you think the title of the article is "The Twin Question: Nature or Nurture?" *(because twins who were separated at birth give researchers the chance to study which has more effect on our lives: genes [nature] or the social influences on our childhood [nurture])*

- Have students read the text. (Or play the audio and have students follow along in their books.) Then have students share their answers with the class.
- Have students discuss the following questions in small groups:
  1. If twins are separated at birth, and if the parents know, should they tell a child that he or she has a twin somewhere? Explain.
  2. Which factors play an important role in shaping personality? Give examples.

After You Read

A. Vocabulary
- Have students find and circle the vocabulary in the text. Encourage them to use the context to figure out the meaning.
- Have students compare answers in pairs. Then go over answers as a class.
- 🕐 Write the following on the board. Have students match the sentence halves:

1. They are	a. between them.
2. She has an outgoing	b. in the mirror.
3. There are many similarities	c. can have an effect on our lives.
4. It is a coincidence	d. personality.
5. He saw his own image	e. identical twins.
6. Environmental factors	f. that they got married on the same day.

B. Comprehension
- Have students choose the answers individually and compare answers in pairs.
- Call on students to say an answer each.

Go to **www.myfocusongrammarlab.com** for an additional reading, and for reading and vocabulary practice.

Step 2: Grammar Presentation (pages 121–124)

See the general suggestions for Grammar Presentation on page 2.

Grammar Charts
- Write one example sentence at a time on the board. Have students rewrite the sentences, changing a sentence with *too* to one with *so* and a sentence with *not either* to one with *neither*. Use colored chalk to highlight the changes in word order.
- Write an example sentence with *but*. Highlight the negative with colored chalk: Andrea stayed in Germany, but Barbara did<u>n't</u>.

Grammar Notes

Note 1
- Point out the need for these forms. Show how awkward language becomes when we don't use them by writing the following sentence on the board:
  Heredity doesn't completely govern our lives, and our environment doesn't completely govern our lives.
- Then draw a line across the phrase *completely govern our lives* in the second clause and write the word *either* above it.
- Have the students look for similarities among their classmates so they can make comparisons. Suggested categories include color of hair, color of eyes, style of clothing, type of backpacks, height, and ways of walking, laughing, speaking, smiling, and carrying books. Encourage simple sentences. Examples: *Greta and Theo have blue eyes. Paulo and Elsa don't have blue eyes. Both Alma and Enrique smile a lot.* As you get feedback from students, write sentences using additions with *so* and *but* on the board. Examples:
  1. Greta has blue eyes, and so does Theo.
  2. Greta and Theo have blue eyes, but Paulo and Elsa don't.
  3. Alma smiles a lot, and so does Enrique.
- Do not erase the examples.

Note 2
- Use the ideas from Note 1 to form sentences with *too*, *neither*, and *not either*. Examples:
  1. Greta has blue eyes, and Theo does too.
  2. Paulo doesn't have blue eyes, and neither does Elsa.
  3. Paulo doesn't have blue eyes, and Elsa doesn't either.
  4. Alma smiles a lot, and Enrique does too.
- Use the examples you wrote on the board for this and the previous note to point out:
  — the use of *so*, *too*, *either*, and *not either* to show how people or things are similar
  — the use of *so* and *too* after affirmative statements
  — the use of *either* and *not either* after negative statements
  — the word order after *so* and *neither*

Note 3
- Point out that *but* is used to show how two people or two things are different. Write new examples on the board:
  Lee loves mysteries, but Chou doesn't.
  Chou doesn't like mysteries, but Lee does.
- Point out the negative addition after the affirmative statement and the affirmative addition after the negative statements.
- Have students provide their own examples using *but* to express contrast.

Note 4
- Point out the rules for additions:
  — *be* in the main statement means *be* in the addition
  — a modal in the main statement means a modal in the addition
  — neither *be* nor a modal in the main statement means a form of *do* in the addition
- Mention that these rules hold true in additions with *so*, *neither*, *not either*, and *but*.
- Do a quick drill. Write on the board:
  Maria _____, and so _____ her sister.
  Say the following statements one at a time, and have students provide the additions: "Maria is tall. Maria has a cat. Maria can dance really well. Maria had a happy childhood. Maria will go to college. Maria has visited 10 countries."
- Point out the *Be Careful!* note. Verbs must agree with subjects in additions.

Note 5
- Brainstorm a list of modals and modal-like verbs and write them on the board, for example: can, won't, should, want to, have to, would like to
- Form pairs. Have students take turns using the words on the board in sentences about themselves and using short responses to express agreement or disagreement. Examples: A: *I can't skydive.* B: *Neither can I.*

⏱ **Identify the Grammar:** Have students identify the grammar in the opening reading on page 118. For example:
  Mark was a firefighter, and **so was Gerald**.
  Mark has never been married, and **neither has Gerald**.
  Mark likes hunting . . . **Gerald does too**.
  Tamara loves Chinese food, **but Adriana doesn't**.
  . . . heredity doesn't completely control our lives. Our environment **doesn't either**.

Go to **www.myfocusongrammarlab.com** for grammar charts and notes.

Step 3: Focused Practice (pages 124–127)

See the general suggestions for Focused Practice on page 4.

Exercise 1: Discover the Grammar
- Go over the example with the class. Ask: "Why is the statement true?" (*because* so do I *expresses similarity*)
- Have students complete the exercise individually and compare answers in pairs.
- Elicit the correct answers from the class.

Exercise 2: Additions
- Go over the example with the class.
- Have students read the text for meaning before choosing their answers.
- Call on a student to read the paragraph aloud.
- ⏱ Books closed. Give the twin who has written the story in this exercise a name, for example, Max. Have pairs write four or five sentences about the text using additions. Examples: *Max didn't cheat. Neither did Joe. / The twins were amused, but Mr. Jacobs wasn't.* To review, have students share their sentences with the class.

Exercise 3: Short Responses
- Go over the example with the class. Remind students that the verb comes before the subject after *so* and *neither*.
- Encourage students to identify the verb or auxiliary in each statement so they can decide on the correct verb or auxiliary for the additions.
- Have students complete the exercise individually and compare answers in pairs.
- ⏱ Have pairs role-play the conversation.

Exercise 4: Additions: Similarity or Difference
- Have students study the chart. Ask: "What are the differences between Bob and Randy?"
- Go over the example with the class. Point out that there are two or three ways to complete each sentence.
- Have students complete the exercise individually and compare answers in pairs.
- Go over answers as a class.

Exercise 5: Editing
- Have students read the composition quickly to find out what it is about.

- Ask: "Are Ryan and his brother twins?" *(no)* "What do they have in common?" *(They are the same height; they have straight black hair and brown eyes; they both like soccer and swimming.)* "How are they different?" *(Ryan likes hamburgers and fries, but his brother likes all kinds of foods; Ryan wants to go to college, but his brother doesn't; Ryan is quiet, but his brother is outgoing.)*
- Go over the example.
- Have students find and correct the mistakes individually and compare answers in pairs.
- To review as a class, have students explain why the incorrect structures are wrong.
- ⏱ Ask students to point out examples of correct usages in sentence additions.

Exercise 6: Understanding Additions
- Have students complete the chart individually and compare answers in pairs.
- To review as a class, have students say full sentences. Examples: *Ryan is 18 years old, but his brother isn't. Ryan is 5'10" tall, and so is his brother.*

Go to **www.myfocusongrammarlab.com** for additional grammar practice.

Step 4: Communication Practice (pages 128–132)

See the general suggestions for Communication Practice on page 4.

Exercise 7: Listening

A
- Review how the expressions with *so, too, neither,* and *not either* show that two people agree about things. Only *but* is used to show differences, and *but* can be left out.
  A: I never eat fast food.
  B: I do. Sometimes I'm really in a hurry. *(A doesn't eat fast food, but B does sometimes.)*
- Play the audio. Have students complete the exercise.

B
- Encourage students to pay attention to sentence additions. Play the audio again and have students check the boxes.
- To review as a class, have students say full sentences. Example: *The man loves Italian food, and so does the woman.*
- ⏱ Form pairs. Have students look at the information in the chart and take turns comparing themselves to the man. Example:
  A: *The man loves Italian food, and so do I.*
  B: *I do too!*

Exercise 8: Pronunciation

A

- Play the audio. Have students read along as they listen to the Pronunciation Note.
- Write on the board:
  1. Belle's sister loves chocolate, and so does Belle.
  2. Alex doesn't play football, but Wren does.
- Direct attention to the additions, and have students say which words would normally be stressed. *(1. so, Belle; 2. Wren, does)*

B

- Play the audio. Have students listen and add the stress marks.

C

- Have students repeat the responses. Then have them practice the conversation. Remind them to play both roles.

Exercise 9: Discussion

- Have students write notes about their answers to the questions. Encourage them to write a list of factors that are important in a good match.
- Have students discuss the question in small groups.
- Have students share their ideas with the class.

Exercise 10: Picture Discussion

- Have students work with a partner. Encourage pairs to write down notes for the imagined conversation.
- ⏱ Ask pairs to role-play their conversation for the class.

Exercise 11: Find Someone Who . . .

A

- Encourage students to complete the sentences with information about different topics, for example: free-time activities, vacations, work, future goals, places to live.
- Go over the example. Encourage students to provide an explanation or give an explanation when they express contrast, as shown in the example.

B

- Follow up by having students tell the class which classmate they have more in common with and give examples.

Exercise 12: Compare and Contrast

- Brainstorm what the students notice in the two pictures, for example: the shelves and what is on them, the hairstyles, the glasses, the mustaches, the kind of clothing, the fact that they fold their arms left over right, tidiness. Then have students complete the exercise.
- To review, call on students to read their sentences aloud. You may want to write some of them on the board.

Exercise 13: What Do You Think?

- Go over the example with the class.
- Before students discuss as a class, have students write notes of examples to support their views.
- After students discuss, write *Nature* and *Nurture* on the board, and take a poll to find out what students think is more important in shaping human lives.

Exercise 14: Writing

A

- Write the following topics on the board to help students generate ideas and elicit vocabulary:
  Physical appearance
  Personality
  Likes and dislikes
  Education
  Jobs
  Family
- Have students make notes on some of the topics and use them as a guide as they write.

B

- After students write their paragraphs, have them correct their work using the Editing · Checklist.

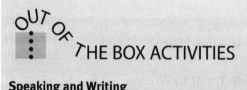

Speaking and Writing

- In small groups, have students discuss growing up. What do they remember learning? How did they have fun?
- Give each student a slip of paper to write a statement about his or her childhood years. Examples: *I learned to swim in a river. I couldn't have a part-time job. I had a pet monkey. I didn't have a bicycle. I learned to ski downhill.*

- Then have students pair up and find out whether their partner had a similar experience or not. They should create sentences like these:

I had a pet monkey, but Yuko had a kitten.
Ahmet learned to swim in a river, and so did I.
I didn't have any brothers, and neither did Maria / Maria didn't either.

Speaking

- Brainstorm a list of topics about which people are likely to have opinions: *sports, food, a law about wearing helmets while bicycling, littering laws (what people should have to clean up if they litter), vegetarianism, high-risk sports.*
- Have students interview someone or several people outside of class.
- Have students come up with reports on their interview findings. *(Mary liked football, and so did Linda. Bob doesn't eat meat, and neither does Michael. Joan and Carlos think bicycle helmets are a good idea, but Karam doesn't and neither does Jaime.)*

Go to **www.myfocusongrammarlab.com** for additional listening, pronunciation, speaking, and writing practice.

Note

- See the *Focus on Grammar Workbook* for additional in-class or homework grammar practice.

Unit 8 Review (page 133)

Have students complete the Unit Review and check their answers on Student Book page UR-2. Review or assign additional material as needed.

Go to **www.myfocusongrammarlab.com** for the Unit Achievement Test.

From Grammar to Writing (pages 134–135)

See general suggestions for From Grammar to Writing on page 9.

Go to **www.myfocusongrammarlab.com** for an additional From Grammar to Writing Assignment, Part Review, and Part Post-Test.

PART IV OVERVIEW

GERUNDS AND INFINITIVES

UNIT	GRAMMAR FOCUS	THEME
9	Gerunds and Infinitives: Review and Expansion	Fast Food
10	*Make, Have, Let, Help*, and *Get*	Zoos and Water Parks

Go to **www.myfocusongrammarlab.com** for the Part and Unit Tests.

Note: PowerPoint® grammar presentations, test-generating software, and reproducible Part and Unit Tests are on the *Teacher's Resource Disc.*

UNIT 9 OVERVIEW

Grammar: GERUNDS AND INFINITIVES: REVIEW AND EXPANSION

Students will learn and practice the meaning and use of gerunds and infinitives.

- Gerunds are base verbs + *-ing* used as nouns. *(I like hiking.)*
- Infinitives are *to* + base verb in form. *(I like to hike.)*
- Often the gerund and the infinitive have essentially the same meaning, so there is a lot of rote memorization involved in learning to use them correctly.

Theme: FAST FOOD

Unit 9 focuses on language that we use to talk about fast food and food preferences.

Because most fast foods are made with taste and not nutrition in mind, they are not necessarily healthy.

Step 1: Grammar in Context (pages 138–140)

See the general suggestions for Grammar in Context on page 1.

Before You Read
- Have students look at the photos and discuss the questions in pairs.
- To review answers as a class, write two column heads—*Reasons for eating fast food* and *Reasons for not eating fast food*—on the board, and write students' ideas under each column.

Read

- To encourage students to read with a purpose, write the following questions on the board:
  1. Why are fast-food restaurants popular? *(because they are fast, convenient, and cheap; the food is familiar and it tastes good)*
  2. Why are some people against them? *(because the food they serve is unhealthy, they prevent families from spending time together around the dinner table, they underpay their workers, they create waste that pollutes the environment)*
- Have students read the text. (Or play the audio and have students follow along in their books.) Call on students to share their answers with the class.
- Have students discuss the following questions in small groups:
  1. What food that is popular in your region could be sold at a fast-food restaurant?
  2. Why do you think so many fast foods are high in sugar, salt, and fat?
  3. How does the fast-food industry affect the environment?

After You Read

A. Vocabulary

- Have students find and circle the vocabulary in the text. Encourage them to use the context to figure out their meaning.
- Have students complete the exercise individually and compare answers with a partner. Then review answers as a class.
- ⏱ To reinforce the vocabulary, prompt the vocabulary words by saying words that are related to them. Example:
  T: *World.*
  Ss: *Globe.*
  Use the words in the following list. *(1. globe; 2. region; 3. consequence; 4. appealing; 5. reliability; 6. objection)*
  1. world
  2. area
  3. effect
  4. attractive
  5. trust
  6. opposition

B. Comprehension

- Have students choose the answers individually. Encourage students to underline the information in the text that supports their answers.
- Have students compare answers with a partner.
- Call on students to say an answer each.

Go to **www.myfocusongrammarlab.com** for an additional reading, and for reading and vocabulary practice.

Step 2: Grammar Presentation (pages 141–143)

See the general suggestions for Grammar Presentation on page 2.

Grammar Charts

- Check that the students know the difference between an infinitive and a gerund by writing a pair of sentences and underlining the relevant parts:
  <u>Eating</u> at McDonald's is easy.
  It's easy <u>to eat</u> at McDonald's.
- Use the example sentences to show the functions of the gerunds and infinitives. For example:
  <u>*Dining*</u> *on fast food* . . . (gerund followed by a prepositional phrase as the subject)
  . . . the speed of <u>ordering</u> and <u>getting</u> served . . . (the two gerunds are objects of the preposition *of*)
  . . . it's <u>easy to see</u> that . . . (the adjective *easy* is followed by the infinitive)
  . . . people <u>don't want to waste</u> time . . . (the infinitive follows the verb *want*)
- Quick pairwork: Have students make up sentences parallel in structure to those in the charts. (From the chart: <u>*Eating*</u> *fast foods is convenient.* Parallel to chart: <u>*Eating*</u> *out is fun.*)

Grammar Notes

Note 1

- Write the following base forms on the board and have students provide the gerunds:
  have   go   take   drive   spend
- Write a list of adjectives on the board:
  easy / difficult, fun / boring, cheap / expensive
  Have students make up sentences with various activities plus the adjectives. *(Taking tests is boring. Shopping is fun.)*

Note 2

- Write on the board:
  1. verb + gerund (I enjoy eating out.)
  2. verb + possessive + gerund (I don't approve of Carla's / her going out.)
- Point out that some verbs like *enjoy* are followed by a gerund. Also point out that you can use a possessive noun *(Carla's)* or possessive adjective *(her)* before the gerund. The possessive before a gerund is normally used in formal English.

- Refer students to Appendix 3 on page A-2. Call on students to provide examples using some of the verbs in the list followed by gerunds.

Note 3
- Write new examples on the board:
  1. I decided <u>to get</u> takeout.
  2. I persuaded <u>him to come</u>.
  3. I want <u>to eat</u> breakfast. OR I want <u>you to eat</u> breakfast.
- Point out that some verbs are followed by an infinitive (Example 1), other verbs are followed by an object and an infinitive (Example 2), and some other verbs can be followed by either an infinitive or an object and an infinitive (Example 3).
- Have students ask a partner: "What do you want to do this weekend?" "What do you want your friend / husband / wife / sister / roommate to do this weekend?" "What does your friend / husband / wife / sister / roommate want you to do this weekend?" Circulate and check grammar and pronunciation (reductions: *whaddya* for *what do you*, *wantcha* for *want you*).

Note 4
- Explain that some verbs can take either a gerund or an infinitive with little or no change in meaning. Examples: *begin, continue, hate, like, love, prefer, start.*
- Point out the *Be Careful!* note. Some verbs can take either a gerund or an infinitive, but there is a difference in meaning. Examples: *forget, remember, try, stop.*
- Have students make sentences with these verbs and add a second sentence to explain the difference in meaning for each example. (*I forgot to water the plants. [I didn't water them at all.] I forgot watering the plants. [Oh, yes, and I almost forgot to tell you: I also watered the plants.]*) You might give the students the situation and have them create the sentences. Say, for example, "A man was working, using both hands, but he wanted a cigarette. He couldn't smoke and work at the same time, so . . ." (*He stopped to smoke.*) Then say, "A man smoked for years but then wanted to become healthier, so . . ." (*He stopped smoking.*)

Note 5
- Have students use the verb + preposition combinations in Appendix 7 (page A-3) to make true sentences about themselves and their friends.

- Remind students that *to* in these cases is a preposition, not an infinitive; hence the tricky *look forward to having.*
- Have students ask their partners: "What are you looking forward to doing tomorrow / this weekend / next year?" Stress the reduction: "*Whadderya.*"

Note 6
- Verbs that can be followed by infinitives are listed in Appendices 4 and 5 on page A-3. Adjectives that can be followed by infinitives are listed in Appendix 9 on page A-4.
- Have pairs practice asking and answering questions like these: "What are you afraid to do?" (*I'm afraid to try skydiving. I'm afraid to swim where there might be sharks.*) Note that some people say, "*I'm afraid of swimming where there might be sharks.*" "What foods are you reluctant to try?" (*I'm reluctant to try raw fish. I'm reluctant to try some tropical fruits.*)
- Point out that almost any noun can be followed by an infinitive phrase in order to provide additional information (for example, *a doll to play with, a day to remember / forget, paper to write on*).
- Have students ask each other: "What do you want to buy, and why?" (*I want to buy some new shoes <u>to wear</u> on Saturday.*)

Note 7
- Remind students that this use of the infinitive is connected to the question *Why? (Why does Doug eat fast food? To save time.)*
- Point out that this also can be seen as an abbreviation of *in order to*. Write on the board:
  Doug eats fast food in order to save time.
  Then cross out *in order*.

Note 8
- As a class, have students do a substitution chain drill with these structures.
  1. Student A creates a sentence with a **gerund** subject. (*Riding an exercycle is good exercise.*)
  2. Student B changes the gerund subject to the <u>it + noun phrase + **infinitive** structure</u>. (*It's good exercise to ride an exercycle.*)
  3. Student C changes the <u>adjective</u>. (*It's boring to ride an exercycle.*)
  4. Student D changes it back to a **gerund** subject. (*Riding an exercycle is boring.*)
- Let students change any part of the sentence. If they get into a rut, you can offer a prompt: "It is . . ." or "Watching television every night . . ."

⏱ **Identify the Grammar:** Have students identify the grammar in the opening reading on page 138. For example:

> . . . you can **expect to hear** this order . . .
> . . . the numbers **keep growing**.
> . . . customers **need to travel** less than four minutes **to arrive** . . .
> **Dining** on fast food has become a way of life . . .

Go to **www.myfocusongrammarlab.com** for grammar charts and notes.

Step 3: Focused Practice (pages 144–148)

See the general suggestions for Focused Practice on page 4.

Exercise 1: Discover the Grammar
- Go over the examples with the class.
- Have students do the exercise individually and compare answers with a partner. **Note:** Students are not expected to complete the questionnaire at this stage. They will do so in Exercise 9.
- Elicit the correct answers from the class.

Exercise 2: Gerund or Infinitive
- Go over the example with the class.
- Have students study the chart and read the statements for meaning before doing the exercise.
- Have students complete the exercise individually and compare answers in pairs. Then go over as a class.

Exercise 3: Verb + Gerund or Infinitive
- Go over the verbs in the box. Have students say if they are followed by a gerund, an infinitive, or either a gerund or an infinitive. Encourage students to refer to the appendices on pages A-2 and A-3 if necessary.
- Have students read the conversations for meaning and match each summary with a verb from the box.
- Have students complete the exercise. Then go over answers as a class.

Exercise 4: Gerund or Infinitive with and without Object
- Go over the example with the class. Point out the subject pronoun *I* in parentheses and the object pronoun *me* in the example. If necessary, remind students that we use object pronouns before infinitives and possessive nouns or adjectives before gerunds.
- Have students read the letters for meaning.

- Have students complete the exercise individually and compare answers in pairs.
- ⏱ Ask the following questions and have students answer in full sentences: "Why did Andre stop using the dining hall?" *(He stopped using it because it wasn't appealing to him.)* "What was M. Rodriguez happy to see as soon as she went into the dining hall yesterday?" *(She was happy to see a Taco Bell sign.)* "What does she think about changing to fast food?" *(She thinks that changing to fast food is the thing to do.)* "What did B. Chen expect to find in the dining hall?" *(He expected to find the usual healthy choices of vegetables and salads.)* "Why does he try to stay away from fast foods?" *(He tries to stay away from fast foods because as a commuter, he needs a healthy meal before class.)* "What does he urge the administration to do?" *(He urges the administration to set up a salad bar.)*

Exercise 5: Editing
- Have students read the posts quickly to find out what they are about.
- Have students number the posts 1–6. Ask the following questions and have students say the post they refer to: "Who is worried about not finding vegetarian dishes while traveling?" *(2)* "Who recommends a restaurant?" *(6)* "Who is interested in international food?" *(4)* "Who is not worried about the consequences of eating fast food?" *(1)* "Who tried seafood and likes it?" *(5)* "Who wants to try typical Japanese food?" *(3)*
- Review the example.
- Have students find and correct the mistakes individually and compare answers in pairs.
- Have students explain why the incorrect structures are wrong.
- ⏱ Ask students to point out examples of correct usages of the gerund and the infinitive.

Go to **www.myfocusongrammarlab.com** for additional grammar practice.

Step 4: Communication Practice (pages 149–154)

See the general suggestions for Communication Practice on page 4.

Exercise 6: Listening
A
- Have students read the statements. Then play the audio.
- Have students complete the exercise individually.

B

- Play the audio again. Have students complete the exercise individually and compare answers in pairs.
- (!) To get students to express their opinion, have pairs of students discuss their ideas about a school's food services. *Should there be fast foods available? Who should decide what kinds of foods students can buy? What kinds of food services are common in other parts of the world? Why do fast-food franchises open restaurants on campuses?*

Exercise 7: Pronunciation

A

- Play the audio. Have students read along as they listen to the Pronunciation Note.
- Write on the board:
  A: Let's get takeout.
  B: Great idea!
- Ask: "How can intonation affect the meaning of the exclamation on the board?" *(If the voice starts high and then drops, the speaker really thinks that getting takeout is a good idea. If the voice starts low and stays flat, the speaker thinks that getting takeout is not a good idea at all.)*

B

- Play the audio. Have students listen and check the boxes.

C

- Have students play both roles.

Exercise 8: Information Gap: The Right Job?

- After students complete Jennifer's quiz, have them makes notes of reasons why the jobs are / aren't good for Jennifer. Encourage them to choose the best job for her.
- Have students explain their reasons why Jennifer is / isn't a good candidate for the jobs in the ads.
- (!) Have students copy the questionnaire on a sheet of paper and complete the questions with information about themselves. Have pairs of students interview each other to see which interests they have in common and discuss which job from the ads would be the most appropriate for them.

Exercise 9: Questionnaire

A

- Have students complete the survey individually.

B

- Have students compare answers in pairs.

- As students compare their answers to the questions, make sure they use gerunds and infinitives correctly. Encourage them to support their answers by giving examples. *(I'm used to eating lunch at fast-food restaurants. I often have lunch at McDonald's on weekdays.)*

C

- Tally the results of the questionnaire. Discuss as a class the results of the survey.

Exercise 10: Cross-Cultural Comparison

A

- Have students think about their answers to the questions. Then have students work in small groups. **Note:** Students can help one another learn about traditional foods from other places. Have students who have similar traditions work together to talk about particular foods.

B

- After students compare their lists in groups, have them share the foods they would like to try with the class. Make a list of typical dishes on the board and have students describe them for the class.

Exercise 11: Problem Solving

A

- Ask small groups of students to prioritize the four problems listed: *people being overweight, traffic, literacy problems,* and *homelessness.*
- Have them explain their reasons. Note that the priorities will vary in different regions.
- As a class, have students decide on a problem for Item 5. Ask students: "What are some issues that people are discussing on television, in the newspapers, and around school?" (Examples: *flooding on the streets after storms, violence in movies and on TV, people throwing trash out on the roads [littering]*)

B

- Have groups compare answers.
- Then have students from different groups share solutions to each of the problems with the class.

Exercise 12: Writing

A

- Have students choose one of the issues and write notes about their opinion. Encourage students to use five or six gerunds and infinitives in their writing. Then have students write their editorial.

B

- Have students exchange editorials with a classmate. Have them write a letter to the editor agreeing or disagreeing with their partner's editorial.

C

- After students write their letters, have them correct their work using the Editing Checklist.

OUT OF THE BOX ACTIVITIES

Speaking

- **Note:** This can be done as a five-minute per class activity over the course of a semester.
- Use the lists from Appendices 3, 4 and 6, pages A-2–A-3 (verbs that can be followed by the gerund, verbs that can be followed by the infinitive, and verbs that can be followed by either the gerund or the infinitive). Type them up in mixed order, and then photocopy so that each student has a list. Ask students, individually, to go over the list and mark "+ inf.," "+ -ing," or "+ inf. or -ing" next to each verb. When they've finished, read the correct answers and have students mark where they made a mistake. Then generate a master list of the class's "problems" from these individual lists (total class time: about 10 minutes).
- Spend five minutes per class on three or four different verbs from this selective list by playing "Going to Jerusalem" in groups of three. Here's how it works: If the verbs for the day are *demand, promise, hesitate, mention*, students make a chain of sentences using these verbs.
  A: I demand to go home.
  B: She demands to go home, and I promise to take her home.
  C: She demands to go home, she promises to take her home, but I hesitate to leave early.
  A: I demand to go home, she promises to take me, he hesitates to leave early, and I mention being tired and hungry.
- **Note:** Sometimes this slips naturally into past tense, which is fine; just make sure the gerunds and infinitives don't change.

Reading and Speaking

- Have students bring classified ads to class.
- As they read the Help Wanted or Job Opening ads, have them discuss the qualifications for the jobs using gerunds. (*A restaurant chef's job includes washing, peeling, and cutting up vegetables. A security officer's job is checking locks and watching for trouble.*) More directly, they could say, *I'm a chef. My job is cutting up vegetables. . . .*
- Have the students write the titles of the jobs they find on index cards with a list of responsibilities under them. Post the cards on the bulletin board.

Go to **www.myfocusongrammarlab.com** for additional listening, pronunciation, speaking, and writing practice.

Note

- See the *Focus on Grammar Workbook* for additional in-class or homework grammar practice.

Unit 9 Review (page 155)

Have students complete the Review and check their answers on Student Book page UR-3. Review or assign additional material as needed.

Go to **www.myfocusongrammarlab.com** for the Unit Achievement Test.

UNIT 10 OVERVIEW

Grammar: *Make, Have, Let, Help,* AND *Get*

Students will learn the meanings and uses of *make, have, let, help,* and *get* as verbs used as auxiliaries to show that one person can *cause* (or *require, permit,* or *persuade*) another person to do something.

Theme: ZOOS AND WATER PARKS

Unit 10 focuses on language that we use to talk about keeping animals in captivity and having them perform in shows.

In general, people naturally seem to distrust animals just as animals distrust people. Perhaps that is why tamed animals are so dear to people who love their pets.

Step 1: Grammar in Context (pages 156–158)

See the general suggestions for Grammar in Context on page 1.

Before You Read

- Have students look at the photos and discuss the questions in pairs. For Question 2, encourage students to use their own experience to answer the question: Have they ever been to a water park or circus? Did they enjoy the show?
- Have students make notes for each question.
- Call on pairs to share their answers to the questions with the class. Encourage students to explain why they think animals should / shouldn't be used for entertainment.

Read

- To encourage students to read with a purpose, write the following questions on the board:
  1. What are the two methods to train animals? *(cruel punishment or positive reinforcement—a kind, humane way)*
  2. When was the second method developed? Why? *(in the 1940s, when trainers wanted to have dolphins do tricks and they could not punish them because they would swim away)*
  3. What is the difference between an elephant trained with each method? *(Punishment makes elephants angry so that they rebel and can become dangerous. Positively reinforced elephants are gentle animals that seem to understand that their trainers want to help them.)*
- Have students read the text. (Or play the audio and have students follow along in their books.) Call on students to share their answers with the class.
- Have students discuss one or all of the following questions in small groups:
  1. What are some basic human rights? Do animals also have rights? What do you think their rights should be? How are animals and people different? The same?
  2. "Vote with your feet." Why do people who work for the freedom of animals urge others to stay away from circuses and animal parks?
  3. Are wild animals always less happy in captivity? What are disadvantages to life in the wild?

After You Read

A. Vocabulary

- Have students find and circle the vocabulary in the text. Encourage them to use the context to figure out their meaning.

- Have students compare answers with a partner. Then review answers as a class.
- ⏱ To reinforce the vocabulary, say the following clues, and have students answer using the vocabulary words. *(1. complicated; 2. a punishment; 3. a reward; 4. physical health; 5. former trainers; 6. humane)*
  1. It is not simple. What is it like?
  2. The elephant rebelled. What did it get?
  3. The monkey did the trick. What did it receive?
  4. This kind of health is as important as emotional health. What is it?
  5. They used to be trainers. What are they?
  6. They are kind to the animals in the zoo. What kind of treatment do the animals get?

B. Comprehension

- Have students choose the answers individually. Encourage them to underline the information in the text that supports their answers.
- Have students compare answers in pairs. Then call on students to say an answer each.

Go to **www.myfocusongrammarlab.com** for an additional reading, and for reading and vocabulary practice.

Step 2: Grammar Presentation (page 159)

See the general suggestions for Grammar Presentation on page 2.

Grammar Charts

- Write *make, have, let, help,* and *get,* on the board. After each one, write an example sentence from the reading. Erase the subject and have the students provide a new one. Next erase the phrase after *make, have, let, help,* or *get.* Have the students write a new sentence ending. Encourage them to find humorous ideas. (For example: *The teacher lets the students sleep in class!*)
- Write the example sentence with *How do trainers get whales to do acrobatic tricks?* on the board. Erase different parts for students to supply new words. (For example: *How could I . . . ?* in place of *How do trainers . . . ?*)

Grammar Notes

Note 1

- Point out that *make, have,* and *get* are very common and often sound more natural (to native speakers) than their equivalents: *force, cause, persuade.*
- Emphasize that *make* and *have* are followed by an object and a base form and that *get* is followed by an object and an infinitive.

- Have students make up answers for each of the following situations. Point out that students should use *make*, *have*, and *get* in their answers, as appropriate.
  1. Gerry is a trainer at a water park. What does he make his dolphin do? *(He makes him do tricks; he makes him jump; he makes him carry a ball on his nose.)*
  2. Sarah had her students work very hard this morning. What did she have them do? *(She had them do research; she had them write an essay; she had them take a test.)*
  3. Brad has a younger sister, Ashley. Last weekend, he got her to do lots of things for him. What did he get her to do? *(He got her to bring him some soda; he got her to make his bed; he got her to prepare breakfast for him.)*
- You may want to point out that *get . . . to do (something)* is common in combination with another verb (for example, *try to* get the kids to practice piano, *can't* get my husband to do the dishes).

Note 2
- Emphasize that *let* is followed by an object and a base form.
- Have students make up answers for the following situation:
  "In return for all the favors Ashley did for her brother, he let her do things he doesn't usually let his sister do. What did he let her do?" *(He let her play in his bedroom; he let her use his computer.)*

Note 3
- Emphasize that *help* can be followed by either an object and a base form or an object and an infinitive.
- Have students give examples of things or activities that help them in their daily lives. *(Exercise helps me (to) have more energy. A diet rich in vegetables helps me (to) stay healthy. My GPS helps me (to) get everywhere on time.)*

(!) **Identify the Grammar:** Have students identify the grammar in the opening reading on page 156. For example:
   . . . sea mammals have been **making audiences say** *oooh* and *aaaah* . . .
   . . . how do trainers **get** *nine-ton whales* **to do** acrobatic tricks or **make** *them* "**dance**"?
   . . . trainers controlled animals with collars and leashes and **made** *them* **perform** . . .
   . . . parks wanted to **have** *dolphins* **do** tricks. You can't **get** *a dolphin* **to wear** a collar.

Go to **www.myfocusongrammarlab.com** for grammar charts and notes.

Step 3: Focused Practice (pages 160–163)
See the general suggestions for Focused Practice on page 4.

Exercise 1: Discover the Grammar
- Go over the example with the class. Ask: "Why is *b* the correct answer?" *(because Ms. Bates got the principal to do it, so she persuaded him / her to do it)*
- Have students identify and circle the forms of *make*, *have*, *let*, *help*, and *get*.
- Have students complete the exercise individually and compare answers in pairs.
- Elicit the correct answers from the class.

Exercise 2: Meaning: *Make, Have, Let, Help* and *Get*
- Go over the example with the class. Remind students that *make*, *have*, and *let* need a base form, *get* needs an infinitive, and *help* can be used with either a base form or an infinitive.
- Have students complete the exercise and compare answers in pairs. Then go over answers as a class.
- (!) For further practice, have students write true or imaginary sentences using the authority figures in the exercise and the verbs they learned in this unit (*make*, *have*, *let*, *help* and *get*).

Exercise 3: Affirmative and Negative Statements
- Go over the example with the class.
- Have students complete the exercise individually and compare answers in pairs. Then go over answers as a class.
- (!) Have pairs write sentences of what you made, let, or helped them do today. Encourage students to write five or six sentences using *make*, *have*, *let*, *help*, and *get*. Students can write about themselves or other students in the classroom. *(You made us work in groups. You helped Aaron answer a question.)* Then call on students to read some of their sentences aloud.

Exercise 4: Affirmative and Negative Statements
- Go over the example with the class.
- Have students complete the exercise individually and compare answers in pairs. Then go over answers as a class.
- (!) In small groups, have students compare what their parents made, let, or helped them do when they were children. Example:
  A: My mother made me wash the dishes.
  B: Mine didn't. But my father made me wash his car.
  C: So did mine!

Exercise 5: Editing

- Have students read the email quickly.
- Ask: "What are the arguments against making orcas perform in water parks?" *(In water parks, orcas don't have physical or emotional health, they may get sick and die, they cannot behave naturally, they cannot have social lives in families, and they don't really help us learn about their lives.)*
- Go over the example.
- Have students find and correct the mistakes individually and compare answers in pairs.
- To review as a class, have students explain why the incorrect structures are wrong.
- (⏱) Ask students to point out examples of correct usages of *make, have, let, help,* and *get.*

Go to **www.myfocusongrammarlab.com** for additional grammar practice.

Step 4: Communication Practice (pages 164–166)

See the general suggestions for Communication Practice on page 4.

Exercise 6: Listening

A
- Have students read the statements.
- Play the audio.

B
- If necessary, have students listen a second time to correct the false statements.
- To review as a class, have students support their answers with details they remember. Example: *1. Simon chose the topic himself, and Ms Jacobson said it was a good topic.*
- (⏱) Ms. Jacobson gives two example questions Simon can use to add more details to the second paragraph of his essay. This paragraph is about Simon's uncle, who used to work at a wildlife park. The questions are: "When did you decide to study zoology? Where were you living at the time?" Have students give examples of other *wh-* questions Simon could use.

Exercise 7: Pronunciation

A
- Play the audio. Have students read along as they listen to the Pronunciation Note.
- Point out that reduced pronouns are not stressed.

B
- Play the audio. Have students listen and complete the sentences.

C
- Have students play both roles.

Exercise 8: Discussion

- Have students discuss their experiences with a partner. Then call on some students to share their ideas with the class.

Exercise 9: For or Against

- Have students write notes of reasons for and against keeping animals captive. Then have students discuss in small groups.
- Call on a few students to share their views with the class. Do most students agree?

Exercise 10: Writing

A
- Write the following sentence starters on the board. Encourage students to include some of them in their writing:
  It is important to let animals . . .
  Some trainers make animals . . .
  It is cruel to make animals . . .
  It is a good idea to have animals . . .
  Some zookeepers have / let animals . . .
  We should help animals . . .
  We should try to get zoos / water parks to . . .

B
- After students write their paragraphs, have them correct their work using the Editing Checklist.

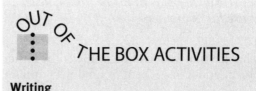

OUT OF THE BOX ACTIVITIES

Writing

- On the board, write the five causative verbs: *make, have, let, help,* and *get.*
- Brainstorm figures of authority: *a police officer, the government, a good boss, a bad boss, my mother, the head of the school.* Write them on the board.
- In pairs or small groups, have students write affirmative and negative sentences using the five verbs. Encourage them to create humorous sentences. *(A police officer made me stop picking flowers in the park. The head of the school got me to try out for the lead in the school play.)*

- Have students share some of their sentences with the class.

Listening and Speaking

- Have students go back to the same working people they interviewed for the Out of the Box Activity in Unit 5. This time they will ask them about their relationships with other people at work, either people they supervise or people who supervise them. What do they have people do, make people do, get people to do during their working day?
- Students then report back to the class. *(I spoke to a doctor. She tries to get patients to eat right. She has them take medicine when they need it. Her job makes her feel tired.)*

Go to **www.myfocusongrammarlab.com** for additional listening, pronunciation, speaking, and writing practice.

Note
- See the *Focus on Grammar Workbook* for additional in-class or homework grammar practice.

Unit 10 Review (page 167)

Have students complete the Review and check their answers on Student Book page UR-3. Review or assign additional material as needed.

Go to **www.myfocusongrammarlab.com** for the Unit Achievement Test.

From Grammar to Writing (pages 168–170)

See general suggestions for From Grammar to Writing on page 9.

Go to **www.myfocusongrammarlab.com** for an additional From Grammar to Writing Assignment, Part Review, and Part Post-Test.

PART V OVERVIEW

PHRASAL VERBS

UNIT	GRAMMAR FOCUS	THEME
11	Phrasal Verbs: Review	Feng Shui
12	Phrasal Verbs: Separable and Inseparable	Telemarketing

Go to **www.myfocusongrammarlab.com** for the Part and Unit Tests.

Note: PowerPoint® grammar presentations, test-generating software, and reproducible Part and Unit Tests are on the *Teacher's Resource Disc*.

UNIT 11 OVERVIEW

Grammar: PHRASAL VERBS: REVIEW

Students will review the meanings and uses of phrasal verbs: transitive and intransitive, separable and inseparable.

- Phrasal verbs, also called two-word verbs, are made up of a verb and a particle (which "looks like" a preposition). Note that the particle often does not help make the meaning clear out of context.
- Most transitive phrasal verbs are separable (meaning that the object can go before or after the particle).
- Intransitive phrasal verbs cannot be separated.

Theme: FENG SHUI

Unit 11 focuses on language that we use to talk about feng shui, our environment, and how we can adjust it to feel better.

There is a great deal that we do not know about the world and how things work. How energy flows may be one of those things. Feng shui is an old idea in China, but it is new in many other parts of the world.

Step 1: Grammar in Context (pages 172–173)

See the general suggestions for Grammar in Context on page 1.

Before You Read

- Write *feng shui* on the board. Call on students to say what they know about it. Encourage simple sentences. *(It's a Chinese art. It's about positive energy. It means wind and water.)* Be sure students pronounce the term correctly (FUNG SHWAY).

- Have students write notes for their answers to each question. For Question 2, have students give examples.
- Call on students to share their answers with the class.

Read
- To encourage students to read with a purpose, write the following questions on the board:
  1. What problem did Ho Da-ming have? *(He had set up a restaurant on a busy street and paid a fortune to decorate it, but it was failing.)*
  2. How did feng shui help solve it? *(The feng shui consultant said the entrance was letting prosperity out. Da-ming tore the old one down and put up a new one, and soon business picked up.)*
- Have students read the text. (Or play the audio and have students follow along in their books.) Call on students to share their answers with the class.
- Have students discuss the following questions in small groups:
  1. Do you believe the arrangement of things in a house can affect people? Why or why not?
  2. Do you like to move things around in your room or your house? How do you feel after you do it?
  3. How does art affect you? Does a painting ever give you really good feelings? Do some paintings depress you? Why do you think you have these reactions?

After You Read

A. Vocabulary
- Have students find and circle the vocabulary in the text. Encourage them to use the context to figure out their meaning.
- Have students complete the exercise individually and compare answers in pairs. Then go over answers as a class.
- ⏱ Write the following sentences on the board. Have students complete them using four of the vocabulary words. Then go over answers as a class. *(1. harmful; 2. complex; 3. environment; 4. consultant)*
  1. Energy can be good or _____.
  2. A theory can be simple or _____.
  3. Your home and workplace are your _____.
  4. To find out more about feng shui, do research or ask a _____.

B. Comprehension
- Have students choose the answers individually. Encourage students to underline the information in the text that supports their answers.

- Have students compare answers in pairs. Then call on students to say an answer each.

Go to **www.myfocusongrammarlab.com** for an additional reading, and for reading and vocabulary practice.

Step 2: Grammar Presentation (pages 174–176)
See the general suggestions for Grammar Presentation on page 2.

Grammar Charts
- Write one sentence with an intransitive phrasal verb on the board. *(His hard work paid off.)* Point out that the two-word verb really has one meaning (*pay off* = be worthwhile).
- Emphasize that phrasal verbs are less formal than single-word verbs and are used more frequently, and that often the single-word equivalent sounds "funny" or overly formal to native speakers, for example *fetch* or *collect* instead of *pick up*.
- Write a transitive sentence with a phrasal verb from the reading on the board. Show how the direct object can move before and after the particle:
  He had <u>set</u> his restaurant <u>up</u> on a busy street.
  He had <u>set up</u> his restaurant on a busy street.
- Point out that the pronoun *it* could take the place of *his restaurant,* but only if the verb *set up* is separated: He <u>set it up</u>. If the direct object is a pronoun, it has to go between the verb and the particle.

Grammar Notes

Note 1
- Write on the board:
  1. I'm looking up at the ceiling.
  2. I'm looking up the new word in my dictionary.
- Circle *up* in both examples. Point out that it is a preposition in Example 1 and a particle in Example 2.
- Explain that particles might look like prepositions, but they act differently. They change the meaning of the verb. Ask: "Which example uses a phrasal verb?" *(2)*

Note 2
- Have pairs add to the sentences with the phrasal verbs in the chart: *come back, figure out, look into, pick up, put up.* (We had to figure out the problem <u>because no one else would do it</u>. We looked into feng shui <u>to find a reason for the problems with our health</u>.)
- Draw attention to the *Be Careful!* note.

Note 3

- Be sure students understand what a transitive phrasal verb is (a phrasal verb that needs an object to go with it). Point out that most transitive verbs are separable.
- Write on the board:
  Separable transitive phrasal verbs
  1. verb + particle + object (noun)
  2. verb + object (noun) + particle
  3. verb + object (pronoun) + particle
- Point out that when the object is a noun, it has two possible positions. When the object is a pronoun, it has only one position.
- Write an example next to each pattern:
  1. He figured out the problem.
  2. He figured the problem out.
  3. He figured it out.
- Have students write their own examples for each of the patterns on the board using phrasal verbs from Appendix 18 on pages A-6–A-7.
- Suggest that students add adjectives to direct objects so that there are more than three words in the direct object and the verb becomes inseparable. More than three words is too long to "fit" between a verb and a particle. Explain that *He looked the number up* or *He looked up the number* are both OK, but not *He **looked** the number of his new classmate with red hair and glasses **up***. Encourage the students to have some fun with this idea by trying to make the sentence longer and longer (but still grammatically correct).

Note 4

- Explain that some phrasal verbs do not take an object—they are intransitive.
- Give each pair of students four intransitive verbs to use in sentences. (Use the list of intransitive verbs in Appendix 19, page A-8.) Have the students share their sentences with the class—one student reading the sentence and the other restating it with the meaning clarified. For example: *The news announcer went on for five more minutes. = The news announcer continued for five minutes. He talked five more minutes.*

⏱ **Identify the Grammar:** Have students identify the grammar in the opening reading on page 172. For example:
  Ho Da-ming couldn't **figure out** why his restaurant was failing.
  He had **set** it **up** on a busy street.
  . . . customers rarely **came back**.
  Mr. Ho **called in** a feng shui consultant to **find out**.

Go to **www.myfocusongrammarlab.com** for grammar charts and notes.

Step 3: Focused Practice (pages 177–181)

See the general suggestions for Focused Practice on page 4.

Exercise 1: Discover the Grammar

A

- Go over the example with the class. Remind students that objects can appear between the verb and the particle or immediately after the phrasal verb. Also remind them that objects can be nouns, noun phrases, or pronouns.
- Have students complete the exercise individually and compare answers in pairs.
- Elicit the correct answers from the class.

B

- Have students refer back to the text if necessary.
- Encourage students to underline the information that supports their answers.
- Go over answers as a class.

Exercise 2: Particles

- Encourage students to choose the particles that sound natural to them, and to refer to the appendices to confirm their choices.
- Call on two students to read the questions and answers aloud.
- ⏱ Write the following on the board. Have pairs match transitive phrasal verbs with the phrases they collocate with and then use them in sentences. *(1. a painting; 2. a book from the library; 3. more about a topic; 4. a tall building; 5. a tree; 6. a word in a list; 7. a problem; 8. the light)*

  1. hang up   a tall building
  2. take out   a problem
  3. find out   a tree
  4. put up   the light
  5. cut down   more about a topic
  6. look up   a word in a list
  7. work out   a painting
  8. block out   a book from the library

Exercise 3: Meaning of Phrasal Verbs

- Go over the meanings of the phrasal verbs in the boxes. Have students refer to the appendices if necessary.
- Have students complete the exercise and compare answers in pairs. Then go over answers as a class.

- ⏱ To extend the activity, have students cover the text and look at the phrasal verbs in the boxes. In pairs, have students take turns using the phrasal verbs in sentences about the text. Ask students to write as many sentences as possible. Call on students to read their sentences aloud.

Exercise 4: Pronoun Objects
- Go over the example with the class. Have students identify the phrasal verb and point out the use of the pronoun *them* in the example.
- Have students complete the exercise individually and compare answers in pairs.
- Call on pairs to read the conversations aloud.

Exercise 5: Editing
- Have students read the entry quickly.
- Ask: "What changes is the student going to make in his or her apartment? Why?" (*buy another lamp to light the apartment up at night; touch up the paint in his / her bedroom because it is chipped; straighten his / her apartment up so it looks more spacious*)
- Review the example with the class.
- Have students find and correct the mistakes individually and compare answers in pairs.
- To review as a class, have students explain why the incorrect structures are wrong.
- ⏱ Ask students to point out examples of correct usages of phrasal verbs.

Go to **www.myfocusongrammarlab.com** for additional grammar practice.

Step 4: Communication Practice (pages 181–184)

See the general suggestions for Communication Practice on page 4.

Exercise 6: Listening
A
- Have students read the statements. Play the audio. If necessary, pause after each conversation to allow students time to answer.
- Have students support their answers. Example: *Ben hasn't finished redecorating his office because he still has to go to a store / pick out a couch.*

B
- Play the audio. The particles are not emphasized, and students might have difficulty hearing them. If necessary, replay the conversations.

Exercise 7: Pronunciation
A
- Play the audio. Have students read along as they listen to the Pronunciation Note.
- Ask: "When is it possible to link verbs with particles?" (*when the verb ends in a consonant and the particle starts with a vowel*)

B
- Have students read the conversations and identify the phrasal verbs. Play the audio. Have students listen and mark the stress and draw the linking lines.

C
- Play the audio again. Have students practice the conversations with a partner. Remind them to play both roles.

Exercise 8: Problem Solving
- Go over the phrasal verbs in the list. Discuss what can be *covered up, lit up, put away,* etc. Examples:
  cover up: a sofa, old boxes
  light up: a room, a corner
  put away: books, clothes
  throw away: old magazines, things that don't work
- Have students share their ideas with the class. List them on the board.

Exercise 9: Compare and Contrast
- Write on the board a list of useful phrasal verbs students can use to describe differences. Examples:

pick up	turn around
throw away	clean up
put away	turn off
touch up	hang up
straighten up	put up
take down	

- ⏱ Have students discuss in general what they have changed or would like to change in the appearance of their bedrooms.

Exercise 10: Writing
- ⏱ Brainstorm as a class a list of decorating ideas that students like. Then brainstorm a list of decorating ideas (or bad housekeeping ideas) that they do not like. Have pairs ask each other how a tidy environment or an attractive environment affects how they feel about working and living in that space. (Or is one partner someone who doesn't seem to notice a pleasant or unpleasant environment?)

A

- Write the following topics on the board to help students generate ideas and elicit vocabulary:

  arrangement of furniture
  arrangement of doors and windows
  light
  colors
  tidiness
  comfort
  temperature
  paint
  decorative objects
  items that are old, torn, broken
  new items that are needed

- Have students make notes for some of the topics and then use them as a guide as they write their paragraphs.

B

- After students complete their paragraphs, have them correct their work using the Editing Checklist.

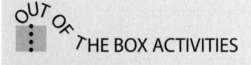

OUT OF THE BOX ACTIVITIES

Writing and Speaking

- Have students work with a partner to find 10 phrasal verbs that neither knows in Appendices 18 and 19, pages A-6–A-8. Then have them write a dialogue using those verbs.
- Have students submit the dialogues to you for correction.
- Have pairs role-play the dialogues for the class.

Listening and Writing

- Have students interview at least two native speakers of English about improvements or changes they have made to their homes. Remind students to take notes.
- Have students write down all the phrasal verbs that the native speakers used (or as many as they can) and share them with the rest of the class, giving context and examples. Some phrasal verbs should come up in several student interviews (for example, *do over, fix up, take apart, put together, take down, put up*).

Go to **www.myfocusongrammarlab.com** for additional listening, pronunciation, speaking, and writing practice.

Note

- See the *Focus on Grammar Workbook* for additional in-class or homework grammar practice.

Unit 11 Review (page 185)

Have students complete the Review and check their answers on Student Book page UR-3. Review or assign additional material as needed.

Go to **www.myfocusongrammarlab.com** for the Unit Achievement Test.

Step 1: Grammar in Context (pages 186–188)

See the general suggestions for Grammar in Context on page 1.

Before You Read

- Have students look at the cartoon and discuss the questions in pairs.
- For Question 2, encourage students to share examples of calls they received.
- Go over answers as a class.

Read

- To encourage students to read with a purpose, write the following questions on the board:
  1. What is telemarketing? *(the practice of selling products and services by phone)*
  2. Why is telemarketing becoming so widespread? *(The number of telephones has gone up and costs of telephones have come down.)*
  3. What are "Do Not Call" lists? *(lists of people who do not want to be called by telemarketers; you can sign up to have your number placed on them)*

4. Why do people have caller ID? *(You can see what number is calling you and answer only the calls you want to receive.)*
5. What is junk mail? *(unwanted offers and requests)*
6. What do we call advertising, free offers, and requests on email? *(spam)*

- Have students read the text. (Or play the audio and have students follow along in their books.) Then call on students to share their answers with the class.
- Have students discuss the following questions in small groups:
  1. Advertisers send out thousands of pieces of mail at one time. It costs a lot less to send many identical pieces of mail. The rates are called bulk mail rates. The people who get this mail call it junk mail. Most people throw away the paper (one problem). However, because of bulk mail income for postal services, the cost of ordinary personal and business letters can be lower (one benefit). Is bulk (junk) mail good or bad?
  2. The job of a telemarketer is a hard one because many people are rude to people who make unwelcome calls. However, telemarketing is a job that helps people support their families. Are the advantages or the disadvantages for society greater?

After You Read

A. Vocabulary

- Have students find and circle the vocabulary in the text. Encourage them to use the context to figure out their meaning.
- Have students complete the exercise and compare answers in pairs. Then go over answers as a class.
- ⏱ To reinforce the vocabulary, ask: "When is a call from a telemarketer illegal?" *(when the name of the person who receives the call is on a Do Not Call list)* "What can you do to identify telemarketers?" *(use caller ID)* "Is it possible to eliminate calls from telemarketers?" *(no, you can only cut them down)* "What is the electronic equivalent of junk mail?" *(spam)* "What can you report to the authorities?" *(illegal calls from telemarketers)*

B. Comprehension

- Have students choose the answers individually. Encourage them to underline information in the article that supports their answers.
- Have students compare answers in pairs
- Call on students to say an answer each.

Go to **www.myfocusongrammarlab.com** for an additional reading, and for reading and vocabulary practice.

Step 2: Grammar Presentation (pages 188–190)

See the general suggestions for Grammar Presentation on page 2.

Grammar Charts

- Write on the board:
  You hesitate to pick up the telephone.
- Show students how the direct object can move. Then substitute a pronoun for the direct object and show how the phrasal verb must separate to allow the pronoun in. Write the following example sentences on the board:
  You hesitate to pick the telephone up.
  You hesitate to pick it up.
- Write the following cues on the board. Have students substitute one item at a time in a chain replacement drill:
  take away, the package
  put away, their library books
  take back, your promise.
- Write on the board:
  1. I got off the phone.
  2. Phone rates come down.
- Have students identify the phrasal verbs in the examples and say if they are transitive or intransitive. *(1. got off: transitive 2. come down: intransitive)*
- Point out that some transitive verbs are inseparable. You cannot say: "I got the phone off." Also point out that all intransitive verbs are inseparable because there is no object to place between the verb and the particle.

Grammar Notes

Note 1

- Have students say phrasal verbs they learned in Unit 11. Write some of them on the board.
- Call on students to use them in sentences.

Note 2

- Ask a student: "What did you take off when you came into the building?" *(I took off my coat.)* Ask another student: "What did [first student's name] do with his or her coat?" *(He / She took it off.)* Do the same with the following questions: "What did you write down in your notebook?" *(I wrote down some answers.)* "What did [first student's name] do with the answers?" *(He / She wrote them down.)* "What forms have you filled out recently?" *(I've filled out a scholarship application form.)* "What did [first student's name] do with the application form?" *(He / She filled it out.)*

- Point out that a few transitive phrasal verbs must be separated. Write only the verbs on the board: ask someone over (invite someone to one's home), bring someone down (depress, cause to lower), do something over (redo, do again), get something out of something (benefit from), keep something on (not take something off), see something through (finish something), start something over (begin again), talk someone into (persuade), turn someone or something into (change from one form to another).
- Clarify the meaning of the phrasal verbs on the board. Point out that some of these verbs frequently occur with a gerund. They always require a gerund if the object of the preposition isn't a noun: get something out of (doing something), talk someone into (doing something).
- Have students work in small groups to make up sentences with these verbs (for example, three verbs per group). Stress that the sentence should be interesting and show the meaning of the verb: I wanted to <u>ask</u> my friends <u>over</u>, but I didn't have any food in the house, so we went out.

Note 3
- As a class, make up sentences using the following inseparable verbs: run into (meet unexpectedly), carry on (continue), stick with (not quit), and come off (become loose or break off). For example: I <u>ran into</u> an old friend at the mall. His son will <u>carry on</u> the business. Pat decided to <u>stick with</u> the company for a few more years. The paint <u>came off</u> in a number of places.

Note 4
- Write the following common phrasal verb + preposition combinations on the board: put up with, get out of, look forward to, keep away from, keep up with, come up with, drop out of.
  Clarify their meanings.
- Have pairs use them to ask and answer questions. Examples: What do you look forward to doing this weekend? What do you always try to get out of doing? Have you ever had trouble keeping up with a class?

⏱ **Identify the Grammar:** Have students identify the grammar in the opening reading on page 186. For example:
> You just **got back** from a long, hard day at the office.
> All you want to do is **take off** your jacket, **put down** your briefcase . . .
> . . . you're about to **sit down** . . .
> You hesitate to **pick** it **up**.

Go to **www.myfocusongrammarlab.com** for grammar charts and notes.

Step 3: Focused Practice (pages 190–194)
See the general suggestions for Focused Practice on page 4.

Exercise 1: Discover the Grammar
A
- Point out that some phrasal verbs are separated (there is an object between the verb and the particle). Also point out that there is one three-word verb.
- Have students complete the exercise individually and compare answers in pairs. Then elicit the correct answers from the class.

B
- Encourage students to use the context to help them figure out the meaning of any unknown phrasal verbs.
- Go over the answers as a class.

Exercise 2: Meaning
- Go over the meanings of the phrasal verbs in the boxes. Have students refer to the appendices if necessary.
- Have students complete the exercise individually. Have them compare answers in pairs and then go over answers as a class.
- ⏱ Ask students to write down a question about each paragraph using one of the phrasal verbs in the boxes. Example: What did the person throw out? Then have pairs close their books and take turns asking and answering the questions about the text.

Exercise 3: Separable Phrasal Verbs and Pronoun Objects
- Go over the example with the class. Point out that all the phrasal verbs in this exercise are separable, so pronouns go between the verb and the particle.
- Have students complete the exercise individually and compare answers in pairs.
- Call on pairs to read the conversations aloud.

Exercise 4: Separable and Inseparable Phrasal Verbs
- Go over the example with the class. Point out that students should separate phrasal verbs whenever possible.
- Have students read the ads for meaning before writing their answers.
- Have students complete the exercise individually and compare answers in pairs. Then go over answers as a class.

- ⏱ To extend the activity, have pairs write their own ad about a product. Encourage the use of phrasal verbs.

Exercise 5: Editing
- Have students read the transcript quickly.
- Ask: "What does the telemarketer want to sell?" *(a 12-month magazine subscription)* "What does he say to try to convince Ms. Linder?" *(that it's a great opportunity / a once in a lifetime chance; that she'll be sorry if she turns the offer down because chances like this don't come around every day)* "How does Ms. Linder handle the call?" *(She says she's not interested and that she'll notify the authorities if he keeps calling. She asks for his phone number to call him back during his dinner.)*
- Go over the example with the class. Point out that there are objects in the wrong position and verbs followed by incorrect particles.
- Have students find and correct the mistakes individually and compare answers in pairs.
- Have students explain why the incorrect structures are wrong.
- ⏱ Ask students to point out examples of correct usages of phrasal verbs.

Go to **www.myfocusongrammarlab.com** for additional grammar practice.

Step 4: Communication Practice (pages 195–198)

See the general suggestions for Communication Practice on page 4.

Exercise 6: Listening
A
- Make sure students are familiar with all of the terms in Mr. Chen's notes: *long-distance, a plan, phone service, included, monthly fee, activation fee.* Play the audio.
- If necessary, play the conversation again and pause the audio after each answer is given.

B
- Have students read the statements before listening. Play the audio.
- Have students support their answers with information from the audio.
- ⏱ Have students discuss why they think the Get Together Program is / isn't a good offer.

Exercise 7: Pronunciation
A
- Play the audio. Have students read along as they listen to the Pronunciation Note.

- Write on the board:
  1. Fill out the forms.
  2. Fill them out.
- Point out that in Example 1, *fill* and *out* receive equal stress, and the noun *forms* is also stressed. In Example 2, *out* receives stronger stress than *fill*, and the pronoun *them* is <u>not</u> stressed.

B
- Have students identify the phrasal verbs. Then play the audio and have students listen and mark the stressed words.

C
- Play the audio again and have students repeat each sentence.
- Then have students practice the conversation with a partner. Remind them to play both roles.

Exercise 8: For or Against
A
- Have students think about the questions individually and write notes about their answers. Or, as a class, brainstorm pros (arguments in favor) and cons (arguments against) about telemarketing and write them in two columns on the board.
- Have students use their notes or the ideas on the board to express in small groups their ideas on telemarketing.

B
- Call on students to share their views with the class.

Exercise 9: Discussion
- Ask students to bring junk mail to class.
- Have students go over the phrasal verbs in the list. Refer them to Appendices 18 and 19 on pages A-6–A-8, if necessary.
- In small groups, encourage students to discuss concepts like intended audience (retired people, teenagers, young parents, grandparents), attractiveness of the junk mail (bright colors, photographs, shiny paper), and misuse of the word "free."

Exercise 10: Writing
A
- Have students discuss the following questions in pairs:
  1. Who calls you on the telephone? *(family and friends, telemarketers, people confirming appointments, bill collectors)*
  2. What do you need to have a telephone for? *(to connect to the Internet, call friends, get information about movie times, order a pizza)*

3. What problems have you had with the telephone? *(wrong numbers, telemarketers, bad connection, confusion over who is calling, confusion over why the person is calling)*

- Have students go over the phrasal verbs in the list and circle the ones they can use to describe their experience. Have students write their paragraphs individually.

B

- After students write their paragraphs, have them correct their work using the Editing Checklist.

OUT OF THE BOX ACTIVITIES

Writing

- Have students use as many separable or inseparable phrasal verbs as they can in a five-sentence paragraph. This assignment might be more fun if you have pairs or small groups of students work together.
- Encourage students to use Appendices 18 and 19 on pages A-6–A-8 as sources for their phrasal verbs. Have them underline the phrasal verbs in their paragraph.
- Give a prize to the student or group with the highest number in five sentences.

Reading and Writing

- Have students find directions for how to make something simple (a candle out of ice using a piece of string, paraffin wax, and a quart milk container; a photo album using squares of cardboard, a hole punch, and ribbon; a special greeting card).
- Write some useful phrasal verbs from Appendix 18 on pages A-6–A-7 on the board: cover up, cut off, cut out, do over, lay out, move around, pick out, pick up, put back, put together, take off, tear up, turn around, turn over. Have students work in pairs to write directions for the projects using phrasal verbs.

Go to **www.myfocusongrammarlab.com** for additional listening, pronunciation, speaking, and writing practice.

Note

- See the *Focus on Grammar Workbook* for additional in-class or homework grammar practice.

Unit 12 Review (page 199)

Have students complete the Review and check their answers on Student Book page UR-3. Review or assign additional material as needed.

Go to **www.myfocusongrammarlab.com** for the Unit Achievement Test.

From Grammar to Writing (pages 200–203)

See the general suggestions for From Grammar to Writing on page 9.

Go to **www.myfocusongrammarlab.com** for an additional From Grammar to Writing Assignment, Part Review, and Part Post-Test.

PART VI OVERVIEW

ADJECTIVE CLAUSES

UNIT	GRAMMAR FOCUS	THEME
13	Adjective Clauses with Subject Relative Pronouns	Friends and Personality Types
14	Adjectives Clauses with Object Relative Pronouns or *When* and *Where*	The Immigrant Experience

Go to **www.myfocusongrammarlab.com** for the Part and Unit Tests.

Note: PowerPoint® grammar presentations, test-generating software, and reproducible Part and Unit Tests are on the *Teacher's Resource Disc.*

UNIT 13 OVERVIEW

Grammar: ADJECTIVE CLAUSES WITH SUBJECT RELATIVE PRONOUNS

Students will learn the meanings and uses of adjective clauses in which the subject is a relative pronoun.

- The subject relative pronouns are *who, which, that,* and *whose* (with a noun).
- These subject relative pronouns are the subjects of clauses within a full sentence.

Theme: FRIENDS AND PERSONALITY TYPES

Unit 13 focuses on language that we use to talk about personality types and friendship.

Step 1: Grammar in Context (pages 206–208)

See the general suggestions for Grammar in Context on page 1.

Before You Read
- Have students discuss the questions in pairs. For Question 1, encourage students to write notes about the typical behavior of an extrovert and an introvert: What do they usually do? For Question 2, encourage students to share their own experiences: Who do they get along with? Do they have a similar or different personality?
- Call on students to share their ideas with the class.

Read
- To encourage students to read with a purpose, write the following questions on the board:
  1. What are some examples of typical behavior of introverts? *(they spend a lot of time alone; they avoid large social gatherings; they hate small talk; they are the first to leave "must-attend" events; they always think before they speak)*
  2. How do introverts and extroverts get their energy? *(introverts: by spending time alone; extroverts: by spending time with others)*
  3. What are some wrong ideas about introverts? *(they are not necessarily shy; they are able to succeed just like extroverts)*
  4. Can an introvert and an extrovert make a good match? *(yes, if they accept each other's needs)*
- Have students read the text. (Or play the audio and have students follow along in their books.) Then call on students to share their answers with the class.
- Have students discuss the following questions in small groups:
  1. The article says that there are introverts and extroverts, and that neither type is better than the other. Do you agree? Explain.
  2. The article says that we are probably all ambiverts—we act like introverts in some situations and extroverts in others. What kind of personality do you have? Are you more of an introvert or an extrovert? Explain.

After You Read

A. Vocabulary
- Have students find and circle the vocabulary in the text. Encourage them to use the context to figure out their meaning.

- Have students complete the exercise and compare answers in pairs. Then go over the answers as a class.
- ⏱ To reinforce the vocabulary, say words or phrases that are related to them. Example:
  T: *The way you are.*
  Ss: *Personality.*
- Use the following list. *(1. personality; 2. assume; 3. contradict; 4. define; 5. unique; 6. require)*
  1. the way you are
  2. believe to be true
  3. say the opposite
  4. describe clearly
  5. special and different
  6. need

B. Comprehension
- Have students choose the answers individually and compare answers in pairs.
- Call on students to say an answer each.

Go to **www.myfocusongrammarlab.com** for an additional reading, and for reading and vocabulary practice.

Step 2: Grammar Presentation (pages 208–210)

See the general suggestions for Grammar Presentation on page 2.

Grammar Charts
- Write on the board:
  Nadia is a person who needs to spend several hours alone.
- Have students identify the adjective clause *(who needs to spend several hours alone)*. Underline it. Draw a circle around *person* and *who* and an arrow from *who* to *person*.
- Point out that we use *who* for people. Erase *who* and write *that* in its place. Point out that *that* is also acceptable and has the same meaning.
- Write on the board:
  She prefers conversations which focus on feelings.
- Have students identify the adjective clause *(which focus on feelings)*. Underline it. Draw a circle around *conversations* and *which* and an arrow from *which* to *conversations*.
- Point out that we use *which* for things. Erase *which* and write *that* in its place. Point out that *that* is also acceptable and has the same meaning.
- Write on the board:
  Extroverts are people whose energy comes from being around others.

- Have students identify the adjective clause *(whose energy comes from being around others).* Underline it. Draw a circle around *people* and *whose* and an arrow from *whose* to *people*.
- Point out that we use *whose* to show possession.
- Use the adjective clauses from the above examples in new sentences to show that adjective clauses can also come inside the main clause. Write on the board:
  A person <u>who needs to spend several hours alone</u> is said to be an introvert.
  Conversations <u>which focus on feelings</u> are her favorite.
  People <u>whose energy comes from being around others</u> are called extroverts.

Grammar Notes

Note 1
- Write the following sentence starters on the board:
  1. I want a [car] that _____.
  2. I'd like a new [girlfriend / boyfriend] who _____.
  3. I know a [clown] whose _____.
  4. I chose this [tiny dog], which _____.
  5. I prefer a [box of chocolates] that _____.
  6. I love to [eat] something which _____.
- Have students work in pairs to finish the sentences. Point out that students can replace the words in brackets. Encourage students to be outrageous. *(I want a diamond ring that costs a lot.)* Call on students to share their sentences with the class.
- Say: "All the adjective clauses in the examples identify nouns except for one, which gives additional information. Which example is it?" *(4)*

Note 2
- Have students make the examples in Note 1 into two individual sentences. *I want a diamond ring that costs a lot. = I want a diamond ring. The ring has to cost a lot.*

Notes 3 and 4
- Have students circle the subject relative pronouns in the reading. Then have them identify the noun each pronoun refers to. Ask: "Can another relative pronoun be used?"
- If helpful, provide two more example sentences:
  We know <u>a man who rides</u> a unicycle. (masculine, singular)
  Our neighbors have <u>two daughters who have long hair.</u> (feminine, plural)

Note 5
- If needed, provide additional examples of subject-verb agreement:
  The <u>chef</u> who <u>cooks</u> at Antonio's comes from Italy.
  The <u>subjects</u> that <u>are</u> offered include the classics.

Note 6
- To explain nonidentifying clauses, write on the board:
  Alberto is a good singer.
- Ask a student to add some "unnecessary" or "extra" information about Alberto: *He likes football. He studied piano for 10 years.* Write two or more of these sentences below the original sentence, and surround them with large and visible commas.
- Draw an arrow from the added sentences to the place in the original sentence where one of them will be inserted, and replace the capital letter with a lower-case letter.
- Point out that, in some situations, this "extra" information might be important, but that it is still set off with commas: *Alberto, who studied piano for 10 years, is a good singer.*
- To explain identifying clauses, write on the board:
  A: I asked Alberto to sing.
  B: I know two Albertos. Which one do you mean?
  A: I mean the Alberto <u>who comes from Venezuela.</u>
- Point out that some clauses—like the one in the example *(who comes from Venezuela)*—help identify the person or thing we are talking about.

Note 7
- Emphasize that the use of commas in written English and pauses in spoken English can change the meaning of a sentence. Write the following examples on the board and read them aloud, pausing as appropriate:
  The students, who studied, passed the test.
    (All of them passed.)
  The students who studied passed the test.
    (Only those who studied passed.)
- Have students, as a class, generate a few examples of sentences that can go either way. List the sentences on opposite sides of the board (one with commas, labeled *identifying*; one without, labeled *nonidentifying*).
- Have students practice reading a sentence to their partner with one of the two possible intonations (with or without a pause). The other student then tells whether he or she heard the sentence as *identifying* or *nonidentifying.*

🕐 **Identify the Grammar:** Have students identify the grammar in the opening reading on page 206. For example:

My friend Nadia, **who needs to spend several hours alone each day**, avoids large social gatherings . . .

. . . at office holiday parties, **which are "must-attend" events**, she's always the first one to leave.

. . . you're even one of those people **that nag a friend like her to get out more.**

Introverts are people **that get their energy by spending time alone**.

Their opposites are extroverts, people **whose energy comes from being around others**.

Go to **www.myfocusongrammarlab.com** for grammar charts and notes.

Step 3: Focused Practice (pages 211–215)

See the general suggestions for Focused Practice on page 4.

Exercise 1: Discover the Grammar

- Go over the example with the class. Remind students that adjective clauses can appear inside the main clause or after the main clause.
- Have students complete the exercise individually and compare answers in pairs.
- Elicit the correct answers from the class.

Exercise 2: Relative Pronouns and Verbs

- Go over the example with the class. Have students identify the noun the clause refers to. *(people)* Then ask: "Is *people* a singular or plural noun?" *(plural)* Point out how the verb *talk* relates to the plural noun *people*.
- Point out that students can circle the nouns the adjective clauses refer to in order to decide whether they need a singular or a plural verb.
- Have students complete the exercise individually and compare answers in pairs. Then go over answers as a class.

Exercise 3: Identifying Adjective Clauses

A
- Have students complete Part A individually and go over answers as a class.

B
- Go over the example. Have students complete the exercise individually.
- Have students compare answers in pairs. Then go over answers as a class.

- 🕐 Have pairs choose two nouns for objects or people from the reading in Exercise 1 and write definitions of these nouns using relative clauses. Students can use a dictionary if necessary. Some examples of useful nouns for this activity are: *photo, glass, friend, job, money, contest, web designer, business, day, night, nickname, president, experts, water.* Then have pairs join another pair. Students take turns reading the definitions and saying the words they refer to. Circulate and listen to the definitions. Make corrections if necessary.

Exercise 4: Nonidentifying Adjective Clauses

- Go over the example with the class. Ask: "Is the relative pronoun *that* also possible in this clause?" *(no, because* that *cannot be used in nonidentifying adjective clauses)*
- Remind students that the relative pronouns *who, which,* and *whose* can introduce nonidentifying clauses.
- Have students complete the exercise individually and compare answers in pairs.
- Call on students to read the sentences aloud.

Exercise 5: Identifying or Nonidentifying Adjective Clauses

- Go over the example with the class. Remind students that adjective clauses directly follow the noun they refer to.
- Have students complete the exercise individually and compare answers in pairs.
- Go over answers as a class.

Exercise 6: Editing

- Have students read the essay quickly to find out what it is about.
- Ask: "Where did the student go in July?" *(to Mexico, to study Spanish for a month)* "Who did he go with?" *(other students and five adult teachers)* "Who did the student make friends with?" *(one of his teachers, Bob Taylor)* "What problem did the student have?" *(He stopped going to classes.)* "How did his teacher help?" *(He helped him get back to his courses.)*
- Review the example.
- Have students find and correct the mistakes individually and compare answers in pairs.
- Have students explain why the incorrect structures are wrong.
- 🕐 Ask students to point out examples of correct usages of adjective clauses.

Go to **www.myfocusongrammarlab.com** for additional grammar practice.

Step 4: Communication Practice (pages 216–219)

See the general suggestions for Communication Practice on page 4.

Exercise 7: Listening

- Prepare students for the listening exercise by having them describe each person in the illustration, starting with the man who is standing. Encourage them to use adjective clauses with subject relative pronouns to make sentences like the following: *The man who is standing is tall. He's talking to a woman who is wearing glasses. The man that is on her right is holding up a coffee pitcher. The woman that's holding a photograph is sitting next to him. At the end of the table a man is talking with a woman who has a scarf around her shoulders. A man who isn't talking to anyone is sitting next to her. The woman who is reaching for the photograph is wearing a lot of jewelry.*

A

- Have students read the statements. Then play the audio.
- Have students complete the exercise. If necessary, play the audio again, stopping after each conversation to review answers.

B

- Have students listen and write the names. Then play the audio again and have them make notes of the information that helped them choose their answers.
- Have students make sentences using adjective clauses. Example: *Ann is the woman who is wearing a scarf / who is wearing a red dress / who is talking to the man in blue.*

Exercise 8: Pronunciation

A

- Play the audio. Have students read along as they listen to the Pronunciation Note.
- Ask: "What kind of clauses need commas in writing and pauses when speaking?" *(nonidentifying clauses)* "Where do we place the commas or make the pauses?" *(before the clause and after the clause if it is in the middle of the sentence)*

B

- Play the audio. Have students listen and add the commas where necessary.

C

- Play the audio again and have students repeat the sentences.

Exercise 9: Discussion

A

- Have students turn to page 212 and take the Personality Quiz.

B

- Have students discuss their answers in pairs. Encourage them to keep the conversation going by giving examples and asking follow-up questions.
- Have students share information about themselves and their partners with the class. Example: *Pamela talks a lot, and so do I.*

Exercise 10: Questionnaire

A

- As students complete the questionnaire, encourage them to think of reasons for their choices or examples to support them. Ask them to make notes.

B

- Write some useful language for expressing agreement and disagreement on the board:
  I absolutely agree.
  I couldn't agree more.
  Well, in my opinion . . .
  I believe that . . .
  You may be right, but . . .
  I'm afraid I don't agree.

C

- As you tally the results, encourage students to find one or more traits most students agree a good friend should have.
- Have students tell their partners the name of a person or descriptive title of a person who . . . . Be sure to encourage them to use "... is someone who" in order to elicit adjective clauses. Students should make other internal changes as appropriate: *My friend Anna is someone who always tells me the truth. Our neighbor Mr. Mickels is someone who has known me for a long time.*

Exercise 11: Quotable Quotes

- Make sure that every quote is addressed by at least one group.
- After students discuss, ask them to pick a quote they like and explain why they like it.

Exercise 12: Writing

A

- Write the following questions on the board to help students generate ideas and elicit vocabulary.

  How long have you been friends?

  Do you have the same or different interests?

  Do you have the same or different personalities?

  What things do you usually do together?

  Why do you consider him or her a good friend?

- Have students write their essays in class or for homework.

B

- After students write their essays, have them correct their work using the Editing Checklist.

OUT OF THE BOX ACTIVITIES

Speaking

- Have the class play the game "I Spy" using adjective clauses in their sentences and questions. Each student looks around the classroom and finds something that the other students will have to guess.

  A: (seeing the globe on a shelf) I spy something that is round.

  B: Is it something that I could eat?

  A: No, it's not.

  C: Is it something that I could hold in my hand?

  A: Yes, it is.

  D: Is it something that is sitting on the shelf?

- The game continues until one student guesses what the object is.

Writing

- Have students write poems about people who have been significant in their lives: mother, father, relative, friend, teacher. Encourage them to use the following form:

  PERSON'S NAME OR RELATIONSHIP TITLE

  Someone who is always . . .

  Someone who is never . . .

  Someone who has always been . . .

  Someone who has never been . . .

  Always (List three adjectives here that describe the person.)

  Dear to me forever

Go to **www.myfocusongrammarlab.com** for additional listening, pronunciation, speaking, and writing practice.

Note

- See the *Focus on Grammar Workbook* for additional in-class or homework grammar practice.

Unit 13 Review (page 220)

Have students complete the Review and check their answers on Student Book page UR-4. Review or assign additional material as needed.

Go to **www.myfocusongrammarlab.com** for the Unit Achievement Test.

UNIT 14 OVERVIEW

Grammar: ADJECTIVES CLAUSES WITH OBJECT RELATIVE PRONOUNS OR *When* AND *Where*

Students will learn the meanings and uses of adjective clauses with object relative pronouns or *when* and *where*.

- The object relative pronouns are *who, whom, which, that.* They can be left out in identifying relative clauses.

- These object relative pronouns are the objects of clauses within a full sentence.

- *When* and *where* can also begin adjective clauses.

Theme: THE IMMIGRANT EXPERIENCE

Unit 14 focuses on language that we use to talk about childhood memories.

Many people look forward to a new life when they emigrate. Few think about what they left behind, because their new life means the hope of better jobs and more prosperity for their families. In *Lost in Translation,* Ewa Wydra (Eva Hoffman) thinks about the change in her life as she tells her story. Ben Fong-Torres, writer of *The Rice Room,* is a first-generation Chinese-American. The gap in his life is the difference between his parents' experience and his own. Emigrating from their home in China was his parents' dream; what was lost in this family is the connection within the family. *Lost in Translation* and *The Rice Room* are examples of autobiography, a person's story told in his or her own words.

Step 1: Grammar in Context (pages 221–223)

See the general suggestions for Grammar in Context on page 1.

Before You Read

- Have students look at the photos and discuss the questions in pairs. As students describe the cities and compare them with their own, encourage them to consider different aspects such as streets, buildings, colors, traffic, signs, people.
- Call on pairs to share their answers to the questions with the class.

Read

- To encourage students to read with a purpose, write the following questions on the board:
  1. What are the two worlds of Eva Hoffman? *(her native Poland and Canada)*
  2. What are the two worlds of Ben Fong-Torres? *(his parents' Chinese-American community and his mainstream society)*
  3. What does Eva Hoffman miss most about life in Cracow? *(the intense lifestyle, the human contact, the cultural values of the community)*
  4. What does Ben Fong-Torres see as the great sadness of his life? *(the language barrier between Chinese and English for his family)*
  5. Why can't Ben discuss family matters with his parents if he spoke Chinese as a child? *(His Chinese did not develop beyond the level of a child's language.)*
- Have students read the text. (Or play the audio and have students follow along in their books.) Have students share their answers with the class.
- Have students discuss the following questions in small groups:
  1. How do people learn languages, either their first language or a second one? Why didn't Ben's Chinese language ability develop as he grew older?
  2. How does a difference in culture affect a person? Why did Eva Hoffman feel "lost" as she got used to her new country?

After You Read

A. Vocabulary

- Have students find and circle the vocabulary in the text. Encourage them to use the context to figure out their meaning.
- Have students compare answers in pairs. Then go over answers as a class.

- ⏱ To reinforce the vocabulary, write the following question on the board, and have students answer it. (*1. poverty; 2. translation; 3. issue; 4. immigration; 5. generation; 6. connection*)
  Which word from the box has to do with . . . ?
  1. having little money
  2. languages
  3. problems
  4. coming into a country
  5. older and younger relatives
  6. a relationship between two things

B. Comprehension

- Have students choose the answers individually. Encourage students to underline information in the text that supports their answers.
- Have students compare answers in pairs. Then call on students to say an answer each.

Go to **www.myfocusongrammarlab.com** for an additional reading, and for reading and vocabulary practice.

Step 2: Grammar Presentation (pages 224–227)

See the general suggestions for Grammar Presentation on page 2.

Grammar Charts

- To explain adjective clauses with object relative pronouns, write on the board:
  It was sad to leave Cracow, which I loved so much.
- Ask students to break the sentence into the two clauses, the main clause and the adjective clause. Write *main clause* and *adjective clause* above the clauses.

Main clause	Adjective clause
It was sad for Eva to leave Cracow,	which she loved so much.

- Have students identify the verb *(loved)* and the subject *(she)* in the adjective clause. Label the example:
  It was sad for Eva
  to leave Cracow,   which she loved so much.
                            ↓   ↓
                         subject   verb
- Point out that that *Cracow* and the relative pronoun *which* both mean the same thing. Say: "She loved Cracow." Point out that *which* is the object of the verb *love*. Add the label "object" to the example on the board:
  It was sad for Eva
  to leave Cracow,   which she loved so much.
                        ↓   ↓   ↓
                     object subject   verb

- To explain adjective clauses with *when* and *where*, write on the board:
  There were moments when Fong-Torres needed to talk with his parents.
  Eva remembers the villages where they took summer vacations.
- Have students identify the clauses and the subject and the verb within each clause.

Grammar Notes

Note 1
- To check comprehension, write on the board:
  1. I borrowed the book that she was reading.
  2. I bought a book which was on sale.
  3. She is the author that I like best.
  4. I like the stories that you are writing.
  5. He is the man who recommended this novel.
- In pairs, have students identify the adjective clauses and the relative pronouns. Then have them decide if the relative pronouns are the subjects *(2 and 5)* or the objects *(1, 3, and 4)* of the verbs in the clauses.
- Ask: "In what position do relative pronouns always come?" *(at the beginning of the adjective clauses)*
- Draw attention to the relative pronoun *that* in Examples 3 and 4. Ask: "In Example 3, does *that* refer to a singular or plural noun?" *(a singular noun)* "In Example 4, does *that* refer to a singular noun or a plural noun?" *(a plural noun)* "Does the relative pronoun change for singular and plural nouns?" *(no)*
- Direct attention to the subject and verb in the clauses in Examples 3 and 4 *(I like; you are writing)*. Point out that in adjective clauses that have relative pronouns as objects, the verb agrees with the subject of the clause.
- Draw attention to the *Be Careful!* note. An adjective clause does not have an object pronoun and an object relative pronoun.

Note 2
- Write on the board:
  1. My friend Sarah, who I have known for years, wrote her autobiography.
  2. That is the woman who I have known for years.
  3. He is the man who told me her story.
- Have students say what kind of adjective clause each example contains.
  (1. nonidentifying adjective clause; 2. identifying adjective clause; 3. identifying adjective clause)

- Ask: "Which relative pronoun can be left out?" (who *in Example 2*) "Why can't the pronoun be left out in Examples 1 and 3?" *(In Example 1, the clause is nonidentifying, so the pronoun cannot be omitted. In Example 3, the clause is identifying, but the relative pronoun is the subject of the clause, so it cannot be omitted.)*

Note 3
- Write on the board:
  He's the man. I saw him at the station.
- Have students use the information on the board to write as many different sentences as possible using adjective clauses. Students will be able to write four sentences. *(He's the man whom I saw at the station. He's the man who I saw at the station. He's the man that I saw at the station. He's the man I saw at the station.)*
- Do the same with:
  This is the prize. She won it.
  Students will be able to write three sentences. *(This is the prize which she won. This is the prize that she won. This is the prize she won.)*
- Do the same with:
  That's the teacher. I loved her class.
  Students will be able to write one sentence. *(That's the teacher whose class I loved.)*

Note 4
- Write *who / whom, that, which,* and *whose* in a vertical list on the board. Before each one, write *That's the one* or *That's the man*. After each one draw a long blank and then write a preposition at the end. Preposition suggestions: *for, to, about,* and *with*.
- On another part of the board, write:
  I donated blood for him. I gave my book to him. I wrote about him. I had lunch with his wife.
- Have students complete the sentences using the information on the board. Go over answers as a class. Write the sentences on the board. Examples:
  1. *That's the man who / that I donated blood for / for whom I donated blood.*
  2. *That's the man who / that I gave my book to. / to whom I gave the book.*
  3. *That's the one which / that I wrote about. / about which I wrote.*
  4. *That's the one whose wife I had lunch with.*

Note 5
- Point out the similarity of *then* and *when* (both time expressions) and *there* and *where* (both place expressions). Some nouns refer to times and places; *when* and *where* are appropriate for use as relative pronouns with these expressions.

- Have students practice with the following examples:

You write		They say
Look at the big house. Ana lives there.	=	"Look at the big house where Ana lives."
It was a great day. I got a good job then.	=	"It was a great day when I got good job."

🕐 **Identify the Grammar:** Have students identify the grammar in the opening reading on page 221. For example:

I'm filled to the brim with . . . images of Cracow, **which I loved as one loves a person** . . .

. . . of the sun-baked villages **where we had taken summer vacations** . . .

. . . of the hours **I spent poring over passages of music with my music teacher** . . .

. . . a place **where life was lived intensely**.

She remembers visiting the city's cafes with her father, **who she watched in lively conversations with his friends**.

Go to **www.myfocusongrammarlab.com** for grammar charts and notes.

Step 3: Focused Practice (pages 227–232)

See the general suggestions for Focused Practice on page 4.

Exercise 1: Discover the Grammar

A
- Go over the example with the class.
- Have students complete the exercise individually and compare answers in pairs.
- Elicit the correct answers from the class.

B
- Go over the example with the class.
- Have students complete the exercise and compare answers in pairs.

Go over the answers as a class. Exercise 2: Relative Pronouns and Verbs
- Go over the example with the class.
- Encourage students to identify the nouns that the clauses refer to in order to decide on the correct relative pronoun. Are they nouns for people, things, places, or periods of time?
- Have students read the interview for meaning. Then have students complete the exercise.
- Call on two students to read the interview aloud.

Exercise 3: Identifying Adjective Clauses
- Go over the example with the class. Ask: "Which other relative pronoun is possible in this sentence?" (which)
- Encourage students to match all the sentences before writing their answers.
- Have students complete the exercise individually and compare answers in pairs. Go over the answers as a class.
- 🕐 Have pairs use sentence starters 1–6 to create their own sentences using adjective clauses with object relative pronouns. Encourage students to be creative.

Exercise 4: Nonidentifying Adjective Clauses
- Go over the example with the class.
- Have students read the text for meaning.
- Have students complete the exercise individually and compare answers in pairs. Then go over answers as a class.

Exercise 5: Identifying and Nonidentifying Adjective Clauses
- Go over the example. **Note:** the relative pronoun *that* should only be used when necessary.
- Remind students that adjective clauses directly follow the noun they modify. Have them identify the noun that the adjective clause refers to in order to decide on the correct place for the clause.
- If students find it easier to write clauses introduced by relative pronouns, allow them to include them, and ask them to insert the relative pronouns between brackets if they are not necessary.
- Have students compare answers in pairs. Then go over answers as a class.

Exercise 6: Editing
- Have students read the essay quickly for meaning.
- Ask: "Where did the student grow up?" (in Tai Dong) "Where is the house he grew up in?" (on the main street in Tai Dong) "What memories does he have about the courtyard?" (It was the place where his mother sold omelets.) "The front room?" (It was the place where his father conducted his business.) "The kitchen?" (It was always full of relatives and customers. It was a fun and noisy place to be.) "His bedroom?" (It was upstairs, where he slept with his brother.)
- Go over the example.
- Have students insert the commas and delete the relative pronouns individually and compare answers in pairs. Then go over the answers as a class.

Go to **www.myfocusongrammarlab.com** for additional grammar practice.

Step 4: Communication Practice (pages 232–235)

See the general suggestions for Communication Practice on page 4.

Exercise 7: Listening

A

- Have students look at the pictures and locate the desk, the chairs, the mirror, the rug, and the guitar. Then play the audio.
- Have students complete the exercise individually.

B

- As students listen, have them check or circle the items they hear described.
- Have students support their answer with information they remember. Example: *There was a beautiful rug under the bed that was not in the corner.*

C

- Play the audio again. Have students support their answer with examples from the audio.
- (🕐) Have students imagine they are Maria Espinosa Martinez and make sentences about the rug, the guitar, the desk, and the mirror using adjective clauses to show where they are in the room. Examples: *The rug, which my sister put her bed on, is near the door. The guitar is on the bed where my sister kept it. The desk is near the window in the corner where there is good light. The mirror is on the wall between the two beds where both of us could use it.*

Exercise 8: Pronunciation

A

- Play the audio. Have students read along as they listen to the Pronunciation Note.
- Ask: "Where should we always pause?" *(around a nonidentifying clause)*

B

- Play the audio. Have students listen and mark the pauses.

C

- Circulate as students practice to make sure they don't pause for too long and sound unnatural.

Exercise 9: What About You?

- Students can also use photos from magazines.

- Encourage students to be creative in making up the stories and to ask follow-up questions to find out more.
- Have pairs of students practice together telling their stories.

Exercise 10: Quotable Quotes

- Use the ideas in the paraphrases of the quotes to get students started.
- Make sure that every quote is addressed by at least one group.
- After students discuss, ask them to pick up a quote they like and explain why they like it.

Exercise 11: Writing

A

- Brainstorm places where people live and write them on the board. Examples: *out in the country (rural areas), in small villages, in farming towns, in factory towns, in small cities with lots of business and industry, in big cities, on islands, in the forest, in barrios, in huge apartment buildings.*
- Have students think of the places and people they will describe in their paragraph and write simple, isolated sentences about them. Examples:
  — *my town: I grew up there. It was near the sea.*
  — *my uncle: He was the oldest person in the village. Everyone in the village knew him. They greeted him with a big smile.*
- Encourage students to combine some sentences into new sentences containing adjective clauses with object relative pronouns or *when* and *where*. Examples: *The town where I grew up was near the sea. My uncle, who everyone greeted with a big smile, was the oldest person in the village.* Then have students write their paragraphs.

B

- After students write their paragraphs, have them correct their work using the Editing Checklist.

OUT OF THE BOX ACTIVITIES

Speaking

- Have fun with this version of "The House That Jack Built." On cards or poster paper, draw the following: a house (square with a roof) with the words *Jack* and *built*; a mouse (two circles with pointed ears and a skinny tail) and *live;* a cat (fluffy tail and whiskers) and *caught;* and a triangle of cheese (add holes) and *was eaten.* Tape the pictures in order on the wall and have the students repeat after you, building the story: *This is the house that Jack built. This is the mouse that lived in the house that Jack built. This is the cat that caught the mouse that lived in the house that Jack built. This is the cheese that was eaten by the mouse that was caught by the cat that lived in the house that Jack built.*

- Have students identify the nouns and object relative pronouns.
- Then have students try it alone.

Speaking

- For this exercise you will need more than twice the number of slips of paper as students and two open shoe boxes or large plastic bowls.
- Create a game by having half of the students write two or three sentence starters about people like these: *There's a person in my class . . . I know an old man . . . We all loved my grandmother . . . I met the most beautiful person in the world . . . I want to marry a person . . .* (You'll want more sentence starters than the number of students in the class.)
- Fold the slips and put them into a bowl or open box.
- Have the other half of the class write two or three adjective clauses that start with *who, whose,* or *that* like these: *. . . who always wears a red hat and something purple . . . whose car is 40 years old . . . that lives in a building that looks like a milk bottle . . . who sings opera while asleep.*
- To play the game, students choose one sentence starter and one adjective clause.
- Take a vote for the funniest sentence.

Writing and Listening

- Have students look around their neighborhoods for unusual people, places, and things. Have them bring back reports of what they have seen.
- Have students write sentences using adjective clauses with object relative pronouns or *when* and *where.* Examples: *I saw a house which is painted purple with chartreuse and navy blue trim. I met a man whose three dogs were wearing ribbons.* Call on students to share sentences with the class.

Go to **www.myfocusongrammarlab.com** for additional listening, pronunciation, speaking, and writing practice.

Note
- See the *Focus on Grammar Workbook* for additional in-class or homework grammar practice.

Unit 14 Review (page 236)

Have students complete the Review and check their answers on Student Book page UR-4. Review or assign additional material as needed.

Go to **www.myfocusongrammarlab.com** for the Unit Achievement Test.

From Grammar to Writing (pages 237–238)

See the general suggestions for From Grammar to Writing on page 9.

Go to **www.myfocusongrammarlab.com** for an additional From Grammar to Writing Assignment, Part Review, and Part Post-Test.

PART VII OVERVIEW

MODALS: REVIEW AND EXPANSION

UNIT	GRAMMAR FOCUS	THEME
15	Modals and Similar Expressions: Review	Social Networking
16	Advisability in the Past	Regrets
17	Speculations and Conclusions About the Past	Unsolved Mysteries

Go to **www.myfocusongrammarlab.com** for the Part and Unit Tests.

Note: PowerPoint® grammar presentations, test-generating software, and reproducible Part and Unit Tests are on the *Teacher's Resource Disc.*

Grammar: MODALS AND SIMILAR EXPRESSIONS: REVIEW

Students will review and practice modals for ability, advice, necessity, prohibition, conclusions, and future possibility.

Modals are auxiliary verbs that express a relationship between the subject of the sentence and its main verb. In this unit students will practice the following modals and uses:

	Ability	Advice	Necessity	Prohibition	Conclusions	Future Possibility
1. can	x					
2. be able to / not be able to	x					
3. could / couldn't	x				x	x
4. can't	x			x	x	
5. must			x		x	
6. must not				x	x	
7. have / has to			x		x	
8. don't / doesn't have to			x			
9. have / has got to			x		x	
10. had better / had better not		x				
11. ought to		x				
12. should / shouldn't		x				
13. may / may not					x	x
14. might / might not					x	x

Theme: SOCIAL NETWORKING

Unit 15 focuses on language that we use to discuss the advantages and disadvantages of social networking, warn about its risks, and give advice about what to do to be safe.

Step 1: Grammar in Context (pages 240–242)

See the general suggestions for Grammar in Context on page 1.

Before You Read

• Have students look at the cartoon and discuss the questions in pairs.

• Discuss as a class. As you get feedback from students about Question 3, write the names of the social networking sites students use on the board. Then take a poll to find out the most popular site among your students. As students provide their answers for Question 4, keep a tally on the board to find out what most students use networking for.

Read

• To encourage students to read with a purpose, write the following questions on the board:
  1. According to the article, how can networking be useful to . . . ?
     • people in general (*It can help them stay in touch with family and friends.*)
     • school students (*It can help them discuss lessons with students from other countries and chat with them.*)
     • college applicants and students (*It can help them provide useful information for college admissions officers, chat with college students to get an inside view of the school, form study groups, organize their schedule.*)
     • job seekers (*It can help them find jobs on job-seeking sites.*)
  2. What are some ways to avoid problems while networking? (*You should keep personal information private, be careful with what you post because it can become public, stay professional on job-seeking sites, know when to say "enough is enough" in order not to waste time*)

• Have students read the text. (Or play the audio and have students follow along in their books.) Then call on students to share their answers with the class.

• Have students discuss the following questions in small groups:
  1. How often do you use networking sites? What do you use them for? Give examples. Does networking stop you from doing other things? Do you think you spend too much valuable time networking? Explain.
  2. Are real-life relationships more important than virtual ones? If so, why do you think people spend so much time making friends and chatting with them on the Internet?

After You Read

A. Vocabulary
- Have students find and circle the vocabulary in the text. Encourage them to use the context to figure out their meaning.
- Have students compare answers in pairs. Then go over answers as a class.
- ⏱ To reinforce the vocabulary, have students complete the following statements with the vocabulary words. *(1. privacy; 2. comments; 3. resource; 4. network; 5. involved; 6. content)*
  1. You should protect your _____ on the Internet.
  2. On a networking site, you can post photos, _____, and videos. (use the plural form)
  3. Networking sites are a good _____ for college applicants and job-seekers.
  4. You can _____ by chatting with people from other countries.
  5. If you get too _____, you should learn how to stop.
  6. The _____ of some sites may not be appropriate for children.

B. Comprehension
- Have students choose the answers individually. Encourage students to underline the information in the text that supports their answers.
- Have students compare answers in pairs. Then call on students to say an answer each.

Go to **www.myfocusongrammarlab.com** for an additional reading, and for reading and vocabulary practice.

Step 2: Grammar Presentation (pages 242–245)

See the general suggestions for Grammar Presentation on page 2.

Grammar Charts
- Select one example sentence at a time from the charts and expand on the context to show students why each example shows ability, advice, necessity, prohibition, conclusions, or future possibility. For example, for the sentence "She can join," you can say: "To join Facebook, you need an email address. She has an email address, so she can join."
- After a few examples, have students expand on the contexts. For example, for the sentence "You had better use Ning," they can say: "If you don't, you won't be able to stay in touch with friends."
- Write the six headers on the board: Ability, Advice, Necessity, Prohibition, Conclusions, Future Possibility.
- Have students circle the modals and modal-like verbs in the reading. Have students discuss with partners which column it should go in.

Grammar Notes

Note 1
- Write on the board:
  Social functions — advice, ability, necessity
  Logical functions — conclusions, future possibility
- Point out that modals do not change. They are the same for all persons. Modal-like verbs do change because they have *be* or *have / has / had* as part of their form, and these words change according to timeframe and person.
- Have pairs write one simple sentence for each of the functions on the board. Example: Advice: You shouldn't reveal personal information.
  Call on students to share their sentences with the class.
- ⏱ Remind students of the importance of pronunciation and stress for modals. Example: the difference between *I can* (kən) *speak <u>English</u>* and *I can't* (kænt) *speak Greek.* Remind them that the modal-like *be able to* and *have to* are almost always reduced. Say: "Name something you can do, something you can't do, and something you've always been able to do." The goal is accuracy with stress and reductions. *(I can cook, but I can't sew. I've always been able to sing.)*

Note 2
- Remind students that the positive and negative forms of *could* and *was / were able to* are used for long time periods in the past.
- Have pairs make up three sentences about things that they *can* do now but *couldn't* (or *weren't able to*) do in the past: *Today I can skydive, but I couldn't in the past.* Then have pairs make up three sentences about things that they *can't* do now but *could* (or *were able to*) do in the past: *When I was younger, I could do karate, but I can't anymore.*
- Point out that for specific times in the past, you can use the positive forms of *could* and both positive and negative forms of *was / were able to.*

Note 3
- Explain that *had better* is stronger than *should*, and *should* is stronger than *ought to*. *Ought not to* is not used often.

- Say: "Name something you ought to do, something you should do, and something you had better do." Point out that *had better* usually occurs as a contraction and also includes the possibility of bad consequence: *I'd better move the car, or I'll get a ticket.*

Note 4

- Point out the order from strongest to weakest: *must, have to, have got to.*
- Write on the board:
  1. oral or written message expressing necessity: friend to friend
  2. oral message expressing necessity: mother to daughter
  3. written message expressing necessity: instructions
  4. oral message expressing prohibition: father to son
  5. oral message expressing that something is not necessary: teacher to student
- Give an example for each of the items on the board. You can say: "1. You have to / have got to buy her a gift. 2. You must tidy your bedroom. 3. You must fill in the form. 4. You can't go out right now. 5. You don't have to answer Question 5."
- Draw attention to the *Be Careful!* note.
- Have pairs write their own examples. Encourage them to look at Note 4 in their Student Book, if necessary. Have some students share examples with the class.

Note 5

- Point out that *must* and *couldn't* both mean certainty about conclusions. *Must not* and *could* are not nearly so certain.
- Ask: "Why do you think [student's name] is absent today?" Have students draw conclusions. Encourage the use of different modals to express different degrees of certainty. Examples: *He can't be ill. I talked to him this morning. / He must be studying. He has an exam tomorrow. / He could be on his way. He's sometimes late.*

Note 6

- Call on students to share their tentative plans for this weekend. Encourage the use of different modals: *may (not), might (not),* and *could.* Write some examples on the board.
- Draw attention to the *Be Careful!* note.

🕐 **Identify the Grammar:** Have students identify the grammar in the opening reading on page 240. For example:
  Blair Thomas's school friends **can find out** what she is doing almost every minute . . .
  I **had to join.** . . .

Her students **are able to discuss** lessons and **chat** with other students . . .
Students **don't have to use** the Ning site . . .
. . . networking **may not** always **be** a good thing.
Both children and adults **have to remember** that . . .
Parents **must teach** children about keeping personal information private.

Go to **www.myfocusongrammarlab.com** for grammar charts and notes.

Step 3: Focused Practice (pages 246–250)

See the general suggestions for Focused Practice on page 4.

Exercise 1: Discover the Grammar

- Brainstorm the modals and similar expressions students have reviewed in this unit. Remind students that there are eleven, and challenge students to say them all. Make a list on the board:
  can, could, be able to, should, ought to, had better, must, have to, have got to, may, might

A

- Go over the example with the class.
- Have students do the exercise individually and compare answers in pairs.
- Elicit the correct answers from the class.

B

- Have students complete the exercise in pairs so they can discuss the meaning of the modals and similar expressions.

Exercise 2: Affirmative and Negative Modals

- Encourage students to read all the posts before choosing their answers.
- Have students compare answers in pairs. Then go over answers as a class.
- 🕐 Form groups of four students. Have students play a game in which they "post" messages on paper. Each student in the group posts a message on a sheet of paper and passes it around. Students reply to the posts. When the sheet of paper gets back to the first student, he or she reads all the posts aloud to his or her group. Remind students that each post should use a modal or similar expression.

Exercise 3: Affirmative and Negative

- Go over the example with the class.
- Have students read the posts for meaning before writing their answers. Point out that students should choose the right modal to express the ideas in parentheses.

- Have students complete the exercise individually and compare answers in pairs.
- Call on students to read the posts aloud.

Exercise 4: Editing
- Have students read the article quickly for meaning.
- Ask: "What are some advantages of Wikipedia?" (*It's fast, convenient, and free. You don't have to register to use it. It's usually more up-to-date than information in books. There are hyperlinks to get more information.*) "What are some disadvantages?" (*The content may not be 100 percent accurate. Facts are not checked by professional editors. People can vandalize articles [insert wrong information or remove important facts].*)
- Go over the example.
- Have students find and correct the mistakes individually and compare answers in pairs.
- Have students explain why the incorrect structures are wrong.
- ⏱ Ask students to point out examples of correct usages of modals and similar expressions.

Go to **www.myfocusongrammarlab.com** for additional grammar practice.

Step 4: Communication Practice (pages 251–255)

See the general suggestions for Communication Practice on page 4.

Exercise 5: Listening

A
- Have students read the statements. Play the audio and have students make observations about the conversation.
- Have students complete the exercise.
- Play the conversation again and stop after each answer is given. Have students support their answers by quoting information from the conversation. Examples: Number 1 is false because the man says, "We've gotta climb the hill today." Number 2 is true because the man says, "I should go first." **Note:** Quoting information from the conversation will prepare students for Part B.

B
- Have students complete the exercise individually. Then play the audio again for students to check their work. Point out that if they chose other modals, these could also be possible in the conversation. Have pairs discuss if the other modals they chose have a similar meaning to the ones used in the conversation.

Exercise 6: Pronunciation

A
- Play the audio. Have students read along as they listen to the Pronunciation Note.
- Point out the schwa at the end of each phrase: *hafta, gotta, oughta,* and *be able ta.* Also point out that the schwa is never stressed. The stress falls in the first syllable of *hafta, gotta, oughta,* and *able.*

B
- Play the audio. Have students listen and write the words they hear.

C
- Play the audio again and have students repeat. Then have students practice the conversation in pairs. Remind students to play both roles.

Exercise 7: Discussion
- After students discuss in pairs, call on students to share their answers to the questions.
- ⏱ Have pairs write sentences warning Blaire about possible risks and giving her advice. Remind students to use modals in their sentences.

Exercise 8: Reaching Agreement
- Have students make notes of their ideas individually.
- Form small groups and have students discuss their ideas. Encourage them to come to a conclusion as a group about what to include.
- Call on students from different groups to share their ideas with the class.
- ⏱ If students show interest, have them implement their ideas and design a class website.

Exercise 9: Problem Solving

A
- Have students take the quiz. Encourage them to make notes of reasons to support their choices.

B
- Have students discuss in small groups. Encourage them to reach a consensus on what to do.
- Have students from different groups explain their choices. Keep a tally on the board. Do most students agree?

Exercise 10: For or Against

A

- Have students write notes for each question individually. Encourage the use of different modals. Examples:

Social networking can / could / may / might help people make friends.

You should / ought to meet people with similar interests.

You may / might / could encounter objectionable content.

You should / must protect your personal information. You shouldn't / mustn't reveal your name.

B

- Have students use their notes to discuss as a class.

Exercise 11: Writing

A

- Write the following topics on the board to help students generate ideas and elicit vocabulary:

studies
housework
free time
diet
getting organized

- Have students make notes on some of the topics and use them as a guide as they write their posts.

B

- After students write their posts, have them correct their work using the Editing Checklist.

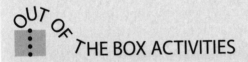
OUT OF THE BOX ACTIVITIES

Writing and Speaking

- Point out that people in some jobs give advice and guidance to others as part of their work. Have students consider *judges* (who evaluate people's bad behavior and decide on punishment), *high school teachers and counselors* (who advise students about academic work, college, and careers), *coaches* (who evaluate athletes and encourage them), *parents* (who make rules for behavior, encourage, discipline, and guide their children), and *police detectives* (who need to get information and make inferences and assumptions based on that information).

- Have students say which modals these groups of people are likely to need.
- Have pairs of students write scripts, practice, and perform a role play about one of the following situations: (a) a judge telling a person what to do to keep out of jail; (b) a school counselor advising a student about getting ready for college; (c) a coach encouraging an athlete to aim high; (d) a parent telling a teenager what the rules are for going to a party; (e) two police detectives discussing the meaning of a broken window, a shirt with blood on the sleeve, a missing television set, and a door that was left open.

Speaking

- Have students talk to coaches, counselors, dorm residents, and teachers to collect complaints and excuses.
- After the class has collected a series of complaints and excuses and the likely responses, have students role-play speaker and advice giver. For example:

A: My grades are terrible.

B: You might have to study more. / You must not be studying enough.

Go to **www.myfocusongrammarlab.com** for additional listening, pronunciation, speaking, and writing practice.

Note

- See the *Focus on Grammar Workbook* for additional in-class or homework grammar practice.

Unit 15 Review (page 256)

Have students complete the Review and check their answers on Student Book page UR-4. Review or assign additional material as needed.

Go to **www.myfocusongrammarlab.com** for the Unit Achievement Test.

Grammar: ADVISABILITY IN THE PAST

Students will learn and practice the use of *should (not) have, ought (not) to have, could have,* and *might have* to express advisability in the past.

Theme: REGRETS

Unit 16 focuses on language that we use to express regrets about things that have happened.

Step 1: Grammar in Context (pages 257–259)

See the general suggestions for Grammar in Context on page 1.

Before You Read
- Have students look at the photo and discuss the questions in pairs. Ask students to make notes for each question.
- Call on students to share their answers to the questions with the class. Write a list of typical things people have regrets about on the board.

Read
- To encourage students to read with a purpose, write the following questions on the board:
  1. Where do feelings come from, according to psychologists? *(from the way we think about reality, not reality itself)*
  2. How can past mistakes help us? *(We can learn from them and improve.)*
  3. How can feeling deep regret be destructive? *(Some people think so much about missed opportunities that they become unable to do anything to improve their current situation.)*
  4. How can a person let go of regrets? *(by realizing that he / she really had no control over the situation anyway)*
- Have students read the text. (Or play the audio and have students follow along in their books.) Then have students share their answers with the class.
- Have students discuss the following questions in small groups:
  1. Have you ever regretted an educational or career decision you made? What was it? What could you have done better or differently?
  2. What should you have done differently when you were younger? What difference could that change have made?

3. When the magazine *Psychology Today* was first published about 35 years ago, most people thought that the writers would quickly run out of topics to write about. To their surprise, the magazine has grown in popularity and scope. Ask: "Why is a magazine that deals with how people think and what they think about so popular?"

After You Read

A. Vocabulary
- Have students find and circle the vocabulary in the text. Encourage them to use the context to figure out their meaning.
- Have students compare answers in pairs. Then go over answers as a class.

B. Comprehension
- Have students choose the answers individually. Encourage them to underline the information in the text that supports their answers.
- Have students compare answers in pairs. Then call on students to say an answer each.
- (!) Have students complete the following sentences with information from the text or their own ideas. (*Possible answers: 1. our feelings result from the way we think about reality; 2. we may not have had the power to do things differently; 3. dealing with regrets; 4. write down the things you regret and then say them aloud; 5. can be very destructive; 6. telling a joke at work*)
  1. According to recent ideas in psychology, . . .
  2. Our feelings of regret are often unrealistic because . . .
  3. There are some good strategies for . . .
  4. A good technique is to . . .
  5. The process called "woulda / coulda / shoulda thinking" . . .
  6. She thought her career was ruined after . . .

Go to **www.myfocusongrammarlab.com** for an additional reading, and for reading and vocabulary practice.

Step 2: Grammar Presentation (pages 260–261)

See the general suggestions for Grammar Presentation on page 2.

Grammar Charts
- Write on the board:

  She   should   have called them.
          ought to
          could
          might

- Have students study the example. Ask: "Which modals can we use to talk about past advisability?" (*should, ought to, could,* and *might*) "What follows the modal?" (have + past participle) Point out that the use of *have* + past participle after the modal indicates that the speaker is talking about the past.
- Point out that for past advisability, the four modals on the board can be used in the affirmative, *should* and *ought to* can also be used in the negative, and only *should* is normally used in questions.
- Erase *ought to, could,* and *might.*
- Erase *She* and *should* and rewrite them in question order: *Should she have . . . ?* Next erase *Should she* and *called them,* leaving *have* in place. Write in *Yes, she should* in front of the *have.* Then erase the *Yes* and replace it with *No.* Ask: "What other change must be made?" (adding *'nt* to *should*). To end this drill, write once more the *yes / no* question *Should she have called them?* and then add a *wh-* question word at the beginning: *When should she have called them?*
- Write on the board:
  He should have explained it.
- Do a chain replacement drill in which pronouns, main verb phrases, and type of sentence (statement, *yes / no* question, *wh-* question, and affirmative and negative short answers) are changed, one element at a time.

Grammar Notes

Note 1
- Make sure students understand what is meant by past advisability. (*that something was convenient, so we regret, blame, or criticize that it was <u>not</u> done* OR *that something was <u>not</u> convenient, so we regret, blame, or criticize that it was done*)
- Have students expand sentences like these two: "I had a chance to travel around the world on a boat but I didn't go." (*I should've gone because I might never get another opportunity like that one. I might've _____.*) "I got into medical school, but I didn't go." (*I should've gone to medical school. I could've become a doctor. I might've _____.*) Let students supply verbs, or prompt with examples such as *might've enjoyed it / might've helped people / might've become rich.*
- Write on the board:
  Think of . . .
  1. Something you (or a person you know) had the chance to buy but didn't do so.
  2. An offer or an invitation you (or a person you know) didn't accept.

  3. A phone call you (or a person you know) didn't make.
- Have students write notes for each item. Form pairs. Have students use their notes and the items on the board to take turns saying sentences with *should / ought to / could / might + have.*

Note 2
- Write the following situations on the board:
  1. He didn't take the train. As a result, he was late.
  2. She left her bags unattended. As a result, they were stolen.
  3. They didn't accept the new credit card offer. We don't know if they did the right thing.
- Have students use the information in Item 1 to make affirmative sentences. Have them use as many modals as possible. (*He should have taken the train. He ought to have taken the train. He could have taken the train. He might have taken the train.*)
- Have students use the information in Item 2 to make negative sentences. Have them use as many modals as possible. (*She shouldn't have left her bags unattended. She ought not to have left her bags unattended*).
- Have students use the information in Item 3 to frame a question. (*Should they have accepted the new credit card offer?*) Have students provide the two possible short answers. (*Yes, they should have. / No, they shouldn't have.*)

Note 3
- Demonstrate the pronunciation of reduced forms of modal phrases: *have* sounds like *of* or even *a.* Mention that when native English speakers are learning to write as children, a very common error is to write *I should <u>of</u> done it.*
- Remind students that the contractions are written only in informal messages. The negative contractions (*shouldn't've*) are never written but are usually pronounced in spoken English.

⏱ **Identify the Grammar:** Have students identify the grammar in the opening reading on page 257. For example:
  It **might have been**.
  . . . you think you **should have done** and did not do . . .
  . . . you **should not have done**.
  . . . she **should have studied** more . . .
  I **ought to have applied** to college.
  I **should've been** rich and famous by now.
  I **could've become** a doctor.

Go to **www.myfocusongrammarlab.com** for grammar charts and notes.

Step 3: Focused Practice (pages 262–264)

See the general suggestions for Focused Practice on page 4.

Exercise 1: Discover the Grammar
- Go over the example with the class.
- Have students do the exercise individually and compare answers in pairs.
- Elicit the correct answers from the class.

Exercise 2: Statements, Questions, and Short Answers
- Go over the examples with the class.
- Have students read the conversation for meaning before choosing their answers.
- Call on four students to read the conversation aloud.
- ⏱ Have students express briefly their view on the problem. Point out that they should use at least one modal for past advisability. Example: *When Greg's boss said "no", he should've asked for credit to buy the sweater.*

Exercise 3: Affirmative and Negative Statements
- Go over the example with the class.
- Have students complete the exercise individually and compare answers in pairs.
- Go over the answers as a class.

Exercise 4: Editing
- Have students read the journal entry quickly to find out what it is about.
- Ask: "What problem does [the author] have?" (*His coworker, Jennifer, was late for work. Their boss, Doug, told him that he wanted to fire her and asked him to make things difficult for her so that she would quit.*) "What does [the author] regret?" (*The way he handled things. He wonders whether he should have confronted Doug, warned Jennifer, and talked to Doug's boss.*)
- Go over the example.
- Have students find and correct the mistakes individually and compare answers in pairs.
- Have students explain why the incorrect structures are wrong.
- ⏱ Ask students to point out examples of correct usages of modals.

Go to **www.myfocusongrammarlab.com** for additional grammar practice.

Step 4: Communication Practice (pages 265–268)

See the general suggestions for Communication Practice on page 4.

Exercise 5: Listening

A
- Point out that this exercise continues the story of Jennifer from Exercise 4.
- Have students read the "To Do" list. Each of the items in the list can be expanded into an advisability sentence. Encourage students to predict what Jennifer will say: *Homework—I should have done my homework.*
- Have students say full sentences. Example: *1. She didn't do her homework.* You may also want to have students say why she regrets having done / not having done the things in the list. Example: *1. She didn't do her homework. Now she has to get up early.*

B
- Have students read the statements. Have them predict what Jennifer will say. Play the audio and have students listen to confirm / correct their guesses.

Exercise 6: Pronunciation

A
- Play the audio. Have students read along as they listen to the Pronunciation Note.
- Point out that the schwa at the end of each phrase—*should've, could've,* and *might've*—is never stressed. The stress falls in the first syllable of *should've, could've,* and *might've.*

B
- Play the audio. Have students listen and write the words they hear.

C
- Have students practice the conversations. Remind them to play both roles.

Exercise 7: Game: Find the Problems
- Have students write descriptions of the picture.
- As students write their sentences, help them with vocabulary if needed: *garbage, cockroaches, leave on, turn off (stove, water,) put away (clothes).* Examples: *She should have taken out the garbage. She shouldn't have left food out to attract cockroaches.*

- ⏱ Have students write sentences about their bedroom / home to answer the questions: What did I leave undone? What did I do that I shouldn't have done? Examples: *I should have turned the heater off. I shouldn't have left my clothes on the floor.*

Exercise 8: Survey

A

- Have students take the survey individually.

B

- Have students compare their survey results in pairs. Call on students to say if they agree / disagree with the result of the test. Encourage them to explain their view.
- ⏱ Have students discuss whether it is good to have a strong sense of obligation.

Exercise 9: Problem Solving

- Have students read Case 1. Go over the examples.
- Ask students: "Was the reporter right to ask the questions?" *(Yes, he was / No, wasn't. He shouldn't have asked her.)* "Was Mustafa right to go back into the building?" *(Yes, he was / No, he wasn't. He shouldn't have gone back.)* "Was the insurance company right to refuse to pay for the medicine?" *(No, it should have paid . . .)*
- Encourage students to explain their views: Did the people act properly? Should they have done things differently?

Exercise 10: Writing

A

- Brainstorm possible dilemmas: *Have you ever run out of money? Have you ever made a serious mistake at school, work, or home? Have you ever been unable to help a friend in need? In any of these situations, what could you / should you / might you have done?*
- As students decide on a dilemma to write about, encourage them to be humorous, and remind them that not all mistakes are tragic or life-altering: *I shouldn't have bought those shoes that hurt my feet. I should never have asked for a pet monkey because a monkey is too much work!*
- Have students choose a title for their writing. A possible title is "That Was a Mistake!" Then have them write their paragraphs.

B

- After students write their paragraphs, have them correct their work using the Editing Checklist.

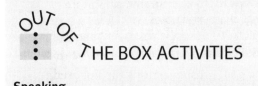

OUT OF THE BOX ACTIVITIES

Speaking

- Have three groups of students create lists of tasks *(household, school, and personal / general)* that they wanted to complete last week. Possible household tasks: *clean my room, take out the garbage, do laundry, pay my bills.* Possible school tasks: *study for the quiz, do my homework, get toner for my printer, buy the textbook I needed.* Suggestions for personal / general: *return books to the library, write home, clean up my email, call my mother.*
- Have students use past modals of advisability and obligation to talk about tasks they did and didn't do. Remind them that *should have* gives a message that the task was <u>not</u> completed. If they did complete the task, they need to change their statements to *I was supposed to . . .* or *I had to . . . and I did.* Encourage them to give themselves advice about how they could have managed better and excuses why they didn't: *I should have cleaned my room, but I had to study for a big test.*

Listening and Speaking

- Have students survey people they know outside of class about regrets or "roads they wish they had taken."
- Have students choose one of the regrets and write it on a card as a statement.
- Mix up the cards in a box or bowl and have each student choose one. Have students work with a partner to describe the problem, express it as a regret, and expand on it. Card example: A car mechanic says, "I decided to become a mechanic instead of going to college to study mechanical engineering." The student changes the statement to something like this: "I should have gone to college to study mechanical engineering." Then the student and partner should expand with reasons and excuses: "I needed money to buy a car of my own, but I might have made a lot more money, and I wouldn't have had to spend so much time now working with dirty, oily cars."
- Have students share their work.

Go to **www.myfocusongrammarlab.com** for additional listening, pronunciation, speaking, and writing practice.

Note

• See the *Focus on Grammar Workbook* for additional in-class or homework grammar practice.

Unit 16 Review (page 269)

Have students complete the Review and check their answers on Student Book page UR-4. Review or assign additional material as needed.

Go to **www.myfocusongrammarlab.com** for the Unit Achievement Test.

UNIT 17 OVERVIEW

Grammar: SPECULATIONS AND CONCLUSIONS ABOUT THE PAST

Students will learn and practice *may (not) have, might (not) have, could (not) have, must (not) have,* and *had to have* to make speculations and draw conclusions about the past.

Theme: UNSOLVED MYSTERIES

Unit 17 focuses on language that we use to speculate about past events.

Prehistory (the time before written records were available) is hidden from us. We have only physical evidence (the Nazca lines in Peru, the pyramids of Egypt and Mexico, the statues of Easter Island, and the great stones of Stonehenge in England) to help us guess why these things exist and how they came to be. Many theories (which can never be proved or disproved) have been published.

Step 1: Grammar in Context (pages 270–272)

See the general suggestions for Grammar in Context on page 1.

Before You Read

• Have students look at the photo and discuss the questions in pairs.
• Call on pairs to share their answers to the questions.

Read

• To encourage students to read with a purpose, write the following questions on the board:
  1. What are the Nazca lines? *(lines in the shapes of animals and geometric forms)*
  2. How many Nazca forms are there? *(over 13,000)*

3. What is Erich von Däniken's theory about the Nazca lines? *(They were made by the Nazcans following instructions from visitors from another planet.)*
4. According to von Däniken, what do the statues on Easter Island prove? *(that ancient cultures had contact with visitors from others planets because the islanders could not have made the statues by themselves)*

• Have students read the text. (Or play the audio and have students follow along in their books.) Have students share their answers with the class.
• Have students discuss the following questions in small groups:
  1. Von Däniken wrote his book *Chariots of the Gods?* in 1972. Why do people continue to read a book that was published so long ago?
  2. What other theories about strange phenomena have you heard?

After You Read

A. Vocabulary

• Have students find and circle the vocabulary in the text. Encourage them to use the context to figure out their meaning.
• Have students compare answers in pairs. Then go over answers as a class.
• (⏱) Write the following on the board or on a handout. Have students match the vocabulary with phrases that are similar in meaning.
  (1. d, 2. e, 3. a, 4. f, 5. b, 6. c)

  1. have evidence
  2. have an encounter
  3. estimate
  4. come to a conclusion
  5. contribute
  6. speculate

  a. judge the value or amount of something
  b. give help or help something happen
  c. guess why something happens
  d. have proof
  e. meet
  f. decide that something is true

B. Comprehension

• Have students choose the answers individually. Encourage students to underline the information in the text that supports their answers.
• Have students compare answers in pairs. Then call on students to say an answer each.

Go to **www.myfocusongrammarlab.com** for an additional reading, and for reading and vocabulary practice.

Step 2: Grammar Presentation (pages 273–274)

See the general suggestions for Grammar Presentation on page 2.

Grammar Charts

- Write on the board:
  He could have seen a ghost.
- Show how the changes are made from statement to *yes / no* question to short answers to *wh-* question: Erase *He* and *could* and rewrite them in question order *(Could he have . . . ?)*. Next erase *Could he* and *seen a ghost?* leaving *have* in place. Write in *Yes, he could* in front of the *have*. Then erase the *Yes* and replace it with *No*. Ask students what other change must be made (adding *not* after *could*) To end this change drill, rewrite the *yes / no* question *(Could he have seen a ghost?)* again and then add a *wh-* question word at the beginning: *When could he have seen a ghost?*
- Write another statement *(It could have been an alien spaceship)* on the board. Ask individual students to go to the board and make the changes that their classmates ask for. Remind the student at the board that he or she can ask another student to say what should be written on the board.
- Do a chain replacement drill in which pronouns, modal expressions, main verb phrase, and type of sentence (statement, *yes / no* question, *wh-* question, and affirmative and negative short answers) are changed one element at a time. Point out that we usually use *could* (not the other modals) in questions about speculations and conclusions about the past.

Grammar Notes

Note 1

- Point out that speculations (some people call them inferences) are based on some evidence, but speculations can be wrong. Mention that there is very little difference between *may have*, *might have*, and *could have* in positive statements, and that these speculations are often preceded by "I don't know, but . . ."
- Ask students: "Who in this classroom got up earliest today? Was it [Gina]? Was it [Tomo]?" *(I don't know, but it could have been [Gina]. She looks tired. I don't know, but it might have been [Tomo]. He was here first today.)*

Note 2

- Point out that conclusions with *must have* and *have to have* are almost certainly true. Give an example: *His hair was all wet when he came in. It must have been raining.*

- Provide a fact and have students draw conclusions. Say: "All the students passed the English test with high grades." *(They must have studied a lot. The test had to have been very easy. They must not have found it hard.)*
- ⏱ Draw a chart on the board to show the difference between positive and negative forms. Use colored chalk, or underline, in order to point out how *might have* and *may have* don't change in degree of certainty between negative and positive, but *could have / couldn't have* are very different.

must have	(95%)	couldn't have can't have
have to have		
	(less than 95% sure)	must not have
could have	(less than 50% sure)	might not have
might have		may not have
may have		

Note 3

- Point out that *couldn't have* emphasizes that the action was impossible—or at least hard to believe.

Note 4

- Point out that *might have* and *may have* are used to ask for permission (as in *May I have another piece of apple pie?* or *Might I have your attention please?*). *Could have* is more commonly used for questions about possibility.

Note 5

- Point out that *be* is added to the short answer *(Yes, it could have been)* whereas other verbs are not.
- Ask students questions with no clear answers:
  Q: Was January 20, 2010, a Monday?
  A: I don't know, but it <u>could have been</u>.
  Q: Was it cold that day in Sweden?
  A: It <u>must have been</u>.
  Q: Did it snow that day in Sweden?
  A: It <u>must have</u>.
  Q: Was it cold that day in Rio?
  A: It <u>couldn't have been / can't have been</u>.
  Q: Did it snow that day in Rio?
  A: <u>It couldn't have</u>. It hardly ever snows there.

Note 6

- Point out that *could have* can sound like *could of* or *coulda*. Have students answer questions or comment on situations with the reduced form of *could have*: *She bought a lottery ticket. She didn't win, but she could have (coulda) won.*

🕐 **Identify the Grammar:** Have students identify the grammar in the opening reading on page 270. For example:

> . . . Xesspe of Peru **must have been** very surprised to see lines . . .
>
> Xesspe **may have been** the first human in almost a thousand years to recognize the designs.
>
> . . . how **could** an ancient culture **have made** these amazing pictures?
>
> What purpose **could** they **have had**?
>
> . . . the people of those cultures **must have believed** that the visitors were gods.

Go to **www.myfocusongrammarlab.com** for grammar charts and notes.

Step 3: Focused Practice (pages 275–279)

See the general suggestions for Focused Practice on page 4.

Exercise 1: Discover the Grammar
- Go over the example with the class.
- Have students do the exercise individually and compare answers in pairs.
- Elicit the correct answers from the class.
- 🕐 Have pairs draw their own conclusions for some of the facts in the exercise. Example: *1. He must have written it in his native language.*

Exercise 2: Questions and Statements
- Have students read the review for meaning.
- Go over the example with the class.
- Have students complete the exercise individually and compare answers in pairs.
- Call on a student to read the review aloud.

Exercise 3: Affirmative and Negative Statements
- Go over the example with the class. Elicit from students how to use modals for speculations and conclusions about the past. Write on the board:
  modal + *(not)* + *have* + past participle
- Have students read the rest of the review for meaning.
- Have students complete the exercise individually and compare answers in pairs.
- Call on a student to read the review aloud.

Exercise 4: Meaning
- Go over the example with the class.
- Have students complete the exercise individually and compare answers in pairs. Then go over answers as a class.

- 🕐 Have students write one or two sentences expressing their opinion about each puzzling event. Point out that they should use modals for speculations and conclusions about the past. Examples for the first event: *A large volcano could have erupted. Ashes may have covered the planet.*

Exercise 5: Short Answers
- Go over the example. Remind students to use subject + modal + *have* in short answers, and to also use *been* if the question includes a form of *be*.
- Have students compare answers in pairs. Then go over answers as a class.

Exercise 6: Editing
- Have students read the essay quickly for meaning.
- Ask: "How could the first settlers have gotten to Easter Island?" *(by boat)* "Where could they have come from?" *(Polynesia, America, or Egypt)* "What made the island a paradise for the first settlers?" *(its fishing, forests, and good soil)* "What happened when they cut down all the trees?" *(With no trees, they couldn't build boats to go fishing and the soil was washed away, so they starved for a period of time.)* "What happened then?" *(They started growing vegetables and learned to live peacefully.)*
- Go over the example.
- Have students find and correct the mistakes individually and compare answers in pairs.
- Have students explain why the incorrect structures are wrong.
- 🕐 Ask students to point out examples of correct usages of modals.

Go to **www.myfocusongrammarlab.com** for additional grammar practice.

Step 4: Communication Practice (pages 280–283)

See the general suggestions for Communication Practice on page 4.

Exercise 7: Listening

A
- Have students look at the pictures, speculate on the uses of the objects, and compare them to common objects today.
- Have students read the statements. Then play the audio. Have students complete the exercise individually.
- Encourage students to support their answers. Example: *1. The woman said it might have been used to cut down grass.*

B

- Play the audio. Stop after each conversation to allow students time to choose the object.
- Encourage students to support their answers. Example: *1. The woman said it looked like a knife.*

Exercise 8: Pronunciation

A

- Play the audio. Have students read along as they listen to the Pronunciation Note.
- Point out that the reduction of *'ve* is not stressed. The stress falls on the modal and the main verb. Write an example on the board, and underline the parts of the verb phrase that are stressed:
  They <u>could</u>'ve <u>tra</u>veled by boat.

B

- Play the audio. Have students listen and complete the conversations.

C

- Play the audio again and have students repeat the responses. Then have students practice the conversations. Remind them to play both roles.

Exercise 9: Picture Discussion

- Have students write notes about their speculations and conclusions individually. Encourage them to be creative in their thinking and to come up with as many uses as they can.
- Have students discuss in small groups. After students discuss, have them read the answer key at the bottom of page 282. You may want to give them more information about the objects:
  1. Ceramic pillow from ancient China (ca. A.D. 900). Ceramic may have been used because it is cool in summer.
  2. Bronze brooch from western or central Europe, probably from Italy (ca. 600 B.C.). Both men and women have been found buried with similar brooches.
  3. Razor and mirror, from Egypt (ca. 1400 B.C.). The mirror has a handle which is held in place by a small bronze peg, with an image of a woman's face with cow's ears.
  4. Pair of snow goggles, from the Canadian Arctic, early 19th century. Goggles like these protected the eyes from the sun and the cold but also prevented the wearer from seeing the ground.

5. Navigation chart from Micronesia, made of sticks. Such charts are still made today, although they are not used for navigation.

Exercise 10: For or Against

A

- Point out that some of the information in the reading supports the von Däniken theory and some contradicts it.
- Have students read the article again. Then have students write supporting and contradictory statements in two columns on the board.

B

- Call on students to share their views. Keep a tally on the board to find out what most students think.

Exercise 11: Writing

A

- Write the following questions on the board to help students generate ideas and elicit vocabulary:
  What was the man doing there?
  Was he alone?
  Why was he carrying a knife, an ax, dried meat, and medicines?
  What caused his death?
  Did his family / friends try to find him?
  Why wasn't he found before?
- Have students make notes on some of the questions and use them as a guide as they write their paragraphs.

B

- After students write their paragraphs, have them correct their work using the Editing Checklist.

OUT OF THE BOX ACTIVITIES

Reading and Speaking

- Have students read the following mysteries.
  1. Police have found an abandoned car in the mountains of British Columbia. It is almost new and in perfect condition. The tank is full of gas, and the keys are in the ignition. The car's owner lives about 500 miles away, but she is on a cruise around the world. She has been gone for two months.

2. Carol James has disappeared. She and her husband Chet have been planning a trip to Bermuda. They were supposed to leave in two days. However, the airplane tickets and a carefully packed suitcase of beach clothes were left, and Carol's car, her winter clothes, her mink coat, all of her jewelry, and all of the money in their bank account are missing. She left no note.

3. Archeologists have found the frozen bodies of three children in a grave on top of a mountain. They were all wearing beautiful clothing and jewelry and were wrapped in nicely woven pieces of cloth. They all had serious head injuries. Tests show that these children died 3,000 years ago.

• Have students discuss in groups. Then call on students to share their speculations and conclusions with the class.

Speaking

• Ask students to bring in the oldest photographs they can find, either of family members or from books or magazines, but not of well-known people.
• Have small groups exchange photographs and make up stories about the people in the photos: *She's wearing a lot of beautiful jewelry. She must have been rich. He looks very tired. He must have worked very hard in his life. She's smiling. She must have been very happy.*

Go to **www.myfocusongrammarlab.com** for additional listening, pronunciation, speaking, and writing practice.

Note
• See the *Focus on Grammar Workbook* for additional in-class or homework grammar practice.

Unit 17 Review (page 284)

Have students complete the Review and check their answers on Student Book page UR-4. Review or assign additional material as needed.

Go to **www.myfocusongrammarlab.com** for the Unit Achievement Test.

From Grammar to Writing (pages 285–287)

See the general suggestions for From Grammar to Writing on page 9.

Go to **www.myfocusongrammarlab.com** for an additional From Grammar to Writing Assignment, Part Review, and Part Post-Test.

PART VIII OVERVIEW

THE PASSIVE

UNIT	GRAMMAR FOCUS	THEME
18	The Passive: Overview	Geography
19	The Passive with Modals and Similar Expressions	The International Space Station
20	The Passive Causative	Personal Services

Go to **www.myfocusongrammarlab.com** for the Part and Unit Tests.

Note: PowerPoint® grammar presentations, test-generating software, and reproducible Part and Unit Tests are on the *Teacher's Resource Disc.*

UNIT 18 OVERVIEW

Grammar: THE PASSIVE: OVERVIEW

Students will learn and practice the general principles of the passive.

Theme: GEOGRAPHY

Unit 18 focuses on language that we use to describe natural and human-made places around the world.

Step 1: Grammar in Context (pages 290–291)

See the general suggestions for Grammar in Context on page 1.

Before You Read
• Write *Geography* on the board. Brainstorm related nouns and write them on the board. (Examples: mountains, rivers, oceans, wildlife, rain forests, population, cities) Then have students provide adjectives to describe them. (Examples: beautiful mountains, winding rivers, deep oceans, rich wildlife, lush rain forests, immigrant population, overpopulated cities)

- Have students discuss the questions in pairs. Call on students to share their answers to the questions:
  - For Question 1, write some definitions on the board. Then have students compare them with the one given in the article.
  - For Question 2, encourage students to give examples of topics they enjoyed / didn't enjoy. Write students' ideas in two columns on the board.
  - For Question 3, encourage students who think geography is important to explain why.

Read
- To encourage students to read with a purpose, write the following questions on the board:
  1. Where and when was the first issue of *National Geographic* published? *(nine months after the National Geographic Society was formed in Washington, D.C., in 1888)*
  2. How did the National Geographic Society change the meaning of geography? *(People used to think of geography as the names of countries, capitals, rivers, and mountain ranges, but the magazine shows how the world looks and feels, how people live, and how important natural resources are.)*
  3. What is the mission of *National Geographic*? *(to spread knowledge of and respect for the world, its resources, and its inhabitants)*
- Have students read the text. (Or play the audio and have students follow along in their books.) Then call on students to share their answers with the class.
- Have students discuss these questions in small groups:
  1. Why do you think the National Geographic Society began publishing a magazine for young people?
  2. Think about people's interest in the *National Geographic* magazine, the television program about different places, and travel to distant places. What do these interests reveal about people all over the world?

After You Read

A. Vocabulary
- Have students find and circle the vocabulary in the text. Encourage them to use the context to figure out their meaning.
- Have students compare answers in pairs. Then go over answers as a class.

B. Comprehension
- Have students answer the questions individually and compare answers in pairs.
- Call on six students to answer a question each.
- (🕐) Have students complete the following sentences with information from the article. Point out that there isn't just one correct answer. *(1. did not enjoy the subject / were forced to memorize information. 2. formed the National Geographic Society in 1888. 3. published the National Geographic magazine. 4. are covered in the magazine. 5. classrooms / school students. 6. was published in 1995 / was the first foreign language edition of the magazine.)*
  1. For decades, geography students . . .
  2. Explorers were among the professionals who . . .
  3. In order to fulfill its mission, the National Geographic Society . . .
  4. Both the world's resources and its inhabitants . . .
  5. *National Geographic Explorer* is a special publication for . . .
  6. The Japanese edition of *National Geographic* magazine . . .

Go to **www.myfocusongrammarlab.com** for an additional reading, and for reading and vocabulary practice.

Step 2: Grammar Presentation (pages 292–293)

See the general suggestions for Grammar Presentation on page 2.

Grammar Charts
- Write an example on the board:
  The magazine is bought by people from all over the world.
- Ask: "Who buys the magazine?" *(people from all over the world)*
- Rewrite the example as an active sentence:
  People from all over the world buy the magazine.
  Underline the object (*the magazine*) in the active sentence and the subject (*the magazine*) in the passive sentence. Draw an arrow to show how it moves to the subject position in a passive sentence. Add labels as indicated below:

The magazine is bought by people from all over the world.
  subject ↑_____ *(passive)*

People from all over the world buy the magazine.
             object   *(active)*

- Draw attention to the passive sentence. Ask: "How do we form the passive?" (*form of* be + *past participle*)
- Have students turn the following sentences into the passive form. (*1. A magazine for classrooms was created. 2. Now geography is taught in an amusing way.*)
  1. They created a magazine for classrooms.
  2. Now they teach geography in an amusing way.

Grammar Notes

Note 1
- Remind students of terminology: the *agent* is the person or thing that does or did the action. The *object* is the person or thing that receives the action.
- Point out that the subject of any sentence (the first part of the sentence) receives the most emphasis, so in passive sentences what was done is more important than *who* or *what* did it.

Note 2
- Point out that the passive requires the addition of some form of *be*: *is* or *are* in the present, *was* or *were* in the past, and *has* or *have been* in the present perfect. The form of *be* is followed by the past participle.
- Draw attention to the *Be Careful!* note. A sentence without a direct object cannot become a passive. (That is, only transitive verbs have active and passive forms.) Put a few examples of intransitive sentences on the board:
  The earthquake happened. A fire broke out. He died.
  Remind the class: no object = no passive form possible.

Note 3
- Point out that there are three advantages to the passive: You leave out unknown or unimportant information, you can choose not to mention who did something, and you can keep a sharp focus on the main topic.
- Write the following active sentences on the board:
  1. The rescue team found the missing climbers.
  2. I'm sorry to say that my assistant mailed the package to the wrong address.
- Have students turn them into the passive, and say why the passive is preferred. (*1. "The missing climbers were found." The passive is preferred because the agent is not as important as the action itself. 2. "I'm sorry to say that the package was mailed to the wrong address." The passive is preferred so as not to blame anyone.*)

Note 4
- Point out that sometimes we want to keep a sharp focus on the main topic, but we also want to mention who or what did something. In such a case, we use *by* + the agent. To give an example, say: "The National Geographic Society was started by a group of scientists, mapmakers, and professors who were concerned about the earth's future." Point out that in this example, the focus is still on the National Geographic Society, but the *by* expression gives information that is also helpful.
- Draw attention to the *Be Careful!* note. Remind students that if the agent is unimportant or obvious, it should be left out.

Identify the Grammar: Have students identify the grammar in the opening reading on page 290. For example:
  They **were forced** to memorize the names of capital cities . . .
  They **were taught** where places were and what **was produced** there.
  But they **weren't shown** how our world looks . . .
  . . . the natural and human-made wonders of our world **have** now **been brought** to life **by** its fascinating reporting . . .
  The National Geographic Society **was formed . . . by** a group of professionals . . .

Go to **www.myfocusongrammarlab.com** for grammar charts and notes.

Step 3: Focused Practice (pages 293–300)

See the general suggestions for Focused Practice on page 4.

Exercise 1: Discover the Grammar
- If necessary, review how the passive is formed. (*form of* be + *past participle*)
- Have students complete the exercise individually and compare answers in pairs.
- Elicit the correct answers from the class.

Exercise 2: Active or Passive
- Have students study the chart. Point out that it gives information about how many people speak each of the languages as a first language.
- Go over the example with the class. Point out that when the numbers are not exact, students can write:
  more than . . . people OR around . . . people.
- Have students compare answers in pairs. Then go over answers as a class.

- ⏱ Ask: "How many languages are spoken in Canada?" (*two, English and French*) "Which are the three most widely spoken languages in Switzerland?" (*German, French, and Italian*) "Which language is spoken as a first, second, or foreign language by most people around the world?" (*English*) "Which language is spoken in Brazil?" (*Portuguese*) "How many languages are spoken in China—over 150, over 250, or over 350?" (*over 250*) "Which language is most widely spoken in China?" (*Mandarin*)

Exercise 3: *Wh-* Questions and Statements

A

- Go over the example with the class. Point out that students are not expected to take the quiz, but they can choose to take it and then check their answers in the *Answers* section.

B

- Have students complete the exercise and compare answers in pairs. Then go over answers as a class.
- ⏱ Form small groups. Have students create a five-question quiz on a city of their choice, using the passive form. Point out that they can use the questions in this exercise as a guide. Have groups exchange quizzes and take them.

Exercise 4: Questions, Statements, and Short Answers

- Point out that a *cultural attaché* is someone who works in an embassy and deals with the way of life of the society of that country.
- Encourage students to read each section for meaning before writing their answers.
- Have students complete the exercise individually and compare answers in pairs.
- Call on two students to read the conversation aloud.

Exercise 5: Affirmative and Negative Statements

A

- Have students read Jill Jones's article and edit it by writing the correct information above each circled item.

B

- Go over the example. Point out that students should write a negative sentence and an affirmative sentence for each item.
- Have students compare answers in pairs. Then go over answers as a class.

Exercise 6: Including or Deleting the Agent

- Go over the example with the class. Remind students that they should choose the correct form for the passive verb—simple present, simple past, or present perfect.
- Have students compare answers in pairs. Then go over answers as a class.

Exercise 7: Editing

- Have students read the biography quickly for meaning..
- Ask: "When did Reza Deghati start his career as a photographer?" (*when he was 25*) "What does Reza do to help children?" (*He donates his photos of children in wars to humanitarian organizations; he has created an organization, whose aim is in part to help children receive an education.*)
- Have students find and correct the mistakes individually and compare answers in pairs.
- Have students explain why the incorrect structures are wrong.
- ⏱ Ask students to point out examples of correct usages of the passive.

Go to **www.myfocusongrammarlab.com** for additional grammar practice.

Step 4: Communication Practice (pages 301–306)

See the general suggestions for Communication Practice on page 4.

Exercise 8: Listening

A

- Have students read the statements before listening. Point out that the information may not be provided in the conversation, in which case they should select the last column.

B

- Play the audio. Stop the recording after each conversation to allow students time to complete the sentences and to review answers. If necessary, play the conversations again so students can correct the answers.

Exercise 9: Pronunciation

A

- Play the audio. Have students read along as they listen to the Pronunciation Note.
- Write an example on the board:
  La Paz isn't located in the north. It's in the west.
- Ask: "Which words should be stressed in the example?" (*north* and *west*)

B

- Play the audio. Have students listen and mark the stressed words.

C

- Play the audio again for students to check their work. Then have students practice the conversation in pairs. Remind them to play both roles.

Exercise 10: Quotable Quotes

- Have students read the proverbs and identify and underline the passive forms in the proverbs. If necessary, clarify the meaning of unknown words: *hailstorm* (rain and ice falling together), *marble* (a hard white rock that can be carved and polished), and *skillful* (good at doing something you have learned and practiced).
- Go over the example with the class. Ask students if similar proverbs exist in their language / culture.
- Discuss the meaning of each proverb as a class. Encourage students to say why they agree / disagree with them.
- ⏱ Take a poll to find out which proverb is preferred by most students.

Exercise 11: Information Gap: The Philippines

- Divide the class into Students A and Students B. Have Students B go to page 306.
- Have students study the symbols and clarify any doubts. Then have them say example questions they can ask to find out the information they need to complete the chart. (Examples: *Is tobacco grown in [Luzon]? Are pigs raised in [Mindanao]? Is gold mined in [Luzon]? Is rubber produced in [Mindanao]?*)
- Call on students to describe each item on the chart using full sentences. (Example: *Tobacco isn't grown in Mindanao.*)

Exercise 12: Game: Trivia Quiz

A

- Have students complete the exercise and compare answers in pairs.

B

- Brainstorm inventions, famous pieces of music, and famous poems or novels. For the blank option, suggest and brainstorm athletes and sports, musicians, magazines and books, or cars / motorcycles / dirt bikes and people associated with them. Be sure to include a topic that is likely to appeal to male students.

Exercise 13: Writing

A

- Have students practice filling in the chart, using local information that the students are likely to know. Point out that many ideas can be expressed using either an active sentence or a passive one. Examples: *We are in southern Wisconsin, where dairy farming is an important industry. (Dairy cows are raised here.) The most important crops are animal foods like alfalfa, corn, and clover. (Alfalfa, corn, and clover are grown.) English is spoken widely, but in some communities you can still hear German, Polish, Italian, and some other European languages. (German, Polish, and Italian are still heard.)*
- Have students complete the chart.

B

- Have students use the information to write their essays.

C

- After students write their essays, have them correct their work using the Editing Checklist.

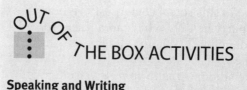

OUT OF THE BOX ACTIVITIES

Speaking and Writing

- Find a game that everyone knows how to play, perhaps Hide and Seek. List what happens on the board.
  — The players gather.
  — The rules are discussed: where "home" is, how far away the players can go, how long they can take to find a hiding place, whether they can move to new hiding places once the seeker ("it") starts looking for the hidden players, etc.
  — The game begins. "It" hides his or her eyes and begins counting. Other players hide. "It" says, "*Ready or not, here I come*" and starts to look for other players. The first player who is found becomes the next "it."
- Have students, individually or in small groups, choose a board or outdoor game they know and write down what is needed to play the game, how the game is played, how the game is won, etc.

- Have students teach their game to another student or group of students. Or have students describe their game without saying the name of the game. The other students guess what it is. Example:

  A: The game is played by two people. A board with red and black squares is used.

  B: I think you mean checkers.

Speaking and Writing

- Ask students to go to resort or apartment complex offices or websites to find schematic drawings or maps. Have the students label the locations where certain activities take place. (Examples: *This is the social center of the apartment complex. This part of the building is used for meetings and parties. This room is reserved for exercise because it holds all kinds of special equipment. Picnics are held in this part of the grounds because there are picnic tables. Renters' cars are parked here, and visitors' cars are parked in this special visitors' parking lot.*)
- Tell students that a wedding reception took place in this social center. Ask: "Where was the party held?" "Which area was reserved for dancing?" "Where were guests' cars parked?"
- Have students make up passive statements about how the facilities were used.

Go to **www.myfocusongrammarlab.com** for additional listening, pronunciation, speaking, and writing practice.

Note

- See the *Focus on Grammar Workbook* for additional in-class or homework grammar practice.

Unit 18 Review (page 307)

Have students complete the Review and check their answers on Student Book page UR-5. Review or assign additional material as needed.

Go to **www.myfocusongrammarlab.com** for the Unit Achievement Test.

Grammar: THE PASSIVE WITH MODALS AND SIMILAR EXPRESSIONS

Students will learn and practice passive constructions with modals *(will, should, ought to, must, can, had better)* and similar expressions *(have (got) to, be going to)* with the corresponding negative and question forms.

Theme: THE INTERNATIONAL SPACE STATION

Unit 19 focuses on language that we use to talk about space projects. It also covers language used to discuss how places could be improved.

In outer space, personal space for astronauts is limited. There is very little room inside space shuttles, but this is not really a problem, since astronauts do not spend much time there. Space stations, where people have to live for long periods of time, are different. Learning to live in these confined areas with people of other cultures presents a great challenge for the astronauts who do it—as well as for the social scientists who study them.

Step 1: Grammar in Context (pages 308–310)

See the general suggestions for Grammar in Context on page 1.

Before You Read

- Write simple definitions of the words *close* and *quarters* on the board:
  close: only a short distance away
  quarters: a room where someone lives
- For Question 1, help students figure out the meaning of the title "Close Quarters" *(a living place where there are too many people and not enough room)*.
- For Question 2, encourage students to think of cultural differences *(language, customs, manners, religion, tastes, etc.)* and make a list of possible problems.
- Call on students to share their answers to the questions with the class.

Read

- To encourage students to read with a purpose, write the following questions on the board:
  1. What is the International Space Station? *(the largest and most complex international project ever in which a multicultural group of astronauts are expected to live and work together in space)*
  2. What are some of the culture-related concerns of its inhabitants? *(the pace at which decisions are made, food and dinner time, privacy, language barriers, cleanup, religious matters like dietary restrictions)*

3. What special benefit do astronauts get from space? *(a unique perspective of Earth with no borders of nations and religions that contributes to the spirit of cooperation that is necessary among them)*
- Have students read the text. (Or play the audio and have students follow along in their books.) Then have students share their answers with the class.
- Have students discuss the following questions in small groups:
  1. The Japanese wondered, "Will decisions be made too fast?" The Americans wondered, "Can they be made quickly enough?" What do these two questions reveal about the Americans and the Japanese?
  2. The article says that astronauts get cross-cultural training. What are some of the things you would expect astronauts to be taught?
  3. Think about body language. How does one person "show" rather than "say" messages like "I'm afraid of you" or "I don't believe you"? What are some other common body language messages? How are these body language messages different among different groups of people?

After You Read

A. Vocabulary
- Have students find and circle the vocabulary in the text. Encourage them to use the context to figure out their meaning.
- Have students compare answers in pairs. Then go over answers as a class.
- ⏱ Write the following on the board or on a handout. Have students match the vocabulary words to the words or phrases that go with them. *(1. b, 2. d, 3. f, 4. a, 5. c, 6. e)*

  1. to assemble   a. undertaking
  2. to benefit   b. a space station
  3. a period   c. perspective
  4. a huge   d. from a discovery
  5. a new   e. on a project
  6. to cooperate   f. of time

B. Comprehension
- Have students choose the answers individually. Encourage students to underline the information in the text that supports their answers.
- Have students compare answers in pairs. Then call on students to say an answer each.

Go to **www.myfocusongrammarlab.com** for an additional reading, and for reading and vocabulary practice.

Step 2: Grammar Presentation (pages 311–312)
See the general suggestions for Grammar Presentation on page 2.

Grammar Charts
- Write on the board:
  The crew <u>will</u> <u>be</u> <u>replaced</u> next month.
  The space station <u>is going to</u> <u>be</u> <u>launched</u> in May.
- Point out that the passive + modal structure contains three elements: modal (or similar expression) + *be* + past participle.
- Write the following questions on the board and elicit the two possible short answers for each question:
  Can decisions be made quickly enough?
  Do they have to be made quickly?
  Are they going to be trained?
- Point out that the modal is used in the short answers and that the *have to* and *going to* expressions use appropriate forms of *do* and *be*, respectively.
- Ask: "Should it be replaced?" "Can it be replaced?" "Will it be replaced?" "Does it have to be replaced?" "Is it going to be replaced?" "Do they have to be replaced?" Signal that you want a *yes* or *no* answer by nodding or shaking your head as you ask. You can add humor by getting faster and faster as you move around the room. If the above sentences seem too easy for your students, you can make them longer and more complicated, just to make the point that even a very long sentence still gets a short simple answer: "Will the faulty computer that the astronauts brought on board the shuttle with them when they first arrived three months ago need to be replaced before it stops working completely?" *(Yes, it will.)*
- Remind students that although the *wh-* question is not included in a box, it follows the same formula as any other *wh-* question, that it is just formed from the *yes / no* question.
- Write on the board:
  Will it need to be replaced?
  What will need to be replaced?

Grammar Notes

Note 1
- Use the same example sentences that are on the board from the grammar charts to remind students of the three necessary elements (modal, *be*, past participle).

Note 2

- Write these two sentences on the board and have students identify the future passive forms. (*will be avoided, is going to be replaced*) Cross-cultural problems will be avoided. The crew is going to be replaced.
- Write the following sentence skeletons on the board and have students make their own sentences or questions. (*1. The street will be repaired next year. / When will it be repaired? 2. The broken clock is going to be replaced next week. / When is it going to be replaced?*)
  1. street / repair / next year
  2. broken clock / replace / next week

Notes 3 and 4

- Point out that the meanings of *can* and *could* for present and past ability and *could, may, might,* and *can't* for future possibility (or impossibility) are consistent with the meanings of these modals in active forms (Unit 15). The addition of the passive doesn't change the meaning of the modal.
- Write active sentences on the board and have students turn them into the passive. (*1. The problem can't be solved. 2. A solution may be found. 3. Instructions could be sent to them. 4. A new space station might be assembled.*)
  1. They can't solve the problem.
  2. They may find a solution.
  3. They could send them instructions.
  4. They might assemble a new space station.

Note 5

- Point out that advisability and necessity as expressed by *should, ought to, had better, must,* and *have (got) to* are also consistent with the meanings of these expressions in active sentences (Unit 15).
- Have students complete the following sentences with their own ideas.

  A space traveler | should be taught . . .
  | must be trained . . .
  | had better be told . . .

- **Identify the Grammar:** Have students identify the grammar in the opening reading on page 308. For example:
  Will decisions **be made** too fast?
  Can they **be made** quickly enough?
  Will dinner **be taken** seriously?
  How **can** privacy **be maintained** in such very close quarters?
  It looked like the ISS **was** finally **going to be launched** that year.
  Could this huge undertaking really **be accomplished** . . . ?
  . . . a . . . great number of technical terms **must be learned** . . .

Go to **www.myfocusongrammarlab.com** for grammar charts and notes.

Step 3: Focused Practice (pages 313–317)

See the general suggestions for Focused Practice on page 4.

Exercise 1: Discover the Grammar

- Go over the example with the class. Review how to form the passive with modals: *modal (or similar expression)* + be + *past participle.* Point out that the interview includes passive structures that do not use modals and should not be underlined.
- Have students complete the exercise individually and compare answers in pairs.
- Elicit the correct answers from the class.

Exercise 2: Affirmative and Negative Statements

- Go over the example with the class. Point out that some of the passive structures do not include modals.
- Have students read the article for meaning.
- Have students complete the exercise and compare answers in pairs. Then go over answers as a class.
- ⏱ Write the topics covered in the article on the board:
  Getting rest, Keeping clean, Dining, Taking it easy, *and* Staying fit.
  For each of the topics, have pairs write something that can't be done in space and something that must / has to be done. Remind students to use the passive with modals. Go over answers as a class. Examples: Ordinary beds can't be used in space. Sleeping bags must be attached to the walls.

Exercise 3: Affirmative and Negative Statements

- Go over the example with the class.
- Have students read the conversation for meaning.
- Have students complete the exercise individually and compare answers in pairs.
- Call on students to read the conversation aloud.

Exercise 4: Editing

- Have students read the journal notes quickly to find out what they are about.

- Ask: "What suggestions does the astronaut have for a better rest?" *(making the restraints more comfortable and designing the sleeping quarters differently)* "Why does he want to get on the exercise bike right away?" *(he is often misunderstood because of his puffy face and red eyes, and exercise can help ease these symptoms)* "Did he enjoy lunch? Why?" *(yes, because he had chicken teriyaki, which was nice and spicy)* "What might happen if he calls his daughter?" *(he might get angry and yell and be overheard by the others)* "What does he say about the view of Earth?" *(it's breathtaking; it has given him a better perspective on his problems with his daughter)*
- Have students find and correct the mistakes individually and compare answers in pairs.
- Have students explain why the incorrect structures are wrong.
- ⏱ Ask students to point out examples of correct usages of the passive with modals and similar expressions.

Go to **www.myfocusongrammarlab.com** for additional grammar practice.

Step 4: Communication Practice (pages 318–321)

See the general suggestions for Communication Practice on page 4.

Exercise 5: Listening

A
- Go over the words *meteorite* (a piece of rock or metal that floats in space) and *manual* (a book that gives instructions about how to do something such as use a machine). Play the audio.
- Encourage students to support their choices with information from the conversation. Example: *1. False. Picarra is calling from a spaceship and she says that they have been hit.*

B
- Go over the stress patterns with positive and negative forms of *can*: *It can be* **helped**. (one stress) / *It* **can't** *be* **helped**. (two stresses)
- Play the conversations again and stop the audio after each answer is given.

Exercise 6: Pronunciation

A
- Play the audio. Have students read along as they listen to the Pronunciation Note.
- Write on the board:
  He couldn't be heard.

Have students practice reading the example aloud pronouncing the modal phrase as "couldn'be." Make sure students stress the first syllable in *couldn't* and the main verb *heard*.

B
- Play the audio. Have students listen and complete the sentences.

C
- Play the audio again. Have students repeat the responses. Then have students practice the conversations in pairs. Remind them to play both roles.

Exercise 7: Reaching Agreement

A
- Brainstorm subtopics for each issue. Write students' ideas on the board. Examples: Food (types of food, meal times, cleaning up) Clothes (what to wear, laundry)
- Have pairs choose three issues to consider. Then have two pairs of students (four students) compare their selections and discuss why they made their selections. Encourage them to come to consensus.

B
- Go over the example and have students identify the passive with modals or similar expressions. Point out that they should also use the passive in their rules.
- Have groups compare their rules. Then call on students to share rules for one of the issues listed in Part A. Continue until all the issues are covered.

Exercise 8: Problem Solving
- Have students describe the picture.
- Go over the example. Remind students about intonation and stress: that modals and auxiliary verbs are stressed less than the past participle. Remind them to use contractions and reductions whenever possible: *It has got to be replaced. = It's gotta be replaced.* List the five things that must be done on the board.
- ⏱ Have students say what could or should be done to improve their classroom. Encourage them to think about what should / could be replaced, cleaned, repaired, painted, or moved to a different place. Ask them why they suggest these improvements.

Exercise 9: For or Against
- Have students brainstorm social problems in addition to public housing that require lots of money: *job development, hunger, natural disaster recovery work, fighting health issues such as the spread of AIDS, care for the elderly,* etc.

- Have pairs of students prioritize these social needs and come up with reasons why they think the most important one should be addressed first.
- Call on students to share their views.

Exercise 10: Writing

A

- Brainstorm things that could be improved / shouldn't be changed in each place. Write students' ideas on the board. Examples:
  Neighborhood: public transport, traffic lights, safety, parks, bridges, trash cans, old buildings
  School: open spaces, benches, lockers, dining room, interactive boards, computer lab
  Workplace: windows, cabinets, shelves, noise, natural light, plants
- Point out that students can use some of the ideas from the Exercise 8 discussion in their paragraphs. Allow time for students to write.

B

- After students write their paragraphs, have them correct their work using the Editing Checklist.

OUT OF THE BOX ACTIVITIES

Speaking

- Have students form "committees" to evaluate several different aspects of the school: the physical plant (condition of the classrooms, restrooms, the grounds); the teaching equipment (DVD players, computers, TV monitors, CD players, screens, overhead projectors); students' supplies and immediate environment (textbooks, dictionaries, desks, work areas, boards); and activities schedule (time in class, time in labs, school trips, extracurricular activities).
- Have them ask questions and then make recommendations.

Speaking

- Ask the class questions about twins: "Should twins have names that are similar? Should parents dress them alike? Should they be in the same class with the same teacher? Should they be treated the same?"

- Encourage students to make up more questions about how twins should be treated. Write these questions on the board, and when there are six questions, have students copy them.
- Have students ask three people outside of class for their opinions. Have the class compare the answers they got. Remind students that besides practicing the passive, this is a chance to review the grammar that they learned in Unit 8. For example: *I asked four people the questions, and so did Kadir. All of my friends thought twins should be dressed alike, but none of Enrique's friends did. Yuko's respondents thought that twins should be placed in the same class, and mine did too.*

Go to **www.myfocusongrammarlab.com** for additional listening, pronunciation, speaking, and writing practice.

Note

- See the *Focus on Grammar Workbook* for additional in-class or homework grammar practice.

Unit 19 Review (page 322)

Have students complete the Review and check their answers on Student Book page UR-5. Review or assign additional material as needed.

Go to **www.myfocusongrammarlab.com** for the Unit Achievement Test.

UNIT 20 OVERVIEW

Grammar: THE PASSIVE CAUSATIVE

Students will learn and practice the use of the passive causative (*have* or *get* + object + past participle).

Theme: PERSONAL SERVICES

Unit 20 focuses on language that we use to talk about what we can do or get done to change our appearance. It also covers the kind of language we use to talk about services we can hire.

People all over the world are concerned with making themselves look good. After body shape and clothing choices, hair and skin treatments are the most obvious adornments.

Step 1: Grammar in Context (pages 323–325)

See the general suggestions for Grammar in Context on page 1.

Before You Read

- Brainstorm forms of body art. Write them on the board. Examples:

hairdo	makeup
haircut	body paint
hair coloring	piercing
tattoo	cosmetic surgery

- Have students discuss the questions in pairs. Encourage students to make notes for each question.
- Call on pairs to share their answers to the questions with the class.

Read

- To encourage students to read with a purpose, write the following questions on the board:
  1. What is the easiest way to change your appearance? *(getting your hair done)*
  2. Why is getting a tattoo an important decision? *(because it's not easy to reverse)*
  3. How is body paint different from a tattoo? *(Body paint can be washed off.)*
  4. What is the most expensive form of changing your appearance? *(cosmetic surgery)*
- Have students read the text. (Or play the audio and have students follow along in their books.) Have students share their answers with the class.
- Have students discuss the following questions in small groups:
  1. What is your opinion of uniforms for medical, military, or school populations? How does wearing a uniform affect a person?
  2. Consider cosmetic surgery. What parts of your body can you have changed easily? Why do people choose cosmetic surgery?

After You Read

A. Vocabulary

- Have students find and circle the vocabulary in the text. Encourage them to use the context to figure out their meaning.
- Have students compare answers in pairs. Then go over answers as a class.
- ⏱ Write the following on the board. Have students complete the sentences using the vocabulary words. *(1. permanent, remove; 2. risk, procedure; 3. options, event)*
  1. Although tattoos are _____, it is possible to _____them.

  2. There is no _____ involved in the chemical _____ that perms your hair.
  3. Getting your hair done is just one of the _____ you can use to change your appearance for a special _____ .

B. Comprehension

- Have students choose the answers individually. Encourage them to underline the information in the text that supports their answers.
- Have students compare answers in pairs.
- Call on students to say an answer each.

Go to **www.myfocusongrammarlab.com** for an additional reading, and for reading and vocabulary practice.

Step 2: Grammar Presentation (pages 326–327)

See the general suggestions for Grammar Presentation on page 2.

Grammar Charts

- Point out that there are two main forms for the passive causative: *get (something) done* and *have (something) done*.
- Have students find the verb phrases that are used with each form in the reading and show them that either *get* or *have* will work in all cases. Emphasize that for this form of passive causative, there is no difference between *get* and *have*.
- Remind students that *have / get* + object + past participle means that another person performed the action.
- Point out that *be going to* can be used for future meaning with the two causative forms: *She is going to <u>have</u> her hair permed, and then she is going to <u>get</u> her nails done.*
- Be sure that your students see that normal rules for *yes / no* questions and *wh-* questions are followed in making passive causative questions, and that they are using *do / does / did* for the questions (rather than "Has she have her hair cut once a month?").

Grammar Notes

Note 1

- Brainstorm a list on the board of all the things that can be done to hair:
  wash it, shave it, cut it, bleach it, curl it, perm it, straighten it, dye it, lengthen it

- Have students make up sentences about their own hair or someone else's, with the two passive causative forms and the various hair-related vocabulary. Encourage the use of more complicated tenses: "My mother has never had her hair permed, but she's been having it colored for years."

Note 2
- Point out the difference between these two similar sentences:
  Ted always washes his car on Saturday. (Ted does it himself.)
  Ted always has his car washed on Saturday. (Another person washes Ted's car.)
- Brainstorm a list on the board of all the things that you can *have done* to your car: wash it, paint it, change the oil, tune up the motor, clean it, rotate the tires on it, fix it
- Have students work in pairs to make up sentences with the two passive causative forms: *I'm going to have my car painted. Bill Gates doesn't wash his car(s) himself; he gets it (them) washed.*
- Draw attention to the *Be Careful!* note.

Note 3
- Point out the difference between these two similar sentences:
  Ted always has his car washed on Saturday. (It doesn't matter who washes it.)
  Ted always has his car washed by the Boy Scouts. (The Scouts having a car-washing service is important because Ted likes to support the Scouts.)

- ⏱ **Identify the Grammar:** Have students identify the grammar in the opening reading on page 323. For example:
  They have **had** *their hair* **shaved, cut, colored, straightened,** and **curled** . . .
  . . . they have **had** *their bodies* **decorated** . . .
  Getting *your hair* **done** is the easiest way to change your appearance.
  . . . both men and women **have** *their hair* **permed**.
  . . . you can, of course, **get** *it* **cut**.

Go to **www.myfocusongrammarlab.com** for grammar charts and notes.

Step 3: Focused Practice (pages 328–331)
See the general suggestions for Focused Practice on page 4.

Exercise 1: Discover the Grammar
- Go over the example with the class. Ask: "Why is the statement false?" *(She says that she's going to get it copied, so someone else is going to do it.)*
- Have students complete the exercise individually and compare answers in pairs.
- Elicit the correct answers from the class.

Exercise 2: Statements
- Go over the example with the class.
- Have students complete the exercise individually and compare answers in pairs.
- Go over answers as a class.
- ⏱ Have pairs play a memory game using the information in this exercise. Student B closes his or her book. Student A says three true or false statements describing the calendar. Student B says if they are true or false. (Example: A: *Debra had her hair colored by a hairdresser.* B: *That's false. She had it permed.*) Then they change roles.

Exercise 3: Statements and Questions
- Go over the example with the class. Point out that *have it shortened* is also possible.
- Have students read the conversations for meaning before writing their answers.
- Have students complete the exercise individually and compare answers in pairs.
- Call on pairs to read the conversations aloud.

Exercise 4: Editing
- Have students read the essay quickly to find out what it is about.
- Ask: "What did Amber's parents do to prepare the house for the party?" *(they had the floors waxed and the windows cleaned)* "What did Amber do to prepare for the party?" *(she had her pink dress shortened and her hair cut by a hairdresser)* "Who prepared the food?" *(Amber's mom made the main dishes and the rest of the food was prepared by a caterer)*
- Have students find and correct the mistakes individually and compare answers in pairs.
- Have students explain why the incorrect structures are wrong.
- ⏱ Ask students to point out examples of correct usages of the passive causative.

Go to **www.myfocusongrammarlab.com** for additional grammar practice.

Step 4: Communication Practice

(pages 332–335)

See the general suggestions for Communication Practice on page 4.

Exercise 5: Listening

A

- Play the audio. Have students listen to the conversation a first time and say the three main topics Amber and her father talk about. *(her car, her apartment, her appearance)*
- Have students read the statements. Play the audio so students can complete the sentences.

B

- Ask students whether they could do the things on Amber's list themselves or whether they would have them done by others. You also could have pairs ask each other: "Do you cut your hair yourself, or do you have it cut?" If you choose this option, circulate to check pronunciation: "your**self**" and "do you have it **cut**?"
- Encourage students to give more information about each item on the list. Example: 1. *She had it done today.*

Exercise 6: Pronunciation

A

- Play the audio. Have students read along as they listen to the Pronunciation Note.
- Write the following examples on the board:
  1. He has the fence painted once a year.
  2. He has painted the fence.
  3. They have cut the grass.
  4. They have the grass cut every week.
  5. They have had the grass cut.
- Ask: "In which examples, can *has* or *have* be contracted?" *(2, 3, and 5)*

B

- Play the audio. Have students listen and complete the conversations.

C

- Play the audio again and have students repeat the responses. Then have students practice the conversation in pairs. Remind them to play both roles.

Exercise 7: Making Plans

A

- Point out that students will be going on a trip to another country. Give examples of things they might need to get done before the trip: *Your best shirt is missing a button. Your coat is dirty and needs to be dry cleaned. Your best shoes are covered with mud. Your jeans have a tear in the pocket.*
- Have students choose a destination, discuss the things they have to get done, and then write a list.

B

- Have students compare their lists. Then call on students to tell the class where they are going and a few important things they need to get done.

Exercise 8: Compare and Contrast

A

- Explain the task. Say: "You will look at the *Before* and *After* pictures of a fashion model and write sentences using the passive causative to describe the things that she had done." Point out that there is a time limit of five minutes.
- Have students open their books and write the sentences.

B

- Have pairs compare lists with another pair.

C

- Have students discuss their observations in pairs or small groups. Then call on students to share their opinion with the class.

Exercise 9: Cross-Cultural Comparison

- As a class, go over the list of procedures and have students share what other cultures do or get done to change their appearance. Write the facts on the board. (**Note:** If necessary, have students do some research before doing this activity.)
- Have students discuss the facts on the board in small groups. Encourage them to think of reasons why they like / don't like what other cultures do. Encourage use of the material from Unit 8: *So do I. / Neither do I.*
- Have students discuss in groups. Call on students to share their views with the class.
- Have pairs choose a special occasion and discuss what they would do to dress up for it.

Exercise 10: Writing

A

- Draw the following chart (without the answers) on the board. Brainstorm services we can hire to change the appearance (or improve the performance) of the items in the chart.

People	Apartment	Car	Clothes
hair / cut, permed, colored, bleached	walls / painted	car / repaired	jacket / dry cleaned
	windows / cleaned	tires / checked	skirt / lengthened
nose / pierced	floors / waxed	oil / changed	pants / shortened
teeth / straightened	air conditioning / fixed	car / washed	dress / pressed
nails / done	picture / framed	brake fluid / changed	
hands / painted	carpet / fitted	motor / tuned up	

- Have students use the ideas in the chart or their own ideas to write their email.

B

- After students write their email, have them correct their work using the Editing Checklist.

OUT OF THE BOX ACTIVITIES

Speaking

- Say: "Usually a hairstylist cuts hair, but what if your hairstylist did something unusual, like pulled out a loose tooth? You'd say, *I had my loose tooth pulled out by my hairstylist!*"
- Have the class make a list of specialists (doctor, dentist, auto mechanic, dressmaker, plumber, fortune teller, tattoo artist, electrician, aerobic instructor, choir director, professor) and a list of actions (hair cut, bathtub fixed, wedding music planned, exercise routine planned, car fixed, tooth fixed, appendix removed, new suit made, fortune told, tattoo applied, course of study outlined).
- Then have them work in pairs to see how many funny sentences they can make using the passive causative.

Speaking (or Writing)

- Have students go to the Internet or to a historical society for historical photographs and modern photographs of the same scene or building. Students can also bring in photographs they have at home. Examples: *the White House in 1850 and today, photos of a family home picture taken 50 years ago and today, the old farm and the farm now.*
- Have students make up eight sentences describing what people had done to make the changes. (Examples: *Dad got the old fence taken down. The new owner had a lot of trees planted and some flower gardens planted.*)

Go to **www.myfocusongrammarlab.com** for additional listening, pronunciation, speaking, and writing practice.

Note

- See the *Focus on Grammar Workbook* for additional in-class or homework grammar practice.

Unit 20 Review (page 336)

Have students complete the Review and check their answers on Student Book page UR-5. Review or assign additional material as needed.

Go to **www.myfocusongrammarlab.com** for the Unit Achievement Test.

From Grammar to Writing (pages 337–338)

See the general suggestions for From Grammar to Writing on page 9.

Go to **www.myfocusongrammarlab.com** for an additional From Grammar to Writing Assignment, Part Review, and Part Post-Test.

CONDITIONALS

UNIT	GRAMMAR FOCUS	THEME
21	Present Real Conditionals	Shopping
22	Future Real Conditionals	Cause and Effect
23	Present and Future Unreal Conditionals	Wishes
24	Past Unreal Conditionals	Alternate Histories

Go to **www.myfocusongrammarlab.com** for the Part and Unit Tests.

Note: PowerPoint® grammar presentations, test-generating software, and reproducible Part and Unit Tests are on the *Teacher's Resource Disc.*

Grammar: PRESENT REAL CONDITIONALS

Students will learn and practice the meaning and use of present real conditionals.

Theme: SHOPPING

Unit 21 focuses on language that we use to discuss online shopping and talk about shopping habits around the world.

Shopping online is becoming more and more popular as companies without doors offer goods and services through the Internet. However, shopping online (or selling online) can be risky because of confidentiality and security with money transactions.

Step 1: Grammar in Context (pages 340–342)

See the general suggestions for Grammar in Context on page 1.

Before You Read

• Have students discuss the questions in pairs. Then poll students to find out how many have / haven't purchased things online.

• Call on students who have shopped online to share their experience with the class. Have them say what they bought and explain the steps they took to shop safely.

Read

• To encourage students to read with a purpose, write the following questions on the board:

1. What are some advantages of shopping online? *(It's fast, convenient, and often less expensive.)*
2. What are some basic precautions you should take regarding payment? *(pay by credit card, only enter your credit card information on a secure site, print out and save a receipt or record of your purchase)*
3. Why is a receipt important? *(If you don't like what you bought, you can return it. A receipt proves that you bought it.)*

• Have students read the text. (Or play the audio and have students follow along in their books.) Then call on students to share their answers with the class.

• Have students discuss the following questions in small groups:

1. Why should you be sure that you buy only on a secure site? Why are prices generally lower from Internet companies?
2. When supermarkets became popular, shoppers began to buy from people they didn't know. They began to shop once a week, or even less often. The result is more isolation. In the same way, will more online shopping mean more isolation? Is online shopping a positive change?
3. What precautions must a person take with credit cards, besides the ones mentioned in the reading? Remind students of the information about credit cards that they discussed in Unit 6.

After You Read

A. Vocabulary

• Have students find and circle the vocabulary in the text. Encourage them to use the context to figure out their meaning.

• Have students compare answers in pairs. Then go over answers as a class.

• ◯ Write the following on the board. Have students match the sentence halves. *(1. e, 2. d, 3. a, 4. b, 5. c)*

1. If you dispute a charge,	a. you find out the conditions to return a product.
2. If a site is secure,	b. you are a smart consumer.
3. If you check the return policy,	c. you should take basic precautions.
4. If you stop and think before you buy,	d. there are no risks involved in shopping on it.
5. If you don't want to have a problem,	e. you ask for all or part of your money back.

B. Comprehension

- Have students complete the exercise individually. Encourage them to underline the information in the text that supports their answers.
- Have students compare answers in pairs. Then go over answers as a class.

Go to **www.myfocusongrammarlab.com** for an additional reading, and for reading and vocabulary practice.

Step 2: Grammar Presentation (pages 343–344)

See the general suggestions for Grammar Presentation on page 2.

Grammar Charts

- Write on the board:
  If I don't want to go out, I shop online.
  I shop online if I don't want to go out.
- Have students study the examples, and ask: "How many clauses are there in each example?" (*two—the* if *clause and the result clause*)
- Mark the two clauses in the examples. Use different colors if possible.
- Ask: "For present real conditionals, what tense do we use in the *if* clause?" *(the simple present)* "And in the result clause?" *(the simple present)*
- Point out that an *if* clause at the beginning of a sentence is always followed by a comma and that no comma is necessary for an *if* clause at the end of a sentence. You can do this by asking: "What's the difference between the first and the second sentence?"
- Write on the board:
  What do you do if the site is not secure?
  Do you shop online if you don't know the company?
- Point out that in both *yes / no* and *wh-* questions, the *if* clause usually comes at the end.

Grammar Notes

Note 1

- Be sure that students understand that *general truths* are phenomena that do not change. Write on the board:

  If you use a credit ⟶ Credit cards are
  card, it's faster.   always faster.
  If it's a holiday, the ⟶ The store is always
  store is closed.   closed on
                            holidays.

- Point out the simple present in both clauses in each example.

- Write the following sentences on the board and have students restate them using the present real conditional. *(If you compare prices, you buy wisely. If you shop during a sale, you save money.)*
  Compare prices and buy wisely.
  Shop during a sale and save money.

Note 2

- Have students list five things that they do every day and expand their statements into if clause statements. Write two examples on the board:

  I get up at seven. ⟶ If I don't get up at seven, I'm late for everything else all day.

  I set my alarm ⟶ If I forget to set my
  clock for six.   alarm clock, it
                        doesn't ring, and I
                        don't get to school
                        on time.

Note 3

- Point out that modals change the meaning of the verb in the result clause. Remind students that modals are not generally used in *if* clauses.
- Write *if* clauses on the board:
  If you don't like it , ...
  If it's too expensive, . . .
  If it's exactly what you wanted, . . .
- Have pairs complete the sentences using result clauses with modals. Then call on students to share some of their sentences with the class. (Examples: *If you don't like it, (then) you should return it. If it's too expensive, you can't buy it. If it's exactly what you wanted, you should get it.*)

Note 4

- Write some *result* clauses on the board:
  . . . wear a hat.
  . . . phone home.
  . . . don't tell your mother.
- Have students work in pairs to create conditions under which the partner would carry out the imperative in the result clause. (Examples: *If it's cold, wear a hat. If you run out of money, phone home. If you get a tattoo, don't tell your mother.*) Encourage students to restate some of their sentences to include *then*.

Note 5

- Have pairs take turns saying conditional sentences and reversing the order of the clauses. (Example: Student A: *If you go to the mall, take these discount coupons.* Student B: *Take these discount coupons if you go to the mall.*)

- Draw attention to the *Be Careful!* note. Remind students that no comma is needed when the result clause comes first. Check pronunciation to be sure that there is no pause when the sentence starts with the result clause.

Note 6
- Write on the board:
  What do you do when / if . . . ?
    you run out of cash
    you get a discount coupon
    you want to buy something online
    you get your credit card bill
- Call on students to share their answer to one of the questions on the board. (Example: *When I run out of cash, I go to an ATM.*)

🕐 **Identify the Grammar:** Have students identify the grammar in the opening reading on page 340. For example:
  If you think it's in Alberta, Canada, you're wrong!
  It doesn't matter if it's a book or a diamond necklace . . .
  If you're looking for the best price, you can easily compare prices . . .
  You are less likely to have a problem if you shop with well-known companies.
  If you don't know the company, ask them to send you information.

Go to **www.myfocusongrammarlab.com** for grammar charts and notes.

Step 3: Focused Practice (pages 345–349)

See the general suggestions for Focused Practice on page 4.

Exercise 1: Discover the Grammar
- Have students complete the exercise individually and compare answers in pairs.
- Elicit the correct answers from the class.
- 🕐 Have students discuss the following questions in small groups: "Have you ever bargained? If yes, where was it? Did you enjoy the experience? If you have never tried it, would you like to try it? Why or why not?"

Exercise 2: Conditional Statements: Modals and Imperatives
- Go over the example with the class. Point out the optional use of *then*.
- Have students complete the exercise and compare answers in pairs. Then go over answers as a class.

- 🕐 Have pairs role-play similar conversations. Student A says what he or she wants to buy and Student B uses a real conditional sentence to give advice. Encourage the use of *ought to, have (got) to, should,* and the imperative in the result clause. Remind students of the optional use of *then*.

Exercise 3: Conditional Statements
- Go over the example with the class.
- Have students complete the exercise and compare answers in pairs. Then go over answers as a class.
- 🕐 Have students look back at the conversation and point out how Legget uses a conditional sentence to answer each question. Challenge students to role-play a short conversation on habits or routines and use conditional sentences in all their answers. (Example: A: *Where do you usually go on vacation?* B: *If I have time and money, I go to Rio.* A: *Sounds fun. What do you do there?* B: *If the weather is nice, I go to the beach.* A: *And do you go out at night?* B: *If I travel with friends, I always do!*)

Exercise 4: Conditional Statements with *When*
- Go over the examples with the class. Point out the use of the present continuous in the second example to describe what is happening in each place.
- Have students complete the exercise individually and compare answers in pairs. Then go over answers as a class.
- 🕐 Have students who have friends or relatives in other countries share similar sentences with the class. (Example: *My parents live in Greece. When I'm going to bed, they're getting up.*)

Exercise 5: Editing
- Have students read the email message quickly to find out what it is about.
- Ask "Where is Claudia flying tomorrow?" *(to Hong Kong)* "Who is she going to be with once there?" *(her husband and son)* "Why is she going to fly at night?" *(to be able to sleep on the plane)* "Why does she like Hong Kong?" *(she always has a great time when she goes there; the shopping is fantastic)*
- Have students find and correct the mistakes individually and compare answers in pairs.
- Have students explain why the incorrect structures are wrong.
- 🕐 Ask students to point out examples of correct usages of present real conditionals.

Go to **www.myfocusongrammarlab.com** for additional grammar practice.

Step 4: Communication Practice (pages 349–354)

See the general suggestions for Communication Practice on page 4.

Exercise 6: Listening

- Have pairs make a sequence of what announcements to expect before boarding an airplane, as they board a plane, and after they are on a plane. Then have them discuss safety on board a plane. Items to consider include baggage, tray tables, oxygen masks, seat belts.

A

- Have students read the statements before listening. Then play the audio. You may want to stop at the end of each announcement to allow students time to choose the words and review answers.

B

- Have students read the statements. Play the audio and have students complete the exercise.
- As you go over the answers, have students support their choices. (Example: *1. It's false because only one piece of carry-on luggage is allowed on board.*)

Exercise 7: Pronunciation

A

- Play the audio. Have students read along as they listen to the Pronunciation Note.
- Write on the board:
  1. If I fly, I travel light.
  2. I pay by check if I don't have cash.
- Ask: "Where does the voice drop?" (*1. in* fly *and* light, *2. in* check *and* cash) "Which example requires a pause?" (*Example 1, after* fly)

B

- Play the audio. Have students listen and add the commas.

C

- Play the audio again and have students repeat. Check that students use the right intonation and pause where needed.

Exercise 8: Reaching Agreement

A

- Have students say if they ever buy gifts online. If they do, have them give examples of gifts they have bought.

- Have students work in pairs. Then call on students to say what they have decided to order. Encourage them to explain their choices. (Example: *Our friend is short and slim. We bought her a small orange T. If it's the wrong size, she can exchange it for a larger one.*)

B

- Have pairs complete the exercise and discuss with another pair.

Exercise 9: Cross-Cultural Comparison

- Have the class say places they have lived in or visited and describe where they are.
- Go over the questions and the example with the class. You may want to write some sentence starters on the board that can be used to answer the questions. Examples:
  If you want to buy local crafts, . . .
  If you like outdoor markets, . . .
  If you need to exchange something, . . .
  If you don't have local money, . . .
  When you bargain, . . .
- Point out that this is an opportunity for review of Unit 3: "Have you ever been to . . . ?" Have students work in pairs to complete the exercise.

Exercise 10: Discussion

- Brainstorm important purchases besides a camera or a car. (Examples: *laptop computer, special software, a new printer*)
- Have students work in small groups to discuss the questions. Call on students to share what they usually do when making an important purchase. Encourage them to give examples of purchases they have made.

Exercise 11: For or Against

- Check that your students are familiar with general shopping vocabulary: *to try on, to fit, too small, too tight, too loose, my size.*
- Write a few questions on the board to help students generate ideas:
  How long are you willing to wait between the time you buy something and the time you have it in your hands?
  How important is it for you to feel / touch what you buy?
  Some stores offer sample or trial products. How useful are these products?
  Do you need to see the item you want to buy in its actual size?
  Are the colors that you see on the computer screen accurate enough for you to choose?

- Draw the following chart on the board and complete it with students' ideas as you get feedback from them. You may want to finish the activity by taking a poll to find out if most students prefer shopping online or in stores.

	Shopping in stores	Shopping online
Advantages		
Disadvantages		

Exercise 12: Writing

A

- Brainstorm topics students can write about. Make a list on the board. Examples:
  Shopping
  Entertainment
  Restaurants
  Historical buildings
  Museums
  Parks
  Beaches
  Sports
- Have students use the topics in the list or their own ideas to write their information sheet.

B

- Have students compare their lists with another pair's list. How were they different?

C

- After students compare their information sheets, have them correct their work using the Editing Checklist.

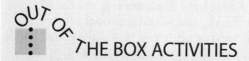

OUT OF THE BOX ACTIVITIES

Reading and Speaking

- Have students imagine they are interested in renting apartments. Distribute copies of the information below from one apartment complex.
  — Apartments can be rented by the month, but they cost 25 percent more than apartments leased for a year.
  — A six-month lease is available, but the cost is more than for a year-long lease.
  — Renters must pay a deposit equal to the first- and last-month's rent when they sign a lease.
  — Apartments have washers and dryers, but there is a charge for using them.
  — There is a $300 pet deposit for each cat or dog.
  — Each apartment has one covered parking space. Additional parking places cost $30 a month each.
  — Apartments on the second floor are $20 a month more than apartments on the first floor.
  — The complex has sports facilities (weight room, swimming pool, exercise equipment), but residents must join the Health Club to use them. Membership is $100 a year for the first resident of an apartment and $50 for each additional resident of the apartment.
  — The second year of a lease entitles a resident to one month's free rent.
  — Packages can be delivered to the main office for a $2 pickup fee.
- Have pairs use the information to make statements using present real conditionals. (Example: *If you have a package delivered to the main office, you have to pay $2 to pick it up.*)

Speaking

- This real-life activity will be different for every student.
- To explain the activity, say: "Think of a daily activity that involves another person and that doesn't vary much from day to day, for example buying a train ticket or speaking with a family member about preparing a meal. Then think of a possible change to this activity and what you would say to ask the other person (ticket agent, family member) about the possible consequences." Give examples: *What if I only buy a three-zone ticket and then I stay on the train for four zones? What if you forget to buy rice today?*
- Have students write down their questions and bring them to class for a role-play exercise in pairs. (Example: A: *You're my sister. You always cook dinner. I ask you, "What if you forget to buy rice?"* B: *If I forget to buy rice, I send you out to buy it!*)

Go to **www.myfocusongrammarlab.com** for additional listening, pronunciation, speaking, and writing practice.

- See the *Focus on Grammar Workbook* for additional in-class or homework grammar practice.

Unit 21 Review (page 355)

Have students complete the Review and check their answers on Student Book page UR-6. Review or assign additional material as needed.

Go to **www.myfocusongrammarlab.com** for the Unit Achievement Test.

UNIT 22 OVERVIEW

Grammar: FUTURE REAL CONDITIONALS

Students will learn and practice the meaning and use of future real conditionals.

Theme: CAUSE AND EFFECT

Unit 22 focuses on language that we use to talk about superstitions. It also covers language that we use to talk about what we will do under certain conditions.

Many cultural beliefs are based on ideas that are superstitious, rather than logical or rational. However, many superstitions have a basis in fact. A black cat may not be bad luck, but a person might trip over a black cat in the dark because the cat is not easy to see. A ladder in itself is not dangerous, but walking under a ladder puts a person in a position where something heavy might fall and cause injury.

Step 1: Grammar in Context (pages 356–358)

See the general suggestions for Grammar in Context on page 1.

Before You Read

- Write two lists—*Superstitions* and *Lucky Items*—on the board. After students discuss the questions in pairs, call on students to explain the superstitions they believe in and / or the lucky items they wear or carry. Write their answers under the correct heading.

Read

- To encourage students to read with a purpose, write the following questions on the board:
  1. When do people tend to be more superstitious? *(when they are worried)*
  2. When do they tend to be less superstitious? *(when they don't have a strong need for control)*

3. What do people who feel lucky usually believe in? And people who feel unlucky? *(People who feel lucky usually believe in good-luck superstitions. People who feel unlucky usually believe in bad-luck superstitions.)*
4. How can a lucky pen help you do better on a test? *(by making you feel more confident)*
- Have students read the text. (Or play the audio and have students follow along in their books.) Then have students share their answers with the class.
- Have students discuss the following questions in small groups:
  1. Superstitions are cause-and-effect sentences. What are real consequences of the following circumstances?
     You break a mirror. *(You have to sweep up the broken pieces and buy a new mirror.)*
     A black cat runs in front of you. *(You have to be careful not to trip over it.)*
     You walk under a ladder. *(Nothing, unless something falls on you! Then you have to take care of your injury.)*
  2. Sports stars tend to be superstitious. They wear lucky hats, take their showers at specific times, refuse to dust themselves off if they fall. What reasons can you think of for this kind if behavior?
  3. What is a lucky number? Do you have one? Why is it your lucky number? Do you have a lucky item? What happens if you lose it?

After You Read

A. Vocabulary

- Have students find and circle the vocabulary in the text. Encourage them to use the context to figure out their meaning.
- Have students complete the exercise individually and compare answers in pairs. Then go over answers as a class.
- ⏱ Write the following sentences on the board, and have students replace the underlined parts with their own ideas.
  1. In my country, there is a widespread belief that <u>red can protect you from envy</u>.
  2. <u>Seeking professional advice</u> can give you some insight into a problem.
  3. About [50] of the students in this class <u>are wearing jeans</u>.
  4. I'm confident that <u>I will pass the exam</u>.
  5. I can anticipate that <u>I will do well</u>.
  6. The right attitude can help you <u>solve a problem</u>.

B. Comprehension

- Have students choose the answers individually. Encourage them to underline the information in the text that supports their answers.
- Have students compare answers in pairs. Then go over answers as a class.

Go to **www.myfocusongrammarlab.com** for an additional reading, and for reading and vocabulary practice.

Step 2: Grammar Presentation (pages 358–359)

See the general suggestions for Grammar Presentation on page 2.

Grammar Charts

- Write an example on the board:
  If he hurries, he will catch the train.
- Have students study the example and name the verb or verb phrase in each clause. (*hurries, will catch*) Underline them as students say them.
- Ask: "For future real conditionals, what tense do we use in the *if* clause? (*the simple present*) "And in the result clause?" (will + *base form*) Point out that *be going to* is also possible. Write on the board:
  If he <u>catches</u> the train, he <u>is going to arrive</u> on time.
- Point out that the *if* clause can come at the beginning of the sentence or at the end of the sentence. It requires a comma if it comes first. Call on a student to reverse the order of the clauses in the examples. Check that he or she doesn't pause between the clauses.
- Show students that the *if* clause can precede a *yes / no* question or a *wh-* question: *If she doesn't pass the exam, will she take it again? If she doesn't pass the exam, what will she do?*
- Call on a student to turn Example 1 into a *yes / no* question and on another student to turn Example 2 into a *wh-* question.

Grammar Notes

Note 1

- Write an example on the board:
  If you spend the money, you won't have it anymore.
- Point out that the purpose of future real conditionals is to state a condition and the result that will occur as a result. Explain the example by saying: "Don't spend the money, and you will still have it."
- Point out that there is no future marker in the *if* clause, but the meaning is future anyway. Write a new example on the board:
  If you <u>are</u> confident, <u>you'll do</u> well on the test.

- Draw attention to the *Be Careful!* note.

Note 2

- Point out that modals can be used in some result sentences in place of *will* or *be going to*.
- Write on the board:

If you feel confident, you	will might should can	improve your test score.

Note 3

- Have pairs change around the order of the conditional sentences in the reading. Check that they pause when the *if* clause comes first in the sentence and that they don't pause between clauses when the *if* clause comes at the end.

Note 4

- Because *unless* is tricky for nonnative speakers of English, do a quick teacher-directed oral drill. Give students a (simple) *if* situation and have them transform it into a sentence with *unless*:
  T: If I'm not hungry, I don't eat.
  Ss: You don't eat unless you're hungry.
  T: If you don't ask, I won't tell you.
  Ss: You won't tell us unless we ask.
  T: If you don't study, you won't pass the test.
  Ss: We won't pass the test unless we study.

Identify the Grammar: Have students identify the grammar in the opening reading on page 356. For example:

If you knock on wood, you'll keep bad luck away.
You'll get a good grade on the test if you wear your shirt inside out.
You'll get a bad grade unless you use your lucky pen.
If you break a mirror, you'll have seven years of bad luck.
If the palm of your hand itches, you're going to get some money.

Go to **www.myfocusongrammarlab.com** for grammar charts and notes.

Step 3: Focused Practice (pages 360–363)

See the general suggestions for Focused Practice on page 4.

Exercise 1: Discover the Grammar

A

- Go over the example with the class.
- Have students complete the exercise individually and compare answers in pairs.
- Elicit the correct answers from the class.

B
- Have students complete the exercise individually. Ask students to read their sentences aloud.

Exercise 2: *If* or *Unless*
- Go over the example with the class.
- Encourage students to pay attention to meaning to choose the right word. Have students complete the exercise individually.
- Call on pairs to read the conversations aloud.

Exercise 3: Simple Present or Future
- Go over the example with the class. Remind students to use the simple present in the *if* clause and *will* + base form in the result clause.
- Have students compare answers in pairs. Then go over answers as a class.
- ⏱ In small groups, have students share similar superstitions they know. (Example: *In Slovakia people believe that if you sit at the corner of the table, you will not get married. In my country, we believe that you will not get married if you help yourself to the last cookie on a plate.*)

Exercise 4: Statements
- Go over the example with the class. Point out that students have to write two sentences. The first is a negative sentence that corrects what Eva says.
- Call on pairs to read the conversations aloud.

Exercise 5: Statements
- Go over the decision tree with the class. Point out that a question mark indicates a possible event or result.
- Go over the examples. Point out that students can start with the *if* clause or the result clause.
- Have students compare answers in pairs. Then go over answers as a class.
- ⏱ Have students discuss in pairs a predicament they may have. Encourage the use of the future real conditional.

Exercise 6: Editing
- Have students read the journal entry quickly to find out what it is about.
- Ask: "What does Yuki have to decide?" (*if she'll campaign for student council president*) "What will happen if she campaigns?" (*She won't have much time to study.*) "What will happen if she doesn't campaign?" (*Todd Laker will become president again, and he will do nothing to solve the problems in the school.*) "Why will she cut her hair?" (*because it brings her good luck*)

- Have students find and correct the mistakes individually and compare answers in pairs.
- Have students explain why the incorrect structures are wrong.
- ⏱ Ask students to point out examples of correct usages of future real conditionals.

Go to **www.myfocusongrammarlab.com** for additional grammar practice.

Step 4: Communication Practice (pages 364–367)
See the general suggestions for Communication Practice on page 4.

Exercise 7: Listening

A
- Brainstorm what a student council does. Write a list of tasks on the board. Examples: hear students' concerns
  communicate with college administration
  communicate with government representatives
  represent students in formal meetings with administration
  provide useful tools and services for students
- Then play the audio and have students complete the exercise individually.

B
- Play the audio. Have students support their choices. (Example: 1. *False. She wants to improve communication with students and will have informal lunch meetings with them.*)

Exercise 8: Pronunciation

A
- Play the audio. Have students read along as they listen to the Pronunciation Note.
- Write on the board:
  1. If it rains, what will you do?
  2. If it rains, will you stay home?
  3. Will you stay home if it rains?
  4. What will you do if it rains?
- Ask: "In which questions does the voice rise at the end?" (*2 and 3*) "In which ones does it fall?" (*1 and 4*)

B
- Play the audio. Have students listen and draw the arrows.

C
- Play the audio and have students repeat the questions. Then have students practice the conversation in pairs. Remind them to play both roles.

Exercise 9: Problem Solving

- Ask *If . . . , then what . . . ?* questions like these: "If you keep careful records of your money, then what?" *(You'll know where it went.)* "If you have house rules where you live, then what?" *(There won't be arguments about small things.)*
- Go over the example. Point out that in order to do this exercise, students will need vocabulary that is not in the book. In the example, they would have needed to think of *police, landlord,* or *move.* If students are having trouble with number 2, you can prompt them with *aspirin, doctor, rest,* or *vacation.*
- Form groups of four or five students. Clarify the task: A student reads a situation and asks a question about it. The other students in the group answer the question using future real conditionals.

Exercise 10: Cross-Cultural Comparison

- If students know only a few superstitions to discuss, you can have them work in small groups to invent some superstitions by completing these *if* clauses or other clauses of their choice:
  If your ears itch, (then) . . .
  If you wear something black, (then) . . .
  If you toss a coin into the air, (then) . . .
- Have students from different groups share some of the superstitions they discussed or made up.

Exercise 11: Writing

A

- Have students answer the following questions in small groups:
  1. What do students need to make studying easier? *(study areas in student unions and classroom buildings, soft music, desks and chairs, . . .)*
  2. What do students need so that education is not so expensive? *(computer labs, public transportation, . . .)*
  3. What can make going to school more enjoyable? *(more on-campus activities, clubs, free concerts, . . .)*
- Have students use the information from the discussions to write their speeches. Then have them share their speeches in small groups.

B

- After students write their speeches, have them correct their work using the Editing Checklist.

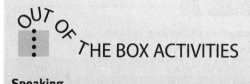

OUT OF THE BOX ACTIVITIES

Speaking

- Have individual students or teams compete with others in the class. One student starts with an *if* clause and a result clause. The next student continues the story by changing the result clause to an *if* clause and making a new sentence. Example:
  A: If I get a part-time job, I'll have more money for entertainment.
  B: If I have more money for entertainment, I won't study as much.
  C: If I don't study as much, my grades will go down.
  D: If my grades go down, I'll lose my scholarship.
  E: If I lose my scholarship, I'll have to drop out of school.
  F: If I drop out of school, I'll have to pay back my student loans.

Speaking

- Have students talk with friends outside of class about making a decision such as whether to buy a secondhand car, whether to get a part-time job, or whether to change majors. Remind students to take notes.
- Have students use the decision-making model in Exercise 5 and create future real conditional sentences about the decision.

Go to **www.myfocusongrammarlab.com** for additional listening, pronunciation, speaking, and writing practice.

Note

- See the *Focus on Grammar Workbook* for additional in-class or homework grammar practice.

Unit 22 Review (page 368)

Have students complete the Review and check their answers on Student Book page UR-6. Review or assign additional material as needed.

Go to **www.myfocusongrammarlab.com** for the Unit Achievement Test.

Grammar: PRESENT AND FUTURE
UNREAL CONDITIONALS

Students will learn and practice the meaning
and use of present and future unreal
conditionals.

Theme: WISHES

Unit 23 focuses on language that we use to
talk about wishes and what would happen if
they came true.

Cultural values are often taught to children
through stories like fairy tales, stories in which
magical things happen. This story is both a
fairy tale and a *fable*—a story that presents
a moral lesson: Ask for what you need, be
willing to work for it, and be satisfied when
you have what you need.

Step 1: Grammar in Context (pages 369–371)

See the general suggestions for Grammar in
Context on page 1.

Before You Read

- Discuss the difference between a fairy tale
  *(story for children in which magical things
  happen)* and a fable *(a traditional short story,
  often about animals, that teaches a moral
  lesson)*.
- For Question 1, encourage students to make
  notes of the elements that make them think
  this is not a true story.
- Go over the answers as a class. Then have
  students name popular fairy tales / fables in
  their culture.

Read

- To encourage students to read with a purpose,
  write these questions on the board:
  1. Who are the main characters of the story?
     *(a fisherman, his wife, and a fish who is an
     enchanted prince)*
  2. Where did the fisherman and his wife live
     at the beginning of the story? *(in a pigpen)*
  3. Where do the fisherman and his wife live
     at the end of the story? *(in a pigpen)*
  4. What kind of human being is the
     fisherman? *(kind-hearted, satisfied, rather
     shy)*
  5. What kind of human being is the
     fisherman's wife? *(dissatisfied, unhappy)*
  6. What is the personality of the fish?
     (reasonable, willing to help)
  7. What is the lesson, or moral, of the story?
     *(A person who asks for too much gets
     nothing.)*

- Have students read the text. (Or play the
  audio and have students follow along in their
  books.) Have students share their answers
  with the class.
- Have students discuss the following questions
  in small groups:
  1. The fisherman and his wife both have
     weaknesses in their personalities. What are
     they and how do these weaknesses bring
     about their downfall?
  2. The writer of the fable tells us about the
     thinking and mood of the enchanted
     prince-fish in an interesting way. What is
     it? *(the color of the seawater and the height
     and strength of the waves)*

After You Read

A. Vocabulary

- Have students find and circle the vocabulary
  in the text. Encourage them to use the context
  to figure out their meaning.
- Have students compare answers in pairs.
  Then go over answers as a class.

B. Comprehension

- Have students choose the answers
  individually. Encourage them to underline
  the information in the text that supports their
  answers.
- Have students compare answers in pairs.
  Then call on students to say an answer each.
- ⏱ To reinforce the vocabulary, read the
  following cues aloud, and have the class
  call out the answers. Be sure students have
  completed the comprehension exercise first.
  1. This character was enchanted. *(the fish)*
  2. This character consented to ask for wishes.
     (the fisherman)
  3. This character could grant wishes. *(the
     fish)*
  4. This character got furious when someone
     else refused to obey him or her. *(the
     fisherman's wife)*
  5. This character felt embarrassed whenever
     he or she asked for more. *(the fisherman)*
  6. This character responded patiently to
     questions. *(the fisherman)*

Go to **www.myfocusongrammarlab.com** for an
additional reading, and for reading and vocabulary
practice.

Step 2: Grammar Presentation (pages 372–373)

See the general suggestions for Grammar
Presentation on page 2.

Grammar Charts

- Write on the board:
  If I were king, I would own all this land.
- Elicit or explain the meaning of the example. Say: "I am not king, and I do not own the land." Show that the example represents a situation in which an unreal condition is stated as a proposition. If the proposition were true (but it's not) then another result would follow.
- Point out that the *if* clause uses the past tense, but it does not refer to the past.
- Point out that in both *yes/no* questions and *wh-* questions, the modal *would* is used in the main clause and *had* or *were* in the *if* clause. Normal word order is used. Short answers follow normal modal-use rules.

Grammar Notes

Note 1

- Write on the board:
  I <u>am</u> rich, so I <u>live</u> in a palace. = If I <u>weren't</u> rich, I <u>wouldn't live</u> in a palace.
- Point out that if the clause in a sentence about a real situation is *positive*, the clause in the related present unreal conditional sentence is *negative*.

Note 2

- Write on the board:
  I <u>don't live</u> in a palace, so I <u>don't give</u> big parties. = If I <u>lived</u> in a palace, I <u>would give</u> big parties.
- Point out that, in a similar way, if the clause in a sentence about a real situation is negative, then the clause in the related present unreal conditional sentence is positive.
- Have students write true simple present tense sentences about situations in their lives that they don't like and their results. Then ask them to imagine a different situation and write related present unreal conditional sentences. (Examples: *I'm a student, so I don't have much money. If I weren't a student, I would have more money.*)
- Draw attention to the *Be Careful!* note. Remind students that *would* is not used in the *if* clause.
- Point out that the correct form of *be* in present and future unreal conditionals is always *were*. (Though some speakers use *was*, many people consider it incorrect. To be correct as far as everyone is concerned, use *were*.)

Note 3

- Point out that the most common modal in the result clause is *would* because it shows certainty: *If X were true, the result <u>would be</u> Y.*
- Remind students that sometimes ability to do something is part of the condition, so *would* is replaced with *could* in the result clause: *If X were true, then Y <u>could do</u> Z.*
- If the result is not certain, then *might* or *could* can appear in the result clause: *If X were true, then (maybe) the result <u>might</u> be Y. If X were true, then (maybe) the result <u>could</u> be Y.*

Note 4

- Point out that the order of the main clause and the *if* clause can be reversed. Give new examples:
  If you knew my real identity, you wouldn't kill me. = You wouldn't kill me if you knew my real identity.
  If we lived in a big stone castle, I would be much happier. = I would be much happier if we lived in a big stone castle.
- Draw attention to the *Be Careful!* note. Remind students that the comma is needed only when the *if* clause comes first.

Note 5

- Have pairs practice giving advice to the fisherman, his wife, and the fish. Examples:
  (to fisherman) *If I were you, I wouldn't do everything your wife asked you to do.*
  (to fisherman's wife) *If I were you, I would be happy with a nice cottage.*
  (to fish) *If I were you, I'd grant fewer wishes.*

Note 6

- Point out that in sentences with *wish*, the result is not stated, but implied: *I wish I had a nice cottage to live in. = If I had a nice cottage to live in, I would be happier.*
- Have students transform their *if* sentences from the Note 2 activity into wishes. Draw attention to the *Be Careful!* note.

Identify the Grammar: Have students identify the grammar in the opening reading on page 369. For example:

If you knew my real identity, you wouldn't kill me.
I wish we had a nice little cottage.
If we had a cottage, I would be a lot happier.
If I asked for a cottage, the fish might get angry.
My wife wishes we had a cottage.

Go to **www.myfocusongrammarlab.com** for grammar charts and notes.

Step 3: Focused Practice (pages 374–378)

See the general suggestions for Focused Practice on page 4.

Exercise 1: Discover the Grammar
- Go over the example with the class. Ask: "Why are statements a and b false?" *(because number 1 expresses an unreal condition—so the reality is that I don't have time—and an unreal result—so the reality is that I don't read fairy tales)*
- Have students complete the exercise individually and compare answers in pairs.
- Elicit the correct answers from the class.

Exercise 2: *If* and Result Clauses: Verb Forms
- Go over the example with the class.
- Have students read the article for meaning before writing their answers.
- Have students complete the exercise individually and compare answers in pairs. Then go over answers as a class.
- In small groups, have students discuss the meaning of the old saying: "If wishes were horses, then beggars would ride."

Exercise 3: Statements
- Go over the example with the class. Remind students to use all subjects + *were* when the verb in the clause is *be*.
- Have students complete the exercise individually and compare answers in pairs. Then go over answers as a class.
- In pairs, have students take turns choosing a sentence from the exercise and replacing one of its clauses with their own ideas. Encourage them to make true sentences about themselves. (Example: *If I weren't so busy, I would take painting lessons.*)

Exercise 4: Wishes About the Present
- Go over the example with the class. Remind students to use *wish* + simple past to express present wishes.
- Have students complete the exercise individually and compare answers in pairs. Then go over answers as a class.
- Have students write three facts about their life that they would like to be different and then write sentences starting with *I wish* about those facts. (Example: *I don't have a car. I wish I had one.*) Have students share their sentences with a partner.

Exercise 5: Questions
- Go over the example with the class. Remind students to use question word order in the result clause (not in the *if* clause).

- Have students complete the exercise individually and compare answers in pairs. Then go over answers as a class.
- Have pairs make up three questions for the fantasy game. (Example: *If you won a trip into space, would you dare go?*) Have students submit the questions to you for correction, and then use them for their discussion in Exercise 9. **Note:** Don't have students answer the questions at this stage.

Exercise 6: Editing
- Have students read the book report to find out what it is about.
- Ask: "What book is the report about?" (The Disappearance, *by Philip Wylie*) "When was it written?)" *(in 1951)* "Which two questions does the book address?" *(Can men live without women? Can women live without men?)* "What conclusion does Wylie come to?" *(Men are too aggressive and women are too helpless to live on their own)* "Would he come to the same conclusion today?" *(no)*
- Have students find and correct the mistakes individually and compare answers in pairs.
- Have students explain why the incorrect structures are wrong.
- Ask students to point out examples of correct usages of the present unreal conditional.

Go to **www.myfocusongrammarlab.com** for additional grammar practice.

Step 4: Communication Practice (pages 379–382)

See the general suggestions for Communication Practice on page 4.

Exercise 7: Listening

A
- Talk with students about things they would wish for if they had a magical wish. (A practical person would ask for an unlimited number of wishes.) Then play the audio.
- Have students complete the exercise.

B
- Play the audio again and have students complete the exercise. Encourage students to support their answers. (Example: *1. False. Cindy wishes she could find her soccer ball because it flew into the woods while she was playing with her friends.*)

Exercise 8: Pronunciation

A

- Play the audio. Have students read along as they listen to the Pronunciation Note.
- Point out that we normally use contractions *('d)* after pronouns.
- Write on the board:
  1. I wish you would stop complaining.
  2. He wishes his mother would get home earlier.
  3. If he had the money, he would buy it.
  4. Our team would have won if we had trained harder.
- Ask: "In which examples can *would* be contracted?" *(1 and 3)*

B

- Play the audio. Have students listen and complete the conversations.

C

- Play the audio again and have students repeat the responses. Then have students practice the conversations in pairs. Remind them to play both roles.

Exercise 9: What About You?

- Have students think about their answers to the questions individually.
- If appropriate, remind students to bring up the questions they made up in Exercise 5 and discuss in small groups.
- Have students share their answers to the questions with the class.

Exercise 10: Problem Solving

- Form groups of three. Have each student contribute a problem to the list.
- After students work in groups, have them share solutions to the problems with the class. (Example: *If you only had $300 to pay a $500 rent, you could get a temporary job.*)

Exercise 11: Discussion

A

- Have students write their wishes individually.

B

- Have students work in pairs to discuss their wishes.
- After students discuss, have them play a chain game in small groups using ideas from the discussion. Example: Students start with the sentence *If I were famous, I wouldn't have any free time,* then change the result clause to the *if* clause and continue. *(If I didn't have any free time, I wouldn't have time to spend with friends. If I didn't have time to spend with friends, I would lose all of the people I love.)*

- Have groups compete to see who can keep the chain going longest.

C

- As a class, discuss the possible positive and negative results of their wishes.

Exercise 12: Writing

A

- Point out that students can use one of the wishes they discussed in Exercise 11.
- Have students complete the following items with notes and then use them as a guide as they write:
  My wish:
  Example:
  What would happen if it came true:

B

- After students write their paragraphs, have them correct their work using the Editing Checklist.

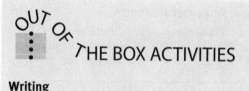

OUT OF THE BOX ACTIVITIES

Writing

- Have students make a list of professions in which people can become famous and maybe also rich like computer billionaire Bill Gates *(scientist, inventor, actor, political leader, clothing designer, musician, athlete, movie star).*
- Then have them name a real person for each profession and create interview questions for that person using present and future unreal conditionals. (Example for Bill Gates: *Bill, what would you do if you lost all your money? Bill, what would you do if someone invented something better than computers and software?*)

Speaking and Listening

- Give students the assignment to find out what people would do if they had a year off from work and enough money so they could go anywhere and do anything.
- Encourage students to interview other teachers, parents, people they work with, hairstylists, and people they meet at places like coffee shops. Remind them to take notes.
- Have them report others' fantasies to the class.

Go to **www.myfocusongrammarlab.com** for additional listening, pronunciation, speaking, and writing practice.

Note
- See the *Focus on Grammar Workbook* for additional in-class or homework grammar practice.

Unit 23 Review (page 383)

Have students complete the Review and check their answers on Student Book page UR-6. Review or assign additional material as needed.

Go to **www.myfocusongrammarlab.com** for the Unit Achievement Test.

UNIT 24 OVERVIEW

Grammar: PAST UNREAL CONDITIONALS

Students will learn and practice the meaning and use of past unreal conditionals.

Theme: ALTERNATE HISTORIES

Unit 24 focuses on language that we use to talk about life-changing events and what would have happened if they hadn't occurred.

Step 1: Grammar in Context (pages 384–386)

See the general suggestions for Grammar in Context on page 1.

Before You Read
- For Question 1, have students make notes of what is different from reality in the cartoon. (Examples: *There is a dinosaur in modern times. The dinosaur is the pet owner and the human is the pet. The dinosaur is wearing clothes. It can understand English.*)
- For Questions 2 and 3, have students identify the *What if?* question implicit in the cartoon (*What if a meteor had never hit Planet Earth?*) and then share other *What if?* questions they might ask themselves.

Read
- To encourage students to read with a purpose, write the following questions on the board:
  1. What are alternate histories? (*stories of what would have happened if a certain event had or had not occurred / stories that answer a* What if? *question*)

2. What would have happened if a meteor hadn't hit the earth 65 million years ago? (*Some types of dinosaur would have continued to develop, become more intelligent, and dominated the world. Humans may or may not have developed alongside dinosaurs.*)
3. How could the *Titanic* disaster have been avoided? (*if the iceberg had been seen earlier, or if the ship had had more lifeboats*)
4. What is the film *Sliding Doors* about? (*two parallel stories of the same woman—the story of the woman if she had gotten on a train and the story of the woman if she had missed the train*)

- Have students read the text. (Or play the audio and have students follow along in their books.) Then have students share their answers with the class.
- Have students discuss the following questions in small groups:
  1. What is your opinion of speculating about the past? Is it just an amusing way to pass the time or can it teach us a lesson? Explain.
  2. What are some big decisions or important events that have changed the course of history? What would have happened if those decisions hadn't been made or if the events hadn't occurred?

After You Read

A. Vocabulary
- Have students find and circle the vocabulary in the text. Encourage them to use the context to figure out their meaning.
- Have students compare answers in pairs. Then go over answers as a class.
- (⏱) Write the following on the board. Have students use the vocabulary words to complete the phrases. (*1. intelligent; 2. outcome; 3. parallel; 4. alternate; 5. version; 6. occur*)
  1. an _____ decision / person / animal
  2. a possible / happy / sad _____
  3. a _____ life / story
  4. an _____ plan / history / past
  5. a new / a different / an old _____
  6. an accident / event can _____

B. Comprehension
- Have students choose the answers individually and compare answers in pairs.
- Then go over answers as a class.

Go to **www.myfocusongrammarlab.com** for an additional reading, and for reading and vocabulary practice.

Step 2: Grammar Presentation (pages 386–387)

See the general suggestions for Grammar Presentation on page 2.

Grammar Charts

- Write on the board:
  If he <u>had been</u> there, he <u>would have helped</u> you.
- Have students study the example. Ask: "For past unreal conditionals, what do we use in the *if* clause?" *(the past perfect)* "And in the result clause?" (would + have + *past participle*)
- Point out that the *if* clause can come at the beginning of a sentence or at the end of a sentence. Call on a student to reverse the order of the clauses in the example. Check that he or she doesn't pause between the clauses.
- Call on a student to turn the example into a *yes / no* question and on another student to turn it into a *wh-* question. (Possible answers: *Would he have helped you if he had been there? If he had been there, would he have helped you? What would he have done if he had been there? If he had been there, what would he have done?*)
- Go over the contractions: *Would have* and *would not have* are contracted as *would've* and *wouldn't have* (or *wouldn't've*, in speech).

Grammar Notes

Note 1

- Remind students that ideas expressed in unreal past conditionals and the results are untrue (perhaps impossible) or imagined. To help clarify, write an example on the board: If I had not gone to college, I wouldn't have become a teacher.
- Say: "I went to college, so the *if* clause is untrue, and I <u>did</u> become a teacher, so the result is also untrue."
- Have pairs add explanatory sentences starting with *but* to some of the boldfaced sentences in the reading. Give an example: *What would have happened if I had stayed in my own country? (But I didn't stay in my own country, so this sentence is unreal.)*
- Point out that a past condition can influence present results as well as past results, depending on the verb and the situation: *If I hadn't taken this class, I never would have met you* (past result) / *I wouldn't know you* (present result).

Note 2

- Point out that the common elements in the *if* clauses are *had* + past participle and the common elements in the result clauses are *would have* + past participle.

- Have students circle the verbs in the *if* clauses and the result clauses with *would* in the boldfaced sentences in the reading.
- Ask: "What would you have done if you hadn't come to class today / yesterday / last week?" *(I would've gone to the beach / stayed home / gone to work / slept late . . .)*
- Point out an easy, quick trick for remembering all the parts of this structure: Use the thumb and fingers of your hand to count off all the parts. Demonstrate as you say: "I <u>would</u> (thumb) <u>have</u> (index) <u>stayed</u> (middle) home if I <u>hadn't</u> (ring) <u>come</u> (pinky) to class." Put the first part of the model question on the board *(What would you have done if . . .)* and have students get up and circulate to ask each other the question while you check for grammar (especially *have;* use the counting-off-on-fingers trick) and pronunciation/reduction: *What wouldja've **done** if you hadn't **come** to class?*

Note 3

- Have students discuss certain and uncertain results of the following questions posed in the reading:
  1. *What if the meteor had missed the earth?*
  2. *Would humans have been able to live alongside dinosaurs?*
  3. *What would have happened if Hitler had never been born?*
  4. *What would have happened if the* Titanic's *lookout had seen the iceberg earlier?*
- Call on students to share their answers with the class.

Note 4

- Remind students that the order of the clauses can be reversed and that a pause is needed when the *if* clause comes first.
- Have students reverse the order of the following sentences adapted from the reading: *More people would have escaped if the* Titanic *had had more lifeboats. World War II could have been avoided if Hitler hadn't been born. If dinosaurs had survived, they might have dominated the world.*

Notes 5 and 6

- Have students think of some situation in which they felt regret and express it with both an "I wish" statement and a past unreal conditional. (Examples: *I wish I had saved my money instead of putting it into a machine at the airport in Las Vegas. If I had known that I would lose every nickel, I wouldn't have put any money into that machine at the airport in Las Vegas.*)

🕐 **Identify the Grammar:** Have students identify the grammar in the opening reading on page 384. For example:

What would have happened if I had stayed in my own country?

What would have happened if I had never met my husband?

. . . life would have been different if certain events had (or had not) occurred.

. . . what if the meteor had missed?

. . . if the meteor had not struck the Earth, some types of dinosaurs would have continued to develop . . .

Go to **www.myfocusongrammarlab.com** for grammar charts and notes.

Step 3: Focused Practice (pages 388–393)

See the general suggestions for Focused Practice on page 4.

Exercise 1: Discover the Grammar
• Go over the example with the class.
• Have students complete the exercise individually and compare answers in pairs.
• Elicit the correct answers from the class.

Exercise 2: If and Result Clauses: Verb Forms
• Go over the example with the class. Remind students that we do not use *may* or *can* in result clauses of past unreal conditional sentences.
• Encourage students to pay attention to meaning to choose the right forms.
• Call on students to read the completed sentences aloud.

Exercise 3: Affirmative and Negative Statements

A
• Go over the events with the class. You may want to express a condition with each event and have students make up results. Examples:
T: *If his shoelace hadn't broken, . . .*
S: *He wouldn't have tripped.*
T: *If the delivery truck hadn't moved, . . .*
S: *It wouldn't have hit the post.*

B
• Have students read the story for meaning before writing their answers.
• Have students complete the exercise and compare answers in pairs. Then go over answers as a class.
• 🕐 Have students who have seen the movie *The Curious Case of Benjamin Button* tell the class about it. Then have students discuss what would / could / might have happened if some of the events in the movie had been different.

Exercise 4: Regrets About the Past
• Go over the example with the class. Remind students to use the past perfect after *I wish.*
• Call on students to read the sentences aloud.
• 🕐 Have students use the statements in this exercise to create past unreal conditional sentences. Example: *If she hadn't taken supplies from her office, her boss wouldn't have fired her.*

Exercise 5: Negative and Affirmative Statements
• Have students read each story and discuss what happened in pairs.
• Have students complete the sentences individually or in pairs. Then review answers as a class.

Exercise 6: Editing
• Have students read the student's book report quickly to find out what it is about.
• Ask: "What book is the report about?" (*What If by Isaac Asimov*) "Who are the main characters in the story?" (*Norman and Livvy.*) "Where do they meet?" (*on a streetcar, when Livvy falls into Norman's lap*) "What does Livvy wonder?" (*what would have happened if they hadn't met on the streetcar*) "How does she find out?" (*a man shows her the answer on a piece of glass*)
• Have students find and correct the mistakes individually and compare answers in pairs.
• Have students explain why the incorrect structures are wrong.
• 🕐 Ask students to point out examples of correct usages of the past unreal conditional.

Go to **www.myfocusongrammarlab.com** for additional grammar practice.

Step 4: Communication Practice (pages 394–397)

See the general suggestions for Communication Practice on page 4.

Exercise 7: Listening

A
• Point out that listening to contractions is very important in understanding conditionals. Review the contractions in the grammar chart in the Grammar Presentation (*would've, wouldn't have*). Mention that spoken English also uses a double contraction (*wouldn't've*) which is not written.
• Have students complete the exercise individually. Go over answers as a class.

B

- Play the audio and have students complete the exercise. Have students support their choices. (Example: 1. *False. The man wasn't injured in a train accident because he missed the train that had the accident.*)

Exercise 8: Pronunciation

A

- Play the audio. Have students read along as they listen to the Pronunciation Note.
- Write on the board:
  1. If they had not missed the train, they wouldn't have met.
  2. If they had met, they would have married.
- In pairs, have students circle the words that can be contracted (*had not* and *had*) and underline the words that are pronounced "of." Have students practice reading the examples using contractions and "of." (*If they hadn't missed the train, they would of met. If they'd met, they would of married.*)

B

- Play the audio. Have students listen and circle the words.

C

- Play the audio again. Have students check their answers and then practice the conversations in pairs. Remind them to play both roles.

Exercise 9: What About You?

- Have students choose a decision or event to share with their group.
- Ask students to make notes of the chain of events that occurred and how things would have been different if the events hadn't occurred.
- After students discuss in groups, call on students to share their story with the class.

Exercise 10: Problem Solving

- Encourage students to use these situations to think of creative solutions and to compare and discuss ethics.
- To make sure they practice past unreal conditionals, write the following sentence starters on the board:
  I would've . . .
  I wouldn't have . . .
  If he'd / she'd . . .
  If he / she hadn't . . .

Exercise 11: Discussion

- Brainstorm past regrets. Write them on the board. Examples:
  a lost friendship, a problem at school, trouble with a family relationship, saying or doing the wrong thing, a missed opportunity for study or travel
- Write the following cues on the board, and have students complete them with notes:
  What you did:
  Why you did it:
  What you wish you had done:
  What would have happened if you had done it:
- Have students discuss in small groups.

Exercise 12: Writing

A

- Brainstorm events than can change a person's life. Write them on the board. Examples:
  having an accident
  getting / losing a job
  meeting someone
  going to college
  overcoming an illness
  getting married
  moving abroad for work or studies
  traveling on business or vacation
  watching a movie
  reading a book
- Have students use the ideas on the board to write their paragraphs.

B

- After students write their paragraphs, have them correct their work using the Editing Checklist.

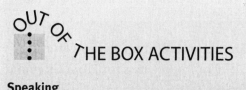

OUT OF THE BOX ACTIVITIES

Speaking

- Have students go back to Unit 16, Exercise 9. Have them consider what *would have happened* if Sheila had been willing to tell the reporter about her mistake and decision never to cheat again (Case 1), if Mustafa had not gone into the building to get the records (Case 2), and if Pierre had not gotten an extra job (Case 3).
- Call on students to share their thoughts about what would / could / might have happened in each case.

Speaking

- Have students take note of some common personal problems in the outside world and be prepared to describe them in class. Suggest that they might find such problems by reading newspaper advice columns, by watching a soap opera or reality television show, by observing, or by asking friends. Each problem should be defined in one or two sentences.
- Have students discuss the problems in small groups. Encourage students to come up with solutions using present unreal conditionals. (Example: *I saw a woman standing by her truck on the side of the freeway. An armchair had fallen out of the back of her truck and was in the middle of a five-lane freeway where it could cause a terrible accident. If that had happened to me, I would have called 911 and gotten police help.*)

Go to **www.myfocusongrammarlab.com** for additional listening, pronunciation, speaking, and writing practice.

Note

- See the *Focus on Grammar Workbook* for additional in-class or homework grammar practice.

Unit 24 Review (page 398)

Have students complete the Review and check their answers on Student Book page UR-6. Review or assign additional material as needed.

Go to **www.myfocusongrammarlab.com** for the Unit Achievement Test.

From Grammar to Writing (pages 399–400)

See the general suggestions for From Grammar to Writing on page 9.

Go to **www.myfocusongrammarlab.com** for an additional From Grammar to Writing Assignment, Part Review, and Part Post-Test.

PART X OVERVIEW

INDIRECT SPEECH AND EMBEDDED QUESTIONS

UNIT	GRAMMAR FOCUS	THEME
25	Direct and Indirect Speech	Truth and Lies
26	Indirect Speech: Tense Changes	Extreme Weather
27	Indirect Instructions, Commands, Requests, and Invitations	Health Problems and Remedies
28	Indirect Questions	Job Interviews
29	Embedded Questions	Travel Tips

Go to **www.myfocusongrammarlab.com** for the Part and Unit Tests.

Note: PowerPoint® grammar presentations, test-generating software, and reproducible Part and Unit Tests are on the *Teacher's Resource Disc.*

UNIT 25 OVERVIEW

Grammar: DIRECT AND INDIRECT SPEECH

Students will learn and practice the uses and forms of direct and indirect speech.

Theme: TRUTH AND LIES

Unit 25 focuses on language that we use to talk about lies that people often tell to avoid hurting feelings or going through unpleasant situations.

To some people, there is a difference between a lie and a *white lie*, a simple untruth told to avoid hurting the feelings of another person. Some people simply avoid saying what they really think; if another person asks, "Do you like my new hairstyle?" the first person will answer, "It's really modern" or "It's an interesting new trend," rather than giving a completely honest answer. Other people lie to avoid an unpleasant truth or situation: They might tell a bill collector that the check is in the mail even though it has not yet been sent at all.

Step 1: Grammar in Context (pages 402–404)

See the general suggestions for Grammar in Context on page 1.

Before You Read

- Have students discuss the questions in pairs. Encourage them to take notes of situations in which it could be right to lie.
- Have students share their views with the class. Then have them say what they would tell the woman in the photo about her hair if she were their best friend, sister, classmate, or co-worker. Would they lie? Why or why not?

Read

- To encourage students to read with a purpose, write the following questions on the board:
  1. What is unusual about the title of this reading? (*The words* truth *and* lying *have opposite meanings.*)
  2. What excuses are given for telling white lies? (*to avoid an unpleasant situation, to be polite, to protect someone's feelings, to appear nicer or more interesting, to feel better, and to get something fast*)
  3. What is the trend in regard to lying? (*People lie more today than they did in the past.*)
- Have students read the text. (Or play the audio and have students follow along in their books.) Then call on students to share their answers with the class.
- Have students discuss these questions in small groups:
  1. What white lies have you told recently? Why did you decide against telling the truth?
  2. Under some circumstances, people decide not to tell the truth at all and feel good about the decision. Is it, for example, good to tell a person who is very ill that she or he is dying? What other circumstances might make people consider not telling the whole story?

After You Read

A. Vocabulary

- Have students find and circle the vocabulary in the text. Encourage them to use the context to figure out their meaning.
- Have students compare answers in pairs. Then go over answers as a class.
- To reinforce the vocabulary, dictate the following questions. Have students underline the vocabulary words in the questions and then answer the questions.
  1. Are you aware of the number of lies you tell each day?
  2. On average, how many lies do you think you tell?

3. How would you justify some of the lies you tell? Do the majority of your lies protect yourself or the person you are talking to?
4. Have you ever revealed the truth after telling a lie? If yes, when was that?

B. Comprehension

- Point out that the article does not use the exact words the person said. Have students complete the exercise individually.
- Have students compare answers in pairs. Then go over answers as a class.

Go to **www.myfocusongrammarlab.com** for an additional reading, and for reading and vocabulary practice.

Step 2: Grammar Presentation (pages 404–406)

See the general suggestions for Grammar Presentation on page 2.

Grammar Charts

- Remind students that a person's words can be reported as direct speech or indirect speech. Direct speech (the exact words of the person) requires quotation marks.
- Point out these three things about indirect speech:
  1. It sometimes requires a change in verb form.
  2. It does not need quotation marks.
  3. It often includes *that* as a clause introducer for the indirect statement (the reworded quotation).

Grammar Notes

Note 1

- Point out that direct speech is a quotation; therefore, you need to tell who said the words. Another person's exact words always require quotation marks. Remind students to follow the punctuation rules for direct speech in Appendix 27, page A-13.
- To help clarify, write an example and draw a diagram on the board:
  He said, "It's raining."

Direct Speech

  ├── use exact words
  └── use quotation marks

Note 2

- Point out that in indirect speech we do not use the exact words the speaker said, so we don't use quotation marks.

- Write a new example and draw a new diagram on the board:
  He said (that) it's raining.

```
┌──────────────────┐
│ Indirect Speech  │
└──────────────────┘
     │
     ├── don't use exact words
     ├── don't use quotation marks
     └── you can use that
```

Note 3
- Write new examples on the board:
  Sam told Sally that he got a new job.
  Sam said to Sally that he got a new job.
  Sam said, "Sally, I got a new job."
  Sam said that he got a new job.
- Use the examples on the board to point out the similarities between *say* and *tell*. They mean essentially the same thing. However, *tell [someone]* is followed by the name of the listener or a personal pronoun (*me / you / him / her / us / them*). *Say [to someone]* (that is, to the listener) is less common. *Say* is usually used alone. Thus, if the listener is mentioned, it is more common to use *tell*.

Note 4
- Point out that in indirect speech the verb form often changes when the reporting verb is in the past. This is especially true when the statement was made some time ago. Write on the board:
  I met Jake yesterday. He said, "Jim is a great guy."
  I met Jake yesterday. He said that Jim was a great guy.
- Quick teacher-directed drill:
  T: I talked to my mother three weeks ago. I said, "I'm coming to see you!" (ask students) What did I say?
  Ss: You said you <u>were</u> coming to see her.
  T: I told her, "You sound happy!" What did I tell her?
  Ss: You told her she <u>sounded</u> happy.
  T: She told me, "I've bought a new car!" What did she tell me?
  Ss: She told you that she <u>had bought</u> a new car.

Note 5
- Remind students that for a newly made statement, an unchanging fact, or a general truth we do not need to change the tense.
- Write the following statements on the board and have students report them. (*1. He just said (that) he is aware of the problem. 2. She said (that) she likes fish. 3. The astronauts said (that) the earth is round.*)

1. He just said, "I'm aware of the problem."
2. She said, "I like fish."
3. The astronauts said, "The Earth is round."

Note 6
- Point out that the simple present stays simple present when the reporting verb is in the simple present. This is often used in newspapers. Write an example on the board: Psychologists <u>say</u> that lying <u>shows</u> a lack of control.
- Bring in some newspaper polls or surveys, and have students report on them in groups. For example, "Our survey says that 50 percent of Americans prefer blue cars."

Note 7
- Write the following statements on the board and have students report them. (*1. Kate told Brad (that) her car had broken down. 2. John told them (that) their meeting was at 10. 3. Sally said (that) she had a party.*)
1. Kate told Brad, "My car broke down."
2. John told them, "Our meeting is at 10."
3. Sally said, "I have a party."

🕐 **Identify the Grammar:** Have students identify the grammar in the opening reading on page 402. For example:
  . . . a supervisor . . . **said Rick's credit card payment was late.**
  "The check is in the mail," Rick **replied** quickly.
  . . . Rick **told his client that traffic had been bad**.
  "It looks great," he **said**.
  . . . he **told himself that sometimes the truth causes too many problems**.
  He **says that lying is a habit** . . .
  . . . we justify the lie by **telling ourselves it was for a good purpose**.

Go to **www.myfocusongrammarlab.com** for grammar charts and notes.

Step 3: Focused Practice (pages 407–410)
See the general suggestions for Focused Practice on page 4.

Exercise 1: Discover the Grammar
- Have students complete the exercise individually and compare answers in pairs.
- Elicit the correct answers from the class.

Exercise 2: *Said* and *Told*; Verb and Pronoun Changes
- Go over the example with the class. Ask: "Why is *told* the correct answer?" (*because the listener—me—is mentioned*)

- Have students read the essay for meaning. Then have them complete the exercise.
- Have students compare answers in pairs. Then go over answers as a class.
- ⏱ Have pairs choose a character—Aunt Leah or her niece—and write three exact quotes. Examples: *Aunt Leah: "I want to show you my new bowl." "I have just bought it." "It really isn't very important."*

Exercise 3: Indirect Speech
- Go over the example with the class. Review tense changes. Elicit that simple present becomes simple past and simple past becomes past perfect.
- You may want to have students underline the words that need changing in each speech bubble before rewriting the statements as indirect speech.
- Have students compare answers in pairs. Then go over answers as a class.

Exercise 4: Indirect Speech
- Go over the examples with the class. Then have students complete the exercise.
- Have students compare answers in pairs. Then go over answers as a class.

Exercise 5: Editing
- Have students read the article quickly to find out what it is about.
- Ask: "What is an Internet hoax?" *(an untrue story that is sent to a lot of people by email)* "What examples of hoaxes does the article give?" *(messages that say that Bill Gates wants to give money away to you, a floor cleaner kills family pets, your computer monitor has taken pictures of you, bananas can kill people, a sunscreen can make people blind)* "Are hoaxes difficult to identify?" *(no, because there are a lot of signs that give them away)*
- Have students find and correct the mistakes individually and compare answers in pairs.
- Have students explain why the incorrect structures are wrong.
- ⏱ Ask students to point out examples of correct usages of direct and indirect speech.

Go to **www.myfocusongrammarlab.com** for additional grammar practice.

Step 4: Communication Practice (pages 411–415)
See the general suggestions for Communication Practice on page 4.

Exercise 6: Listening
- Play the audio. Have students listen and say what each conversation is about. Encourage students to answer in just a few words. *(Conversation 1: an invitation; Conversation 2: spare time / going to the gym; Conversation 3: a report for a meeting; Conversation 4: meat sauce)*

A
- Have students read the statements. Play the audio again. You may want to stop at the end of each conversation to allow students time to choose the words and review answers.

B
- Review the weekly planner and what is already scheduled. Play the audio.
- Have students complete the exercise individually and compare answers in pairs. Ask: Why do you think Lisa told the white lies?

Exercise 7: Pronunciation
A
- Play the audio. Have students read along as they listen to the Pronunciation Note.
- Write on the board:
  He told me that I looked great.
- Ask: "Where would you pause when saying the sentence on the board?" *(after* me*)* "Would you stress *that*?" *(no)*

B
- Play the audio. Have students listen and mark their answers.

Exercise 8: Discussion
- Elicit the six excuses for lying described in the opening reading on page 402. If necessary, have students look back at the reading. Write the excuses on the board as students say them:
  1. to be polite
  2. to protect someone else's feelings
  3. to feel better about yourself
  4. to appear more interesting to others
  5. to get something more quickly
  6. to avoid uncomfortable situations
- Form small groups. Have each student disclose a white lie she or he recently told and justify it. Encourage students to express their views as shown in the example.

Exercise 9: Questionnaire: Honesty

A
- Ask students how often they believe others when they blame traffic for their being late. Ask what other statements or excuses seem like white lies. Then have students complete the questionnaire individually.

B
- Have students compare answers in small groups. Then have them write sentences summarizing their group results. Have groups report their sentences to the class.

Exercise 10: Game: To Tell the Truth
- To help students generate ideas for this contest, ask the following questions, but don't have students answer them: "Have you ever participated in a marathon? Do you have a twin brother or sister? Have you lived in three or more different countries? Have you had cosmetic surgery? Have you ever won a contest or the lottery? Have you ever tried an extreme sport?"

A
- Have students work in groups of three. Each student in the group tells an interesting fact about themselves. The group chooses one fact to share.

B
- Each group shares that fact with the class.

C
- Have the class ask the group questions to determine who the fact is true for.

D
- Have the class decide who is telling the truth and why. Was the class correct?

Exercise 11: Quotable Quotes
- Have students read the proverbs. If necessary, clarify the meaning of unknown words: *inaccuracy* (information that is not true), *at ease* (feeling relaxed).
- Discuss the meaning of each proverb as a class. Encourage students to give examples to show why they agree / disagree with them.
- ⏱ Have students paraphrase one or two of the quotes and then share their paraphrases with the rest of the class.

Exercise 12: Writing

A
- Discuss as a class how students know when someone is upset (besides the things they say). Ask them to describe some body language clues.

- Have students read the conversation and discuss who is lying and why.
- Go over the example with the class. Point out that students can add details that are not in the conversation to enrich their paragraph. (Example: *Rick came home . . .*) Have students write their paragraphs either in class or for homework.

B
- After students write their paragraphs, have them correct their work using the Editing Checklist.

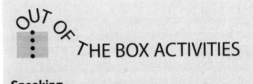

OUT OF THE BOX ACTIVITIES

Speaking
- Write the following three proverbs about honesty on the board:
  Honesty is always the best policy.
  The truth will out. *(You may have to explain that this is a short way of saying that the truth will come out.)*
  A person who always tells the truth doesn't have to remember as much as a person who lies.
- Have students work in small groups to discuss the meaning of these proverbs. Then have them discuss which ones they agree or disagree with. Encourage them to support their reasons with examples.
- Finally, have the groups report their findings to the class using indirect speech *(Marcus said that he agrees with . . . , but Alma said that she . . .).*

Speaking and Writing
- Have students identify three political issues. They can decide to use campus issues, like the need for emergency phone stations; local issues, like changes in parking regulations; or global concerns, like global warming or the spread of AIDS.
- Have groups of students make survey statements about each of the chosen issues. *(Parking should be free on Sundays.)*
- Then send students out with survey forms to interview three people each with answers such as: *agree strongly, have no opinion, disagree somewhat,* and *disagree strongly.*

- Have them write up the responses they gathered and report them to the class in indirect speech. Tally the responses. Summarize the responses with indirect speech (*Most of the people in our survey said that they . . .*).

Go to **www.myfocusongrammarlab.com** for additional listening, pronunciation, speaking, and writing practice.

Note
- See the *Focus on Grammar Workbook* for additional in-class or homework grammar practice.

Unit 25 Review (page 416)

Have students complete the Review and check their answers on Student Book page UR-7. Review or assign additional material as needed.

Go to **www.myfocusongrammarlab.com** for the Unit Achievement Test.

UNIT 26 OVERVIEW

Grammar: INDIRECT SPEECH: TENSE CHANGES

Students will learn and practice the tense changes in indirect speech.

Theme: EXTREME WEATHER

Unit 26 focuses on language that we use to talk about people's experiences with extreme weather conditions.

Floods are usually caused by long rainstorms and the rapid melting of snow. For this reason, people hope for gentle rain over a period of months and a long, cool spring. The flood in this reading was caused by one heavy late-summer storm.

Step 1: Grammar in Context (pages 417–419)

See the general suggestions for Grammar in Context on page 1.

Before You Read
- After students discuss the questions in pairs, call on students to describe the pictures and explain the title of the article.
- ⏱ Have students share their experiences by asking: "Have you ever experienced a flood in your city? How long did it rain? Where were you? What did you do?"

Read
- To encourage students to read with a purpose, write the following questions on the board:
  1. What caused the flood in central Europe in 2002? *(heavy rain for more than 24 hours)*
  2. Why are Prague and Dresden historically important? *(because they are the homes of treasures of art and architecture)*
  3. What natural disasters followed the flood of 2002? *(a heat wave in 2003 and another flood in 2006)*
  4. What do experts believe could stop the weather-related disasters? *(government policies and laws that will control the causes of climate change)*
- Have students read the text. (Or play the audio and have students follow along in their books.) Then have students share their answers with the class.
- Have students discuss the following questions in small groups:
  1. Land along rivers, lakes, and oceans is beautiful. The article says that statistical studies concluded that people ought to stop building so close to water. What are some possible problems with building houses in such places?
  2. What seems to be the reason for global warming and changes in weather patterns? What could be done to stop global warming?

After You Read

A. Vocabulary
- Have students find and circle the vocabulary in the text. Encourage them to use the context to figure out their meaning.
- Have students compare answers in pairs. Then go over answers as a class.
- ⏱ Write the following on the board. Have students match the sentence halves. *(1. e, 2. d, 3. a, 4. c, 5. b)*

Before, during, or after a natural disaster . . .
1. Bridges can   a. evacuated.
2. Works of art are   b. optimistic.
3. Cities are   c. damage.
4. Floods are causing more d. restored.
5. People should try to be e. collapse.

B. Comprehension
- Have students complete the exercise individually. Point out that the article does *not* use the exact words the person said.
- Have students compare answers in pairs. Then go over answers as a class.

Go to **www.myfocusongrammarlab.com** for an additional reading, and for reading and vocabulary practice.

Step 2: Grammar Presentation (pages 420–422)

See the general suggestions for Grammar Presentation on page 2.

Grammar Charts

- Point out that moving from direct to indirect speech is moving one step into the past.
- Write the column heads *Direct Speech* and *Indirect Speech* on the board. Then add the first column of verbs and have students supply their equivalent in indirect speech. Complete the second column as you get feedback from students.

Direct Speech	Indirect Speech
is	(was)
are	(were)
move	(moved)
moved	(had moved)
am looking	(was looking)
have looked	(had looked)
will stay	(would stay)
can go	(could go)
may stay	(might stay)
have to go	(had to go)
must visit	(had to visit)

- Point out that the only verbs that do not change are those that don't really have another form, like past modals. Add to the verbs on the board:

should go	remains	should go
ought to go	remains	ought to go
could go	remains	could go
would go	remains	would go
might go	remains	might go

- Point out that past perfect verbs and present and past unreal conditionals have no further past form to move to, so they stay the same: Add to the verbs on the board:

had seen	remains	had seen

- Elicit a present unreal conditional sentence from a student and report it. For example:
  S: *If I had time, I would go.*
  T: *[Student's name] said that if he/she had time, he/she would go.*
- Do the same with the past unreal conditional.
- Do not erase the lists on the board.

Grammar Notes

Notes 1 through 5

- After going over the notes, use what you have written on the board during the presentation of the Grammar Charts for oral practice of all of these forms. Give your students a sentence and then ask them: "What did I say?" For example, "It's a nice day. What did I say?" *(You said it was a nice day.)* "He must leave this place. What did I say?" *(You said he had to leave this place.)*

- **Identify the Grammar:** Have students identify the grammar in the opening reading on page 417. For example:
  . . . John Hooper reported **that it has been raining for more than 24 hours straight**.
  The journalist noted **that people were already evacuating Prague and were just beginning to leave Dresden**.
  . . . Mayor Igor Nemec told reporters **that the historic Old Town should remain safe**.
  She told Hooper sadly **that many original copies of the most treasured poems in the Czech language had been lost**.
  He told reporter Julian Coman . . . **that with another few feet of water, nothing would be safe**.

Go to **www.myfocusongrammarlab.com** for grammar charts and notes.

Step 3: Focused Practice (pages 422–427)

See the general suggestions for Focused Practice on page 4.

Exercise 1: Discover the Grammar

- Have students complete the exercise individually and compare answers in pairs.
- Elicit the correct answers from the class.

Exercise 2: Indirect Statements and Tense Changes

- Go over the example with the class. Have students point out the changes. *(changed–had changed; last night–the night before)* Remind students that *that* is optional.
- Have students complete the exercise individually and compare answers in pairs.
- Have a student read the direct speech statement and another student report it.

Exercise 3: Indirect Statements and Tense Changes

A

- Have students read the interview silently. Clarify any vocabulary students are not sure of.

B

- Go over the example with the class. Emphasize that students should provide the correct information by reporting what Dr. Myers said.
- Have students complete the exercise individually and compare answers in pairs. Then go over answers as a class.
- (!) Have pairs find and read an interview (or part of it) in a magazine or on the Internet. Then have them take turns saying false statements about what the people said and correcting them.

Exercise 4: Direct Speech

- Go over the example with the class.
- Have students complete the exercise individually and compare answers in pairs. Then go over answers as a class.

Exercise 5: Editing

- Have students read the report quickly to find out what it is about.
- Ask: "What happened in the Nemec family's city last month?" *(there were floods)* "What did the Nemecs lose?" *(all their belongings)* "How long did they take to clean their house?" *(one week)* "What happened to Anna's dollhouse?" *(It was damaged, but Anna and her father were able to restore it.)*
- Have students find and correct the mistakes individually and compare answers in pairs.
- Have students explain why the incorrect structures are wrong.
- (!) Ask students to point out examples of correct usages of indirect speech.

Go to **www.myfocusongrammarlab.com** for additional grammar practice.

Step 4: Communication Practice (pages 428–430)

See the general suggestions for Communication Practice on page 4.

Exercise 6: Listening

A

- Ask: "What kind of weather warnings are there in your area? What are people usually advised to do? What do schools, public offices, and businesses usually do?"
- Play the audio. Have students complete the exercise individually.

B

- Point out that the information will come very fast, so students should leave items blank if they are unsure of an answer. They will discuss answers with their group in Part C. Play the audio and have students complete the exercise.

C

- Have students compare their answers. Point out that students should use reported speech to discuss the answers. Play the audio again for students to check their answers.

Exercise 7: Pronunciation

A

- Play the audio. Have students read along as they listen to the Pronunciation Note.
- Write on the board:
  1. Alice said she would be late for dinner.
  2. She told me that the roads were blocked.
- Ask: "Which words should we stress in each example?" *(1. Alice, said, late, dinner; 2. told, roads, blocked)*

B

- Play the audio. Have students listen and put the stress marks.

C

- Play the audio and have students repeat the answers. Then have them practice the conversations in pairs. Remind them to play both roles.

Exercise 8: Game: Telephone

- Point out that students should not repeat what they have said.
- Have students play the game three or four times. Have different students start the game each time.

Exercise 9: Interview

- Go over the words in the list. Clarify the meaning of any unknown words: *hurricane* (a storm that has very strong, fast winds and that usually moves over water); *tornado* (an extremely violent storm consisting of air that spins very quickly and causes a lot of damage); *drought* (a long period of dry weather when there is not enough water).
- As students interview their classmates, encourage them to take notes. Point out that they will use their notes when reporting their findings.

Exercise 10: Writing

A

- If students decide to interview another person, have them prepare basic questions for their interview. Examples:

  Have you ever experienced extreme weather conditions?

  When was that?

  Where were you?

  What did you do?

  Did the weather service issue a warning?

  Were people told to evacuate?

  Was there a lot of damage?

  Did any buildings collapse?

  When did life go back to normal?

B

- After students write their paragraph, have them correct their work using the Editing Checklist.

OUT OF THE BOX ACTIVITIES

Speaking

- On individual index cards, write statements using a variety of verb tenses and modals. Make as many cards as you have students. Examples:
  — My grandmother is sending me a check for a thousand dollars.
  — You can have my two free tickets to Hawaii for spring break.
  — You should pay the electricity bill as soon as possible.
  — You ought to get the windshield on your car fixed.
  — I'm going to start a new job tomorrow.
  — My family has to find a new place to live because of the fire in their building.
  — I have to write an essay for class tomorrow.

- Form groups of three students. Pass a card to each student. Student A picks up a card and reads it aloud. Student B asks, "What did she say?" Student C repeats the message using indirect speech and moving one step into the past whenever possible. Example:

  A: My grandmother is sending me a check for a thousand dollars.

  B: (to C) What did she say?

  C: She said that her grandmother was sending her a check for a thousand dollars.

- When each group has finished with its cards, it can pass them along to another group of students.

Reading, Speaking, and Listening

- Have students look up news articles about events of the past. Possible topics are unusual weather conditions, a natural disaster like a forest fire or an earthquake, a crime that made headlines, or a sports event of some importance.

- Have students read the article and report back to the class about what happened.

Listening and Writing

- Many communities have storytellers' clubs. If there is one in your area, invite a member to class to tell stories, which the students can then write up using indirect speech.

Go to **www.myfocusongrammarlab.com** for additional listening, pronunciation, speaking, and writing practice.

Note

- See the *Focus on Grammar Workbook* for additional in-class or homework grammar practice.

Unit 26 Review (page 431)

Have students complete the Review and check their answers on Student Book page UR-7. Review or assign additional material as needed.

Go to **www.myfocusongrammarlab.com** for the Unit Achievement Test.

Grammar: INDIRECT INSTRUCTIONS, COMMANDS, REQUESTS, AND INVITATIONS

Students will learn and practice how to give indirect instructions, commands, requests, and invitations.

Theme: HEALTH PROBLEMS AND REMEDIES

Unit 27 focuses on language that we use to talk about insomnia and other health problems and tips to solve them.

Sleep disruption, according to psychologists, is a major reason for emotional and other mental disturbances. People who are deprived of sleep tend to be more nervous, hold more water in their bodies, and have more headaches. They are also more easily angered, frustrated, and moved to tears.

Step 1: Grammar in Context (pages 432–434)

See the general suggestions for Grammar in Context on page 1.

Before You Read

- Have students discuss the questions in pairs. Then go over answers as a class.
- Ask: "Have any of you ever felt the way the man feels?" Encourage students who answer "yes" to briefly describe their experience.

Read

- To encourage students to read with a purpose, write the following questions on the board:
  1. Who is the director of the Sleep Disorders Clinic? *(Dr. Thorton Ray)*
  2. What is the topic of the interview? *(sleep disorders, particularly insomnia)*
  3. What is insomnia? *(a problem with getting to sleep or staying asleep)*
  4. In Dr. Ray's opinion, why is insomnia a problem? *(because it can cause costly accidents)*
  5. Of all the recommendations Dr. Ray makes, choose one that you consider useful. *(Possible answers: Stop drinking coffee and cola later in the day, eat a high-carbohydrate snack before going to bed, exercise regularly but not just before going to bed, do something boring when you can't sleep)*
- Have students read the text. (Or play the audio and have students follow along in their books.) Then have students share their answers with the class.

- Have students discuss the following questions in small groups:
  1. Are you a morning person or a night owl? When do you do your best studying? Your best creative work?
  2. What happens to you when you are tired? Are you able to express yourself as well as usual? Are you as fast in the work you do?
  3. Have students, working in groups of three or four, find out how many hours of sleep the group averages per night. Do they think it is enough?

After You Read

A. Vocabulary

- Have students find and circle the vocabulary in the text. Encourage them to use the context to figure out their meaning.
- Have students compare answers in pairs. Then go over answers as a class.
- (🕐) To reinforce the vocabulary, write the following on the board or on a handout, and have students cross out the word or phrase that is *not* a possible answer: *(1. a snack; 2. a solution; 3. your thoughts; 4. your eyes; 5. hard work; 6. warm)*
  1. What can be astonishing?
     a fact, a snack, a sight
  2. What can persist?
     a problem, a headache, a solution
  3. What can be monitored?
     your work, your thoughts, your sleep
  4. What can interfere with your sleep?
     your eyes, your worries, your diet
  5. What can fatigue cause?
     insomnia, accidents, hard work
  6. What kind of remedies are there?
     home, warm, natural

B. Comprehension

- Have students choose the answers individually.
- Have students compare answers in pairs. Then go over answers as a class.

Go to **www.myfocusongrammarlab.com** for an additional reading, and for reading and vocabulary practice.

Step 2: Grammar Presentation (page 435)

See the general suggestions for Grammar Presentation on page 2.

Grammar Charts

- After students study the charts, have them report the following statements: "Read the examples again." *(You said to read the examples again.)* "Can you open the door?" *(You asked us to open the door.)* "Why don't you write an example?" *(You told us to write an example.)*
- Then have students report instructions or requests that you gave or made since you walked into the classroom today. Challenge them to report as many as they can remember. (Examples: *You said to read the text. You asked us to do Exercise B. You told us to pay attention. You asked Pete to clean the board. You told us not to speak Japanese. You asked Brenda to lend you a pen. You told us to be silent.*)

Grammar Notes

Note 1

- Point out that Appendix 14 on page A-5, has a list of reporting verbs for giving instructions, commands, requests, and invitations. Discuss which verbs are used for each purpose.
- Have pairs of students create at least two sentences for each instruction, command, request, and invitation. Have them share their sentences with their classmates. Examples:
  A: Could you open the window?
  B: She asked me if I could open the window.
  A: Give me the pen.
  B: He asked me to give him the pen.

Note 2

- Point out that *not* precedes the *to* of the infinitive.
- Have the students make negative instructions, commands, requests, and invitations out of their sentences from the Note 1 activity.

⏱ **Identify the Grammar:** Have students identify the grammar in the opening reading on page 432. For example:
  . . . we've invited Dr. Thorton Ray **to talk to us about insomnia.**
  Then I ask them **to think about what can happen if they drive when they're tired.**
  . . . what would you advise me **to do**?
  . . . I would tell you **to stop.**
  We tell patients **to have a high-carbohydrate snack like a banana before they go to bed.**
  My doctor told me **to get more exercise** . . .

Go to **www.myfocusongrammarlab.com** for grammar charts and notes.

Step 3: Focused Practice (pages 436–439)

See the general suggestions for Focused Practice on page 4.

Exercise 1: Discover the Grammar

- Warn students that not every reporting verb in this exercise is used to give an indirect instruction, command, request, or invitation.
- Go over the example with the class.
- Have students complete the exercise individually and compare answers in pairs.
- Elicit the correct answers from the class.
- ⏱ Encourage students to remember a time when they helped a friend make a decision. Form pairs and have students share their experiences. Example: *Once a friend was unsure about which car to buy. I advised him to buy a small car. I told him to check prices on the Internet. I advised him not to go into deep debt.*

Exercise 2: Indirect Instructions: Affirmative and Negative

- Go over the health issues with the class. Clarify any unknown words or expressions: *sore throat* (if your throat is sore, it is painful), *cramps* (a severe pain in a part of your body when a muscle becomes too tight), *stains on teeth* (if your teeth have stains, they have marks that are difficult to remove), *poison ivy rash* (red spots on your skin that hurt and itch, caused by touching a plant that has leaves with three parts and white berries).
- Have students complete the exercise individually. Then go over answers as a class.
- ⏱ Form small groups. Have students share small health problems and give one another advice. Point out that they can make up the problems. After students work in groups, have them report to the class on some of the problems they discussed. Example: *I said I sometimes had a pain in my back. Anna told me to take an aspirin. Steve said not to take any medications. He advised me to go to the doctor.*

Exercise 3: Direct and Indirect Speech

- Have students look at the cartoon and say what they think the dream is about.
- Go over the underlined fragments to make sure students have selected the right information. Then have students complete the cartoon.

Exercise 4: Editing

- Have students read the journal entry quickly to find out what it is about.

- Ask: "What did the student's teacher ask her to do?" *(write a story and then read it in class)* "What did the student have trouble with?" *(getting ideas for her story)* "What did her classmate suggest?" *(getting ideas from her dreams)*
- Have students find and correct the mistakes individually and compare answers in pairs.
- Have students explain why the incorrect structures are wrong.
- ⏱ Ask students to point out examples of correct usages of the indirect instructions, commands, requests, and invitations.

Go to **www.myfocusongrammarlab.com** for additional grammar practice.

Step 4: Communication Practice (pages 440–443)

See the general suggestions for Communication Practice on page 4.

Exercise 5: Listening

A
- Play the audio and have students complete the exercise.
- Have students support their answers with additional information they remember. (Example: *1. He says he has had a lot of headaches lately.*)

B
- Have students read and discuss the eight suggestions. Ask if they think there is likely to be any truth about these suggestions. Tell them that you will play the recording twice. The first time they listen have them make a small *X* next to the items they hear. Have them check "Not Mentioned" for the remaining items. For the second listening, suggest that they listen for what the experts told Juan to do and *not* to do.

Exercise 6: Pronunciation

A
- Play the audio. Have students read along as they listen to the Pronunciation Note.
- Write on the board:
  1. He told me to exercise.
  2. He told me not to exercise.
- Ask: "How many words are stressed in Example 1?" *(two)* "Which ones?" *(told, exercise)* "How many words are stressed in Example 2?" *(three)* "Which ones?" *(told, not, exercise)*

B
- Play the audio. Have students listen and circle the words.

C
- Play the audio and have students repeat the answers. Then have them practice the conversations in pairs. Remind them to play both roles.

Exercise 7: Problem Solving

A
- Go over possible new vocabulary: *hiccup* (usually plural, a sudden repeated stopping of the breath, usually caused by eating or drinking too fast); *blister* (a swelling on your skin containing clear liquid, caused for example by a burn or continuous rubbing).
- Have pairs make notes of *Do's* and *Don'ts* for some health problems. (Example: *Insect bites: Put some vinegar on it. Don't scratch it.*) Point out that they will use their notes when reporting to the class.

B
- Have students report their suggestions to the class. Possible answers: put cold water and then aloe vera on minor kitchen burns; drink warm milk for insomnia; make a paste of baking soda and water and put it on insect bites; take aspirin for headaches; turn the snoring sleeper on his or her side; swallow a spoonful of dry sugar fast to stop hiccups; take vitamin C for colds; wash the skin with strong soap and avoid scratching for poison ivy; drink hot water with lemon juice and honey for sore throats.

Exercise 8: Picture Discussion
- Be sure that students know the meaning of the word *nightmare* (a very frightening dream).
- ⏱ After students discuss the picture in pairs, have them share a personal anecdote about a day when their parents gave them instructions that they didn't follow. Encourage them to say what happened next. Did their parents find out?

Exercise 9: Writing

A
- Have pairs tell each other about good dreams or nightmares in preparation for this assignment. Have students plan their writing by making notes for (some of) the following items:
  Place:
  Time of the day:
  People in my dream:
  Comments they made:
  Instructions / commands they gave:
  Requests / invitations they made:

- Allow time for students to write their paragraphs.

B

- Have students exchange papers and draw a sketch of their partner's dream. Remind them to include the direct speech. Ask: Did your partner understand your dream correctly from your paragraph?

C

- After students write their paragraphs, have them correct their work using the Editing Checklist.

OUT OF THE BOX ACTIVITIES

Speaking

- Form small groups. Have each group choose a different person to give advice to (a person looking for an apartment, someone buying a used car, a college student).
- Then have the group create a list of instructions and advice for that person using imperative statements like *find a good advisor.*
- Have the groups exchange lists and change the imperative statements to indirect instructions and commands: *They told me to find a good advisor.*

Speaking

- Brainstorm places where a person can get help in the community. The Chamber of Commerce helps new business owners; the tourism office helps tourists and businesses that are related to tourism; newspapers help people buy and sell things; various government entities (like social security offices, the post office, an unemployment office) give instructions and advice on many different topics. As a class, create a list of places to go and what to ask.
- Send pairs or small groups to different offices to get information, instructions, and advice.
- Have them report their findings to the class or make a poster that can be displayed in the classroom.

Go to **www.myfocusongrammarlab.com** for additional listening, pronunciation, speaking, and writing practice.

Note

- See the *Focus on Grammar Workbook* for additional in-class or homework grammar practice.

Unit 27 Review (page 444)

Have students complete the Review and check their answers on Student Book page UR-7. Review or assign additional material as needed.

Go to **www.myfocusongrammarlab.com** for the Unit Achievement Test.

UNIT 28 OVERVIEW

Grammar: INDIRECT QUESTIONS

Students will learn and practice how to make and use indirect questions.

Theme: JOB INTERVIEWS

Unit 28 focuses on language that we use to talk about experiences with job interviews.

There are laws that prevent employers from asking specific kinds of questions of prospective employees so that all people have equal chances to get good jobs, regardless of age, religion, marital status, gender, and race. For example, without these laws, a woman of 40 who has five children to support might not get a job even if she is well-qualified because an employer might think she would miss a lot of work time because of her children's needs and might decide not to hire her for that imagined reason.

Step 1: Grammar in Context (pages 445–447)

See the general suggestions for Grammar in Context on page 1.

Before You Read

- Have students discuss the questions in pairs. Then call on students to say how they would have felt if they had been in the woman's place. Would they have reacted in the same way?
- Have students form groups and write a list of four or five typical questions for a job interview and then share them with the class.

Read

- To encourage students to read with a purpose, write the following questions on the board:
    1. What is a stress interview? *(a type of job interview that features tough, tricky questions, long silences, and negative evaluations of the candidate)*
    2. What is its purpose? *(to determine whether a job candidate can handle pressure of the kind that a job might include)*
    3. How did Melissa react to it? *(She was shocked.)*
    4. What disadvantage might it have for a company? *(A good candidate for a job might decide he/she does not want to work for a company that would stress a candidate so much during an interview and refuse the job offer.)*
- Have students read the text. (Or play the audio and have students follow along in their books.) Then have students share their answers with the class.
- Have students discuss the following questions in small groups:
    1. How can a person prepare for a stress interview? Do you think it helps to be prepared for a stress interview? How so?
    2. What kind of investigation into a company should any job applicant do? Why is it important to know about the company?
    3. Is it a good idea to send thank-you cards to people who have interviewed you when you are looking for a job? What is the effect of such a personal communication as thanking an interviewer for having taken the time to talk with you?

After You Read

A. Vocabulary

- Have students find and circle the vocabulary in the text. Encourage them to use the context to figure out their meaning.
- Have students compare answers in pairs. Then go over answers as a class.

- ⏱ Write the following on the board or on a handout. Have students match the items in each list. *(1. b, 2. e, 3. d, 4. f, 5. c, 6. a)*

    1. potential employer
    2. job candidate
    3. appropriate reply
    4. job evaluation
    5. be under pressure
    6. handle something well

    a. deal with a difficult situation successfully
    b. a person who might give you a job
    c. have difficult or complicated things to do
    d. a good response for a particular question
    e. a person who applies for a job
    f. your employer's feedback on how well you're working

B. Comprehension

- Have students choose the answers individually. Point out that the article does not use the exact words the person said.
- Have students compare answers in pairs. Then go over answers as a class.

Go to **www.myfocusongrammarlab.com** for an additional reading, and for reading and vocabulary practice.

Step 2: Grammar Presentation (pages 448–450)

See the general suggestions for Grammar Presentation on page 2.

Grammar Charts

- Explain the meaning of *spreadsheet* (a computer program that can show and calculate financial information).
- Write on the board:
  He asked, "Did you → He asked if / whether
  have an interview?"   (or not) she had
                         had an interview.
- Point out that *yes / no* questions that become indirect questions use *if* or *whether (or not)*.
- Write on the board:
  Who told her about → He asked who told
  the job?   her about the job.
- Point out that *who* and *what* can take the place of the subject, so no change in word order is required with these two *wh-* words.
- Write on the board:
  Where <u>did</u> I <u>work</u>? → He asked where I <u>worked</u>.

  What <u>can</u> a cook → The chef asks what
  <u>make</u> with tomatoes?   the cook <u>can make</u>
                              with tomatoes.

- Point out that when the *wh-* word takes the place of part of the predicate, the helping verb *(do / did)* is dropped and any modal (such as *can* or *might*) moves to the regular sentence word order position after the subject.

Grammar Notes

Note 1
- Have students ask each other two questions that start with *do you* and two that start with *are you.* Then go around the room having students report what they asked their partners. (*I asked my partner if he likes pizza. I asked my partner whether she is comfortable with spreadsheets.*)

Note 2
- Brainstorm *wh-* words and write them on the board. (*what, where, when, why, who(m), whose, which, how, how much, how many, how long*)
- Write on the board:
  1. He asked _____ she had gone.
  2. She asked _____ students had failed the exam.
  3. They asked _____ he wanted.
- In pairs, have students complete the indirect questions with as many wh- words as possible. Go over answers as a class.
  (*1. where, when, why, how, how long ago; 2. which, whose, how many, why; 3. what, how much, how many*)
- Do not erase the *wh-* words.

Note 3
- Write on the board:
  Who is that man? ⟶ I asked who that man was.
  What does he want? ⟶ I asked what he wanted.
- Use the examples on the board to point out the statement word order (subject + verb) in the indirect questions.
- Have pairs take turns asking each other *wh-* questions (point out the *wh-* words on the board) and *yes / no* questions. (Example: *Where do you live? Do you like the area?*)
- Then call on students to tell the class the questions they were asked. (Example: *Mandy asked me where I lived. She also asked me if I liked the area.*)

Note 4
- Point out that an indirect question is not a true question, so it does not need a question mark.
- Draw attention to the *Be Careful!* note. Remind students that *be* changes word order in indirect questions.

Note 5
- Repeat the rule that *do, does,* and *did* are not needed in indirect questions because statement word order is used.

- ⏱ **Identify the Grammar:** Have students identify the grammar in the opening reading on page 445. For example:
  . . . the interviewer asked **why she couldn't work under pressure**.
  . . . he asked **if she had cleaned out her car recently**.
  . . . he wanted to know **who had written her application letter for her**.
  She asked the interviewer **whether he was going to ask her serious questions**.
  . . . reporters ask **how the accident could have occurred**.

Go to **www.myfocusongrammarlab.com** for grammar charts and notes.

Step 3: Focused Practice (pages 450–454)

See the general suggestions for Focused Practice on page 4.

Exercise 1: Discover the Grammar

A
- Go over the example with the class.
- Have students complete the exercise individually and compare answers in pairs.
- Elicit the correct answers from the class.

B
- Have students complete the exercise individually. Then go over answers as a class.
- ⏱ With books closed, have students play a memory game about the questions that the interviewer asked Melissa. Have pairs write down as many indirect questions as they remember and then compare answers with another pair. Have them use the following format and add arrows to the diagram as necessary:
  The interviewer asked ⟶ how much . . .
  Melissa

Exercise 2: Word Order
- Go over the example with the class. Point out the statement word order in the indirect question: subject + verb *(it was).*
- Have students compare answers in pairs. Then go over answers as a class.

Exercise 3: Indirect Questions: Verb and Pronoun Changes

- Have pairs go over the questions and decide if they were asked by Jaime or Ms. Stollins. Have them write "J" for Jaime and "S" for Ms. Stollins at the end of each question.
- Have students write the indirect questions. Remind them to use statement word order (subject + verb) and that the verb moves one step into the past in indirect speech.
- Have students compare answers in pairs. Then go over answers as a class.
- ⏱ Have students imagine Jaime was asked the inappropriate questions listed in the article on page 446. In pairs, have them take turns reporting them as if they were Jaime. (Examples: Student A: *He asked me how old I was.* Student B: *He asked me what my religion was.*)

Exercise 4: Editing

- Have students read the memo quickly to find out what it is about.
- Ask: "Who did Ken Marley interview?" *(Carlos Lopez, a candidate for the administrative assistant position)* "Did Marley ask any tricky questions?" *(yes)* "How did Lopez respond to them?" *(He was able to handle them really well.)* "Does Marley think he is a good candidate for the job?" *(yes)*
- Have students find and correct the mistakes individually and compare answers in pairs.
- Have students explain why the incorrect structures are wrong.
- ⏱ Ask students to point out examples of correct usages of indirect questions.

Go to **www.myfocusongrammarlab.com** for additional grammar practice.

Step 4: Communication Practice (pages 455–459)

See the general suggestions for Communication Practice on page 4.

Exercise 5: Listening

A

- After students read the checklist, have them supply possible questions for some of the items in the lists. (Examples: *What kind of experience do you have? How much would you like to earn? Where were you born? Have you ever been arrested?*)
- Play the audio and have students check the subjects they hear.

B

- Play the audio again. If necessary, stop the audio after each illegal question to allow students time to write. Then play the audio again (without stopping) and have students make any necessary corrections.

C

- Before students report the questions, review the direct questions by calling on students to write them on the board.

Exercise 6: Pronunciation

A

- Play the audio. Have students read along as they listen to the Pronunciation Note.
- Write on the board:
  1. Did you quit your previous job?
  2. Why did you quit your previous job?
  3. He asked me if I had quit my previous job.
- Ask: "In which question does the voice go up?" *(1)* "Why?" *(because it is a yes / no question)* "Why doesn't the voice go up in Question 2?" *(because it is not a yes / no question; it is a* wh- *question)* "Why doesn't the voice go up in Question 3?"*(because it is an indirect* yes / no *question)*

B

- Play the audio. Have students listen and draw the arrows at the end of each question. Go over the answers as a class.

C

- Play the audio again. Then have students practice the conversations with a partner.

Exercise 7: Role Play: A Job Interview

A

- Go over the résumé and the advertisement with the class. Point out the term *associate's degree*, and explain that it is a two-year degree from a community college. You may want to ask questions to check comprehension. You can ask: "Is Pat working at the moment?" "Where?" "When did he finish high school?" "Does he have computer skills?" "What is the advertisement for?"
- Have students work in small groups to write the questions.
- Point out that students can use both legal and illegal questions in their interviews.

B

- Ask for volunteers to act out the role play.

C

- Have students prepare for the discussion by thinking about their answers to the questions individually. Then discuss as a class. Ask: "Do you think the interview was fair to the interviewee?"

Exercise 8: Questionnaire: Work Values

A

- Point out that the acceptability of some personal questions (about, for example, one's origins, family, financial matters, marital status, education, life goals, weight, age) varies from one culture to another. Discuss with your class what things are inappropriate to ask before they interview one another.
- Encourage students to ask each other follow-up questions. (Example: Student A: *Where do you prefer to work?* Student B: *I'd like to travel.* Student A: *Would you like to travel abroad?*)

B

- Have pairs join another pair and tell about their conversation with their partner.

Exercise 9: What About You?

- Point out that students can make up the information if necessary.
- Discuss the questions that students were asked and determine which questions were difficult to answer. Help the students come up with ways of avoiding such questions. Sometimes the best way is with another question: *Is the number of languages I can speak an important part of this job?*
- Call on students to share one of their partner's experiences with the class. (Example: *Alice said that she had an interview two months ago. The interviewer asked her why she was interested in working for that company . . .*)

Exercise 10: Writing

A

- Have pairs write four or five questions and share them with the class. Write a list of students' questions on the board.
- Have students select the questions they want to use for their interview.

B

- **Note:** If students do not have a chance to interview someone, have them research the information they need to answer the questions they chose.
- Have students practice changing their questions into indirect questions before they begin to write their reports.

C

- After students write their reports have them correct their work using the Editing Checklist.

OUT OF THE BOX ACTIVITIES

Speaking

- Form groups of three. Prepare information cards, one for Student A and one for Student C.
  Student A's card says:
  I'm arriving at the airport at three o'clock on Thursday afternoon.
  Can you pick me up then?
  Do you have a bed for me so that I can stay overnight?
  Student C's card says:
  Which airline are you coming in on?
  Will you have a lot of baggage?
  How long are you going to stay with us?
- Set up the chairs so that Students A and C have their backs to each other and Student B is between them. Student A and C are talking on the phone, but they have a very bad connection. Student B is the operator, helping them to understand each other's questions.
  A: I'm arriving at the airport at three o'clock on Thursday afternoon.
  C: (to B) What did he say?
  B: He said he's (or he was) arriving at the airport at three o'clock on Thursday.
  C: (to B) Ask him which airline he's coming in on.
  B: (to A) Which airline are you coming in on?
- Continue until all the questions have been asked and answered. If you make each set of question cards slightly different (for example: *I'm arriving at the train station. Can you send a taxi for me? Can you reserve a hotel room for me?*), the groups can exchange cards and roles and do the activity again. Then everyone will have a chance to be Student B.

Reading and Speaking

- Bring in want ads from the local newspaper. Have students work in pairs to choose jobs that appeal to them (whether they are presently qualified for those jobs or not).

- Have them create a list of five questions for each job.
- Have them role-play the interviews in pairs.
- Then have two pairs join together and explain to each other (using indirect questions) what they asked.

Go to **www.myfocusongrammarlab.com** for additional listening, pronunciation, speaking, and writing practice.

Note
- See the *Focus on Grammar Workbook* for additional in-class or homework grammar practice.

Unit 28 Review (page 460)

Have students complete the Review and check their answers on Student Book page UR-7. Review or assign additional material as needed.

Go to **www.myfocusongrammarlab.com** for the Unit Achievement Test.

UNIT 29 OVERVIEW

Grammar: EMBEDDED QUESTIONS

Students will learn and practice the use of embedded questions with *if* or *whether*, *wh-*words, and infinitives.

Theme: TRAVEL TIPS

Unit 29 focuses on language that we use to talk about tipping customs.

Tipping for good service is a custom that is common in many places. However, both who is tipped and how much he or she is tipped vary significantly from place to place. Most commonly, food servers, bartenders, and taxi drivers expect tips. Hotel housekeepers, doormen, hairstylists, manicurists, and delivery people may also expect tips. In the United States, tips for good service range from 10 to 20 percent.

Step 1: Grammar in Context (pages 461–463)

See the general suggestions for Grammar in Context on page 1.

Before You Read
- Draw attention to the unit title "Travel Tips" and the title of the article "The Tip: Who? When? and How much"? Ask: "What does the word *tip* mean in the unit title?" *(a piece of advice)* "What does it mean in the article?" *(a small amount of money that you leave for a service performed)*
- Call on students to say if they have ever been in a situation where they didn't know whether to tip or how much to tip. Have volunteers briefly explain their experiences.

Read
- To encourage students to read with a purpose, write the following questions on the board:
  1. Where did it use to be illegal to tip? *(China)*
  2. Where is a tip added to the bill? *(Germany)*
  3. Who did *World Travel* magazine interview? *(Irene Frankel)*
  4. What did she write? *(a book about tipping customs)*
  5. Who was the book initially aimed at? *(people from cultures where tipping is not a custom)*
  6. Who did it turn out being aimed at in the end? *(people traveling to the United States and people living there)*
- Have students read the text. (Or play the audio and have students follow along in their books.) Then have students share their answers with the class.
- Have students discuss the following questions in small groups:
  1. What are some tipping customs in your country? Do you follow them? Why or why not?
  2. When you travel, you may not know what the tipping customs are. What do you do about tipping? How do you feel about it?

After You Read

A. Vocabulary
- Have students find and circle the vocabulary in the text. Encourage them to use the context to figure out their meaning.
- Have students complete the exercise individually and compare answers in pairs. Then go over answers as a class.

- 🕐 Write the following on the board. Have students match the sentence halves. *(1. d, 2. c, 3. a, 4. b)*

    1. If something is a custom,
    2. If something is logical,
    3. If something is ordinary,
    4. If you clarify something,

    a. there is nothing special about it.
    b. you explain it.
    c. there is a reason for it
    d. a lot of people do it.

B. Comprehension
- Have students choose the answers individually. Encourage them to underline the information in the text that supports their answers.
- Have students compare answers in pairs. Then go over answers as a class.

Go to **www.myfocusongrammarlab.com** for an additional reading, and for reading and vocabulary practice.

Step 2: Grammar Presentation (pages 463–465)

See the general suggestions for Grammar Presentation on page 2.

Grammar Charts
- Point out that an embedded question is different from an indirect question: When you use an embedded question, you don't report what someone else said. You choose to ask a question in an indirect way. Write examples on the board:
    Direct question: Where is the cat?
    Embedded question: Do you know where the cat is?
- Point out that questions are embedded in two ways: The whole question is embedded *(People will tell you <u>what most customers do</u>.)* or a *wh-* word + infinitive structure is used *(Does your book explain <u>who to tip</u>?).*

Grammar Notes

Note 1
- Write the following examples on the board. (**Note:** You will be using these examples for Grammar Notes 1 through 6.)
    1. I wonder if I can pay by credit card.
    2. I don't know how much the bill is.
    3. Can you tell me where I should park?
    4. Do you know whether the park closes at six?
    5. I'm not sure who to ask.
- Have students study the examples and identify the embedded questions. Underline them as students read them aloud.

- Ask: "Which embedded questions are inside a statement?" *(1, 2, and 5)* "Which ones are inside another question?" *(3 and 4)*
- Draw attention to the *Be Careful!* note. Punctuation marks depend on whether the questions are embedded in statements or questions.
- Do not erase the examples on the board.

Note 2
- Be sure that students know the meaning of the term *service charge* (an amount of money that is added to the price of something in order to pay for extra services that you use when buying it).
- Point out that direct questions sometimes seem abrupt and impolite, but embedded questions are softer: *Can / Could you tell me . . . ? Would you mind telling me . . . ?*
- Direct attention to the examples on the board. Ask: "Which embedded questions express something you don't know?" *(1, 2, and 5)* "Which ones ask politely for information?" *(3 and 4)*
- Have students ask each other personal questions such as, "How old are you?" using the polite embedded question form. Their partners can then answer, "I'd rather not say."

Note 3
- Point out that embedded *yes / no* questions are like the indirect questions of Unit 28. The difference is that the verbs are more likely to be ones such as *know, wonder,* or *can't decide* rather than *say* or *tell.*
- Direct attention to the examples on the board. Ask: "Which examples include embedded *yes / no* questions?" *(1 and 4)* "What do embedded *yes / no* questions start with?" (if *or* whether) "Which examples include embedded *wh-* questions?" *(2, 3, and 5)* "What do embedded *wh-* questions start with?" (wh- *words*)

Note 4
- Note that the rules for use of *do / does / did* are the same as for indirect questions.
- Point out that the word order changes for *wh-* questions are the same as for indirect questions.
- Direct attention to the examples on the board. Ask: "Which embedded questions use statement word order: subject + verb?" *(1, 2, 3, and 4)* Have students call out the subjects + verbs in the examples. *(1. I can pay; 2. the bill is; 3. I should park; 4. the park closes)*
- Draw attention to the *Be Careful!* note. Remind students of word order changes with *be.*

Note 5

- Direct attention to the examples on the board. Ask: "Which example uses an infinitive in the embedded question?" *(5)*
- Have students identify the embedded questions that use the infinitive in the reading.
- Have students expand the embedded questions with infinitives into full questions.
  Does your book ⟶ *Does the book explain*
  explain who to tip? *who I should tip?*
- Draw attention to the *Be Careful!* note. Remind students not to use the infinitive after *if* or *why*.

Note 6

- Direct attention to the examples on the board. Have students identify the phrases that are followed by embedded questions and read them aloud. *(I wonder . . . , I don't know . . . , Can you tell me . . . ?, Do you know . . . ? I'm not sure . . .)*
- Have students write some embedded questions about tipping using the question openers in this note.

⏱ **Identify the Grammar:** Have students identify the grammar in the opening reading on page 461. For example:

Do *you* often wonder **what to do** about tipping?

. . . *Tips on Tipping: The Ultimate Guide to **Who, When**, and **How Much to Tip***, answers all your questions . . .

Tell me **why you decided to write a book about tipping**.

. . . I found that Americans were also unsure **how to tip** . . .

Does your book explain **who to tip**?

It tells you **who to tip, how much to tip,** and **when to tip**.

. . . it tells you **when not to tip**.

Go to **www.myfocusongrammarlab.com** for grammar charts and notes.

Step 3: Focused Practice (pages 466–470)

See the general suggestions for Focused Practice on page 4.

Exercise 1: Discover the Grammar

- Go over the example with the class.
- Have students complete the exercise individually and compare answers in pairs.
- Elicit the correct answers from the class.
- ⏱ In small groups, have students discuss why they would / wouldn't be interested in reading the book. Encourage them to share questions that they would like the book to answer.

Exercise 2: Embedded Questions

- Go over the example with the class. Remind students to use statement word order.
- Call on pairs to read the questions and answers aloud.

Exercise 3: Embedded Questions

- Go over the example. If necessary, remind students not to use auxiliaries and to use statement word order.
- Encourage students to read each conversation for meaning before choosing the questions.
- Call on pairs to read the conversations aloud.

Exercise 4: Question Word + Infinitive

- Go over the example with the class.
- Have students read the whole conversation before writing their answers.
- Call on a pair to read the conversation aloud.
- ⏱ Have students imagine that a friend, Brandon, is celebrating his birthday at his place next week. Have pairs create a conversation in which they ask each other embedded questions with infinitives. Write the following cues on the board:
  1. what / wear
  2. what time / arrive
  3. what / buy as a gift
  4. how / get / Brandon's place

Exercise 5: Editing

- Have students read the post quickly to find out what it is about.
- Ask: "Where does Jenna need to go?" *(to the hairdresser's)* "Which people doesn't Jenna know whether to tip?" *(the person who washes your hair, the one who cuts it, and the one who colors it)* "Jenna doesn't know where to leave the tip. Which options does she mention?" *(leaving it on the counter, in the person's hands, or in the person's pocket)*
- Have students find and correct the mistakes individually and compare answers in pairs.
- Have students explain why the incorrect structures are wrong.
- ⏱ Ask students to point out examples of correct usages of embedded questions.

Go to **www.myfocusongrammarlab.com** for additional grammar practice.

Step 4: Communication Practice (pages 471–476)

See the general suggestions for Communication Practice on page 4.

Exercise 6: Listening

A

- Have students complete the exercise individually. When going over answers as a class, encourage students to provide information from the call to support their choices. (Example: 1. *He said that a service charge is added to the bill, so people don't leave a tip.*)

B

- Prepare students for the exercise by anticipating (inferring from the information there) what the first two questions might be. If the correct answer to the first question is *between 15 and 20 percent of the bill* and the wrong answer is *the server,* then the question must be about how much to tip a server in a restaurant. Clues for Caller Two show that the question must be about a taxi ride and whether a driver should be tipped. (Note that this anticipation gives the students more practice with making embedded questions.)
- Be sure students understand that the answer is not given in the audio, so they should choose the option that answers the caller's question appropriately.

Exercise 7: Pronunciation

A

- Play the audio. Have students read along as they listen to the Pronunciation Note.
- Write on the board:
  1. Can you tell me whether I should leave a tip?
  2. I don't know who I'm supposed to tip.
- Ask: "In which example does the voice go up?" *(1)* "Why doesn't the voice go up in Example 2?" *(because the voice goes down at the end of statements)*

B

- Play the audio. Have students listen and draw the arrows.
- For additional practice, have students practice the conversations with a partner. Remind them to play both roles.

Exercise 8: Information Gap: Eating Out

- Go over the menu with the class. Review terms they might not know: *catch of the day, soup of the day, side dishes,* da Luigi.
- Brainstorm question openers students can use in the conversation. Write them on the board:
  It doesn't say . . .
  Let's ask . . .
  I wonder . . .

I'd like to know . . .
I'm not sure . . .
I don't know . . .
Can you tell me . . . ?
Do you know . . . ?

- Then have students work in groups to complete the exercise.

Exercise 9: Discussion

- You may want to point out that there is one advantage that tipping provides. In a place where there is no tipping, servers are less likely to be pleasant, to be quick about serving you, or to check to be sure you are happy with the food.
- Brainstorm question openers students can use during the discussion. Write them on the board. Examples:
  I wonder . . .
  I'm not sure . . .
  I don't know . . .
  I can't imagine . . .
  We should find out . . .
  Do you know . . . ?
- Then have students work in groups to discuss.

Exercise 10: What About You?

A

- Model a first-time experience for your students: "I remember the first time I went skiing. I didn't know whether everyone there would know how to ski really well. I didn't know what I should bring. I didn't know if I would need my own skis. I didn't understand what the customs were about getting skiing lessons. And I didn't know if I should have money for tips for the instructor or where to keep that money."
- Have students make notes about their own experience. Encourage the use of *I didn't know . . . , I didn't understand . . . , I wasn't sure . . . , Now I can't remember . . .*

B

- Have students work in pairs. Encourage them to ask each other questions using: *Can you remember . . . ? Did you know . . . ? Did you find out . . . ?*

Exercise 11: Role Play: Information Please!

- Write useful question openers on the board:
  Can / Could you tell me . . . ?
  I'd like to know . . .
  Do you know . . . ?
  Can / Could you explain . . . ?
- Have students practice in pairs. Then ask for volunteers to perform for the class.

Exercise 12: Writing

A

- Brainstorm a list of the kinds of problems students are likely to have had and then add related words. Examples:

  MONEY—*cash, travelers' checks, coins, ATM, receipt*

  TRANSPORTATION—*ticket, ticket sellers, kiosk, conductor, bus driver, transfers*

- You may also want to write the following questions on the board to remind students of the information they can include in their paragraph:

  Where were you?

  When?

  What confused / surprised you?

  What didn't you know?

  What couldn't you understand?

  What did you wonder?

  What did you have to find out?

- Allow time for students to write their paragraphs.

B

- After students write their paragraphs, have them correct their work using the Editing Checklist.

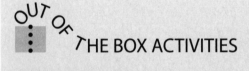

OUT OF THE BOX ACTIVITIES

Writing and Speaking

- Point out that people who have jobs at information booths have to give information, advice, and guidance to others as part of their everyday work. As a class, discuss what a new interpreter at a tourist information office will have to ask the expert in order to give good answers to the questions.

- Have pairs of students write scripts, practice, and perform a role play with questions from foreign visitors about the distance to a tourist site, how long it takes to visit the site, what to take, whether there is any danger in visiting the site, etc. Tell students that these particular foreign visitors are very polite and don't want to risk offending anyone by asking questions too directly.

Reading and Writing

- Have students collect tourist brochures. They might contact embassies or consulates to find information on tourist attractions they know well (a historical site, museum, palace, park, shrine, or gallery).

- Ask students to imagine that they are going to work at a tourist information booth. Have them write down questions with embedded questions inside that they might be asked.

- Have them share their questions with the class. Posting the brochures with the questions would make a nice display.

Go to **www.myfocusongrammarlab.com** for additional listening, pronunciation, speaking, and writing practice.

Note

- See the *Focus on Grammar Workbook* for additional in-class or homework grammar practice.

Unit 29 Review (page 477)

Have students complete the Review and check their answers on Student Book page UR-8. Review or assign additional material as needed.

Go to **www.myfocusongrammarlab.com** for the Unit Achievement Test.

From Grammar to Writing (pages 478–480)

See the general suggestions for From Grammar to Writing on page 9.

Go to **www.myfocusongrammarlab.com** for an additional From Grammar to Writing Assignment, Part Review, and Part Post-Test.

STUDENT BOOK AUDIOSCRIPT

EXERCISE 4 (page 8)

1.

A: Hi, Janine. What are you doing?

B: Looking at photos. Want to see?

A: Sure. I love photos. Oh, who's that?

B: My niece Alex. Isn't she cute?

A: Alex? Isn't that actually a boy's name?

B: Not anymore. Well, maybe some people still consider it a boy's name, but more and more parents are giving girls names like Alex, too. It's the style now.

2.

A: Now *he's* kind of cute.

B: Who?

A: The guy who's wearing glasses.

B: Oh. That's my friend, Red.

A: Red?

B: Yeah, you can't tell from this photo, but he's got *really* read hair.

3.

A: Who's the boy who's holding his head? He looks like he has a headache.

B: That's my nephew, Michael. He doesn't have a headache. He's just kidding around. That's why everyone calls him "Bozo."

A: Bozo? As in "Bozo the clown"? I bet he hates it.

B: Not really. He knows we mean it affectionately. Anyhow, he just makes a joke out of it—like with everything else.

4.

A: And who's that?

B: That's my cousin. We call her "Sunshine."

A: Sunshine? How come?

B: Because she smiles so much.

A: But she's not smiling in *this* picture! In fact, she looks pretty serious.

B: You're right. She doesn't look happy at all. Well, so much for nicknames!

5.

A: That guy looks familiar. Who is he?

B: Oh, you know who that is! That's my brother, Karl.

A: Karl! I didn't recognize him. Doesn't he wear glasses?

B: Yeah. Usually. But he doesn't like how he looks in them. *I* think he looks great in glasses, but I can't convince him. That's why he isn't wearing them in the picture.

6.

B: Now, guess which one is Bertha.

A: Bertha? That's easy. Bertha's the woman who's wearing the hat.

B: Wrong! That's my Aunt Vicki.

A: You're kidding! She looks more like a Bertha to me!

B: Why do you say that?

A: Oh, I don't know. Bertha sounds kind of old-fashioned. The name Vicki sounds like it belongs to someone young and sexy—like the other woman.

B: Nope. Bertha's her daughter!

A: Strange.

EXERCISE 6 (page 22)

INTERVIEWER: So, tell me. How did you and your husband meet?

WOMAN: Well, actually it's a pretty romantic story. John and I were both working for a newspaper. We didn't know each other well at the time, but one day we got an assignment together. (I was a photographer, and he was a writer.)

INTERVIEWER: What was the assignment?

WOMAN: Let's see. We were covering this story about the new murals on Market Street. John was doing the research about the artists, and I was taking photos of the art. Well, anyhow, we were doing this story outside when it started to rain. I mean, it was really coming down hard. When it started thundering and lightening too, we ran into the nearest coffee shop we could find. As soon as we sat down, lightning struck nearby and the place lost its electricity. Luckily, the coffee shop had candles on the table, so it was no problem.

INTERVIEWER: Oh. So while it was thundering and lightening outside, the two of you were sitting there talking by candlelight. You're right. It does sound romantic. How long did the storm last?

WOMAN: Oh, about an hour, I suppose.

INTERVIEWER: So I guess you two both got to know each other pretty well.

WOMAN: Yes. You know, at work there was never enough time to talk—we were always working against some deadline. So, anyway, John was just beginning to tell me a little about his childhood when the lights came back on. We were going to leave and get back to work, but then we just sat there another two hours talking. When we finally left, the sky was clear and the sun was shining. It all seemed so symbolic. A month later, we were married.

UNIT 3

EXERCISE 5 (page 33)

JASON: Hi, honey. I'm calling from the passport office. You wouldn't believe the lines down here. I've been waiting for 40 minutes.

JOY: Well, that's what happens when you leave things till the last minute. What about the plane tickets?

JASON: I got them on the way over here.

JOY: Is there anything you can do while you're waiting? What about that skydiving guide I gave you to read?

JASON: I've read it. I found some fantastic locations. I'll tell you about them later. That reminds me—have you made the hotel reservations?

JOY: I've been calling Hotel Splendor all morning but I haven't gotten through. Oh—I went to the post office to arrange for our mail to be held. The lines were long there too. I had to wait more than half an hour.

JASON: Well, at least it's taken care of. Did you look for a bathing suit?

JOY: Well, I've *been* looking, but . . .

JASON: Don't worry. You'll find one. And when we get all this stuff done, let's celebrate with a nice dinner. Oops, got to go. It's almost my turn. See you later.

JOY: Love you.

JASON: Love you too.

EXERCISE 6 (page 34)

1. **A:** Did you hear about Jason and Joy?
   B: Yeah, they just got engaged. It's great.
2. **A:** Has he taught Joy to skydive yet?
   B: Yes. She's already made three jumps.
3. **A:** How did you meet them?
   B: A friend introduced us.
4. **A:** Have you tried skydiving?
   B: No, extreme sports are too dangerous.
5. **A:** Did he graduate ?
   B: No. One more year to go!
6. **A:** Did he move here from Perth?
   B: Yes. Three years ago.

7. **A:** Have you known them a long time?
   B: No, just a couple of years.

UNIT 4

EXERCISE 9 (page 50)

HOST: Good evening, and welcome to Classical Notes. I'm your host Elena Rodriguez Hernando, and tonight we are joined by five young, exciting musicians: Julio Rivera, Marta Lopez, Klaus Berger, Ling Wong, and Antonio Moreno. . . . Julio, you play the trombone. Tell me, how did you choose the trombone as your instrument?

JULIO: *I* didn't choose the trombone. It chose me.

HOST: What do you mean?

JULIO: Well, I hadn't really been planning to study the trombone. I'd wanted to play the flute. But my school didn't have any flutes available at the time, so they gave me a trombone.

HOST: Marta, you and Julio got married last year. How did the two of you meet?

MARTA: Well, it was 2009. We'd been playing in the same orchestra. In fact, we had both just signed two-year contracts. But we really hadn't spoken very much. Then there was this concert in Berlin, and we were both travelling there in the same bus. It was a long trip and we really got to know each other quite a bit.

JULIO: We sure did. And the rest, as they say, is history.

HOST: Klaus, you used to play in a jazz band. Now you're a classical pianist. What happened?

KLAUS: I was visiting my cousin in Caracas, and he'd gotten us tickets for a concert. Gustavo Dudamel was the guest conductor. I hadn't seen him conduct before. In fact, I'd never even *been* to a classical music concert in my life. The concert was awesome and it changed how I felt about classical music. So, I started studying classical piano right after that.

HOST: What about you, Ling? How did you choose the violin as *your* instrument?

LING: The choice was obvious. My older sister was taking violin lessons and I'd been dreaming of getting a violin of my own. So by the time my parents asked me what I wanted for my tenth birthday, I'd already decided.

HOST: Was your sister happy with your choice?

LING: Yes. It was great. In a little while we were playing duets together.

HOST: Antonio, you grew up in Venezuela. In fact, you were a graduate of El Sistema, weren't you?

ANTONIO: That's right. I was pretty typical of kids in my town. I hadn't been doing my school work. I'd been hanging out on the streets with my friends, and

I'd been getting into a lot of trouble. But, like I said, once I started the program, everything changed. El Sistema really transformed my life.

UNIT 5

EXERCISE 7 (page 72)

LORNA: You know, interest is really growing in housing development on Venus. Some people with very innovative ideas are working on it. I really think we should try to organize a conference there this summer.

SKYLER: Good idea. But it's going to be a big challenge for us to find a time we're all available. We're all so busy.

JAREK: Well, we won't know unless we try. Come on, maybe we'll find a creative solution. Skyler, what are your summer plans?

SKYLER: I don't know exactly, Jarek. I do know that I'm taking a vacation with my family the last two weeks of August. What about you, Jarek?

JAREK: Well, I won't be going on vacation, but I'll be going on a business trip to Mars the second week of July.

LORNA: How long will you be staying?

JAREK: I'll be leaving the beginning of the second week of July and staying through the third week. What about you Lorna? What are your plans?

LORNA: Well, it's already the end of June, and I'll need to tell my boss at least two weeks before I leave.

JAREK: Hmm. So, let's see, Lorna. That means the earliest you could go would be the third week of July. Zindra, what about you? Any plans?

ZINDRA: You know I hate this planet in the summer. Too many tourists from other planets. I'm going to be getting away from Earth as much as I can.

LORNA: Really? Where will you be going, Zindra?

ZINDRA: Well, I'll be flying to Mars to visit my sister every other weekend, starting the second week in July.

JAREK: Hmm. Every other weekend starting the second week of July . . . the conference has to run through the weekend, so the second and fourth weeks of July won't be good for you, Zindra.

LORNA: And the second and fourth weeks of August aren't good either. What about the rest of the time, Zindra?

ZINDRA: Well, I won't be going into the office, but I'll be doing research the third week in July. And with a little luck, I'll be traveling to Jupiter with my new boyfriend the third week in August.

JAREK: Well, then, according to my calculations, that leaves only one week that we all have free . . .

UNIT 6

EXERCISE 6 (page 91)

THEA: The kids' summer vacation will be over in a month, and we won't have even left Seattle. Next year, I want to *go* somewhere during the summer.

DON: Well, we've decided not to use credit for vacations. That means we'd better start planning right now if we want to save enough for next year.

THEA: OK. Let's get out the budget and calculator . . . Hmmm . . . You know, your food budget seems awfully high. Why don't you try packing your lunch?

DON: Do you really think it's worth it?

THEA: Well . . . let's figure it out. How much do you spend on lunch every day?

DON: Uh . . . the minimum I spend is $8 . . . five days a week . . . uhmmm . . . that's $40 a week.

THEA: $40 a week. Well, it only costs *me* $4 a day at the most to pack my lunch, so I only spend about $20 a week . . . Hmm . . . That means you can save $20 a week on lunch if you pack your own lunch too.

DON: OK—so figure 50 weeks of work. That means by the end of the year, I'll have saved . . . uhmmm . . . $1,000. Just on lunches! Wow! $1,000! That's a lot of money!

THEA: Uh-huh. It adds up, doesn't it?

DON: Now, what about clothing? You're going to need some new things this year, aren't you? How much do you want to budget for that?

THEA: I can just buy some new scarves and earrings to make my suits look new. Actually, I think I'll only need about $500 for those purchases. That's only half of what I spent last year.

DON: So, you can save $500 that way. That's great—if you're sure you don't mind. And if Ned and Valerie will wear some things from the thrift shop, we can save another $500 on clothes. That means we'll have saved $1,000 on clothing.

THEA: That's terrific. OK, now, let's look at transportation. You know, I've been thinking that we could save some money taking the commuter van instead of driving into the city. Two monthly van tickets cost $150.

DON: Well, right now, we're spending about $300 a month on gas and parking downtown.

THEA: OK. Let's try the commuter van, then. We'll save $150 a month. So, how much will we have saved by next summer?

DON: Let's see . . . If we go on vacation in August, that's 12 months from now. We'll have saved $1800 dollars on transportation alone. Wow! Why didn't we think of this sooner?

THEA: Now, can we cut back on entertainment?

DON: I think so. We could rent DVDs online instead of going to the movies and order a pizza instead of eating dinner in a restaurant. By next summer, we'll have saved $780 just by watching movies and having pizza at home.

THEA: How did you figure that?

DON: Look—the four of us go out for dinner and a movie about once a month, and on a typical night out, we spend a minimum of $100 for our meal, movie tickets, and snacks at the movie. We can rent movies online for just $10 a month, and a large pizza costs only $25, delivered. We save approximately $65 a month times twelve months. That's $780.

THEA: This is going to be a great vacation. What's our total so far?

DON: Well, so far I figure we'll have saved . . . let's see . . . uhhhh . . .

EXERCISE 7 (page 92)

1. **A:** We're doing really well with our savings plan.
   B: You're right. By next summer, we'll have saved enough for a great vacation.
2. **A:** How are the kids?
   B: Great. In May, my daughter will have been working on her degree for almost a year.
3. **A:** Uh-oh. I think this is your credit card bill.
   B: No problem! As of this month, I won't have made a late payment for two years.
4. **A:** Your English is so good! How long have you been living here?
   B: Let me think . . . On December 1st, I'll have been living in this country for three years.
5. **A:** Do you think Ned's team will win again today?
   B: I hope so. If they do, they won't have lost a game all year.
6. **A:** In June, Don and Thea will have been married for fifteen years.
   B: Let's throw a party for them!
7. **A:** What's up? You're looking very pleased with yourself.
   B: And I should! By 6:00 this evening, I won't have smoked a cigarette for six months.
8. **A:** As of this Saturday, my girlfriend and I will have been seeing each other for three years.
   B: Congratulations! What will you do to celebrate?

UNIT 7

EXERCISE 9 (page 113)

Conversation 1

A: I just got back from Rio. I think I'd like to move there! It's beautiful!

B: Rio isn't the capital of Brazil, is it?

Conversation 2

A: It's a great city. There's so much to do there.

B: I've heard that. They have an exciting night life, don't they?

Conversation 3

A: Anton! Hi! I haven't seen you around in ages!

B: I was in Korea for six months.

A: Oh, that's right. You were teaching a course there, weren't you?

Conversation 4

A: I'm looking for an apartment. Do you know of anything?

B: No, sorry. It's hard to find an apartment in Berlin, isn't it?

Conversation 5

A: So, how do you like Cairo?

B: Oh, it's a fascinating city. And the people are great.

A: You don't speak Arabic, do you?

Conversation 6

A: It gets really hot here.

B: Yes. And isn't the traffic terrible?

Conversation 7

A: I just found a great apartment in Vancouver. I'm glad Anne was with me. She knew just where to look.

B: Oh, that's right. Anne's from Vancouver, isn't she?

Conversation 8

A: I'd *love* to visit Vancouver some day.

B: It's a really great city. You'll love it.

A: You're not originally from there, are you?

Conversation 9

A: Hi, Tom.

B: Hi, Alicia. Nice day, isn't it?

Conversation 10

A: I just got back from Scotland.

B: Scotland? Weren't you in England?

UNIT 8

EXERCISE 7 (page 128)

A: This is a great restaurant. I really love Italian food.

B: So do I. Do you cook?

A: Not really.

B: I do. I love trying out new recipes.

A: Me, I eat out a lot.

B: Oh, so do I.

A: Or I buy some take-out food after work and watch a movie on TV. I love old movies.

B: I do too . . . Uh . . . do you like to read?

A: Uh-hmm. Especially biographies.

B: So do I! What about novels?

A: I don't actually read much fiction.

B: Me neither. I prefer history or travel books. Things about *real* people and places. . . . So, what about sports? Do you do any sports?

A: Nah. I don't really play any sports. What about you?

B: I do. A lot! I play tennis and volley ball every week. But I never watch sports on TV.

A: Me neither. I watch a lot of news programs, though.

A: So do I. In fact, there's an interesting documentary on tonight at 8:00. It's about identical twins.

B: Hmm. It's seven o'clock now. If we leave right away, we can watch it.

A: That sounds good. You know, I think we have a lot in common!

B: Me too!

UNIT 9

EXERCISE 6 (page 149)

LILY: Yuck!

VICTOR: I warned you not to get the meat loaf, didn't I?

LILY: I don't remember your saying anything. I can't wait to fill out that survey.

VICTOR: Well then, let's do it now. How about lending me a pencil?

LILY: Here you go. Do we support introducing Burger Queen? Yes! We do! Hey, wait a minute. I refuse to check that one. I think it's wrong to sell fast food in a school dining hall. It has too much fat and salt. They shouldn't encourage students to eat it.

VICTOR: Come on—you're not the food police. You can't keep students from eating fast food.

LILY: I guess not. But you can avoid selling it to them. And I think showing the fat and calorie content of foods is a good idea. That way, you can choose between having a burger with 18 grams of fat and a piece of chicken with 8.

VICTOR: That sounds appealing! I don't feel like seeing that information before I eat. It ruins my appetite. No, I definitely *don't* want to know about fat and calories. But I'm not opposed to them having more healthy choices.

LILY: I think that's a good idea too. Look at the next one. Do you care about lowering prices? The food is already pretty cheap.

VICTOR: You're right. It is.

LILY: Then I would like them not to lower prices, but to improve the quality of the food—starting with this meat loaf!

VICTOR: That's a good point. I agree with you on both items. Now, you can't object to their offering Chinese food.

LILY: Chinese food would be great. But they'd better hire a chef to prepare it. Remember, they can't even cook meat loaf here.

VICTOR: They'll probably hire someone to do it. Having some international foods makes sense since we have so many international students here now.

LILY: Right. So we both approve of offering Chinese food. Oh, look at number 7. They're asking about starting breakfast at 6:30.

VICTOR: Oh yeah? Right!

LILY: Why do you say that? I run early in the morning. I'd be happy to be able to buy breakfast at 6:30.

VICTOR: I work here, remember? I can't *imagine* getting up any earlier.

UNIT 10

EXERCISE 6 (page 164)

SIMON: Hi, Ms. Jacobson. I wanted to talk to you about my essay. I know that I chose the topic, but I think I'd like to change it.

MS. JACOBSON: Let's see. You're writing about wild animals in zoos. It's a good topic, and you've already done a lot of work on it. Why don't you keep this topic and just add more details to the second paragraph?

SIMON: OK, but that's my problem. I can't think of anything more to say.

Ms. Jacobson: Didn't your uncle work with animals? I remember your writing about him in your journal. I think you said his work made you want to learn more about animal behavior.

Simon: Oh, yeah. He was great. He worked at a wildlife park near the Caribbean Sea. He used to let me come with him when I wasn't in school. And he taught me a lot about sea turtles and the orcas in the sea near Costa Rica.

Ms. Jacobson: Why don't you include that in your essay?

Simon: OK. I'll try. Is that what you meant about adding details?

Ms. Jacobson: That's part of it. You could also try answering some *wh-* questions. For example, when did you decide to study zoology? Where were you living at the time?

Simon: Oh, we were living in Costa Rica. Both my mother and my uncle worked with animals. OK. I see what you mean. I'll use *wh-* questions to add details.

Ms. Jacobson: Great. Anything else?

Simon: Um, yes. I'm confused about this sentence. Like, why can't I say, "Get zoos to release orcas is my dream"?

Ms. Jacobson: When you use a verb form for a subject, what should you do?

Simon: Uh . . . use a gerund? So should I say, "Getting zoos to release orcas is my dream"?

Ms. Jacobson: Exactly. Very good!

Simon: Would you mark all the gerund mistakes on this paper? I'd like to work on them.

Ms. Jacobson: Why don't *you* go through the paper and underline the gerunds? Then we'll talk about any problems you're having.

Simon: OK. Can I make an appointment for another conference on Wednesday?

Ms. Jacobson: Sure. I can see you again at 3:00. And don't worry, Simon. It's going to be a great essay!

EXERCISE 7 (page 165)

1. **A:** Was she happy with the essay topic?
   B: Yes, her teacher let her write about pets.
2. **A:** Where did they go for their class trip?
   B: The teacher took them to the children's zoo.
3. **A:** Did he enjoy the trip?
   B: Yes. They let him feed the rabbits.
4. **A:** What are the elephants doing?
   B: The trainer got them to stand on one foot!
5. **A:** Is Ellie walking the dog?
   B: Yes, we finally got her to do it.
6. **A:** Why does Jack look so angry?
   B: They made him stop taking pictures of the monkey.

UNIT 11

EXERCISE 6 (page 181)

1. **Amy:** It's good to be home. How's the temperature in here?
   Ben: It's a little too cold for me. Do you mind if I turn the air conditioner down?
2. **Amy:** This information on feng shui is really interesting. I'm looking forward to redecorating with the help of this book. What did you think about it?
   Ben: I haven't had the chance to look it over yet.
3. **Amy:** Have you finished redecorating your office?
   Ben: Almost. I'm going to the furniture store today to pick out a new couch.
4. **Amy:** The living room is a mess. Your books are all over the place.
   Ben: Don't worry. I'll put them back as soon as I'm done with my homework.
5. **Amy:** I really don't like those new curtains.
   Ben: Neither do I. I'm going to take them down tomorrow.
6. **Amy:** This mattress isn't as comfortable as it used to be.
   Ben: I know. I think we need to turn it around.
7. **Amy:** What color should we paint the kitchen?
   Ben: I don't know. Let's look up some colors online.

UNIT 12

EXERCISE 6 (page 195)

Mr. Chen: Hello?

Brenda: Hi! This is Brenda Williams from Cheatim Telecommunications? Is this Mr. Chin?

Mr. Chen: No, this is Mr. *Chen*.

Brenda: Well, Mr. Chen, it looks like you've been paying too much for your phone service. But we think we can help you out with our new low rates.

Mr. Chen: Oh, really?

Brenda: That's right . . . When you sign up for our Get Together Program, you'll be paying just 5 cents a minute on all your long distance calls.

Mr. Chen: Actually, I'm only paying 5 cents a minute now . . .

Brenda: But wait till you hear the rest! The Get Together Program offers cell phone service! When you add on our cell phone service, you'll get unlimited cell phone minutes for just one low monthly fee! You will never run out of minutes again!

Mr. Chen: Never run out of minutes? How much is the program?

Brenda: The program is just $49.95 a month.

Mr. Chen: $49.95 a month.

Brenda: That's right. And what a lot of people like is, it eliminates extra paperwork. Instead of separate phone bills, we put all your phone charges together on one convenient bill. So, Mr. Chen, can I sign you up today?

Mr. Chen: Are there any other charges?

Brenda: Just a small fee for setting up the new plan.

Mr. Chen: How much?

Brenda: That will be just $20. It'll show up on your first bill.

Mr. Chen: How about activation fees?

Brenda: Well, sure, there's a small charge to program your cell phone and turn the service on. That's just $30.

Mr. Chen: And how about the phone? Is *that* free?

Brenda: We have a great offer for you! Normally, we charge $59 for the cell phone. But if you sign up right now, we'll send you a rebate card with the phone. Send in the card, and we'll give you $20 back!

Mr. Chen: So, the cost of the phone actually comes out to $30. You know, I have to talk this over with my wife. It sounds like we might end up paying more after all these fees. Can I call you back?

Brenda: I'm really sorry, Mr. Chin . . .

Mr. Chen: Chen.

Brenda: . . . Mr. Chen, but I can only make this offer for one day. If you put it off until tomorrow, you won't have another chance. Think about it! Low long distance rates and unlimited cell phone minutes. This offer is too good to pass up.

Mr. Chen: I guess I'll just stick with the service I have. But thanks, anyway.

Brenda: But, wait, Mr. Ch. . . .

Mr. Chen: Goodbye.

UNIT 13

EXERCISE 7 (page 216)

A: Wow, people have really changed!

B: You're not kidding! Can you recognize anyone at that table over there?

A: Uhmm. Let's see. Isn't that Bob Gramer?

B: Bob Gramer? Which one?

A: The man who's standing up.

B: You know, I think you're right! That's Bob! Wow! He looks even taller!

A: And isn't that Ann Richardson over there?

B: Ann? Where? The woman sitting next to Bob?

A: No. The one who's wearing a scarf.

B: You're right! That *is* Ann with the scarf!

A: And that's Kado!

B: Kado? I remember him. Which one is he?

A: The man who's talking to Ann.

B: Yeah. You're right! That's Kado. . . . So, who's the woman sitting next to Bob?

A: The one wearing glasses? You know, that must be Pat. Remember Pat Wayne? She and Bob used to work on the school newspaper.

B: Do you think they both became writers?

A: I don't know. Maybe. . . .Who's the woman who's wearing all the jewelry?

B: You mean the one sitting across the table from Bob?

A: Uh-huh. The one who's looking at the photo. Do you think that could be . . . uhmm . . . what's-her-name . . . Kasha?

B: You mean Asha!

A: Yeah, that's the one. Didn't she always use to wear a lot of unique jewelry, even to school?

B: Yes! You're right! That's Asha! . . . Asha got married to Raza Gupta, didn't she?

A: I assumed she did. But that' s not Raza who's sitting next to her, is it?

B: No. It looks more like Pete Rizzo.

A: Pete Rizzo? Who's he? The name sounds familiar.

B: Oh, you remember Pete. He was the guy who ran for class president in our senior year.

A: Uh-huh. He's changed a lot, but I'm pretty sure it's Pete.

B: Well, why don't we go over and find out if that's Pete?

A: Good idea. Then we can find out who the couple is that's sitting between Asha and Pat.

B: Yeah. I don't have a clue who they are!

UNIT 14

EXERCISE 7 (page 232)

Host: Good afternoon, and welcome to Book Notes. Childhood memories can be bitter or sweet. Sometimes they are both. Today our guest is author Maria Espinosa Martinez, who will read to us from the new English translation of her book, *Broken Mirrors*. Maria, who is fluent in both Spanish and English, wrote this fine translation herself. Welcome, Maria.

Maria: Thank you. The passage which I'm going to read is from Chapter Two of my book. I remember my childhood bedroom very well. It was a small room, which I shared with my older sister, Katie. There were two beds. The one which I slept in was in a corner. My sister's bed, under which was a large beautiful old rug, was in the middle of the room against the wall. To the left of my bed was a window through which we could see a tree. There was also a big wall mirror in which we both enjoyed looking at our own reflections. That was in the corner that was nearest my sister's bed. Across from my bed was a desk at which we both did our homework after dinner, which we always ate in the kitchen with the rest of the family. My sister, whose greatest passion in life those days was music, kept her guitar on her bed, where she would practice for hours after our homework was done. I remember those as happy times, when we were both young and full of hope and excitement. . . .

UNIT 15

EXERCISE 5 (page 251)

A: Lea, you really must join Facebook. You're my only friend who isn't on it.

B: I just don't have time for it. There are too many other things that I've got to do.

A: You must have *some* free time.

B: Sure I do. But I can't afford to spend it online. Besides, isn't it a little dangerous?

A: Not really. Of course, you have to be careful and use common sense. Just like with other things.

B: Well, I guess you could be right.

A: Trust me. It's a lot of fun. And you can meet a lot of interesting people that way. Like me, for example!

B: I don't have to join Facebook to meet interesting people. But on second thought, I suppose it might be fun to reconnect with old friends.

A: Exactly. You really ought to give it some thought. Will you think about it?

B: Will we be able to chat online if I join?

A: Sure.

B: In that case, I might!

EXERCISE 6 (page 252)

1. **A:** You ought to join Facebook. It's a lot of fun.
   B: I know. But first I have to get a new email address.
2. **A:** Do you have to post a photo of yourself?
   B: No. But you've got to give information about yourself.
3. **A:** You ought to see Jason's new photos. They're great.
   B: I've heard about them, but I wasn't able to sign on last night.

4. **A:** Will you be able to email me the photos?
   B: No problem. I just have to find them on my computer.
5. **A:** I've got to write a report about social networking.
   B: You ought to look it up on Wikipedia first.

UNIT 16

EXERCISE 5 (page 265)

What a day! I really messed up in a big way. For starters—I could have done my homework. Now I've got to get up early tomorrow morning, and it's already midnight. What a bummer! I'm going to be exhausted tomorrow. And I shouldn't have walked to work today. I was late again, and I could see that Doug was really annoyed. Then I got a notice from my bank that one of my checks bounced! Now I'm afraid I'm going to bounce another one. I really ought to have made that $100 deposit today. I'll never learn. Speaking of money, I shouldn't have bought that new coat. That was really foolish of me. My old one's good enough, and I could use the extra money. I just don't have any self-control. Oh, and now Aunt Rose is furious with me. I didn't send her a card for her birthday. I might have at least called to wish her a happy birthday. I only think of myself. On the other hand, I shouldn't have called Ron. All he does is complain. He regrets this, he regrets that . . . Now I feel depressed, but I guess I asked for it! Let's see . . . what else? Uh, oh yeah. I ought to have gone to the supermarket before it closed. I never plan ahead. And now there's nothing in the house to eat. Oh, and I should have finished that David Burns book. Maybe then I'd know how to feel better. Oh, well, maybe there's something amusing on TV tonight. And there's always tomorrow.

EXERCISE 6 (page 266)

1. **A:** Doug ought to have sent that email.
   B: I know. But you should have told him that yesterday.
2. **A:** We should have taken the train.
   B: You're right. We might have been home by now.
3. **A:** I guess I ought to have accepted that job.
   B: Well . . . maybe you could have waited a few days before deciding.
4. **A:** You should have washed that T-shirt in cold water.
   B: I guess I could have read the label before I washed it.
5. **A:** I should have asked my sister to lend me some money.
   B: She's your *sister*! She could have *offered* to help.

EXERCISE 7 (page 280)

Conversation 1

A: Wow! Look at that! It's got a blade. And this looks like a handle.

B: Yeah. It kind of looks like a knife. It might have been some kind of tool, like a sickle.

A: A sickle? What's that?

B: It's a kind of farming tool. Something used to cut down high grass.

A: You mean like wheat?

B: Yeah. They could have harvested wheat with this.

Conversation 2

A: That's a strange-looking design.

B: Yeah. They must have seen one of those astronauts that von Däniken writes about!

A: Right. What do you think they used it for?

B: Well, look at the hole. They may have worn it on a string around their necks for good luck or something.

A: That's right. They could have.

Conversation 3

A: Hey, look at this ring. What do you suppose they used it for?

B: Hmm. Good question. I guess it could have been part of a shoe.

A: Part of a shoe? What do you mean?

B: Like an eyelet—you know—the holes in a shoe?

A: Oh. You mean the holes for shoelaces?

B: Yeah. They could have pulled some kind of shoelace through the hole, and then tied the laces.

A: I see what you mean.

Conversation 4

A: That's beautiful. What do you think it came from?

B: Well, from the round shape and from the design, I'd say it must have been part of a vase.

A: Or it could have been a cooking or serving dish.

B: Yeah, the design looks like some kind of border.

A: It could have been part of the base.

B: No, it's too narrow for the bottom. It must have been part of the top—the neck. They could have poured water or soup out of this part.

A: You're right.

Conversation 5

A: That looks like a pretty complicated instrument!

B: Is it a pump?

A: A pump? I don't think so. I remember reading about something like this in one of our books. I think they could have used this to make fire!

B: Really? How would they have made fire with it?

A: Well, they could have had a tinder inside the cylinder—that's this long, round part on the bottom—see?

B: OK, I see. But what's a tinder?

A: A tinder is something that burns easily, like dry leaves. Look—when they pushed this piece on the top down into the cylinder, it quickly compressed the air.

B: Compressed—that means it pushed it into a small space, right? And that made the air hot!

A: Right! So then the tinder could start to burn.

B: Incredible! How did they figure that out!? They must have been very intelligent!

A: Yeah, really!

Conversation 6

A: What's that you've got there? It looks just like a rock.

B: Yeah, it looks like a rock, but I don't think it actually *is* a rock. Someone must have made it.

A: You know, you're right. It couldn't have just formed like that naturally. Someone must have chipped away at it to produce all those different angles. What do you think it was used for?

B: I think it must have been used as some kind of tool.

A: Hmm. They could have used it to cut hard material—like wood.

B: You mean like a hand axe?

A: Exactly. Like a hand axe.

EXERCISE 8 (page 281)

1. **A:** What was that used for?
   B: I'm not sure. It could have been a spoon.
2. **A:** I called Rahul yesterday afternoon, but there was no answer.
   B: Oh. He might have gone to the museum
3. **A:** Is Sara still on Easter Island?
   B: I'm not sure. She may have left already.
4. **A:** I think I saw John yesterday.
   B: You couldn't have seen him. He's in Peru.
5. **A:** Do you agree with the author's conclusion?
   B: I don't know. He might have been wrong.
6. **A:** Alice got an A on her archeology test.
   B: She must have been happy.
7. **A:** Could they have sailed that far in small boats?
   B: Sure they could have. They were expert sailors.

EXERCISE 8 (page 301)

Conversation 1

A: I just saw this month's *National Geographic*. Great cover!

B: Yeah. I love the photo of the desert.

A: Me too. Ana's a great photographer.

B: Oh. It wasn't taken by Ana.

Conversation 2

A: When did you get back from Peru?

B: Yesterday.

A: I like your hat! Did you buy it there?

B: Yes, but it wasn't made there.

Conversation 3

A: I haven't seen Jill lately. Is she on vacation?

B: No. Haven't you heard what happened?

A: No. What happened?

B: She was sent to Morocco to cover a story.

Conversation 4

A: There's a mistake in this article about the Andes.

B: Really? What does it say?

A: It says corn is grown in the mountains.

B: Oh, that's wrong. Corn isn't grown in the mountains. Potatoes are grown there.

Conversation 5

A: I just got the latest copy of *National Geographic*.

B: Have you read the article about Bolivia?

A: Yes. It was really interesting.

B: It was written by a friend of mine.

Conversation 6

A: Is *National Geographic* sold in Korea?

B: It is. Why?

A: I want to get a subscription for my niece.

UNIT 19

EXERCISE 5 (page 318)

Conversation 1

PICARRA: Spaceship *Endeavor* calling Earth. This is Captain Picarra speaking. We've been hit by a meteorite.

EARTH: Earth to spaceship *Endeavor*. Is anyone hurt, Captain Picarra?

PICARRA: No, everyone is safe.

EARTH: You'd better start repairing the damage immediately.

PICARRA: It can't be repaired out here.

Conversation 2

PICARRA: We'll be approaching Planet CX5 of the Delta solar system in a few hours. Is their language on our computer, Dr. Sock?

SOCK: I'm checking now . . . Hmm. Sorry, Captain Picarra. I see that we don't have a language for planet CX5 on the computer. But look here! We have one for CX4. Shall we try it?

PICARRA: OK, Sock, let's try it. But we'd better be very careful. Our messages could be misunderstood.

Conversation 3

SOCK: I've just spoken to Lon, Captain. He wants you to send him to find help on CX5. He says he's been to CX5 before. He knows the language and the people.

PICARRA: No, Sock. Lon takes too many risks. He can't be trusted on such an important mission. I'll send Torsha instead.

SOCK: But Captain, we know that Lon will be taken seriously down there. Why not send both of them?

PICARRA: OK, Sock, you've convinced me. I'll send Lon *with* Torsha.

Conversation 4

LON: OK, Torsha. It looks like we're ready to leave. Let's go.

TORSHA: Uhhh, Lon, I think you forgot something. Where's your oxygen?

LON: Oxygen? Why? Isn't the atmosphere on CX5 just like Earth's?

TORSHA: I think you've been in space too long, Lon. Read your manual. Oxygen must be used in this situation.

Conversation 5

PICARRA: Sock, I've lost contact with Lon and Torsha. I hope their equipment works on CX5.

SOCK: Don't worry. They'll be picked up by the radar.

Conversation 6

LON: Look at those plants, Torsha! They're huge. I want to take some back to the ship.

TORSHA: They're really amazing plants, Lon, but they can't be grown in space. We've already tried.

LON: That's right. I forgot.

Conversation 7

CX5: What do you want to ask us, Earthlings?

LON: Our vehicle was hit by a meteorite. We request permission to land on your planet.

CX5: Permission granted. Our engineers will be ready for you.

Lon: Thank you. As you know, we have to be helped with the repairs.

EXERCISE 6 (page 319)

1. **A:** Could you see Tokyo or was it too cloudy?
   B: Too cloudy. Tokyo couldn't be seen at all.
2. **A:** Should I tell Commander Kotov about the problem?
   B: No. He shouldn't be disturbed right now.
3. **A:** Did they decide on the new crew yesterday?
   B: No. It couldn't be decided then.
4. **A:** They haven't fixed our Internet connection yet.
   B: I know. But it must be fixed by tomorrow.
5. **A:** When should we eat dinner?
   B: It probably shouldn't be served before 6:00.
6. **A:** Mikel's working late on that experiment.
   B: Yeah. He says it must be finished by next week.

UNIT 20

EXERCISE 5 (page 332)

Amber: Hi, Dad.

Jake: Hi, honey. How are things going with your new apartment?

Amber: Great. I really like my roommate, and I can drive to school in 15 minutes.

Jake: Good. Hey—speaking of driving, remember that you have to change the oil in your car every 3,000 miles. It must be almost time.

Amber: I remembered. I had it changed today.

Jake: Did you change the locks on your apartment door?

Amber: Of course, Dad. I got them changed right after we moved in. Don't worry. This is a really safe neighborhood.

Jake: OK, but you know we can't help worrying a little. Your mother said the apartment needs painting. Maybe I could come up next weekend and paint it for you. You probably need some bookshelves, too. I could put those up, too.

Amber: That's OK, Dad. We had a painting party last weekend. Li and I invited some friends over, and we painted the apartment ourselves. It looks great. And I got the bookshelves put up as soon as the paint was dry.

Jake: Wow. That must have been a fun event! It sounds like you've really settled in.

Amber: Just about. I had to buy a computer desk and some lamps. They fit right into the car, so I didn't even have to have them delivered.

Jake: Well, your mom and I would really love to see you soon—even if you don't have any chores for us to do.

Amber: I'd love to see you too, Dad. Why don't you come up next weekend? Oh, I should warn you. I had my hands painted. Don't be shocked when you see me.

Jake: OK. I'll warn your mother. Anything else we should know about?

Amber: I cut my hair, too. It's pretty short now. And I had it colored.

Jake: Hey—will we be able to recognize you?

Amber: Well . . . Maybe we'd better meet at the apartment!

EXERCISE 6 (page 333)

1. **A:** Marta's hair looks great.
   B: Yes. She's had it colored.
2. **A:** Do you do your own taxes or do you have them done?
   B: I have them done.
3. **A:** Is Anton's car OK now?
   B: Yes. He's had it repaired. 4. **A:** Does Amy wash her own car?
   B: She has it washed once a month.
5. **A:** What color is your new apartment?
   B: I've painted it green.
6. **A:** Your hair looks different!
   B: Yes. I've colored it.

UNIT 21

EXERCISE 6 (page 349)

Announcement Number 1

Flight 398 nonstop to Taipei will be ready to board at Gate 8C in just a few minutes. Please have your boarding passes and passports ready. If you have more than one piece of carry-on luggage, you must check it at the gate. Only one piece of carry-on luggage will be permitted on board. We will begin boarding in about five minutes. Thank you.

Announcement Number 2

Flight 398 nonstop to Taipei is now ready for boarding. If you are traveling with a small child, or if you need extra time, please go to the gate now. If you are flying standby, please wait until all other passengers have boarded. If you are sitting in rows 17 to 24, please proceed to the gate for boarding. All other passengers, please wait until your row is called.

Announcement Number 3

Flight 398 is now continuing to board. If you are sitting in rows 7 to 16, please proceed to the gate for boarding. Please have your boarding pass and passport ready. If you are traveling standby, please continue to wait until all other passengers have boarded.

Announcement Number 4

Welcome to Flight 398 nonstop to Taipei. Please pay careful attention while the flight attendants review some important safety procedures. In the unlikely event that the cabin loses pressure, oxygen masks will automatically descend from the overhead panels. If you are traveling with a child, put your own mask on first. Then assist the child. This cabin is equipped with six emergency exits. Please take the time to locate the one nearest you.

Announcement Number 5

Good morning. This is Captain Huang Wen-Chu speaking. We hope you're enjoying the flight. We are flying at an altitude of 35,000 feet, with light winds and clear skies. For passengers sitting on the left—if you look out your window, you can see the lights of Tokyo. We're expecting to arrive on schedule, and the weather in Taipei should be good.

Announcement Number 6

We are beginning our initial descent into the Taipei area. The temperature is a comfortable 26 degrees Celsius—that's around 78 degrees Fahrenheit—and the skies are pretty clear. If you need information about a connecting flight, be sure to check the overhead monitors in the airport terminal. Please put your seats and tray tables in an upright and locked position and make sure all carry-on luggage is safely stowed under the seat in front of you or in the overhead compartments. We should be landing in Taipei in approximately 10 minutes. We thank you for flying UPAir and hope you have had a pleasant trip.

UNIT 22

EXERCISE 7 (page 364)

INTERVIEWER: Welcome to "Meet the Candidates." Tonight we are talking to Yuki Tamari, who, as most of you know, is running for student council president. Welcome, Yuki.

YUKI: Thanks, Daniel. It's a pleasure to be here.

INTERVIEWER: What will you do first if you become our student council president?

YUKI: Students don't think the student council is listening to them. That attitude is very widespread. And that's why, if I'm elected, I'm going to improve communications with students. I want to be available to students and hear what they have to say.

INTERVIEWER: How do you plan to do that?

YUKI: First, by a lot of personal contact. If I'm elected, I'll have informal lunch meetings with students. In the evenings, I'll be at the Student Union and other places where students meet. Unless I talk to a lot of students personally, I won't be able to hear their concerns. That has been the problem of our student council for a while.

INTERVIEWER: What else do you have in mind?

YUKI: Again, I want to talk about communication. If I become president, I'm going to appoint a committee to improve the student council's website. A lot more information should be available to students. Teacher evaluations, for example. If we publish evaluations on the Web, it'll give the students more insight, and it'll be much easier for them to choose their courses. The email addresses of student council representatives should also be on our website. Students can't participate in student government unless they know how to contact their representatives.

INTERVIEWER: Do you have any plans for other student services?

YUKI: I have a lot of plans, but I'll just mention one right now. If I become president, I'll try to get the college to provide a bus service between the airport and the college at the beginning and end of every semester. It won't be free, but if students use the bus, they won't have to pay those very expensive taxi fares. This will also be a much friendlier welcome for international students when they arrive here for their first semester.

INTERVIEWER: What about educational issues?

YUKI: The college should offer more majors. A lot of students are interested in mass communications, for example, but there's no mass communications major. International studies is another important major that the college doesn't offer. If I'm elected, I'm going to encourage the administration to develop more major areas of study. Many students will take these courses if we offer them.

INTERVIEWER: College tuition has been increasing very quickly. Is there anything the student council can do about that?

YUKI: This is a state college, but our tuition has been rising too. Unless we can keep tuition costs down, a lot of good students aren't going to be able to afford a college education. If I'm elected, I will ask our student council to create a committee to meet with state lawmakers. Many state colleges have committees that do this. If I get support for this idea, we will be able to discuss tuition costs with the state government.

INTERVIEWER: Thanks, Yuki. You have a very ambitious platform. Good luck at the polls tomorrow.

YUKI: Thank you. I'm wearing my lucky charm, so I'm going to win!

INTERVIEWER: Oh! Are you superstitious?

YUKI: Not really. I believe if I prepare well for something, I'll do fine. As for my lucky charm? I figure it can't hurt!

UNIT 23

EXERCISE 7 (page 379)

Once there was a young girl named Cindy who was very good at math, sports, and languages. She wanted to be a scientist when she grew up so she could help many people. One day, while Cindy was playing soccer in the park with her friends, the ball flew into the woods. She looked and looked for the ball, but she couldn't see it anywhere.

"I wish I could find that soccer ball," Cindy muttered angrily. At that she heard a strange sound. "Ree-beep. Ree-beep. Over here! Your ball is over here." She looked in the direction of the sound, and she saw the soccer ball in the middle of some bushes. Next to the ball was a large toad.

"Thanks for finding the ball," she told the toad. "You're welcome," said the toad. "But before I give it to you, you have to grant me one wish." Cindy started to run toward the ball, but she couldn't get through the bushes. There was some sort of magic spell around them. "What's your wish?" she asked the toad. "Please hurry up. We want to finish our game."

"I wish that you would marry me." "Yuk!" screamed Cindy. "You're a toad. I'm a girl. I can't marry you." "I'm not really a toad," he replied. "I'm an enchanted prince. I'm under a spell. If you married me, you would break the spell. I would become a handsome prince. And if I were a prince, you would be my princess."

Cindy thought about the princesses she had read about in magazines. "I don't think so, Toad," Cindy told him. "You see, I plan to become a scientist and help a lot of people when I grow up. If I were your princess, I'd have to spend a lot of time having my photograph taken and going to ceremonies. If I did that, I'd be too busy to study science. But thanks anyway." Cindy turned to leave the woods.

The toad was furious. "Wait!" he shouted. "If you really wanted to help people, you wouldn't leave me here in these bushes." Cindy stopped. "If you give me back the soccer ball, I'll try to help you. But no wedding." The toad agreed, and Cindy picked up the ball.

"So, who put you under the spell?" she asked.

"A magician turned me into a toad. He also gave me some magic powers. He keeps telling me that if I used my powers properly, I'd find a way to become a prince again. But so far, nothing has worked."

"Can you grant wishes?" asked Cindy. "Just one," responded the toad.

"Then I wish you would turn me into a scientist right now. If I were a scientist, I would find a way to turn you back into a prince."

The frog consented, and in a flash, Cindy and the toad found themselves in a large, modern laboratory. Cindy thought hard and worked long hours. At last she succeeded in turning the toad back into a prince. The prince became a good king, and Cindy worked hard in her laboratory. Her discoveries helped many people.

EXERCISE 8 (page 380)

1. **A:** I want to give one big party this year.
   B: If I were you, I wouldn't give it during the holidays.
2. **A:** Karen's soccer team has a big game today.
   B: I know. I wish she'd play.
3. **A:** Is Don coming over?
   B: Probably not. If he came, he wouldn't stay for dinner.
4. **A:** She always looks upset. Does she tell you what's wrong?
   B: No. But if she told me, I'd be able to help.
5. **A:** I hate to keep reminding Debra about her homework.
   B: If you didn't remind her, she wouldn't remember by herself.
6. **A:** The kids don't read enough.
   B: If I were you, I'd read to them.

UNIT 24

EXERCISE 7 (page 394)

Conversation 1

A: Sorry I'm late. The train doors closed just as I got to the platform.

B: Oh, that was bad timing.

A: Actually it was very *good* timing!

B: *Good* timing? What do you mean?

A: Well, it turns out that the train was in an accident just five minutes after it left the station! If I had been on it, I could have been injured—or worse!

Conversation 2

A: So, how did you become an English teacher?

B: It was really just by chance. I was living in Germany and a friend of mine was teaching at this language school. One day she got sick and couldn't go in. The director of the school was desperate and called me to ask if I could teach that afternoon.

A: But you had never taught before.

B: Right. I guess he thought that just because I spoke English I could teach! Well, anyway, I went in, taught the class, and really enjoyed it. Then I went on to graduate school to get training.

A: You mean if your friend hadn't been sick that day, you wouldn't have become a teacher?

B: That's right. I don't think I would ever have thought of it!

Conversation 3

A: This is a great apartment. How did you find it?

B: Well, I'd been looking for an apartment for months—searching online, reading the paper, asking friends. But nothing. Then one day, I was trying to find a bookstore and I got totally lost. All of a sudden, I passed this building and it had a For Rent sign on it. I rang the manager's bell, saw the apartment, and decided on the spot to take it.

A: That was lucky!

B: Yeah. If I hadn't gotten lost I'd never have found this place.

Conversation 4

A: How was the movie last night?

B: It was great.

A: Oh, I wish I had gone with you.

B: Why didn't you? You would have liked it.

A: I wanted to. But I had to study for my history test. If I hadn't had the test, I definitely would have gone.

Conversation 5

A: Phew. I can't believe how lucky I am.

B: Why? What happened?

A: I lost my wallet on the train yesterday.

B: How did that happen?

A: I'm not sure. I guess it fell out of my pocket. Anyhow, I was really upset. There was a lot of money in it plus a couple of credit cards.

B: What did you do?

A: When I got home, there was a message on my machine from the police. Someone had found it and turned it in to them.

B: Wow! That's great. What would you have done if you hadn't gotten the call. Would *you* have called the police?

A: I might have.

Conversation 6

A: So how did you and Marla end up owning this café?

B: Well, one day I got laid off from my job at the bank.

A: Oh, really? You worked at a bank?

B: Yep. I worked at that big bank right across the street. Anyway, the day I was laid off, I was pretty depressed. I didn't want to go home and tell Marla right away, so I walked around the neighborhood looking for a place to sit and have a cup of coffee. But I couldn't find one.

A: That's funny. This is the perfect spot for a neighborhood café.

B: Well, that's what I thought too. So when I got home, I said to Marla, "Let's open a café across from the bank."

A: So you did! And it's great—I love this place. Could you have opened this place if you hadn't lost your job?

B: Never! We love doing this. But if they hadn't fired me, I'd never have thought of it. I often think about what we would have missed.

EXERCISE 8 (page 395)

1. **A:** Did Mike go to the movie with you?
   B: No, but, if his cousin hadn't been in town, he would've gone.
2. **A:** Did you get to the theater by 8:00?
   B: Well, if I had taken a different train, I couldn't have done it.
3. **A:** What's the matter? You look upset.
   B: I wish I'd invited Jason to go with us.
4. **A:** Did you like the movie?
   B: Not really. If I'd understood more of the English, I could've enjoyed it.
5. **A:** I called you at 11:00, but there was no answer.
   B: Well, I would've been home if I hadn't walked.
6: **A:** What would you have done instead?
   B: I would've taken a taxi.

UNIT 25

EXERCISE 6 (page 411)

Conversation 1

ALEX: Hi, Lisa. This is Alex. Let's have dinner together Saturday night. I know you don't like to eat meat, so I found this great new vegetarian restaurant on the West Side.

LISA: I'd really love to, Alex, but my parents are in town for the weekend. I want to spend some time with them on Saturday night. Let's do it another weekend, OK?

Conversation 2

Lisa: So, what do you do in your spare time, Ben?

Ben: I like to go to the gym when I get a chance. I usually work out about three times a week.

Lisa: Oh really? So do I. I'm even taking aerobics on Sunday, and I love it. I never miss a class.

Conversation 3

Lisa: Hi, Mark. This is Lisa. How's the report coming?

Mark: Pretty well. Let's see . . . Today's Monday. I'll have it ready for you tomorrow morning.

Lisa: Gee, Mark. I really need to have it today.

Mark: Oh? What's the rush?

Lisa: Our weekly staff meeting is Monday afternoon. I need to have the report before the meeting.

Mark: I wasn't aware that the meeting was this afternoon. I thought it was Tuesday. OK. I'll do my best.

Conversation 4

Lisa: Dinner looks absolutely wonderful, Chris.

Chris: Try the meat sauce. I want to know what you think.

Lisa: Mmm. I love it. It's just delicious. How did you make it?

Chris: Oh, it's an old family recipe. But I can give it to you if you like.

Lisa: Yes, please do. I'd love to make this sauce.

UNIT 26

EXERCISE 6 (page 428)

The weather service has issued a winter storm warning. About a foot of snow has fallen in our area since early this morning, and more snow is expected during the day. All schools closed by ten o'clock. We advise students, teachers, and other employees to return home immediately. Schools may remain closed tomorrow, so keep listening for further reports.

Snow and high winds are causing dangerous conditions on the roads. Drivers must drive slowly and with a great deal of caution to avoid accidents. If possible, everyone should avoid driving until conditions improve. If you *must* drive, you should take along extra clothing and blankets. You should also make certain you have plenty of gas.

Many government offices will close today. Libraries are closing at 1 P.M. However, post offices will stay open until five o'clock. All government offices will be closed tomorrow. Many businesses in the area are also closing early because of the storm.

Banks are closing at noon to allow employees time to get home safely. Most supermarkets and gas stations will remain open until this evening. You are advised to stock up on food and other necessary items since driving could be difficult for several days.

UNIT 27

EXERCISE 5 (page 440)

Ann: Hi, Juan. How are you doing?

Juan: Oh, well, actually not that great. I've been having a lot of headaches lately. In fact, I just got back from a headache clinic.

Ann: Really? What did they tell you?

Juan: Let's see . . . They told me to keep a journal and monitor the headaches—you know, write down when I get a headache and what I was doing before I got it.

Ann: Did they tell you how to prevent them?

Juan: They made some suggestions. First, they said to get regular exercise. I think I'm going to start running every day. Oh, and they also told me to get eight hours' sleep. They said that fatigue causes headaches, and I've had insomnia lately.

Ann: That's interesting. You work at a sleep clinic and you haven't been getting enough sleep. Do you think it's because you've been working the night shift?

Juan: I think so. Working at night really interferes with my sleep.

Ann: That must be hard. Did they give you some painkillers? Some people really need medicine for the pain.

Juan: No, not yet. They told me not to take painkillers right now. If the headaches persist, they'll prescribe them. But they said to try to treat the headaches without medication first.

Ann: That sounds good. Did they recommend any natural remedies?

Juan: Uhmm . . . they said to use an ice pack.

Ann: That's a good idea. Did they say anything about massaging around your eyes?

Juan: They didn't tell me to do that. Does it help?

Ann: I think so. It works for me. Why don't you try it? What else did they say about preventing headaches?

Juan: Oh, they said not to eat three big meals a day. They told me to eat several small meals instead.

Ann: Do you have to avoid certain foods?

Juan: Yeah. Chocolate. They said not to eat chocolate.

ANN: How about cheese? I've heard that cheese can cause headaches.

JUAN: They didn't tell me to avoid cheese. Hey, you seem to know a lot about this.

ANN: Oh, I've been going to a headache clinic for a long time. Let me show you how to massage around your eyes. That really helps me.

EXERCISE 6 (page 441)

1. **A:** What did the doctor say?
   B: She told me not to eat a lot of cheese.
2. **A:** What time are you going to the sleep clinic?
   B: Well, they asked me to arrive before 8:00.
3. **A:** How can I remember my dreams?
   B: I'd advise you to sleep for a long time, if possible.
4. **A:** Is Ella jogging with us today?
   B: No. Her doctor told her not to exercise in the morning.
5. **A:** This article says that vinegar is good for a sunburn.
   B: Really? My mother always said not to use that.
6. **A:** Did you tell your boss you needed a new schedule?
   B: Yes. I asked him to put me on the night shift.

UNIT 28

EXERCISE 5 (page 455)

INTERVIEWER: Your resume is very impressive, Ms. . . . uhmm . . .Tsourikov.

TSOURIKOV: That's Tsourikov.

INTERVIEWER: Tsourikov. So, tell me, Ms. Tsourikov, why did you leave your job at Q & L Enterprises?

TSOURIKOV: Well, I had worked there for more than 15 years. Two years ago, I went back to school and got my degree in accounting. I want a position that uses my new skills, and there's nothing available at Q & L right now and no potential openings in the near future.

INTERVIEWER: Fifteen years. Hmm. That's a pretty long time. How old are you?

TSOURIKOV: Let's just say that I'm old enough to have a lot of valuable experience and still young enough to bring a lot of energy to the job.

INTERVIEWER: I'm sure you are. Are you married?

TSOURIKOV: Er, yes. I'm married and I have two grown children.

INTERVIEWER: I see. What do you know about this company? I mean, why do you want to work for us?

TSOURIKOV: I know you're one of the three leading producers of household appliances and that your products have a reputation for excellence. I would

like to be part of your company, and I know I could make a significant contribution.

INTERVIEWER: Tsourikov. That's an unusual name. What nationality are you?

TSOURIKOV: Well, I took my husband's last name . . .

INTERVIEWER: Oh, yes. What does your husband do, Mrs. Tsourikov?

TSOURIKOV: Tsourikov. He's a data processor.

INTERVIEWER: Do you owe anyone any money?

TSOURIKOV: Uh . . . We owe some money on our credit cards . . . and uhmm, we do still have a mortgage on our home . . .

INTERVIEWER: OK . . . Tell me, what computer programs are you familiar with?

TSOURIKOV: I've used Word, Filemaker Pro, and Excel.

INTERVIEWER: Have you ever been arrested?

TSOURIKOV: Excuse me?

INTERVIEWER: Have you ever been arrested?

TSOURIKOV: Er, no. Why do you ask?

INTERVIEWER: Just checking. We have to be very careful who we hire these days . . . Why don't you tell me a little more about yourself. Do you consider yourself successful?

TSOURIKOV: Yes. I was very successful at my last job, as I'm sure my employer would tell you. I always received very high evaluations.

INTERVIEWER: Good. How tall are you, Mrs. Tsourikov?

TSOURIKOV: How tall am I? I'm sorry, but before I answer that question, can you tell me how it specifically relates to this job?

INTERVIEWER: Yes? . . . Uhmm, would you excuse me a moment? I have to take this call.

UNIT 29

EXERCISE 6 (page 471)

HOST: Good morning. You're listening to WYAK talk radio. I'm your host, Emma Collins, and our topic this morning is tipping—when, who, where, and how much. For those of you who've just tuned in, we've been talking to Alicia Marksen, who owns and operates a travel agency. Ms. Marksen is now ready to answer any and all of your questions about tipping. Caller number 1, you're on the air.

CALLER 1: I'm from Norway, and I'm visiting the United States for a few weeks. Your tipping customs here are pretty unfamiliar to me. Where I come from, restaurants add a service charge to the bill. They just add an additional 10% to the total, so we usually don't leave a tip. Can you tell me how much to tip in a U.S. restaurant?

HOST: Caller number 2, go ahead.

CALLER 2: I don't take taxis very much, so when I do take a taxi, I always have a problem with the tip. I never know exactly how much to tip the driver. Sometimes I think I overtip. You know, I end up giving the driver too much.

HOST: Caller number 3, you're on the air.

CALLER 3: I just got to this country, and I've been eating out a lot in restaurants where, you know, you don't pay the server, you pay at the cashier instead. My problem is this—I'm never sure where to leave the tip. I don't know if I should leave it on the table or try to find my server. Could you help clarify this for me?

HOST: Caller number 4, you're on the air.

CALLER 4: I'm going to France on business, and I'll probably go to the theater. Someone told me that it's the custom to tip in a French theater. Can you tell me who I'm supposed to tip?

HOST: Caller number 5, please ask your question.

CALLER 5: I just had an awful experience in a restaurant. Our server was slow, forgot things, and on top of it all, wasn't even polite. Please tell me what to do if I don't like the service in a restaurant.

HOST: Caller number 6, please go ahead.

CALLER 6: I recently started going to a hairdresser. I know I'm supposed to tip the person who washes my hair, but when I'm ready to leave, she's often busy with another customer and I don't want to interrupt. Besides, her hands are all wet! Can you tell me where I should leave the tip?

HOST: Caller number 7, what's your question?

CALLER 7: I'm going to be traveling a lot for my new job. I need reliable cultural information for all the places I'm going to be visiting. For example, I wonder how to find information on tipping practices before I travel.

HOST: We have time for just one more question. Caller number 8, please go ahead.

CALLER 8: My roommate and I are exchange students from Pakistan. We need to find out how much to tip when we order takeout. It's kind of urgent! We just ordered a pizza.

STUDENT BOOK ANSWER KEY

In this answer key, where the short or contracted form is given, the full or long form is also correct (unless the purpose of the exercise is to practice the short or contracted form). Where the full or long form is given, the contracted form is also correct.

UNIT 1 (pages 2–11)

AFTER YOU READ

A. 1. a **2.** c **3.** b **4.** c **5.** b

B. 1. False. She is now in Canada.
   2. True
   3. False. In Russia, she calls her teacher by his first and middle name.
   4. False. Jorge is in Canada.
   5. True
   6. False. He's not going to change his first name.

EXERCISE 1

Are you living or working in a foreign country? Do you worry about making a mistake with someone's name or title? You are right to be concerned. Naming systems vary a lot from culture to culture, and people tend to have very strong feelings about their names. Well, now help is available in the form of an interesting and practical book by Terri Morrison. *Kiss, Bow, or Shake Hands: How to Do Business in Sixty Countries* gives information on cross-cultural naming customs and much more. And it's not just for businesspeople. In today's shrinking world, people are traveling abroad in record numbers. They're flying to all corners of the world, and they're exchanging emails with people they've never actually met. So, if you're doing business abroad or making friends across cultures, I recommend this book.

EXERCISE 2

A. 2. does . . . come
   3. means
   4. do . . . do
   5. sell
   6. 'm working
   7. owns
   8. 're joking
   9. guess
   10. influence

B. 1. 'm trying
   2. Do . . . know
   3. mean
   4. calls
   5. 's always winning OR always wins

C. 1. hear
   2. are expecting
   3. 're looking for
   4. do . . . think of
   5. sounds
   6. do . . . spell

D. 1. wants
   2. smells
   3. don't drink
   4. is boiling
   5. does . . . boil
   6. boils

EXERCISE 3

Hi, everybody. ~~I write~~ *I'm writing* this note to introduce myself to you, my classmates in English 047.

Our teacher ~~is wanting~~ *wants* a profile from each of us. At first I was confused by this assignment because my English dictionary ~~is defining~~ *defines* profile as "a side view of someone's head." I thought, "Why does she ~~wants~~ *want* that? She sees my head every day!" Then I saw the next definition: "a short description of a person's life and character." OK, then. Here is my profile:

My name is Peter Holzer. Some of my friends ~~are calling~~ *call* me Pay-Ha because that is how my initials actually ~~sounding~~ *sound* in German. I am ~~study~~ *studying* English here in Miami because I want to attend the Aspen Institute of International Leadership in Colorado.

Maybe ~~are you~~ *you are* asking yourself, "Why ~~he wants~~ *does he want* to leave Miami for Colorado?" The answer is: snow! I ~~am coming~~ *come* from Austria, so I love to ski. It's part of my identity. In fact, my nickname in my family is Blitz (lightning) because ~~always~~ I am *always* trying to improve my speed.

EXERCISE 4

A. a. "Sunshine"
   b. Alex
   c. Red
   d. Karl
   e. "Bozo"
   f. Bertha and Vicki

B. 2. hair
   3. doesn't have
   4. doesn't match
   5. doesn't recognize
   6. mother and daughter

EXERCISE 5

B. 1. B: She often drinks coffee, but at the moment she's drinking tea.

2. B: I'm not making dinner. I'm eating dinner.

3. B: I often study at home, but these days I'm studying at the library.

4. B: She normally wears red, but right now she's wearing black.

5. B: They usually call him Bill, but today they're calling him William.

6. B: He doesn't speak Spanish, but he reads it very well.

7. B: He generally takes the bus, but this week he's taking the train.

EXERCISES 6–7

Answers will vary.

UNIT 2 (pages 13–24)

AFTER YOU READ

A. 1. research
2. couple
3. opponent
4. recover
5. influential
6. cover

B. 1. during
2. after
3. after
4. Before
5. before
6. during
7. during
8. after

EXERCISE 1

2. T   **3.** F   **4.** F   **5.** F   **6.** T

EXERCISE 2

A. 2. were
3. doing
4. were dancing
5. Did
6. get
7. gave
8. Did
9. bring
10. fell
11. bumped
12. found

B. 1. were
2. doing
3. sprained
4. playing
5. were pretending
6. hurt
7. was hitting

C. 1. Were
2. crying
3. did
4. know
5. wasn't crying
6. came
7. Did you ever see
8. was watching
9. was thinking
10. recovered

EXERCISE 3

A. 2. were smiling
3. was watching
4. looked
5. did . . . meet
6. didn't come
7. was covering
8. changed

B. 1. found
2. was surfing
3. did . . . become
4. was reading
5. decided
6. wanted
7. was studying
8. started

C. 1. Did . . . surprise
2. came
3. was watching
4. knocked
5. ended
6. had
7. were eating
8. asked

EXERCISE 4

1. She met Paul when she moved to Australia. OR When she moved to Australia, she met Paul.

2. She got married while she was studying medicine. OR While she was studying medicine, she got married. OR She was studying medicine when she got married. OR When she got married, she was studying medicine.

3. She was living in Australia when she got married. OR She got married when / while she was living in Australia. OR While she was living in Australia, she got married.

4. She got her first job when she had her medical degree. OR She had her medical degree when she got her first job.

5. She was practicing medicine at Lenox Hospital when she had her son. OR When she had her son, she was practicing medicine at Lenox Hospital. OR She had her son while she was practicing medicine at Lenox Hospital. OR While she was practicing medicine at Lenox Hospital, she had her son.

6. She wrote a book while she was working at Lenox Hospital. OR While she was working at Lenox Hospital, she wrote a book. OR When she wrote a book, she was working at Lenox Hospital. OR While she was working at Lenox Hospital, she was writing a book. OR While she was writing a book, she was working at Lenox Hospital.

7. She did a TV interview when she finished her book. OR When she finished her book, she did a TV interview.

8. She left her job when her book became a success. OR When her book became a success, she left her job.

EXERCISE 5

I was writing chapter two of my new book when I
~~was thinking~~ *thought* of you. The last time I saw you, you
~~walked~~ *were walking* down the aisle to marry Dave. That was more
than two years ago. How are you? How is married
life?

A lot has happened in my life since that time.
While I ~~worked~~ *was working* at Lenox Hospital, I began writing.
In 2004, I ~~was publishing~~ *published* a book on women's health
issues. It was quite successful here in Australia. I
even got interviewed on TV. When I ~~was getting~~ *got* a
contract to write a second book, I decided to quit my
hospital job to write full-time. That's what I'm doing
now. Paul, too, has had a career change. While I was
writing, he was attending law school. He ~~was getting~~ *got*
his degree last summer.

Oh, the reason I thought of you while I ~~wrote~~ *was writing* was
because the chapter was about rashes. Remember
the time you ~~were getting~~ *got* that terrible rash? We
~~rode~~ *were riding* our bikes when you ~~were falling~~ *fell* into a patch of
poison ivy. And that's how you met Dave! When you
~~were falling~~ *fell* off the bike, he offered to give us a ride
home. Life's funny, isn't it?

Well, please write soon, and send my love to Dave.
I miss you!

EXERCISE 6

A. c
B. 2. True
   3. False. They were covering a story about the
      new murals on Market Street.
   4. False. They didn't have an appointment. or
      They ran into a coffee shop when it started to
      rain.
   5. True
   6. False. They got married a month later.

EXERCISE 7

B. 1. A: What did you do when the rain started?
     B: When it started to rain, we went inside.
   2. A: What did you do during the storm?
     B: While it was raining, we were talking.
   3. A: What did you do after the storm?
     B: When the storm was over, we left.
   4. A: What happened while you were leaving?
     B: While we were leaving, the sun came out.
   5. A: What did you do when you got home?
     B: When we got home, we turned on the TV.

6. A: When did you get the phone call?
   B: While I was exercising, the phone rang.

EXERCISES 8–10

Answers will vary.

UNIT 3 (pages 26–36)

AFTER YOU READ
A. 1. a   **2.** b   **3.** a   **4.** c   **5.** b   **6.** a
B. Finished: 2, 5, 6
   Unfinished: 1, 3, 4

EXERCISE 1

A.

Nancy Board and Erden Eruc of Seattle,
Washington, have always loved the outdoors, so
Alaska was a natural choice to celebrate their
wedding. Nancy flew there for the June 7 ceremony,
but Erden started in February and rode his bike.
Then he climbed Mt. Denali. Unfortunately, he ran
into some bad weather, so the historic event was a
week late. Nancy understood. She herself has been
doing extreme sports for years.

Erden, an engineer, has earned degrees from
universities in Turkey and the United States. He has
been climbing since he was 11. In 2003, he left his
job to begin an around-the-world trip powered only
by human effort. Since then, he has been climbing,
hiking, biking, and rowing his way across several
continents. So far, he has climbed Mount Denali in
Alaska, and he has rowed across two oceans (the
Atlantic and the Pacific).

Nancy, a psychotherapist, recently founded a
new business in Seattle. She and her co-founder
have been using their outdoor experience to teach
leadership skills to women in Australia, Canada,
South Africa, and the U.S.

B. 2. F   **5.** ?   **8.** ?
   3. T   **6.** T   **9.** ?
   4. F   **7.** T   **10.** T

EXERCISE 2

Circled verbs
   2. got
   3. appeared
   4. sold out
   5. became
   6. have visited
   7. started
   8. has been keeping
   9. bought
  10. Have you found

EXERCISE 3

A. **2.** bought
   3. was
   4. took
   5. changed
   6. has been shooting OR has shot
   7. has competed
   8. won

B. **1.** began
   2. got
   3. hasn't stopped
   4. has become
   5. joined
   6. have been performing OR have performed
   7. has given

C. **1.** found
   2. has been working OR has worked
   3. saved
   4. got
   5. began
   6. has been buying OR has bought
   7. has been trading OR (has) traded
   8. has found

EXERCISE 4

have been doing
I ~~am doing~~ adventure sports since I got engaged,
joined
and this year I've ~~been joining~~ a climbing club.
have been following
All the members ~~followed~~ your fantastic trip on
the *Around-n-Over* website since last January, but I
haven't ~~been~~ written to you before. I have a few
climbed
questions. I know you~~'ve been climbing have been~~
~~climbing~~ Mt. Erciyes in Turkey many years ago.
Will you climb it again on this project? Also, you've
traveled OR *been traveling*
~~traveling~~ to different continents. How have you
communicated with people? Did you study other
saw
languages before your trip? Last month, I~~'ve seen~~ an
article about your project in *Hooked on the Outdoors*
become
Magazine. You've ~~became~~ famous! Have you received
started
many emails since you ~~start~~ your project? Thanks for
answering my questions, and good luck!

EXERCISE 5

A. **2.** got
   3. 've read
   4. 've been calling . . . haven't gotten
   5. had to
   6. Did you look

B. **Items checked:**
   read skydiving guide
   stop mail for two weeks

EXERCISE 6

B. **1.** Did you hear
   2. Has he taught
   3. did you meet
   4. Have you tried
   5. Did he graduate
   6. Did he move
   7. Have you known

EXERCISES 7–9

Answers will vary.

UNIT 4 (pages 38–53)

AFTER YOU READ

A. **1.** transformed
   2. enthusiastic
   3. conducted
   4. ethnic
   5. participated
   6. contract

B. **1.** He started taking music lessons.
   2. He turned four.
   3. He became part of El Sistema.
   4. Music saved him.
   5. He became conductor of the Simón Bolívar National Youth Orchestra.
   6. He became music director of the Los Angeles Philharmonic.

EXERCISE 1

2. ?   **4.** F   **6.** T
3. ?   **5.** T   **7.** F

EXERCISE 2

2. had already begun
3. had not yet begun
4. had already become
5. had not yet gotten
6. had already won
7. had already moved

EXERCISE 3

2. **A:** Had she started rehearsing . . .
   B: Yes, she had.
3. **A:** Had she eaten . . .
   B: Yes, she had.
4. **A:** Had she had . . .
   B: No, she hadn't.
5. **A:** Had she shopped . . .
   B: No, she hadn't.
6. **A:** Had she done . . .
   B: Yes, she had.
7. **A:** Had she ordered . . .
   B: Yes, she had.
8. **A:** Had she eaten . . .
   B: No, she hadn't.

EXERCISE 4

2. had been studying
3. had . . . been observing
4. had been hoping
5. had been playing
6. had been winning
7. had been waiting
8. had been treating
9. had not been competing

EXERCISE 5

2. Had she been living in Los Angeles before (OR when) she signed a contract with the L.A. Philharmonic?
3. Had she been practicing long before (OR when) she gave her first solo performance?
4. Had she been competing a long time when (OR before) she won first prize in the Paganini Violin Competition?
5. How long had she been playing when (OR before) her bow broke?
6. Had the newspaper reporters been following her when (OR before) they took pictures of her in front of her home?
7. How long had they been dating before (OR when) she married the conductor Lorenzo Russo?
8. Where had they been living when (OR before) Ling and her husband moved to Rome?

EXERCISE 6

2. had been teaching
3. had been observing
4. had come up
5. had shown up
6. had received
7. had helped
8. had been
9. had . . . been
10. had been working
11. had been living
12. had . . . arrested
13. had been hoping

EXERCISE 7

2. I had been performing with a group at college . . . my professor recommended me.
3. . . . I had been working there for only a month, the company closed.
4. . . . City Orchestra called me, I had been teaching in a community music program.
5. I had almost decided to stop performing . . . I loved working with those kids.
6. We had been planning an orchestra for the kids . . . I left.

EXERCISE 8

Measha Brueggergosman was born in 1977 in New Brunswick, Canada. Her first-grade teacher urged Measha's parents to give her music lessons. They did, and by age fifteen, she ~~had been deciding~~ *had decided* on a singing career. Not growing up in a large cultural center, she didn't have the chance to attend concerts or the opera. However, by the time she enrolled at the University of Toronto, she ^*had been* listening to classical music on the radio for years and she ~~participated~~ *had participated* OR *had been participating* in her church's music program since she was a child.

After receiving her degree in Toronto, Brueggergosman moved to Düsseldorf, Germany to study. By age 25, she had been performing internationally for several years, and had won a number of important prizes. One enthusiastic judge said she'd never ~~been meeting~~ *met* so young a singer with such perfect vocal control.

By her thirtieth birthday, Brueggergosman ~~has~~ *had* become both a classical music sensation[2] and a popular celebrity. A diva with a Facebook fan club, she ~~had been developed~~ *had developed* OR *had been developing* her own unique fashion. She had also ~~appearing~~ *appeared* OR *been appearing* on popular TV shows. Things had been going along fine when, in June 2009, she experienced a health crisis that led to emergency surgery. She had to cancel many performances, but she recovered in time to sing at the *Bienvenido Dudamel!* concert in LA four months later. When she took the stage at the Hollywood Bowl, it was clear why the soprano ~~had been made~~ *had made* OR *had been making* such an impression on critics and audiences for the last ten years. They had all fallen in love with her style as well as her beautiful voice. Brava Brueggergosman!

EXERCISE 9

A.
2. We'd
3. He'd
4. I'd
5. I hadn't

B.
2. False. They became good friends after the concert.
3. False. Klaus had never seen Dudamel conduct before the concert in Caracas.
4. True
5. True

EXERCISES 10–12

Answers will vary.

EXERCISE 13

Possible answer:

By six o'clock, the drummer had joined the violinists.

EXERCISE 14

Answers will vary.

1

2. don't know	**16.** had been
3. thought	**17.** was pretending
4. judged	**18.** got
5. spoke	**19.** laughed
6. said	**20.** made
7. seemed	**21.** stopped
8. didn't care	**22.** have been carrying
9. wanted	OR have carried
10. was	**23.** (have been) expressing
11. read	OR (have) expressed
12. pretended	**24.** have prepared OR have
13. came	been preparing
14. was reading	**25.** am applying
15. had . . . seen	**26.** feel

2

2. Since that day   **3.** Now

3

Paragraph Section	Information	Form of the Verb
Topic Sentence • what the writer is like now	*a serious student*	*simple present*
Body of the Paragraph • habits and feelings during the phase	*thought about clothes and makeup; spoke in stereotyped phrases; judged people by appearances and possessions; didn't want people to know she was interested in school; read the newspaper secretly; pretended to be unprepared for tests*	*simple past*
• the event that ended the phase	*brother laughed at her*	*simple past*
• behavior since the phase ended	*has stopped trying to hide her real interests; has carried news magazines proudly; has expressed opinions in class; has prepared openly for tests*	*present perfect; present perfect progressive*
Conclusion • the results of the change	*is applying for college; feels proud of being a change good student*	*present progressive and simple present*

4–7

Answers will vary.

UNIT 5 (pages 60–77)

AFTER YOU READ

A. 1. a   **2.** b   **3.** c   **4.** b   **5.** a
B. Now: 1, 3, 5
    In the Future: 2, 4, 6

EXERCISE 1

A.
HAPIN: Nouvella! It's nice to see you. <u>Are you presenting</u> a paper today?
EON: Hi, Will! Yes. In fact my talk <u>starts</u> at two o'clock.
HAPIN: Oh. I think <u>I'll go</u>. What do you plan to talk about? <u>Will you be discussing</u> robots?
EON: Yes. <u>I'm focusing</u> on personal robots for household work. My talk is called Creative Uses of Home Robots.
HAPIN: I want one of those! But seriously, you promised me an interview on personal robots. <u>Will you be getting</u> some free time in the next few weeks?
EON: I'm not sure. <u>I'll get back</u> to you, OK?
HAPIN: Great! Where's your son, by the way? Is he with you?
EON: No. Rocky stays in Denver with his grandparents in the summer. <u>I'm going to visit</u> him right after the conference. <u>He'll be</u> ten years old in a few days. I can't believe it!
HAPIN: It's his birthday, huh? Here, take this little model of the flying car for him.
EON: Oh, <u>he's going to love</u> this! Thanks, Will. So, what are you working on these days?

(continued on next page)

HAPIN: Well, *Futurist Magazine* just published my story on cities of the future. And I'm still with the World Future Association. In fact, I'm speaking at a news conference next month about the space elevator.

EON: That will be exciting! Good luck with it!

B. 2. starts: Schedule

3. 'll go: Quick Decision

4. Will you be discussing: Plan

5. 'm focusing: Plan

6. Will you be getting: Plan

7. 'll get back: Promise

8. 'm going to visit: Plan

9. 'll be: Fact

10. 's going to love: Prediction

11. 'm speaking: Plan

12. will be: Prediction

EXERCISE 2

2. it's going to rain

3. I'll talk

4. I'll call

5. I'm going

6. I'm sending

7. I'm giving

8. will you be, lands, I'll see

9. Are we going, you're going to like

EXERCISE 3

3. won't be presenting

4. 'm going to be attending

5. are . . . going to be doing

6. are . . . going to be helping

7. will be improving

8. 'll be cooking

9. 'll be performing

10. are . . . going to be buying

11. No, I won't

12. Is . . . going to be changing

13. Yes it is

14. 'll be selling

15. 'm going to be testing

16. Will . . . be driving

EXERCISE 4

3. At 10:05 he'll be (OR he's going to be) dusting.

4. At 11:05 he won't be (OR he's not going to be) doing laundry. He'll be (OR he's going to be) shopping for food.

5. At 12:05 he won't be (OR he's not going to be) making lunch. He'll be (OR he's going to be) doing laundry.

6. At 1:05 he'll be (OR he's going to be) recycling the garbage.

7. At 2:05 he'll be (OR he's going to be) paying bills.

8. At 3:05 he'll be (OR he's going to be) giving Dr. Eon a massage.

9. At 5:05 he'll be (OR he's going to be) making dinner.

10. At 6:05 he won't be (OR he's not going to be) playing cards with Rocky. He'll be (OR he's going to be) playing chess.

EXERCISE 5

2. will be (OR 's going to be) lifting

3. is

4. 're enjoying (OR enjoy)

5. is going to be (OR will be) pointing out

6. know

7. 'll be (OR 're going to be) getting ready

8. unpack

9. 'll be (OR 're going to be) joining

10. 'll be (OR 're going to be) watching

11. are relaxing (OR relax)

12. 'll be (OR 're going to be) putting on

13. won't be (OR aren't going to be) thinking

EXERCISE 6

Your class starts in ten minutes, but you're stuck in traffic. Don't panic. With just a press of a button, your car will ~~lifts~~ *lift* off the ground, and you'll be on your way to school. No bad roads, no stop signs, no worries! Welcome to the future! It seems like science fiction, but it isn't. Engineers have been working on flying cars for decades, and they have already solved many of the big challenges. They predict that we'll all be ~~use~~ *using* these amazing vehicles one day.

According to *Car Trends Magazine*, one model, part car and part plane, is going *to* be on the market in the not-so-distant future. It will look like a regular car when it's on the road, but its wings will unfold when the driver ~~will decide~~ *decides* to take to the skies. It will ~~runs~~ *run* on the same fuel for both land and air travel, and you'll be able to keep it in your garage. (But you're still going *to* need an airport to take off and land.)

A better model will be a vertical take off and landing vehicle (VTOL). You won't need to go to the airport anymore, and all controls will ~~being~~ *be* automatic. Imagine this: You'll be doing your homework while your car ~~will be~~ *is* getting you to school safely and on time.

And what ~~does~~ *will* this future dream car cost? Well, fasten your seatbelts—the price will ~~going to~~ *will* be sky-high. At first it will be about a million dollars, but after a few years, you'll be able to buy one for "only" $60,000. Don't throw away your old driver's license just yet!

EXERCISE 7

A. **2.** False. Jarek won't be going on vacation.
   3. True
   4. True
   5. False. Zindra is flying to Mars every other weekend.
   6. False. Zindra will be doing research the third week in July

B.

	July				August			
Weeks:	1	2	3	4	1	2	3	4
Skyler							X	X
Jarek		X	X					
Lorna	X	X						
Zindra		X	X	X		X	X	X
When they're all available:				_Week 1 in August_				

X = not available

EXERCISE 8

B. 1. B: No, he won't be running. He'll be swimming.

  2. B: No, I won't be leaving for vacation, but I'll be leaving for a business trip.

  3. B: Oh, she won't be going into the office tomorrow. She'll be working in the library.

4. B: We'll be working Saturday, but we won't be working Sunday.

5. B: Well, I'll be visiting my sister. But my brother isn't there now.

6. B: We'll be meeting in August. In July a lot of people will be on vacation.

EXERCISES 9–10

Answers will vary.

EXERCISE 11

(See chart below)

EXERCISE 12

Answers will vary.

UNIT 6 (pages 79–94)

AFTER YOU READ

A. 1. a   **2.** b   **3.** b   **4.** c   **5.** a   **6.** b

B. 1. False. The show wasn't traveling two months ago.
   2. T
   3. T
   4. T
   5. T
   6. False. It's a good idea to use a credit card wisely when you're a student.

FEBRUARY						2115
SUNDAY	**MONDAY**	**TUESDAY**	**WEDNESDAY**	**THURSDAY**	**FRIDAY**	**SATURDAY**
1 fly to Tokyo	2 meet with Dr. Kato	3 attend World Future Conference	4	5	6	7 →
8 take Bullet Train to Osaka	9 sightseeing	10	11 →	12 fly to Denver	13 Visit Mom and Dad →	14 →
15 fly home	16 give speech at Harvard University	17 meet with Dr. Rover	18 attend energy seminar →	19	20 →	21 shop with Rocky and Asimo
22 relax!	23 work at home	24	25	26	27 →	28 take shuttle to Mars

EXERCISE 1

2. b **3.** b **4.** b **5.** a **6.** a

EXERCISE 2

2. By 2015, Debbie won't have gotten married.
3. By 2015, she'll have moved into an apartment.
4. By 2015, she won't have moved to Miami.
5. By 2015, she'll have spent a summer in France.
6. By 2015, she'll have started working at a bank.
7. By 2015, she'll have bought a used car.
8. By 2015, she won't have bought a house.
9. By 2015, she won't have graduated from college.
10. By 2015, she won't have become a parent.

EXERCISE 3

2. By the time she moves into an apartment, she won't have gotten married yet.
3. By the time she starts college, she won't have bought a used car yet.
4. By the time she graduates from college, she will have already moved into an apartment.
5. By the time she spends a summer in France, she won't yet have found a job at a bank.
6. By the time she graduates from college, she will have already spent a summer in France.
7. By the time she gets married, she will have already graduated from college.
8. By the time she moves to Miami, she won't have bought a house yet.
9. By the time she becomes a parent, she will have already graduated from college.
10. By the time she buys a home, she won't have become a parent yet.

EXERCISE 4

(Note: The clause with *by* can go either at the beginning or at the end of the sentence.)

2. **Q:** By April 19, how much will Valerie have saved?
   A: By April 19, she will have saved $35.
3. **Q:** By June 16, how many books will Sung have read?
   A: By June 16, he will have read 15 books.
4. **Q:** How long will Don have been running by May 29?
   A: By May 29, he will have been running for five weeks.
5. **Q:** How many miles will Tania have run by May 29?
   A: By May 29, she will have run 72 miles.
6. **Q:** Will Rick have saved $100 by March 27?
   A: No, he won't.
7. **Q:** How many apartments will Tim have painted by May 29?
   A: By May 29, he will have painted six apartments.

8. **Q:** Will he have finished by June 19?
   A: Yes, he will.
9. **Q:** Will Talia have lost 20 pounds by May 21?
   A: Yes, she will.
10. **Q:** How long will Erik have been studying by April 26?
    A: By April 26, he will have been studying for nine weeks.
11. **Q:** How much interest will Jeff have paid by the end of June?
    A: By the end of June, he'll have paid $40 interest.

EXERCISE 5

I have five credit cards. If nothing changes, I *will* have

doubled the credit card debt I had as a freshman by the time I graduate. According to statistics, that makes me a typical college student. But I've decided to change. By this time next year, I'll ~~has~~ *have* gotten my debt under control. I won't ~~had~~ *have* become debt-free, but I'll have made a good start. Here's my debt-free timeline so far:

- I just found a part-time job, and when I start working, I'll use that money to pay debts.
- By February, I'll have ~~been recorded~~ *been recording* OR *recorded* all my spending for a month. Then I'll be able to make a spending plan. Only essentials—food, basic clothes, tuition—will be on this budget.
- By March 1st, I'll only have two credit cards left. By that time I'll already have ~~been transferring~~ *transferred* all my balances to those two cards with the lowest interest rate. And I'll have ~~closing~~ *closed* six accounts by then, too!
- When I graduate, ~~I've~~ *I'll have* been paying more than the minimum on my cards for three months, so I might be able to get a lower interest rate. I expect a lot of financial challenges after I graduate, but by then I ~~had~~ *'ll have had* experience in managing debt. I'll add goals to the timeline and record my progress during the year.

I'd love to hear stories and suggestions from readers about getting debt free. If you're a college student in my situation, send in your timeline and let's change the statistics together. How much progress will we "typical" college students have ~~been making~~ *made* by next January 1?

EXERCISE 6

A. **2.** Thea
3. Ned and Valerie
4. Thea and Don
5. Thea, Don, Ned, and Valerie

B. Lunches, $1,000, Clothing $1,000
Transportation $1,800, Entertainment $780
Total of all categories: $4,580

C. **1.** a car trip to British Columbia, renting camping equipment
2. a car trip to British Columbia, staying in motels

EXERCISE 7

B. **1.** 'll have saved
2. will have been working
3. won't have made
4. 'll have been living
5. won't have lost
6. will have been
7. won't have smoked
8. will have been seeing

EXERCISES 8–10

Answers will vary.

PART II   From Grammar to Writing
(pages 96–98)

1

As of today, I'm a working man! ~~By the time you~~ *By the time you get this letter,* ~~get this letter.~~ I'll have been taking tickets at Ciné Moderne for more than a week. It's going to be hard to work and go to school full time, but you'll understand why I'm doing it *when you hear my plans.* ~~When you hear my plans.~~ ~~As soon as school ends. My~~ *As soon as school ends, my* brother Alex and I are going to take a trip to Greece and Turkey. I plan to buy a used car, and we'll camp most of the way. By the end of January, I'll have been saving for more than a year for this trip—and I'll have enough to buy a car.

Why don't you come with us? Your exams are over on May 31, but mine don't end until June 10. That means you'll have already finished *while I'm still taking* ~~While I'm still taking~~ my finals. Maybe you can come early and do some sightseeing until I'm ready to leave. Alex has some business to complete *before he goes on* ~~Before he goes on~~ vacation. He won't have finished until July 15, but he can join us then.

I'm leaving Paris on June 17. I'll drive through Italy and take the ferry from Brindisi to Greece. I'll *until Alex joins me.* stay in Greece ~~Until Alex joins me.~~ Just think—while your friends are in summer school you could be swimming in the Aegean! We'll be leaving Greece *as soon as Alex arrives,* ~~As soon as Alex arrives~~ so we'll have a month in Turkey. We'll start back around August 20. Your classes won't have started by then, will they? I hope you'll be able to join us for this trip. Alex is looking forward to seeing you again too.

2

December 10	Philippe starts his new job.
January 31	Philippe will have saved enough for a car.
May 31	Jamie finishes his exams.
June 10	Philippe finishes school.
June 17	Philippe leaves Paris.
July 15	Alex finishes his business and joins Philippe in Greece.
August 20	Alex and Philippe start back.

3–6

Answers will vary.

UNIT 7   (pages 100–117)

AFTER YOU READ

A. **1.** c   **2.** c   **3.** a   **4.** b   **5.** c   **6.** b

B. **1.** False. She has seen him on TV.
2. False. He thinks she isn't originally from Rio.
3. False. He thinks the cold weather bothers Kada.
4. False. The reporter didn't buy anything at the market.
5. False. He thinks Bradley comes from England.
6. True

EXERCISE 1

PETRA: Hi, Ken. Nice day, isn't it?
KEN: Sure is. What are *you* doing home today? Don't you usually work on Thursdays?
PETRA: I took the day off to help my son. He just got back to Berlin, and he's looking for an apartment. You don't know of any vacant apartments, do you?
KEN: Isn't he going to stay with you?
PETRA: Well, he just got a new job at an architecture firm downtown, and he wants a place of his own in a quiet neighborhood. Do you know of anything?

(continued on next page)

KEN: As a matter of fact, I do. The Edwards family lives in a nice residential neighborhood near the river. You know them, don't you?

PETRA: Yes, I think Anton went to school with their son. But they're not moving, are they?

KEN: Yes, they're moving back to Vancouver next month.

PETRA: Are they? What kind of apartment do they have?

KEN: A one-bedroom.   It's very nice . . . The owner is Canadian too.

PETRA: It's not furnished, is it? Anton really doesn't have any furniture.

KEN: Can't he rent some? I did that in my first apartment.

PETRA: I don't know. Isn't it less expensive to buy?

EXERCISE 2

2. h	**4.** d	**6.** g	**8.** b
3. e	**5.** a	**7.** c	

EXERCISE 3

2. haven't you
3. did you
4. doesn't it
5. haven't they
6. aren't you
7. don't you
8. isn't it

EXERCISE 4

2. Haven't you seen; No, I haven't. OR Didn't you see; No, I didn't.
3. Aren't; Yes, they are.
4. Isn't there; No, there isn't. OR Doesn't it have; No, it doesn't.
5. Aren't you going to paint; Yes, I am.
6. Isn't it; Yes, it is.
7. Isn't it; Yes, it is.

EXERCISE 5

2. Don't you have a class today? OR You have a class today, don't you?
3. Isn't it only 2:30 now? OR It's only 2:30 now, isn't it?
4. Don't you have your bike with you? OR You have your bike with you, don't you?
5. Isn't Vancouver a beautiful city? OR Vancouver is a beautiful city, isn't it?
6. Aren't you coming to see my film tonight? OR You're coming to see my film tonight, aren't you?
7. Isn't your class that way? OR Your class is that way, isn't it?

EXERCISE 6

2. Didn't he take piano lessons? OR He took piano lessons, didn't he?
3. Didn't he (OR they) move to Tokyo? OR He (OR They) moved to Tokyo, didn't he (OR they)?

4. Didn't he originally study music composition there? OR He originally studied music composition there, didn't he?
5. Didn't he write traditional music? OR He didn't write traditional music, did he?
6. Didn't he paint on paper? OR He didn't paint on paper, did he?
7. Didn't the structure use 1,003 TV monitors? OR The structure used 1,003 TV monitors, didn't it?
8. Didn't he do installations after that? OR He didn't do installations after that, did he?
9. Didn't he become a U.S. citizen? OR He became a U.S. citizen, didn't he?
10. Wasn't he 75 years old? OR He was 75 years old, wasn't he?

EXERCISE 7

BEN: It's been a long time, Joe, ~~haven't~~ *hasn't* it?

JOE: That depends on what you mean by a long time, doesn't ~~that?~~ *it?*

BEN: ~~Are not you~~ *Aren't you* afraid to show your face here in Vancouver?

JOE: I can take care of myself. I'm still alive, *aren't I?* ~~amn't I?~~

BEN: Until someone recognizes you. You're still wanted by the police, ~~are~~ *aren't* you? ~~Don't~~ *Doesn't* that bother you?

JOE: I'll be gone by morning. Look, I need a place to stay. Just for one night.

BEN: I have to think about my wife and kid. Don't you have any place else to go?

JOE: ~~Yes, I do~~ *No, I don't*. There's no one to turn to but you. You have to help me.

BEN: I've already helped you plenty. I went to jail for you, ~~haven't~~ *didn't* I? And didn't I ~~kept~~ *keep* my mouth shut the whole time?

JOE: Yeah, OK, Ben. Don't you remember what happened in Vegas, ~~do you~~? [OR You remember what happened in Vegas, don't you?]

BEN: Don't ever think I'll forget that! OK, OK. I can make a call.

EXERCISE 8

B. Rising intonation: 2, 5, 6, 8, 9
   Falling intonation: 1, 3, 4, 7, 10

EXERCISE 9

A. Expects other person to give information: 1, 5, 8, 10
   Expects other person to agree: 2, 3, 4, 6, 7, 9

B. True: 1, 2, 5, 7, 8, 9, 10
False: 3, 4, 6

EXERCISE 10

London

2. is, isn't it OR isn't, is it
3. a river OR the ocean, doesn't it
4. two OR thirty-two, doesn't it
5. has, doesn't it OR doesn't have, does it
6. Many, don't they OR Not many, do they
7. is, isn't it OR isn't, is it

Vancouver

2. lies, doesn't it OR doesn't lie, does it
3. has, doesn't it OR doesn't have, does it
4. is, isn't it OR isn't, is it
5. Many, don't they OR Not many, do they
6. can, can't you OR can't, can you
7. is, isn't it OR isn't, is it

EXERCISES 11–12

Answers will vary.

UNIT 8 (pages 118–133)

AFTER YOU READ

A. 1. identical   4. outgoing
2. coincidence   5. Despite
3. image   6. factor

B. 1. marriage histories, types of jobs, hobbies
2. effects of nature and nurture on
3. first names, marriage histories, job histories
4. difficult
5. hair color
6. partly controls

EXERCISE 1

2. F	5. T	8. T
3. T	6. T	9. T
4. F	7. F	10. F

EXERCISE 2

2. too   6. didn't
3. neither   7. either
4. did   8. So
5. hadn't   9. but

EXERCISE 3

2. did I   6. do I
3. can I   7. can I
4. do too   8. would I
5. do I

EXERCISE 4

2. but Randy isn't.
3. and so does Randy. OR and Randy does too.
4. and so does Randy. OR and Randy does too.
5. and Randy doesn't either. OR and Neither does Randy.
6. and so does Randy. OR and Randy does too.
7. and so does Randy. OR and Randy does too.
8. but Randy didn't.
9. and so has Randy. OR and Randy has too.
10. but Randy does.
11. but Randy didn't.
12. and neither does Randy. OR and Randy doesn't either.

EXERCISE 5

My brother is just a year older than I am (I'm 18). We have a lot of things in common. We look alike. In fact, sometimes people ask us if we're twins. I am 5'10", and so ~~he is~~ *is he*. I have straight black hair and dark brown eyes. So does he. We share some of the same interests too. I love to play soccer, and he *does* too.

Both of us swim every day, but I can't dive and ~~either~~ *neither* can he.

Although there are a lot of similarities between us, there are also many differences. For example, he likes eating all kinds of food, but I don't. Give me hamburgers and fries every day! My brother doesn't want to go to college, but I ~~don't~~ *do*. I believe it's important to get as much education as possible, but he wants to get real-life experience. I think our personalities are an important factor in these choices. I am quiet and easygoing, but ~~he doesn't~~ *he's not* OR *he isn't*. He's very outgoing and talks a lot. When I think about it, despite the many things we have in common, we really are more different than similar.

EXERCISE 6

	Ryan	Ryan's Brother
2. is 5'10" tall	✓	✓
3. has black hair	✓	✓
4. has dark brown eyes	✓	✓
5. loves soccer	✓	✓
6. swims	✓	✓
7. dives	☐	☐
8. prefers hamburgers and fries	✓	☐
9. wants to go to college	✓	☐
10. prefers real-life experience	☐	✓
11. is quiet and easygoing	✓	☐

EXERCISE 7

A. 1. don't know
2. in a restaurant
3. new
4. history
5. play tennis
6. TV show

	Man	Woman
B. 2. cooks	☐	☑
3. eats out a lot	☑	☑
4. enjoys old movies	☑	☑
5. reads biographies	☑	☑
6. enjoys fiction	☐	☐
7. plays sports	☐	☑
8. watches sports on TV	☐	☐
9. watches news programs	☑	☑
10. wants to see the documentary	☑	☑

EXERCISE 8

B. 1. So did I

2. Mine haven't either

3. but Kate doesn't

4. Neither do I

5. and I am too

6. Bob's is

7. So does Steve

8. I should too

EXERCISES 9–11

Answers will vary.

EXERCISE 12

Possible answers:
Michael wears glasses, and so does Matthew.
Michael reads French, but Matthew doesn't.
Michael is married, but Matthew isn't.
Michael doesn't have a beard, but Matthew does.
Michael plays sports, and so does Matthew.

EXERCISES 13–14

Answers will vary.

PART III   From Grammar to Writing
(pages 134–135)

1

Citizens of Brasília and citizens of Washington, D.C., live on different continents, but their cities still have a lot in common. Brasília is its nation's capital, <u>and so is Washington</u>. Brasília did not exist before it was planned and built as the national capital. <u>Neither did Washington</u>. Both cities were designed by a single person, and both have a definite shape. However, twentieth-century Brasília's shape is modern—that of an airplane—<u>but the shape of eighteenth-century Washington's isn't</u>. Its streets form a wheel.

The cities reflect their differences in location and age. Brasília is located in a dry area in the highlands, while Washington was built on wet swampy land. As a result, Brasília has moderate temperatures all year, <u>but Washington doesn't</u>. Washington is famous for its cold winters and hot, humid summers. Brasília was built 600 miles from the Atlantic coast in order to attract people to an unpopulated area. Washington, near the Atlantic coast, includes old towns that had already existed. Brasília is home to many famous theaters and museums, <u>and so is the city of Washington</u>. However, as a new city, Brasília has not yet become its nation's real cultural center. <u>Washington hasn't either</u>. Washington is its country's capital, but it is not its country's most popular city. <u>Neither is Brasília</u>. Many people still prefer the excitement of Rio and New York.

2

Possible answers:
Brasilia: in South America, twentieth century, shape of an airplane, located in a high and dry area, moderate temperatures all year, 600 miles from the coast, built in an unpopulated area
Both cities: national capital, didn't exist before it was planned as a city, designed by one person, definite shape, national theater, famous museums, not the cultural center, not the favorite city of residents
Washington, D.C.: in North America, eighteenth century, shape of a wheel, located in a swamp, hot summers and cold winters, near the coast, includes older towns

3–6

Answers will vary.

AFTER YOU READ

A.
1. globe
2. objection
3. region
4. reliability
5. consequence
6. appealing

B. 1. c **2.** b **c.** a **4.** a **5.** b **6.** b

EXERCISE 1

Underlined words (gerunds)
2. eating
4. selecting
6. going
7. seeing

Circled words (infinitives)
3. to eat
5. to eat
8. to include

EXERCISE 2

Number of calories given are exact. Student answers will be approximate.
2. eating
3. to consider
4. Ordering
   Exact number of calories: 540
5. Having
   Exact number of calories: 200
6. to lose
7. eating
   Exact number of calories: 285
8. to gain
   Exact number of calories: 370
9. eating
   Exact number of calories: 424
10. choosing
    Exact number of calories: 207
11. to stay away
    Exact number of calories: 110

EXERCISE 3

2. recommended ordering
3. volunteered to throw out
4. has stopped (OR stopped) eating
5. deserved (OR deserves) to receive
6. is trying to decide
7. admits (OR admitted) stopping
8. remember playing

EXERCISE 4

2. Andre's (OR Andre) choosing to go
3. stopped using (OR had stopped)
4. finding
5. to see
6. changing
7. to do

8. support their (OR them) selling
9. appreciate my friend's (OR my friend) encouraging
10. to express
11. having
12. expected (us) to find
13. didn't expect (OR hadn't expected) to see
14. to bring
15. eating
16. need to have
17. try to stay away
18. urge the administration to set up
19. keep on buying

EXERCISE 5

Re: love those tacos

I love ~~eat~~ *eating OR to eat* tacos for my lunch. I think they are delicious, convenient, nutritious, and inexpensive. I don't even mind ~~to have~~ *having* the same thing every day. And I'm not worried about any health consequences. What do you think?

Re: vegetarian travel

I'm a vegetarian. I stopped ~~to eat~~ *eating* meat two years ago. I feel a little nervous about traveling to other countries. I'm going to Ghana in September. Is to find meatless dishes there ~~easy~~ *it easy*?

Re: takoyaki

Hi! I am Paulo and I come from Brazil. I travel a lot and I enjoy trying different foods from all over the globe. I hope I have a chance ~~trying~~ *to try* takoyaki (fish balls made with octopus) when I go to Japan. Is there a takoyaki shop you can recommend my going to? I look forward to ~~hear~~ *hearing* from you.

Re: recipe exchange

My name is Natasha. I'm interested in ~~exchange~~ *exchanging* recipes with people from other countries. If you want to know about Russian food, I'd be glad ~~sending~~ *to send* you some information.

Re: calamari

Hi! I was in Italy last month. The region I was visiting is famous for seafood. I don't usually like eating seafood, so I was not eager ~~trying~~ *to try* calamari (squid). I was surprised ~~finding~~ *to find* that I liked it! I

(continued on next page)

to be
expected it ~~being~~ tough, but it's actually quite tender if prepared well.

Re: cheap and delicious in Taiwan

trying
Are you going to Taiwan? If so, I suggest ~~to try~~ the appealing little restaurants around the National
Eating
University in Taipei. ~~Eat~~ there is cheap and it's easy to find the neighborhood. The dumpling shops are great—once you eat one there, you won't want
to stop.
~~stopping.~~

EXERCISE 6

A. 2. disgusting
3. pencil
4. fast food
5. cheap
6. cook Chinese food
7. get up earlier

B. Items checked
Lily: 2, 3, 5, 6, 7
Victor: 1, 3, 5, 6

EXERCISE 7

B. Sincere: 1, 4, 6
Sarcastic: 2, 3, 5

EXERCISE 8

JOB/PERSONALITY QUIZ

Name: _____ *Jennifer Johnson* _____

1. I enjoy _____ *working with others* _____ .

2. I expect _____ *to make a lot of money* _____ .

3. I'm good at _____ *talking to people* _____ .

4. I dislike _____ *working inside* _____ .

5. I don't mind _____ *working nights* _____ .

6. I'm willing _____ *to learn new skills* _____ .

7. I never complain about _____ *following orders* _____ .

8. I'm eager _____ *to meet new people* _____ .

9. I plan _____ *to major in business* _____ next year.

10. I dream about _____ *owning my own business* _____ one day.

11. I can't stand _____ *rushing* _____ .

12. I expect people _____ *to be friendly* _____ .

Answers in discussion will vary.

EXERCISES 9–12

Answers will vary.

AFTER YOU READ

A. 1. b **2.** c **3.** a **4.** b **5.** a **6.** c
B. 1. False. It's not easy to train orcas and dolphins.
2. False. You can't get a dolphin to wear a collar.
3. True
5. True
6. True

EXERCISE 1

2. b **4.** a **6.** a **8.** b
3. a **5.** a **7.** b

EXERCISE 2

2. h, made
3. e, made
4. a, got
5. g, let
6. b, had
7. i, had
8. d, let
9. f, made

EXERCISE 3

2. made Ana (or her) work
3. had Fernando (or him) clean
4. got Uri and Greta (or them) to research
5. helped Uri (or him) find
6. had Hector (or him) ask

EXERCISE 4

2. made (or had) her (or María) drive or got her (or María) to drive
3. let him (or John) borrow
4. didn't let him (or John) use
5. helped them (or the class) choose (or to choose)
6. didn't get him (or John) to read

EXERCISE 5

Orcas are beautiful and intelligent, so aquariums
to buy
easily get audiences ~~buy~~ tickets for orca shows. What does this mean for the orcas? In the wild, an orca may swim up to 100 miles a day and dive hundreds of feet below the surface of the water. In captivity, an orca can't have normal physical or emotional health.
live
We make this animal ~~lives~~ in a small, chemically-treated pool where it may get sick and die of an infection. Is that humane? Some people argue that
learn OR *to learn*
captive orcas have helped us ~~learned~~ about these animals. However, orcas cannot behave naturally in an aquarium. In captivity, trainers make them
OR *get them to*
~~to~~ perform embarrassing tricks for a "reward." In the wild, these animals have rich and complicated social lives in families. How can watching tricks help

us
~~we~~ learn about their lives? Orcas don't belong in aquariums!

suffer
Don't let these beautiful animals ~~suffering~~ in order to entertain us! First, help us stop aquarium shows. Stop going to these shows and get your

to stop
friends and family ~~stop~~ also. Next, we must make aquariums stop buying orcas. Write to your mayor and tell him or her how you feel. Can former captives live in the wild? It's a difficult question, but

retrain
aquariums must let others ~~retrained~~ these animals and release them to a normal life.

Help us help the orcas! It's the humane thing to do. Sign this e-letter and send it to your friends.

EXERCISE 6

A. 2. wildlife park
  3. *wh-* questions
  4. gerund
  5. another conference
B. 2. False. She didn't let him change the topic of his essay.
  3. False. She had him add some details to his second paragraph.
  4. True
  5. True
  6. False. Simon didn't get Ms. Jacobson to correct the gerunds in his essay. She had him correct them.
  7. True
  8. True

EXERCISE 7

B. 1. let her
  2. took them
  3. let him
  4. got them
  5. got her
  6. made him

EXERCISES 8–10

Answers will vary.

PART IV   From Grammar to Writing (pages 168–170)

1

It's October 1957, and the Soviet Union has just launched Sputnik. Homer, a teenage boy (played by Jake Gyllenhaal), watches the satellite fly over his poor coal-mining town in West Virginia and dreams

launching
of building and ~~to launch~~ his own rocket. He teams up with three friends, and "The Rocket Boys" start to

fire
put together and ~~firing~~ their homemade missiles. The boys' goal is to win the regional science fair. First prize will bring college scholarships and a way out of Coalwood. The school science teacher, Miss Riley, encourages him, but Homer's father (played by Chris Cooper) is angry about the boys' project. He wants

work
Homer to follow in his footsteps and ~~working~~ at the mine. Nevertheless, the boys continue launching

learning
rockets, failing in different ways, and ~~to learn~~ with each failure. People begin changing their minds and

admiring
~~to admire~~ the Rocket Boys. Some even help them. However, success does not come easily in Coalwood. When a forest fire starts nearby, a rocket is blamed, and the boys must give up their project. Then Homer's father is injured, and Homer quits school to support his family as a miner. His father is proud of him, but Homer can't stand giving up his dream and

working
~~to work~~ in the mine. He uses mathematics to prove a rocket did not start the fire. Then he tells his father

return
he plans to leave the mine and ~~returning~~ to school.

The Rocket Boys win first prize at the science fair, and all four of them receive scholarships. The whole town celebrates, and Homer wins another very valuable prize—his father attends the science fair and launches the rocket. It's clear that the father and

respect
son will try to make peace and ~~respecting~~ each other.

2

Answers may vary. See diagram on next page.

3–6

Answers will vary.

UNIT 11   (pages 172–184)

AFTER YOU READ

A. 1. consultant
  2. theory
  3. complex
  4. environment
  5. harmful
B. 1. False. He called in a consultant to find out why his restaurant was failing.
  2. False. Mr. Ho did spend a lot of money on the restaurant's appearance.
  3. True
  4. True
  5. False. He put up a new entrance.
  6. True
  7. False. To find out more about feng shui, look up the topic online or pick up a book on basic feng shui.

MOVIE TITLE: _October Sky_

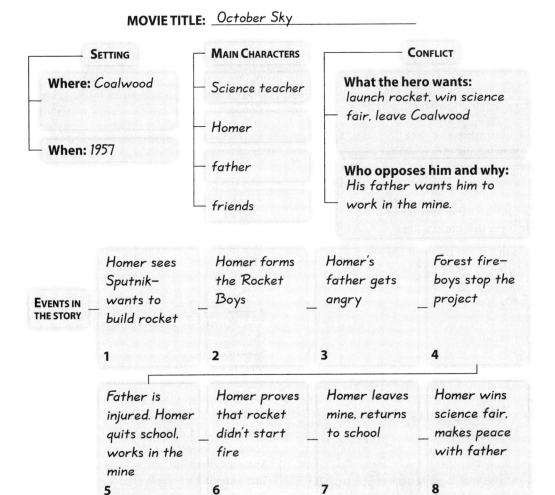

SETTING

Where: _Coalwood_

When: _1957_

MAIN CHARACTERS

- _Science teacher_
- _Homer_
- _father_
- _friends_

CONFLICT

What the hero wants: _launch rocket, win science fair, leave Coalwood_

Who opposes him and why: _His father wants him to work in the mine._

EVENTS IN THE STORY

1. _Homer sees Sputnik— wants to build rocket_
2. _Homer forms the Rocket Boys_
3. _Homer's father gets angry_
4. _Forest fire— boys stop the project_
5. _Father is injured. Homer quits school, works in the mine_
6. _Homer proves that rocket didn't start fire_
7. _Homer leaves mine, returns to school_
8. _Homer wins science fair, makes peace with father_

EXERCISE 1

A.

Have you noticed that some spaces cheer you up and give you energy, while others bring you down? This feng shui diagram uses mythological animals to explain why. Look it over, and then imagine yourself in the center. According to feng shui theory, a phoenix takes off in front of you and gives you inspiration. Behind you, a tortoise guards you from things you cannot see. On your left and right, a dragon and a tiger balance each other. The dragon floats above the floor and helps you take in the big picture, not just small details. The tiger's energy gives you courage.

These symbols can be important in setting up a work environment. Dana, for example, needed ideas and energy in order to get ahead. Unfortunately, her undecorated, windowless cubicle took away most of her powers. After she hung up a scenic poster in the phoenix area in front of her desk, she began to feel more inspired. She gave her tiger some power by picking out plants to put on the file cabinet to her right. For her dragon, she hung a cheerful mobile from the top of the left wall of her cubicle. Try these ideas out in your own work area and see what happens!

B. 2. False. The phoenix takes off in the space in front of you.

3. False. The dragon floats above the floor and helps you understand an overall plan.

4. True

5. False. From the beginning, Dana's work area took away her powers.

6. False. She hung up a poster in the area in front of her desk.

7. True

EXERCISE 2

2. down	**9.** up
3. up	**10.** down
4. out	**11.** out
5. out	**12.** out
6. over	**13.** out
7. out	**14.** up
8. together	

EXERCISE 3

2. put up
3. settle on
4. turned out
5. tear down
6. figure out
7. put on
8. went up
9. letting in
10. kept on
11. set up
12. go back
13. give up

EXERCISE 4

2. took them down
3. cheer him up
4. try them out OR try some out
5. light it up
6. touch it up

EXERCISE 5

I just read an article about feng shui. The author
suggests sitting ~~up~~ *down* in your home and thinking about
how your environment makes you feel. I tried ~~out it~~ *it out*.

My apartment is bright and sunny. This cheers
me ~~out~~ *up*. At night, it's very dark, but I've figured ~~up~~ *out*
what to do. I'm going to buy another lamp to
light up the apartment at night OR
light the apartment up at night
~~light the apartment at night up~~. I'll leave it on when
I go out at night, so I can see light as soon as I come
in. I also like the light green walls in my bedroom,
but the chipped paint has been bringing ~~down me~~ *me down*.
I'm going to touch it ~~over~~ *up* soon.

My apartment is too small, but I can't tear ~~up~~ *down*
the walls. I think it'll look more spacious if I just
straighten it up. I'll try to put books back after I
take them off the shelves and ~~hang away~~ *hang up* OR *put away* my clothes
at night. With just a few small changes, I'll end up
feeling happier in my home. It's worth trying ~~on~~ *out*. And
I won't even need a consultant!

EXERCISE 6

A. 2. True
3. False. Ben has almost finished redecorating his
office.
4. True
5. True
6. False. The mattress isn't as comfortable as it
used to be.
7. True

B. 2. over
3. out
4. back
5. down
6. around
7. up

EXERCISE 7

B. Linked words:
1. A: find out
   B: look over
2. A: made up
   B: come up
3. A: hang up
   B: pick up
4. A: light up
   B: pick out
5. A: put away
   B: clean out
6. A: turn on
   B: turn off

EXERCISE 8

Answers will vary.

EXERCISE 9

Possible answers:
She turned the light off.
She cleaned up the table.
She moved the table.
She took off the bedspread.
She took the curtains down.
The weather cleared up.
She emptied the garbage pail.
She put away the clothes.
She touched up the paint.
One of the dresser handles fell off.
The cat woke up.
She put up a shelf.
She took down the photos.
She put up a poster.

EXERCISE 10

Answers will vary.

UNIT 12 (pages 186–198)

AFTER YOU READ

A. 1. always
2. control
3. disappears
4. the same
5. sales methods
6. know

B. 1. False. He got a call from a telemarketer in the
evening (when he got home from the office).
2. True
3. False. Most people don't welcome these calls.
4. True
5. False. You can't do anything to stop all of these
unwanted calls. You can stop some of them.
6. True

EXERCISE 1

A. Underlined verbs

HOLD ON, PLEASE! Your phone number is on the Do Not Call list, but you keep on receiving telemarketing calls. Constantly. Why not have some fun with them? We came up with these amusing tactics:

- When the telemarketer asks, "How are you today?"—tell her! Don't leave anything out. Say, "I have a headache you wouldn't believe, and my back is acting up again. Now I can't figure out the instructions for my DVD player . . ."
- When a telemarketer calls during dinner, request his home telephone number so you can call him back. When he refuses, ask him to hold on. Put the phone down and continue eating until you hear the dial tone.
- Ask the telemarketer to spell her first and last name and the name of the company. Tell her to speak slowly—you're taking notes. Ask questions until she hangs up.
- To credit card offers, say, "Thanks a lot! My company just laid me off, and I really need the money!"

B.
1. acting up
2. keep on
3. hangs up
4. laid off
5. came up with
6. hold on
7. leave out
8. call back
9. put down
10. figure out
11. writing down

EXERCISE 2

2. end up with
3. let . . . down
4. hang up
5. got to
6. help out
7. fall for
8. watch out for
9. give . . . back
10. go along with
11. find out
12. turn . . . down
13. put on
14. pick out
15. turned up
16. fill out
17. count on

EXERCISE 3

2. turn it down
3. filled it out
4. leave them out
5. called her back
6. wrote them down
7. take it off
8. turn it off

EXERCISE 4

2. give them up
3. fill you up
4. Try our plan out
5. Find them out
6. sign up for our plan
7. Fill it out
8. stick to our plan
9. take you off

1. Turn your hobby into
2. takes $2,000 in
3. turn work down
4. take employees on
5. go after those jobs
6. set it up
7. send the materials out
8. Check them out
9. send them back
10. put it off
11. pass it up
12. cash in on this great opportunity

EXERCISE 5

TM: Hello. Ms. Linder?

JL: Yes. Who's this?

TM: This is Bob Watson from *Motorcycle Mama*. I'm calling to offer you a 12-month subscription for the low price of just $15 a year. Can I sign ~~up you~~ *you up*?

JL: No, thanks. I'm trying to eliminate clutter, so I'm not interested in signing ~~in~~ *up* for any more magazine subscriptions. Besides, I just sat ~~up~~ *down* for dinner.

TM: Why don't you at least try ~~out it~~ *it out* for six months? Don't pass this great opportunity ~~down~~ *up*! It's a once in a lifetime chance!

JL: Sorry, I'm really not interested. I don't even have a motorcycle.

TM: Well then, this is a great opportunity to find ~~all about them out~~ *out all about them*! We'll send you a free copy and you can look ~~over it~~ *it over*.

JL: You're not going to talk me ~~in~~ *into* it! In fact, I'm going to hang the phone ~~down~~ *up* right now. And please take my name ~~out~~ *off* your list. If you keep calling, I'll notify the authorities.

TM: No, hold ~~out~~ *on*! Don't go away! Don't turn this great offer down! You'll be sorry if you do. Chances like this don't come around every day! Don't miss ~~it out on~~ *out on it*!

JL: OK. I have an idea. Why don't you give me your phone number, and I'll ~~call back you~~ *call you back* during YOUR dinner?

[click as the telemarketer hangs *up* OR *up* the phone.]

JL: Hello? Hello?

EXERCISE 6

A. **2.** $49.95 **8.** $59
   3. set up   **9.** sign up
   4. show up   **10.** give
   5. $30   **11.** back
   6. turn   **12.** one day
   7. on

B. **2.** True
   3. False. He'll never run out of cell phone minutes.
   4. True
   5. False. It will cost $39. ($59 and a $20 rebate)
   6. False. Mr. Chen must decide immediately.
   7. False. He isn't going to sign up. He's going to keep the service he has.

EXERCISE 7

B.
   1. A: Don't pick up the phone. It's probably a telemarketer.
      B: Don't worry. I won't pick it up.

   2. A: Did the phone wake up the baby?
      B: No. It didn't wake her up.

   3. A: Can you write down the information?
      B: Sure. I'll write it down on the pad.

   4. A: Did you fill out the form?
      B: I filled it out yesterday.

   5. A: I think you left out your phone number.
      B: I didn't leave it out. Here it is.

   6. A: Did you turn down the offer?
      B: Yes. I turned it down.

   7. A: Let's turn off the phone and have dinner.
      B: I already turned it off.

EXERCISES 8–10

Answers will vary.

PART V   From Grammar to Writing (pages 200–203)

1

2. l	**5.** k	**8.** n	**11.** c	**14.** e
3. d	**6.** o	**9.** j	**12.** a	**15.** b
4. i	**7.** g	**10.** h	**13.** m	

2

Note to Van:
   2. got on
   3. signed up
   4. give up
   5. fix up
   6. picked up
   7. put together
   8. 'm looking into
   9. light up

Note to Mr. Livingston:
   1. discarded
   2. indicated
   3. examine
   4. support
   5. appear
   6. meet

3

Possible answers:
   3. fix up the lobby OR fix the lobby up
   4. clean up the lobby OR clean the lobby up OR clean it up
   5. empty out the trash can OR empty the trash can out
   6. fill in the manager's phone number on the sign OR fill the manager's phone number in on the sign
   7. take down the old poster OR take the old poster down
   8. turn the couch around
   9. take away the ladder OR take the ladder away
   10. keep out the cats OR keep the cats out

4–6

Answers will vary.

AFTER YOU READ

A. 1. personality
  2. sensitive
  3. contradict
  4. require
  5. unique
  6. define
B. Introvert: 1, 4, 6, 7
  Extrovert: 2, 3, 5, 8

EXERCISE 1

Look at the photo. Do you see a glass which is half full or a glass which is half empty? For optimists, people who believe that things in the future will work out fine, the glass is half full. On the other hand, for pessimists, people who expect things to go badly, the glass is half empty.

Most of us know people who have a strong tendency to be either optimistic or pessimistic. I have a friend whose life motto is "Things have a way of working out." Even when something bad happens, Cindi remains optimistic. Last year, she lost a job that was extremely important to her. She didn't get depressed; she just thought "Well, maybe I'll find a new job that's even better than this one!" But then there is the example of Monica, who always sees the dark side of every situation, even when something good happens. She recently won a lot of money in a contest. Is she happy about this windfall? Not really. She worries that she won't know how to spend the money wisely. And now she's also worried that her friend Dan, a talented web designer who is struggling to start a business, will be jealous of her.

Cindi and Monica are women whose outlooks on life are as different as day and night. But the two women are best friends! Is it true what they say? Do opposites attract? Cindi says that their very different ways of seeing things help balance each other.

Sometimes Monica has views that are more realistic than her friend's. Right after Cindi was laid off, for example, Monica persuaded her to take a temporary job. "Just until you find that dream job," she said. On the other hand, Monica admits that she's sometimes too negative, and that Cindi, whose nickname is "Miss Sunshine," often gets her to see opportunities in a difficult situation. "Why not invest in Dan's business?" Cindi suggested the other day.

Former U.S. president Harry Truman defined the two personalities well: "A pessimist is one who makes difficulties of his opportunities and an optimist is one who makes opportunities of his difficulties." However, as Cindi and Monica are learning, we can learn to make these tendencies less extreme. Today's experts agree: Half full or half empty—you may not be able to change how much water is in your glass, but you can often change how you view the situation and how you respond to it. Optimists and pessimists may be able to help each other do this more appropriately.

EXERCISE 2

  1. who (OR that) talk
  2. who (OR that) takes
  3. who (OR that) leaves
  4. who talks
  5. which (OR that) focus
  6. whose . . . is
  7. whose . . . are
  8. who (OR that) . . . sees
  9. which (OR that) provide
  10. who (OR that) are

EXERCISE 3

A. 2. j   **5.** i   **8.** g
  3. e   6. d   **9.** c
  4. a   7. b   **10.** f

B. 2. An extrovert is a person (OR someone) who (OR that) requires a lot of time with others.
  3. An introvert is a person (OR someone) who (OR that) requires a lot of time alone.
  4. An opportunity is a situation that (OR which) gives you a chance to experience something good.

5. Opposites are people who (OR that) have completely different personalities.

6. An optimist is a person (OR someone) who (OR that) usually sees the bright side of situations.

7. An outlook is an attitude that (OR which) shows your ideas about your future.

8. A pessimist is a person (OR someone) who (OR that) usually sees the dark side of situations.

9. Creativity is an ability that (OR which) makes you able to produce new ideas.

10. A windfall is money that (OR which) is unexpected.

EXERCISE 4

3. He drives to school with his sister Jena, who wants to go to law school.

4. Jena, who loves to argue, is always contradicting him.

5. That never annoys cheerful Sami, who just laughs.

6. Jena, whose personality is perfect for a lawyer, is going to have a great career.

7. I always look forward to the class, which meets three days a week.

8. San Antonio, which is in Texas, has a lot of community colleges.

9. My school, which is one of the largest colleges in the country, has students from all over the world.

EXERCISE 5.

2. The office party is going to be at the restaurant which is (OR that's) across the street from the library.

3. I liked that speaker who talked about optimists.

4. Bill and Sue aren't close friends with the Swabodas, whose interests are very different from theirs.

5. I loaned some chairs to the new neighbors, who are having a party tonight.

6. I'm watching an old video of Jason which (OR that) totally defines his personality. OR I'm watching an old video of Jason, who was telling jokes when he was five.

7. My boyfriend, who's visiting Venezuela with some friends, left me a lot of plants to water.

EXERCISE 6

A writer once said that friends are born, not made. I think he meant that friendship is like love at first sight—we become friends immediately with people who ~~they~~ are compatible with us. I don't agree with this writer. Last summer I made friends with some
who are OR *who were*
people ~~who's~~ completely different from me.

In July, I went to Mexico City to study Spanish for a month. In our group, there were five adults,
who
~~which~~ were all language teachers from our school. Two teachers stayed with friends in Mexico City, and we only saw those teachers during the day. But we saw the teachers who stayed with us in the dormitory both day and night. They were the ones who ~~they~~ helped us when we had problems. Bob Taylor, who is much older than I am, became a really

good good friend. After my first two weeks, I had a problem that was getting me down. Mexico City,
which
~~that~~ is a very exciting place, was too distracting. I'm a real extrovert—someone who wants to go out all the time—and I stopped going to my classes. But my classes required a lot of work, and my grades suffered as a result. When they got really bad, I
has
wanted to leave. Bob, who ~~have~~ studied abroad a lot, was very sensitive to those feelings. But he was also a lot more optimistic about my situation. He helped me get back into my courses, which were actually

pretty interesting. I managed to do well after all!
whose
After the trip I kept writing to Bob, ~~who's~~ letters are always friendly and encouraging. Next summer, he's
that
leading another trip ~~what~~ sounds great. It's a three-week trip to Spain, which is a place he knows a lot about. I hope I can go.

EXERCISE 7

A. 2. a scarf
3. woman
4. worked on the school paper
5. a photo
6. Raza Gupta
7. don't know

B. Ann—wearing scarf
Kado—lower right, talking to Ann
Pat—wearing glasses, sitting next to Bob
Asha—wearing jewelry
Pete—not talking to anyone, sitting next to Asha

EXERCISE 8

B. 1. (no commas)
2. My neighbor, who is an introvert, called me today.
3. My brother, who is one year older than me, is an extrovert.
4. (no commas)
5. My friend, who is in the same class as me, lent me a book.

(continued on next page)

4. [comma] where (OR in which) all the children worked.

5. [comma] that he heard on the radio.

6. [comma] where they opened another Chinese restaurant.

7. [comma] for which he won an award. OR which he won an award for.

8. [comma] who he married in 1976,

EXERCISE 5

2. I lived with my parents and my siblings, who (OR that, OR whom) you've met.

3. I had two sisters, who (OR whom) I got along well with (OR with whom I got along well), and an older brother.

4. My sisters and I shared a room, where we spent nights talking.

5. My brother, who (OR whom) I hardly ever saw, slept on the living room couch.

6. It was a large old couch, which my father had made himself.

7. My best friend, whose family I loved, lived across the hall.

8. We went to the same school, where we both studied English.

9. Mr. Robinson, who (OR whom) everyone was a little afraid of (OR of whom everyone was a little afraid), was our English teacher.

10. After school I worked in a bakery that (OR which) my aunt and uncle owned.

11. They sold delicious bread and cake, which people stood in line for hours to buy.

12. My brother and sisters, who (OR whom) I miss, live far away now.

13. When we get together we like to talk about the old days when we all lived at home.

EXERCISE 6

Tai Dong , where I grew up , is a small city on the southeast coast of Taiwan. My family moved there

when OR *that* (OR *no pronoun*)

from Taipei the summer ~~where~~ I was born. I don't

which

remember our first house, we rented from a relative,

but when I was two, we moved to the house that I grew up in. I have a very clear image of it. The

where OR *in which*

house, ~~which~~ my parents still live, is on a main street in Tai Dong. To me, this was the best place in the world. My mother had a food stand in our

where OR *from which*

front courtyard ~~whom~~ she sold omelets early in the

who OR *whom*

morning. All her customers, ~~which~~ I always chatted with, were very friendly to me. On the first floor, my father conducted his tea business in the front room.

After school, I always went straight to the corner where he sat drinking tea with his customers. In the back was our huge kitchen with its stone floor and brick oven. I loved dinnertime because the kitchen was always full of relatives and the customers, that my father had invited to dinner. It was a fun and noisy place to be. Next to the kitchen, there was one small bedroom. My oldest cousin, whose father wanted him to learn the tea business, slept there. Our living room and bedrooms were upstairs. My two older sisters slept in one bedroom, and my older brother and I slept in the other. My younger sister

who

shared a room with my grandmother, ~~whose~~ took care of her a lot of the time.

EXERCISE 7

A. 2. True
3. True
4. False. There was a rug under her sister's bed.
5. True
6. False. They did their homework at a desk in their bedroom.
7. False. Her sister played the guitar.
8. True

B. The correct picture is A.

C. The description is in formal English.

EXERCISE 8

B. 1. Hoffman / who spent her childhood in Poland / moved to Canada / when she was 13.

2. Her autobiography describes her experiences / as she leaves her beloved Cracow / and struggles to find herself / in a new place / and a new language.

3. She visited the city's many cafés with her father / who she watched / in lively conversations / with his friends.

4. As she grew up / her friendship with Marek / whose apartment she visited almost daily / deepened / and the two always believed / that they would one day be married.

5. At her new school in Vancouver / Ewa is given her English name / Eva / which her teachers find easier / to pronounce.

6. All her memories and feelings / are still in her first language / Polish.

7. The story of Eva / as she grows up / and comes to terms / with her new identity and language / is fascinating / and moving.

EXERCISES 9–11

Answers will vary.

1

Octavio Paz is considered one of the greatest writers <u>that the Spanish-speaking world has produced</u>. He was born in Mexico in 1914. As a child, he was exposed to writing by his grandfather and father. His childhood was hard because of his father's political activities, <u>which forced his family into exile and poverty</u>.

Paz began writing <u>when he was very young</u>. He published his first poem at age 16. He attended law school in Mexico City, <u>where he joined a Marxist student group</u>. Around the same time, he married his first wife, Elena Garro. Paz's literary career received a boost in his early twenties, <u>when he sent a manuscript to the Chilean poet Pablo Neruda</u>. Neruda was impressed, and he encouraged Paz to go to Spain to attend a writing conference. Paz remained there and joined the forces <u>that were fighting against General Franco in the Spanish Civil War</u>. Later, he went on to become a diplomat, representing his country in France, Japan, the United States, and India.

Paz wrote both poetry and prose. He is most famous for *The Labyrinth of Solitude*, a collection of essays <u>that deal with the character of the Mexican people</u>. He also founded *Vuelta*. In 1990 he received the Nobel Prize for Literature. He died eight years later.

2

2. Around the same time, he married his first wife, Elena Garro, who was also a writer.
3. Paz's literary career received a boost in his early twenties, when he sent a manuscript to the Chilean poet Pablo Neruda, who was already famous in Spain and Latin America.
4. He also founded *Vuelta*, which was one of Latin America's most famous literary magazines.

3–6

Answers will vary.

UNIT 15 (pages 240–255)

AFTER YOU READ

A. 1. c **2.** e **3.** b **4.** f **5.** d **6.** a
B. 1. False. Vince joined MySpace because he wanted to stay in touch with his family.
2. True
3. True
4. False. . . . it's not a good idea to post messages with abbreviations.

5. False. Social networking is a great resource for college students.
6. False. She thinks everyone ought to learn how to use social networking.

EXERCISE 1

A.
How do I join Facebook?
It's easy. You just <u>have to complete</u> an online form with some basic information—your name, birthday, relationship status, etc. Oh, and you <u>must have</u> an email address.

Are there any age restrictions?
Yes. You <u>must be</u> 13 or older to join.

I'm worried about privacy. Do I really <u>have to provide</u> personal information such as my date of birth?
Yes you do. But you <u>will be able to hide</u> personal information if you'd like.

Do I <u>have to post</u> a photo of myself?
It's not required, but most people do. To get the full benefit of making connections, you <u>ought to give</u> as much information as you feel comfortable with. Remember: Facebook is a great resource, so get involved!

<u>Can someone post</u> a photo of me without my permission?
Yes. As long as it doesn't break any of Facebook's rules, people <u>don't have to ask</u>. However, if the photo is embarrassing, a lot of users feel the poster ***really ought to get*** permission.

What if I don't like a photo that someone has posted of me?
Unfortunately, Facebook <u>cannot remove</u> a photo if it hasn't broken any rules. If you're unhappy, however, you <u>can choose</u> to remove your name from it.

There must be some dangers in social networking. What <u>should I do</u> to protect myself?
The number 1 rule is this: You <u>must not give</u> your password to anyone. Ever. Also, you <u>should never give out</u> information that strangers <u>could use</u> to contact you in the real world.
And remember: Facebook tries to make the environment as safe as possible, but one day you <u>may encounter</u> objectionable content
B. Ability:
1. will be able to hide
2. can someone post
3. cannot remove
4. can choose
Advice:
1. ought to give
2. ought to get
3. should do
4. should never give out

Necessity:
1. have to complete   4. have to provide
2. must have   5. have to post
3. must be   6. don't have to ask

Prohibition: 1. must not give

Future Possibility:
1. could use
2. may encounter

Conclusions: 1: must be

EXERCISE 2

1. **b.** has got to
   c. 'd better
   d. should
2. **a.** 'll be able to
   b. can't
   c. ought to
   d. 'll have to
   e. may not
   f. Should
3. **a.** can
   b. could
   c. can
   d. must
   e. be able to
   f. could
4. **a.** must
   b. should
   c. may not
   d. has to
   e. couldn't
   f. must

EXERCISE 3

2. couldn't be
3. can OR is able to keep
4. may OR might OR could get rid of
5. should OR ought to be
6. had to go
7. must not know
8. won't have to worry about
9. may OR might OR could go
10. should OR ought to get on
11. might OR could win

EXERCISE 4

Wikipedia (pronounced WIK-i-PEE-dee-a) It's fast (*wiki* means *quick* in Hawaiian), it's convenient (you
don't have to
~~must not~~ go to the library), and, best of all, it's free. It's the world's most popular online encyclopedia, and you don't even have to register to use it. It's called "the free encyclopedia that anyone can
edit
~~edits~~." Volunteers around the world contribute to the millions of articles on its website, which are usually more up-to-date than what you may find in
can
a book. You ~~can't~~ also click on hyperlinks to get more
to
information. But, critics say, users ought ^ be aware that the content may not always be 100% accurate. A "paper" encyclopedia has professional editors who fact check every article. Not so with Wikipedia. As
not
a result, many teachers say their students should ^ rely on it when they write reports. It's wrong to think that just because an article is on a famous
might
website, it must be reliable. It ~~mights~~ be a good starting point when researching a topic, but writers should then check the facts with other sources. Then there is always the issue of plagiarism. Remember: Wikipedia information is free to use and edit, but
must not OR *can't*
you ~~don't have to~~ copy other people's writing without giving them credit. It's against the law!

Along with the freedom of Wikipedia, come some dangers. People can "vandalize" articles. This means that they maliciously insert wrong information into a text or remove important facts. Wikipedia says it deals quickly with these attacks, but, again, users
have
~~has~~ to be aware that information could be wrong.

Online encyclopedias have changed the way we
Could
get information. ~~May~~ they one day replace paper encyclopedias? It's possible. But for now, it might be a good idea to hold on to that library card. In the meantime, it's safe to say that despite some
can
disadvantages, an online encyclopedia ~~can't~~ be a very useful resource if you are careful and use common sense.

EXERCISE 5

A. 2. True
   3. False. The man doesn't think Facebook is dangerous.
   4. False. The woman would like to connect with old friends online.
   5. True
   6. True
   7. False. The woman might consider joining.
B. 2. 've got to   8. don't have to
   3. must   9. might
   4. can't   10. ought to
   5. have to   11. Will . . . be able to
   6. could   12. might
   7. can

EXERCISE 6

B. **1.** **A:** ought to
   B: have to
   2. **A:** have to
   B: 've got to
   3. **A:** ought to
   B: wasn't able to
   4. **A:** be able to
   B: have to
   5. **A:** 've got to
   B: ought to

EXERCISES 7–11

Answers will vary.

UNIT 16 (pages 257–269)

AFTER YOU READ

A. **1.** a   **2.** c   **3.** b   **4.** a   **5.** b   **6.** a

B. **2.** improve   **5.** unrealistic
   3. paralyzes   **6.** laugh
   4. questioning   **7.** silly

EXERCISE 1

2. b   **4.** b   **6.** b
3. a   **5.** a   **7.** a

EXERCISE 2

4. shouldn't have taken
5. should . . . have used
6. might've asked
7. could've paid
8. ought to have worn
9. should . . . have fired
10. shouldn't have
11. should . . . have handled
12. ought to have warned
13. shouldn't have . . . fired

EXERCISE 3

Answers may vary slightly. Possible answers:
2. I might have warned him.
3. I shouldn't have eaten all the chocolate.
4. She might have called.
5. She could have listened to me.
6. I shouldn't have jogged five miles.
7. I should have applied for the job.
8. I ought to have done the laundry.
9. I should have invited her to the party.
10. He might have sent me a card.

EXERCISE 4

About a week ago, Jennifer was late for work again, and Doug, our boss, told me he wanted to fire her. I was really upset. Of course, Jennifer shouldn't *have* ~~had~~ been late so often, but he might ~~has~~ *have* talked to her about the problem before he decided to let her go. Then he laughed and told me to make her job difficult for her so that she would quit. He thought it was amusing! I just pretended I didn't hear him. What a mistake! It was unrealistic to think the problem would just go away. I ought ^*to have* confronted him right away. Or I could at least have warned Jennifer. Anyway, Jennifer is still here, but now I'm worried about my own job. Should I have ~~telling~~ *told* Doug's boss? I wonder. Maybe I should ~~handle~~ *have handled* things differently last week. The company should never ~~has~~ *have* hired this guy. I'd better figure out some techniques for handling these situations.

EXERCISE 5

A. **Checked items**
   Walk to work
   Buy coat
   Call Ron
B. **2.** shouldn't have walked
   3. should've made
   4. shouldn't have bought
   5. might've . . . called
   6. ought to have gone
   7. should've finished

EXERCISE 6

B. **1.** **A:** ought to have
   B: should've
   2. **A:** should've
   B: might've
   3. **A:** ought to have
   B: could've
   4. **A:** should've
   B: could've
   5. **A:** should've
   B: could've

EXERCISE 7

Answers will vary. Possible answers:
She shouldn't have left the window open.
She should have cleaned up her room.
She should have washed the dishes.
She should have fed the cat.

She should have studied for her test.
She should have watered her plant.
She shouldn't have left the stove on.

EXERCISES 8–10

Answers will vary.

UNIT 17 (pages 270–284)

AFTER YOU READ

A. 1. evidence   4. speculate
    2. contribute   5. conclusion
    3. estimate   6. encounter

B. Certain: 1, 4
   Possible: 2
   Impossible: 3

EXERCISE 1

2. d   **4.** c   **6.** b   **8.** g
3. h   **5.** f   **7.** a

EXERCISE 2

2. carved   **7.** have drawn
3. have   **8.** could
4. must   **9.** Could
5. could   **10.** have
6. have

EXERCISE 3

2. must not have had
3. couldn't have supported
4. could have developed
5. must have made
6. must have fished
7. must have eaten
8. may have lived
9. could have made
10. had to have come
11. could . . . have called
12. must have had
13. might have moved
14. couldn't have created

EXERCISE 4

2. Dinosaurs must not have survived the cold.
3. A huge meteor might have hit the Earth.
4. A Bigfoot couldn't have kidnapped Ostman.
5. Ostman must have seen a bear.
6. Ostman could have dreamed (OR dreamt) about a Bigfoot.
7. He might have made up the story.
8. The man had to have changed the photo.
9. The man might have seen a large fish.

10. The man may have seen a dead tree trunk.
11. A dinosaur couldn't have been in the lake.

EXERCISE 5

2. They couldn't have been.
3. They might have.
4. They could have.
5. They must have.
6. They may have.
7. He may not have.
8. He might not have been.
9. He must have.

EXERCISE 6

   Rapa Nui (Easter Island) is a tiny island in the middle of the Pacific. To get there, the first settlers had to ~~had~~ *have* traveled more than 1,000 miles in open boats. Some scientists believed only the Polynesians of the Pacific islands could have ~~make~~ *made* the journey. Others thought that Polynesians couldn't have carved the huge stone statues on Rapa Nui. They speculated that Mayans or Egyptians ~~maybe~~ *might* OR *may* OR *could* have traveled there. (Some people even said that space aliens might *have* helped!) Finally, a University of Oslo scientist was able to study the DNA from ancient skeletons. Professor Erika Halberg announced, "These people ~~has~~ *had* to have been the descendants of Polynesians."

   We now know that the islanders built the statues, but we have also learned that they must ~~had~~ *have* solved even more difficult problems. The first settlers came some time between the years 400 and 700. At first, Rapa Nui must ~~be~~ *have been* a paradise with its fishing, forests, and good soil. Their society may have grown too fast for the small island, however. Botanical studies show that by the 1600s they had cut down the last tree. The soil must ~~not~~ have washed away, so they couldn't farm. And with no wood for boats, they couldn't have *been* able to fish. For a period of time, people starved and fought violently, but when the Dutch discovered Rapa Nui in 1722, they found a peaceful, healthy population growing fields of vegetables. How ~~the islanders could~~ *could the islanders* have learned in this short period of time to live peacefully with so few resources? For our troubled world today, this might be the most important "mystery of Easter Island."

EXERCISE 7

A. 2. True
  3. True
  4. False. The man thinks this piece came from the top of the object.
  5. True
  6. False. The man thinks this object is a tool.

B. a. 2 **b.** 6 **c.** 5 **d.** 3 **e.** 4 **f.** 1

EXERCISE 8

B. 1. could have
  2. might've
  3. may've
  4. couldn't have
  5. might've
  6. must've
  7. could've

EXERCISES 9–11

Answers will vary.

PART VII   From Grammar to Writing
(pages 285–287)

1

Underlined sentences

He might have even decided that I couldn't afford to send a gift.

He couldn't have been angry with me!

Bracketed sentences

[He could've sent me an invitation and let me decide for myself.]

[I should have called him to discuss it.]

[He shouldn't have decided for me.]

2

  1. 3 **2.** 1 **3.** 4 **4.** 2

3

Possible answers:

Paragraph 2

You might have even decided that I couldn't afford to send a gift.

You couldn't have been angry with me!

Paragraph 3

You could've sent me an invitation and let me decide for myself.

You shouldn't have decided for me.

On the other hand, I should have called you to discuss it.

4–7

Answers will vary.

AFTER YOU READ

A. 1. d **2.** a **3.** b **4.** f **5.** c **6.** e

B. 1. students
  2. fascinating reporting and beautiful photographs
  3. Reza Deghati
  4. a group of professionals or geographers, explorers, teachers, and mapmakers
  5. people in over 160 million homes OR people in more than 140 countries
  6. It includes worlds beyond Earth.

EXERCISE 1

Active: 2, 4, 8, 10
Passive: 1, 3, 5, 6, 7, 9, 11

EXERCISE 2

  2. speak Russian
  3. by 23.2 million people
  4. 1,231 million people speak
  5. Korean is spoken
  6. Japanese is spoken
  7. speak English
  8. Turkish is spoken by

EXERCISE 3

A. 2. was . . . established (1548)
  3. are produced (agricultural tools)
  4. is . . . called (El Prado)
  5. is played (soccer)

B. 1. is surrounded
    is covered
  2. was established
  3. are made
  4. is known
  5. was formed

EXERCISE 4

  3. was created
  4. Is . . . grown
  5. No, it isn't
  6. is . . . spelled
  7. 's been eaten OR has been eaten
  8. are . . . used
  9. aren't raised OR 're not raised
  10. is . . . mined
  11. are found
  12. 's produced OR is produced
  13. are spoken
  14. Are . . . seen
  15. Yes, they are

EXERCISE 5

B. 2. Quinoa isn't spelled with a *k*. It's spelled with a *q*.

3. Llamas aren't raised only for transportation. They're raised for many uses.

4. Llamas aren't raised for meat in the lowlands. Cattle are raised for meat in the lowlands.

5. Rubber isn't found in that region. Oil, petroleum, and natural gas are found in that region.

6. The parrot isn't seen in the highest mountains. The condor is seen in the highest mountains.

7. A great civilization wasn't created on the shores of the Pacific. It was created on the shores of Lake Titicaca.

8. Portuguese isn't spoken in the government. Spanish is spoken in the government.

EXERCISE 6

3. are not allowed

4. is controlled by the feet, the head, and the body

5. wasn't played

6. has been made popular by Pelé, Beckham, and other international stars

7. have been played by different cultures

8. was enjoyed

9. was banned by King Edward III of England

10. were played

11. are held by the World Cup Association

EXERCISE 7

Reza Deghati ~~is~~ *was* born in Tabriz, Iran, in 1952. When he was only 14 years old, he began teaching himself photography. At first, he took pictures of his own country—its people and its architecture. When he was 25, he ~~was~~ decided to become a professional photographer. During a demonstration he was asked by a French news agency to take photos. He only shot one and a half rolls of film (instead of the usual 20 to 40), but his photos ~~was~~ *were* published in *Paris Match* (France), *Stern* (Germany), and *Newsweek*, (U.S.A).

Reza, as he is ~~knew~~ *known* professionally, has covered several wars, and he has ~~be~~ *been* wounded on assignment. Among all his assignments, the project dearest to his heart is photographing children, who he calls "the real victims of war." He has donated these photos to humanitarian organizations. Always concerned with the welfare of children, Reza has made it his life's mission to help them receive an education. His organization AINA *was* created, in part, to achieve this goal.

When he was interviewed ~~by an interviewer~~, Reza was asked to give advice to wannabe photojournalists. Reza replied, "There is a curtain between the photographer and the subject unless the photographer is able to break through it. . . . Open your heart, to them, so they know you care."

Today Reza Deghati lives in Paris. His photos ~~is~~ *are* widely distributed in more than 50 countries around the world, and his work is published in *National Geographic* as well as many other internationally famous publications.

EXERCISE 8

A. 2. ?
3. ?
4. F
5. T
6. T

B. 2. wasn't made
3. was sent
4. are grown
5. was written
6. is . . . sold

EXERCISE 9

B. 2. It wasn't taken in Bolivia. It was taken in Peru.

3. No. It wasn't written by him. It was edited by him.

4. It wasn't written in 1950, it was published then.

5. It wasn't translated into French. It was translated into Spanish.

6. No, John's story wasn't published, Tom's was.

EXERCISES 10–13

Answers will vary.

UNIT 19 (pages 308–321)

AFTER YOU READ

A. 1. assemble
2. period
3. undertaking
4. cooperate
5. benefit
6. perspective

B. 1. False. Japanese and Amercian astronauts worried about decision making.
2. True
3. False. Astronauts from 16 countries have been operating the ISS.

(continued on next page)

4. True

5. ?

6. False. Astronauts always spend meal times together.

EXERCISE 1

CM: Some parts of the ISS <u>had to be cancelled</u>, and some parts were delayed. But the whole station has finally been assembled. What an undertaking this has been! When was it completed?

BK: It was finished at the end of 2010. In February of that year, the last major sections—Tranquility and the Cupola—were attached. In Tranquility, oxygen <u>can be produced</u> and waste water <u>can be recycled</u>. Tranquility's equipment will support life on the ISS if communication with Earth <u>can't be maintained</u> for a period of time.

CM: And the Cupola? I understand it was built by the European Space Agency.

BK: Yes, it was. It's amazing. It <u>should be considered</u> one of the most important parts of the station. It's got seven huge windows, and the views of Earth and space are spectacular.

CM: Why the big windows?

BK: Because robots <u>have to be used</u> for maintenance outside the space station. Astronauts can observe and control them more easily from these windows. But I think that the perspective of Earth and space that we gain from these views might be just as important.

CM: Why is that?

BK: Observing the Earth and space keeps the astronauts in touch with the importance of their mission. Originally the station was going to include sleeping cabins with windows, but that part of the project <u>couldn't be accomplished</u> for a number of reasons. Now the sleeping cabins are windowless, and the Cupola is everyone's favorite hangout.

CM: Now that the station is complete, <u>will more scientific work be done</u> on the ISS?

BK: <u>Yes, it will</u>. The ISS is the first step to further exploration of our solar system. On the ISS, ways to grow food in space <u>can be developed</u>, and new materials <u>can be tested</u>, for example. But most important of all, human interactions <u>have got to be understood</u> better. An international crew from 16 different countries makes the ISS a wonderful laboratory for cross-cultural understanding. This could be one of the great benefits of the ISS.

CM: I guess we don't know what <u>might be discovered</u>, right?

BK: Right. That's what makes it so exciting.

EXERCISE 2

2. can be protected

3. can't be considered

4. can be compared

5. must be attached

6. can't be used

7. might be damaged

8. has to be sucked

9. could be washed

10. don't have to be concerned

11. can be sent

12. burned up OR burnt up

13. should be taken

14. doesn't have to be squeezed

15. can be heated

16. eaten

17. must be attached

18. has got to be provided

19. can be used

20. could be accessed

21. can be exchanged

22. are going to be enjoyed

23. must be allowed

24. will be lost

EXERCISE 3

2. can be sent

3. might not be accepted

4. shouldn't be rejected

5. 's got to be trained

6. can't be done

7. should be sent

8. have to be approved

9. will be shared

10. could be done

11. 're going to be surprised

EXERCISE 4

6:15 A.M. I used the sleeping restraints last night, so my feet and hands didn't float around as much. I slept a lot better. I'm going to suggest some changes in the restraints though—I think they ought to be ~~make~~ *made* more comfortable. I felt really trapped. And maybe these sleeping quarters could _be_ designed differently. They're too small.

10:45 A.M. My face is all puffy, and my eyes are red. Exercise helps a little—I'd better ~~be gotten~~ *get* on the exercise bike right away. I can be ~~misunderstanding~~ *misunderstood* very easily when I look like this. Sometimes people think I've been crying. And yesterday Max thought I was angry when he turned on *Star Trek*. Actually, I love that show.

1:00 P.M. Lunch was pretty good. Chicken teriyaki.

It's nice and spicy, and the sauce can actually ~~been~~ *be* tasted, even at zero gravity. They'd better fly in some more of it for us pretty soon. It's the most popular dish in the freezer.

4:40 P.M. I'm worried about my daughter. Just before I left on this mission, she said she was planning to quit school at the end of the semester. That's only a month away. I want to call her and discuss it. But I worry that I might get angry and yell. I might *be* ^ overheard by the others. They really should figure out some way to give us more privacy.

10:30 P.M. The view of Earth is unbelievably breathtaking! Tonight I spent a long time just looking out the window—watching Earth pass below. At night a halo of light surrounds the horizon. It's so bright that the tops of the clouds can ~~see~~ *be seen*. It can't be described. It simply ~~have~~ *has* to be experienced. I think it's even given me a better perspective on my problems with my daughter.

EXERCISE 5

A. **2.** True

3. True

4. False. Lon doesn't think oxygen is necessary on the planet.

5. True

6. False. The plants can't be grown in space.

7. True

B. **2.** could

3. will

4. must

5. be picked up by

6. can't

7. be helped

EXERCISE 6

B. **1.** can't be

2. shouldn't be

3. couldn't be

4. won't be

5. shouldn't be

6. must be

EXERCISES 7–10

Answers will vary.

UNIT 20 (pages 323–335)

AFTER YOU READ

A. **1.** event

2. option

3. risk

4. appearance

5. permanent

6. remove

B. **1.** False. Every culture has a different ideal of beauty.

2. True

3. ?

4. False. This form of body art was created thousands of years ago.

5. False. Tattoos are not permanent. You can get a tattoo removed.

6. True

7. True

8. ?

9. False. Some ways of changing your appearance are expensive and permanent.

EXERCISE 1

2. F **4.** T **6.** T **8.** T

3. T **5.** F **7.** F

EXERCISE 2

2. Debra got her hair permed on the 7th.

3. Amber had the dog groomed on the 14th.

4. They're going to get the windows washed on the 16th.

5. They had the carpets cleaned on the 13th.

6. Amber is going to have (OR is having) her ears pierced on the 25th.

7. Jake got his hair cut on the 12th.

8. They're going to have food and drinks delivered on the 20th.

EXERCISE 3

2. have / get it dry cleaned

3. 're going to have / get them washed OR 're having / getting them washed

4. 'm going to have / get it cut OR 'm having / getting it cut

5. have / get it colored

6. have / get it removed

7. 've . . . had / gotten it repaired

8. Did . . . have / get it painted OR Have . . . had / gotten it painted

EXERCISE 4

The party was tonight. It went really well! The house looked great. Last week, Mom and Dad had the floors waxed and all the windows ~~clean~~ *cleaned* professionally *painted* OR *had painted* so everything sparkled. And of course we ~~had~~ the whole house ~~painted~~ ourselves last summer. (I'll never forget that. It took us two weeks!) I wore my pink *had* dress that I ~~have~~ shortened by Bo, and my best friend Alicia, wore her new black gown. Right before the

(continued on next page)

party, I got ~~cut my hair~~ *my hair cut* by André. He did a great job. There were a lot of guests at the party. We had almost 50 people ~~invited~~ *invited*, and they almost all showed up for our family event! The food was great too. Mom made most of the main dishes herself, but she had the rest of the food ~~prepare~~ *prepared* by a caterer. Mom and Dad had hired a professional photographer, so at the end of the party we ~~took~~ *had* our pictures *taken*. As you can see, they look great!

EXERCISE 5

A. 2. car
   3. safe
   4. painting
   5. a computer
   6. face
B. Amber did the job herself: 3, 5, 7
   Amber hired someone to do the job: 1, 2, 4, 6, 8

EXERCISE 6

B. 1. 's had it colored
   2. have them done
   3. 's had it painted
   4. has it washed
   5. 've painted it
   6. 've colored it

EXERCISE 7

Answers will vary.

EXERCISE 8

Answers may vary. Possible answers:

She had her nose shortened. She had her chin lengthened. She had her lips enlarged. She had her tattoo and mole removed. She had her teeth straightened. She had her hair cut, permed, and colored. She had the lines around her mouth and eyes removed (OR filled in). She had her left ear pierced.

EXERCISES 9–10

Answers will vary.

1

   Two Buddhist monks built Haeinsa Temple in the year 802. The king gave them the money to build the temple after the two monks saved his queen's life. Haeinsa burned down in 1817, but the Main Hall was rebuilt in 1818 on its original foundations. Today, Haeinsa is composed of several large, beautiful buildings. It contains many paintings and statues. Someone carved three of the statues from a single ancient tree. Behind the Main Hall is a steep flight of stone stairs that leads to the Storage Buildings. These buildings, which escaped the fire, were constructed in 1488 in order to store wooden printing blocks of Buddhist texts. It was believed that these printing blocks could protect the country against invaders. Monks carved the 81,258 wooden blocks in the 13th century. A century later, nuns carried them to Haesina for safekeeping. Architects designed the Storage Buildings to preserve the wooden blocks. For more than five hundred years, the blocks have been kept in perfect condition because of the design of these buildings. Haeinsa, which means *reflection on a smooth sea*, is also known as the Temple of Teaching because it houses the ancient printing blocks.

2

   2. Three of the statues were carved from a single ancient tree.
   3. The 81,258 wooden blocks were carved (by monks) in the 13th century.
   4. A century later, they were carried (by nuns) to Haeinsa for safekeeping.
   5. The Storage Buildings were designed to preserve the wooden blocks.

3

   1. 802
   2. Two monks.
   3. *Possible answers:* To store wooden printing blocks of Buddhist teachings. OR Because the king gave money to two monks who had saved the queen's life.
   4. *Possible answers:* Beautiful buildings, stone stairs, many paintings and statues, special storage buildings
   5. Ancient printing blocks of Buddhist texts

4–7

Answers will vary.

AFTER YOU READ

A. 1. policy
2. consumer
3. precaution
4. secure
5. site
6. dispute

B. 1. c 2. b 3. b 4. a 5. b 6. c 7. a

EXERCISE 1

You're shopping in a foreign city. Should you pay full price, or should you bargain? <u>If you don't know the answer</u>, <u>you can pay too much or miss a fun experience</u>. <u>Bargaining is one of the greatest shopping pleasures</u> <u>if you know how to do it</u>. The strategies are different in different places. Check out these tips before you go.

Hong Kong

Hong Kong is one of the world's greatest shopping cities. <u>If you like to bargain</u>, <u>you can do it anywhere except the larger department stores</u>. The trick is not to look too interested. <u>If you see something you want</u>, <u>pick it up along with some other items and ask the prices</u>. Then make an offer below what you are willing to pay. <u>If the seller's offer is close to the price you want</u>, <u>then you should be able to reach an agreement quickly</u>.

Italy

Bargaining in Italy is appropriate in outdoor markets with street vendors. In stores, <u>you can politely ask for a discount</u> <u>if you want to bargain</u>. Take your time. <u>Make conversation</u> <u>if you speak Italian</u>. Show your admiration for the object by picking it up and pointing out its wonderful features. When you hear the price, look sad. Make your own offer. <u>Then end the bargaining politely</u> <u>if you can't agree</u>.

Mexico

In Mexico, people truly enjoy bargaining. There are some clear rules, though. <u>You should bargain only if you really are interested in buying the object</u>. <u>If the vendor's price is far more than you want to pay</u>, <u>then politely stop the negotiation</u>. <u>If you know your price is truly reasonable</u>, <u>walking away will often bring a lower offer</u>.

Remember, bargaining is always a social interaction, not an argument. <u>And it can still be fun even if you don't get the item you want at the price you want to pay</u>.

EXERCISE 2

2. If you'd like to buy some nice but inexpensive clothes, take the train to outdoor markets in towns *outside* of the city. OR Take the train to outdoor markets in towns outside of the city if you'd like to buy some nice but inexpensive clothes.

3. If you want to go shopping in the Grand Bazaar, you have to go during the week. OR You have to go during the week if you want to go shopping in the Grand Bazaar.

4. If your son wants to buy computer games, he should try the Panthip Plaza. OR Your son should try the Panthip Plaza if he wants to buy computer games.

5. If you plan to buy some silver jewelry in Mexico, you'll be able to get something nice at a very good price. OR You'll be able to get something nice at a very good price if you plan to buy some silver jewelry in Mexico. OR If you plan to buy some silver jewelry in Mexico, try bargaining. OR Try bargaining if you plan to buy some silver jewelry in Mexico.

6. If you'd like to find some nice secondhand clothing shops, try the Portobello market on the weekend. OR Try the Portobello market on the weekend if you'd like to find some nice secondhand clothing shops.

EXERCISE 3

2. You can make better business decisions if you have good business skills.

3. A buyer needs great interpersonal skills if she's negotiating prices.

4. If there's a big international fashion fair, I'm usually there.

5. If I go to a fair, I can see hundreds of products in a few days.

6. I usually stay two weeks if I'm traveling to Europe.

7. If my husband can come, he and our son, Pietro, do things together.

8. Pietro comes to the fair with me if my husband can't get away.

9. I always go shopping if I have free time.

EXERCISE 4

Answers will vary. Possible answers:

3. When people are watching the sun rise in Honolulu (OR Wellington), people are watching the sun set in Johannesburg (OR Madrid).

4. When it's midnight in Jakarta, it's 6:00 P.M. in Madrid.

5. When people are eating lunch in Montreal, people are eating dinner in Johannesburg (OR Madrid).

6. When people are getting up in Honolulu, people are going to bed in Bombay (OR Jakarta).

7. When it's 7:00 A.M. in Honolulu, it's 7:00 P.M. in Johannesburg.

8. When it's 5:00 A.M. in Wellington, it's 9:00 A.M. in Los Angeles.

EXERCISE 5

Tomorrow I'm flying to Hong Kong for a fashion show! My son, Pietro, is flying with me, and my husband is already there. Whenever Pietro's off

from school, I ~~liked~~ _like_ to take him on trips with me. If

my husband comes too, they ~~are going~~ _go_ sightseeing during the day. Our plane leaves Los Angeles around midnight.

If we ~~flew~~ _fly_ at night, we can sleep on the plane. (At least that's the plan!)

I love Hong Kong. We always have a great time when we ~~will~~ go there. The shopping is really fantastic. When I'm not working, I'm shopping.

I'll call you when I arrive at the hotel (around

7:00 A.M.). When it ~~will be~~ _'s_ 7:00 A.M. in Hong Kong, it's midnight in London. Is that too late to call? If

you want to talk, just ~~calling~~ _call_. And, of course you can always email me.

EXERCISE 6

A. 2. no
   3. boarding passes and passports
   4. emergency exits
   5. on time
   6. warm
B. 2. F   **3.** T   **4.** F   **5.** T   **6.** F

EXERCISE 7

B. 1. If I have time, I like to go to the mall.
   2. (no commas)
   3. If I like something, I sometimes buy two.
   4. When I shop online, I only use secure sites.
   5. (no commas)
   6. (no commas)
   7. If I don't like something, I return it.
   8. When I shop with friends, I always buy more.
   9. If the mall is crowded, I don't stay long.
   10. (no commas)

EXERCISES 8–12

Answers will vary.

UNIT 22 (pages 356–367)

AFTER YOU READ

   1. e   **2.** d   **3.** f   **4.** b   **5.** a   **6.** c
B. 1. False. Most people are superstitious.
   2. False. Most people will react superstitiously if they are worried.
   3. True

   4. False: 15 percent of people who study science are superstitious.
   5. True

EXERCISE 1

A. 2. e   **3.** f   **4.** a   **5.** c   **6.** b
B. 2. If I give my boyfriend a new pair of shoes, he'll walk out of the relationship.
   3. If I use my lucky pen, I'll get 100 percent on the test.

EXERCISE 2

2. unless	**7.** If	**12.** If
3. If	**8.** unless	**13.** if
4. If	**9.** Unless	**14.** if
5. if	**10.** If	**15.** unless
6. If	**11.** if	

EXERCISE 3

3. washes	**11.** itches
4. 'll rain	**12.** 'll give
5. walk	**13.** throws
6. 'll have	**14.** 'll start
7. sweep	**15.** sit
8. 'll sweep	**16.** won't get
9. is	**17.** throw
10. 'll get	**18.** 'll have

EXERCISE 4

2. If you take the job, you won't have the chance to travel a lot. You'll never leave the office.
3. If you stay at ZY3, you won't get a raise every year. You'll get one (OR a raise) every two years.
4. If you join ZY3, you're not going to have wonderful health care benefits. You'll have terrible health care benefits.
5. If you accept ZY3's offer, it won't be the best career move of your life. It will be the worst.

EXERCISE 5

Answers will vary. Possible answers:
3. If I take out student loans, I'll have to depend on my family. OR I'll have to depend on my family if I take out student loans.
4. If I go to law school, I'll earn more money. OR I'll earn more money if I go to law school.
5. If I earn more money, I'll pay back my loans quickly. OR I'll pay back my loans quickly if I earn more money.
6. If I pay back my loans quickly, I'll put my sister through college. OR I'll put my sister through college if I pay back my loans quickly.
7. If I go to law school, I may (OR might OR could) go into politics. OR I may (OR might OR could) go into politics if I go to law school.

8. If I go into politics, I'll be able to improve life for others. OR I'll be able to improve life for others if I go into politics.

9. If I go into politics, I might (OR may OR could) get elected to city council. OR I might (OR may OR could) get elected to city council if I go into politics.

10. If I get elected to city council, I might (OR may OR could) run for mayor. OR I might (OR may OR could) run for mayor if I get elected to city council.

EXERCISE 6

Should I campaign for student council president? I'll have to decide soon if I ~~wanted~~ *want* to run. If ~~I'll be~~ *I'm* busy campaigning, I won't have much time to study. That's a problem because I'm not going to get into law school ~~if I get~~ *unless I get* OR *if I don't get* good grades this year. On the other hand, the problems in this school are widespread, and nothing ~~is getting~~ *will get* done if Todd Laker becomes president again. I'm 100 percent certain of that, and most people agree with me. But will I know what to do if ~~I'll~~ *I* get the job? Never mind. I shouldn't anticipate difficulties. I really need to have a better attitude. I'll deal with that problem, if I win. I know what I'll do. If I become president, I *'ll* OR *'m going to* cut my hair.

That always brings me good luck!

EXERCISE 7

A. Issues checked: 1, 3, 4
B. 2. True
3. False. She thinks student council representatives should have their email addresses on the website.
4. False. The bus service won't be free. (It'll be less expensive than a taxi.)
5. True
6. False. She will ask the student council to create a committee to meet with state lawmakers.
7. True
8. True

EXERCISE 8

B. 1. (falling)   4. (rising)
2. (rising)   5. (rising)
3. (falling)   6. (falling)

EXERCISES 9–11

Answers will vary.

AFTER YOU READ

A. 1. a   2. b   3. c   4. a   5. c   6. b
B. 1. False. He and his wife lived in a pigpen.
2. True
3. True
4. False. The wife wasn't satisfied with the stone castle. (OR The wife wanted to be King.)
5. True
6. False. The fish didn't grant her wish.

EXERCISE 1

2. a. T	5. a. T	8. a. T
b. F	b. T	b. T
3. a. F	6. a. F	9. a. F
b. F	b. T	b. T
4. a. F	7. a. F	10. a. T
b. T	b. F	b. T

EXERCISE 2

2. wouldn't be
3. were
4. would moan
5. were
6. could wish
7. had
8. wouldn't have to deal
9. were
10. could find
11. thought
12. realized
13. would understand
14. might have to wait
15. insisted
16. were
17. could ride

EXERCISE 3

2. My husband would ask for a raise if he were ambitious. ~~OR If my husband were ambitious, he would ask for a raise.~~
3. I'd play sports if I were in shape. ~~OR If I were in shape, I'd play sports.~~
4. If I had enough time, I would (plan to) study for the exam. ~~OR I would (plan to) study for the exam if I had enough time.~~
5. If I weren't too old, I'd go back to school. ~~OR I would go back to school if I weren't too old.~~
6. ~~If my boss explained things properly, I could (OR would be able to) do my job.~~ OR I could (OR would be able to) do my job if my boss explained things properly.
7. If I were good at math, I'd balance my checkbook. ~~OR I would balance my checkbook if I were good at math.~~
8. ~~If I didn't feel nervous all the time, I could (OR would be able to) stop smoking.~~ OR I could (OR I'd be able to) stop smoking if I didn't feel nervous all the time.
9. If I weren't so tired, I wouldn't get up so late. ~~OR I wouldn't get up so late if I weren't so tired.~~

EXERCISE 4

2. I wish I were a handsome prince.
3. I wish I didn't live in the sea.
4. I wish I lived in a castle.
5. I wish I were married to a princess.
6. I wish the fisherman didn't come here every day.
7. I wish his wife didn't always want more.
8. I wish she were satisfied.
9. I wish they left (OR would leave) me alone.
10. I wish I could grant my own wishes.

EXERCISE 5

2. If you were the leader of this country, what would you do?
3. How would you feel if you never needed to sleep?
4. What would you do if you had more free time?
5. If you had three wishes, what would you ask for?
6. What would you do if you didn't have to work?
7. If you had a ticket for anywhere in the world, where would you travel?
8. If you could build anything, what would it be?
9. If you could meet a famous person, who would you want to meet?
10. Who would you have dinner with if you could invite three famous people?

EXERCISE 6

What would happen to the women if all the men
in the world ~~would disappear~~ *disappeared*? What would happen
to the men ~~when~~ *if* there were no women in the world? Philip Wylie's 1951 science-fiction novel, *The Disappearance*, addresses these fascinating questions. The answers show us how society has changed since the 1950s.

According to Wylie, if men and women ~~live~~ *lived* in different worlds, the results would be a disaster.

In Wylie's vision, men are too aggressive to survive on their own, and women are too helpless. If women didn't control them, men ~~will~~ *would* start more wars. If men ~~aren't~~ *weren't* there to pump gas and run the businesses, women wouldn't be able to manage.

If Wylie ~~is~~ *were* alive today, would he write the same novel? Today, a lot of men take care of their children, and a lot of women run businesses. In 1951, Wylie couldn't imagine these changes because of his opinions about men and women. I wish that Wylie ~~was~~ *were* here today. If he were, he might ~~learns~~ *learn* that men

are not more warlike than women, and women are not more helpless than men. His story might be very different.

EXERCISE 7

A. 2. marry
3. magic powers
4. scientist
5. worked in her laboratory
6. king

B. 2. True
3. True
4. False. Cindy wishes she could become a scientist.
5. False. If Cindy became a princess, she'd be too busy to study science.
6. True
7. True
8. False. Cindy and the prince didn't get married.

EXERCISE 8

1. wouldn't
2. 'd
3. wouldn't
4. 'd
5. wouldn't
6. 'd

EXERCISES 9–12

Answers will vary.

UNIT 24 (pages 384–397)

AFTER YOU READ

A. 1. e 2. c 3. a 4. f 5. d 6. b

B. 1. past
2. an accident
3. military events
4. possible
5. necessary
6. missed train

EXERCISE 1

1. **b.** T
2. **a.** F
   b. F
3. **a.** T
   b. F
4. **a.** F
   b. T
5. **a.** F
   b. T
6. **a.** T
   b. T
7. **a.** F
   b. T
8. **a.** F
   b. F
9. **a.** F
   b. T
10. **a.** T
    b. T

EXERCISE 2

2. would have gone . . . hadn't lost
3. could have gone . . . hadn't gotten
4. wouldn't have felt . . . had found
5. had . . . been
6. wouldn't have known . . . hadn't shown
7. hadn't rescued . . . wouldn't have saved
8. hadn't helped . . . might have gone
9. wouldn't have been . . . hadn't met
10. would have been . . . hadn't been

EXERCISE 3

B. 1. hadn't broken
   3. hadn't moved
   4. had been
   5. hadn't broken up
   6. had set
   7. had gotten up
   8. hadn't stopped
   9. had remembered
  10. had gotten
  11. would have crossed
  12. would have driven

EXERCISE 4

2. I wish I had caught my train. I wish I hadn't had to find a taxi.
3. I wish she hadn't gotten mugged near my taxi. I wish she hadn't needed to go to the hospital.
4. I wish Helen hadn't seen me with Lydia. I wish Helen hadn't left me.
5. I wish I hadn't started seeing Gerry again. I wish I hadn't broken up with him.
6. I wish I had told Helen about my wife. I wish I hadn't lost her trust.
7. I wish James had called me. I wish I hadn't gotten so depressed.
8. I wish James hadn't lied to Helen. I wish he hadn't hurt her.

EXERCISE 5

1. **b.** if she had planned ahead, I might not have met the love of my life.
  c. If she hadn't been so disorganized, my next trip to Jamaica wouldn't have been for my honeymoon.
2. **a.** if I had broken my leg, I couldn't have accepted her dinner invitation.
  b. If I hadn't gone skiing that day, she wouldn't have knocked me over.
  c. if she hadn't knocked me over, we wouldn't have gotten married.
3. **a.** If he hadn't been such a good writer, I wouldn't have thought about contacting him.
  b. If I had known, I might not have been brave enough to write him.

  c. If we had met right away, I might not have realized that.

EXERCISE 6

Have you ever had a small accident that made a
big difference in your life? If it ~~haven't~~ *hadn't* happened,
would your life have been much different? A lot of
people think so. They wish they ~~were~~ *had* avoided a mistake.
Or they worry that today's good luck *was* just a
mistake. Isaac Asimov's short story, *What If –*
suggests another way to look at life. Norman and
Livvy are traveling to New York to celebrate their
fifth wedding anniversary. The two met on a streetcar
when Livvy accidentally fell into Norman's lap.
Although they're happy, Livvy always thinks about
other possible outcomes of their lives. Now, on the
train to New York, she asks her favorite question:
"Norman, what if you ~~would have~~ *had* been one minute
later on the streetcar corner and had taken the next
car? What do you suppose would ~~had~~ *have* happened?"
Minutes later, a man carrying a box sits in the seat
across from them. He takes out a piece of glass that
looks like a TV screen and shows them the answers
to Livvy's question.

    Sadly, the couple sees that if Livvy hadn't fallen,
the two wouldn't *have* connected that day. Then the
screen shows Norman's marriage—to Livvy's friend
Georgette. Upset, Livvy now thinks Norman only
married her because she fell into his lap. "If I hadn't,
you would have married Georgette. If she ~~hasn't~~ *hadn't*
wanted you, you would have married somebody
else. You would have ~~marry~~ *married* anybody." However, the
couple next sees a New Year's Eve party with a very
unhappily married Norman and Georgette. The truth
is clear—Norman could never have forgotten Livvy,
even if they ~~did~~ *had* not married. But ~~will~~ *would* Norman and
Georgette have stayed together? Now *Norman* needs
to know! What would they be doing right now, he
wonders—"This very minute! If I ~~have~~ *had* married
Georgette." In the final scene, the couple sees
themselves, married (after Norman and Georgette's
divorce), and traveling on the same train, at the
same time, headed for their honeymoon in New
York. If Livvy hadn't fallen into Norman's lap,
nothing would have ~~changes~~ *changed*! At the end, Livvy sees
that her *What if* questions have caused pain, and that
". . . all the possibles are none of our business. The
real is enough."

EXERCISE 7

A. 1. late
   2. became a teacher
   3. an apartment
   4. woman
   5. lost
   6. café
B. 2. True
   3. True
   4. False. She didn't go to the movie.
   5. False. He might have called the police.
   6. True

EXERCISE 8

B. 1. hadn't
   2. couldn't have
   3. I'd
   4. could've
   5. I hadn't
   6. would've

EXERCISES 9–12

Answers will vary.

PART IX From Grammar to Writing
(pages 399–400)

1

   My biggest problem in school is my fear of talking in class. <u>My hands always shake</u> if <u>I answer a question or present a paper.</u> If <u>it is a big assignment, I even feel sick to my stomach.</u>

   There are several reasons for my problem, but my family's attitude is the most important. My family motto is, "Children should be seen, but not heard." Because <u>my parents never ask for our opinions,</u> <u>we never give them.</u> <u>I can feel my mother's disapproval</u> if <u>a talkative friend visits.</u> In addition, my parents classify their children. My older brother is the "Smart One." I am the "Creative One." I think <u>I would do better in school</u> if <u>they expected more,</u> but <u>they don't expect much.</u> Therefore, <u>I have not tried very hard.</u>

   Recently I decided to do something about my problem. I discovered that <u>I feel less nervous about giving a speech in class</u> if <u>I role-play my presentation with a friend.</u> <u>I have also joined discussion club.</u> As a result, <u>I get a lot of practice talking.</u> <u>My problem has causes,</u> so <u>it must have solutions</u>!

2

   2. I became more courageous because he believed in me. OR Because he believed in me, I became more courageous.

---

   3. We worked in groups, so I got used to talking about ideas with classmates.
   4. I have gotten a lot of practice. As a result, I feel more confident.
   5. Sena didn't understand the question. Therefore, she didn't raise her hand.

3–6

Answers will vary.

UNIT 25 (pages 402–415)

AFTER YOU READ

A. 1. a   **2.** c   **3.** b   **4.** c   **5.** b
B. 1. "Your credit card payment is late."
   2. "Traffic was bad."
   3. "I run a mile every day."
   4. "I'm fine."
   5. "People were more honest 10 years ago."

EXERCISE 1

   <u>"Lying during a job interview is risky business,"</u> says Martha Toledo, director of the management consulting firm Maxwell. <u>"The truth has a funny way of coming out."</u> Toledo tells the story of one woman applying for a job as an office manager. The woman told the interviewer <u>that she had a B.A. degree.</u> Actually, she was eight credits short. She also said <u>that she had made $50,000 at her last job.</u> The truth was $10,000 less. <u>"Many firms really do check facts,"</u> warns Toledo. In this case, a call to the applicant's company revealed the truth. <u>"She was a strong applicant,"</u> says Toledo, <u>"and most of the information on the resume was true. Nevertheless, those details cost her the job."</u>

   Toledo relates a story about another job applicant, George. During an interview, George reported that <u>he had quit his last job.</u> George landed the new job and was doing well until the company hired another employee, Pete. George and Pete had worked at the same company. Pete later told his boss <u>that his old company had fired George.</u> After George's supervisor became aware of the lie, he stopped trusting George, and their relationship became difficult. Eventually, George quit.

EXERCISE 2

   2. wanted **6.** said **10.** told
   3. her   **7.** her   **11.** said
   4. said   **8.** told **12.** felt
   5. had   **9.** wasn't **13.** she

EXERCISE 3

2. He said (that) his car had broken down (OR broke down).

He (OR Mr. Brown) said (that) he had missed the (OR missed) the meeting.

3. He said (that) he had to drive his aunt to the airport.

She (OR Tina) said that she had already bought (OR already bought) movie tickets.

4. He said that she looked (OR looks) very fit.

She said (that) she exercised (OR exercises) every day.

5. He (OR Mr. Morgan) said (that) his bill was (OR is) overdue.

He said (that) he had just mailed (OR he just mailed) the check.

6. He said (that) he was (OR he's) 35.

She said (that) he didn't (OR doesn't) look 35.

EXERCISE 4

3. She (OR Lisa) said (that) they hadn't revealed the starting salary.

4. He (OR Ben) said (that) he needed (OR needs) a lot of money to pay off his student loans.

5. She (OR Lisa) said (that) they wanted (OR want) someone with some experience as a programmer.

6. He (OR Ben) told her (that) he worked (OR works) as a programmer for Data Systems.

7. She (OR Lisa) said (that) they needed (OR need) a college graduate.

8. He (OR Ben) told her (that) he had graduated (OR graduated) from Florida State.

9. She (OR Lisa) said (that) they didn't (OR don't) want a recent graduate.

10. He (OR Ben) told her (that) he had gotten (OR got) his degree four years ago.

11. She (OR Lisa) told him (that) she hadn't been (OR wasn't) aware of that.

12. He (OR Ben) said (that) he really appreciated the information.

13. She (OR Lisa) told him (that) her boss had just come in and (that) she had to go.

EXERCISE 5

Everyone gets urgent email messages. They
                                    wants
tell you that Bill Gates now ~~wanted~~ to give away
                            OR *tell you*
his money—to YOU! They say ~~you~~ that a popular
floor cleaner kills family pets. They report that your
                    has
computer monitor ~~had~~ taken photographs of you.
Before I became aware of Internet hoaxes, I used to
forward these emails to all my friends. Not long

                    explained
ago, a very annoyed friend ~~explains~~ that the story
about killer bananas was a hoax (an untrue story).
        said OR *told me*
He ~~said me~~ ×that the majority of those scary emails
were hoaxes.× He told me about these common
telltale signs of hoaxes:

                                is
! The email always says that it ~~was~~ very urgent. It
has lots of exclamation points.

        you
! It tells ˄ that it is not a hoax and quotes important

people. (The quotations are false.)

! It urges you to send the email to everyone you
know.

        said OR *told me*
He also ~~told~~ that a lot of Internet sites reveal
information about Interent hoaxes. With this
information, you can avoid the embarrassment of
forwarding all your friends a false warning. So,
                                has
before *you* announce that sunscreen ~~had~~ made
people blind, check out the story on a reliable
website.

EXERCISE 6

A. 1. b. her parents
  2. a. work out
    b. attend
  3. a. Monday
    b. Tuesday
  4. a. opinion of
    b. will

Answers may vary slightly.

2. She said (OR told Ben) (that) she never missed (OR misses) an aerobics class, but she's going to sleep late on Sunday.

3. She said (OR told Mark) (that) the weekly staff meeting was on Monday, but it's on Tuesday.

4. She said (OR told Chris) (that) she loved the meat sauce, but she's a vegetarian.

EXERCISE 7

1. Doesn't believe
2. Believes
3. Doesn't believe
4. Doesn't believe
5. Believes
6. Believes

EXERCISES 8–12

Answers will vary.

AFTER YOU READ

A. 1. optimistic
   2. evacuate
   3. bear
   4. collapse
   5. restore
   6. damage

B. Items checked:
   1. "It has been raining for more than 24 hours."
   2. "Many treasured poems in the Czech language have been lost."
   3. "I'm back in my hometown this summer to help."
   4. "With another few feet of water, nothing will be safe."
   5. "Governments have to do something about climate change."

EXERCISE 1

2. c	**5.** a	**8.** b
3. c	**6.** c	**9.** a
4. a	**7.** b	**10.** a

EXERCISE 2

2. They said (that) it was going to pass (OR is going to pass) north of here.
3. They said (that) the bridge had collapsed yesterday afternoon.
4. They said (that) it wasn't (OR isn't) really a hurricane, just a big storm.
5. They said (that) people in Dresden were evacuating.
6. They said (that) they wouldn't (OR won't) restore the electricity until today.
7. They said (that) they couldn't (OR can't) reopen the schools because of the damage.
8. They said (that) we ought to use bottled water for a few days.

EXERCISE 3

B. *Answers may vary slightly.*
2. That's right. He said (that) floods were (OR are) the most widespread of all natural disasters.
3. That's wrong. He said (that) floods were (OR are) usually caused by intense, heavy rainfall.
4. That's wrong. He said (that) tsunamis are often caused by earthquakes.
5. That's wrong. He said (that) a flash flood was (OR is) a flood that comes with little or no warning.
6. That's right. He said (that) a flash flood was (OR is) the most dangerous type of flood.
7. That's wrong. He said (that) flash floods caused (OR cause) 75 percent of all flood-related deaths.

8. That's right. He said (that) we had (OR have) made progress in predicting floods.
9. That's wrong. He said (that) people had to (OR must) improve their protection of the Earth and the environment.
10. That's wrong. He said (that) we should restore those green areas.
11. That's right. He said (that) many scientists believe (OR believed) that global warming was (OR is) causing an increase in the number of floods.
12. That's wrong. He said (that) we couldn't (OR can't) completely stop floods from happening.
13. That's true. He said (that) he's optimistic that we can (OR could) predict floods better and prevent flood damage from increasing.

EXERCISE 4

2. I'm worried about you and Eva.
3. If you weren't so stubborn, you'd pack up and leave right now.
4. I've had some experience with floods.
5. You have to put sandbags in front of your doors.
6. You ought to fill the sinks and bathtubs with clean water.
7. You should buy a lot of batteries.
8. ~~We (OR Uta and I) are worried.~~ We can't stay here.
9. We want to stay with you (OR you and Eva).
10. We're leaving tonight.
11. Uta and I should have called sooner.
12. The storm will hit tonight.
13. The rainfall is going to be very heavy.
14. The storm may (OR might) last for several hours.

EXERCISE 5

What is it like to live through a flood? For my report, I interviewed the Nemec family, who experienced last month's floods in our city. They reported that ~~we~~ *they* had experienced fear and sadness. On September 14, the family went to a movie. Jerzy, a high school student, said they ~~can't~~ *couldn't* drive the car home because their street was flooded. He ~~told~~ *said OR told me* it had happened in only three hours. Mrs. Nemec said that all their belongings were ruined, but that their cat ~~has~~ *had* gone to an upstairs bedroom. They were sad about losing so many items, but she said she ~~will~~ *would* have been much sadder to lose the family pet. Jerzy's father also said their home had been a complete mess, and the family had worked all *that* ~~this~~ week to clean out the house.

Anna, who is in junior high school, wanted to keep her old dollhouse. It had belonged to her mother and her mother's mother. At first, her father told her that she ~~can't~~ *couldn't* keep it because seeing it would just make her sad. Anna replied that she saw memories in that dollhouse—not just broken wood. She said ~~I~~ *she* couldn't bear to throw it away. In the end, they kept it. Mr. Nemec said that he and Anna ~~are~~ *were* able to restore the dollhouse a few weeks later. Mrs. Nemec said that Anna had taught them something important ~~today~~ *that day*.

EXERCISE 6

A. 1. has fallen
  2. Schools
  3. conditions
  4. gas
  5. open
  6. evening
  7. won't

B. Items checked
  2. should go home immediately
  3. may stay closed
  4. are dangerous
  5. drive slowly
  6. avoid driving
  7. will close at 1:00
  8. will stay open until 5:00
  9. will be closed tomorrow
  10. will close at noon
  11. will stay open until evening
  12. are open now

EXERCISE 7

1. Tom said they would leave after breakfast.

2. He said they weren't dangerous.

3. No. He told me he'd call us later.

4. They said that the storm could get bigger.

5. No. I told you we needed some yesterday.

6. Definitely. You told me that I should pack it.

7. He told me to drive carefully.

EXERCISES 8–10

Answers will vary.

AFTER YOU READ

A. 1. b **2.** c **3.** b **4.** a **5.** c **6.** b
B. Items checked: 1, 3, 5, 6

EXERCISE 1

2/18 **11:00 A.M.** The clinic called and asked me to arrive at 8:30 tonight. They told me to bring my nightshirt and toothbrush. They told me people also like to bring their own pillow, but I decided to travel light.
  8:30 P.M. I arrived on schedule. My room was small but cozy. Only the video camera and cable told me I was in a sleep clinic. Juan Estrada, the technician for the night shift, told me to relax and watch TV for an hour.
  9:30 P.M. Juan came back and got me ready for the test. He pasted 12 small metal disks to my face, legs, and stomach. I asked him to explain, and he told me that the disks, called electrodes, would be connected to a machine that records electrical activity in the brain. I felt like a character in a science fiction movie.
  11:30 P.M. Juan came back and asked me to get into bed. After he hooked me up to the machine, he instructed me not to leave the bed that night. I fell asleep easily.

2/19 **7:00 A.M.** Juan came to awaken me and to disconnect the wires. I told him that I didn't think insomnia was my problem—those electrodes hadn't interfered with my sleep at all! He invited me to join him in the next room, where he had spent the whole night monitoring the equipment. I looked at the pages of graphs and wondered aloud whether Juan and Dr. Ray would be able to read my weird dream of the night before. Juan laughed and told me not to worry. "Those just show electrical impulses," he assured me.
  8:00 A.M. Dr. Ray reviewed my data with me. He told me I had healthy sleep patterns, except for some leg movements during the night. He told me to get more exercise, and I promised I would.

EXERCISE 2

  3. She said to sip some hot herbal tea with honey.
  4. She told her not to drink black tea.
  5. She said to pinch the place between her upper lip and her nose.
  6. She told him to make a toothpaste of one tablespoon of baking soda and a little water.
  7. She said to brush as usual.

(continued on next page)

8. She told him to spread cool, cooked oatmeal over the rash.
9. She said to try soaking the rash in a cool bath with a quarter cup baking soda.
10. She told him not to scratch the rash.
11. She said to eat onions or garlic every day.
12. She told him to ask his doctor about a vitamin B supplement.

EXERCISE 3

I dreamed that an extraterrestial came into my room. He told me to get up. Then he said to follow him. There was a spaceship outside the clinic. It was an astonishing sight! I asked the creature from outer space to show me the ship, so he invited me to come aboard. Juan, the lab technician, was on the ship. Suddenly, Juan told me to pilot the ship. He ordered me not to leave the controls. Then he went to sleep. Next, Dr. Ray was at my side giving me instructions. He told me to slow down. Then he said to point the ship toward the Earth. There was a loud knocking noise as we hit the ground, and I told everyone not to panic. Then I heard Juan tell me to wake up. I opened my eyes and saw him walking into my room at the sleep clinic.

Answers may vary slightly.
2. Follow me.
3. Come aboard.
4. Lead the way!
5. Pilot the ship.
6. Don't leave the controls.
7. Slow down.
8. Point the ship toward the Earth.
9. Don't panic.
10. Wake up.

EXERCISE 4

                                                          to
In writing class today, the teacher asked Juan ‸

read one of his stories. Juan, who works in a sleep clinic, read a story about someone with insomnia. It was wonderful and everyone in class enjoyed it a
                                                 to
lot. After class, the teacher invited me ‸ read a story in

class next week. I don't feel ready to do this. I asked
       not
her ~~no~~ to call on me next week because I'm having trouble getting ideas. She told me ~~that~~ not to worry, and she said to wait for two weeks. I was still worried about coming up with an idea, so I decided
                                                      to
to talk to Juan after class. I asked him ‸ tell me the

source for his ideas. He was really helpful. He said that they came from his dreams. I was astonished— I'd never thought of using my dreams!
              told
He ~~said~~ me to keep a dream journal for ideas. Then he invited me ✗ to read some of his journal. ✗ It was very interesting, so I asked him to give me some tips on remembering dreams. (Juan says that everyone dreams, but many people, like me, just don't remember their dreams in the morning.)
                                        to get
Again, Juan was very helpful. He said ~~getting~~ a good night's sleep because the longer dreams come
                                          told
after a long period of sleep. He also ~~tell~~ me to keep my journal by the bed and to write as soon as I wake
            not to
up. He said ~~to no~~ move from the sleeping position.
                                        to
He also told me not ‸ think about the day at first. (If

you think about your day, you might forget your dreams.) Most important—every night he tells himself ~~that~~ to remember his dreams. These all sound like great ideas, and I want to try them out right away. The only problem is—I'm so excited about this, I'm not sure I'll be able to fall asleep!

EXERCISE 5

A. 2. False. At the clinic, they said that fatigue causes headaches.
   3. True
   4. False. The clinic told him not to use painkillers right now.
   5. True
   6. False. At the clinic they said to eat several small meals every day.
   7. False. Ann has been going to a headache clinic for a long time.
B. Items checked:
   Do: 1, 2, 4
   Don't Do: 3, 6, 7
   Not Mentioned: 5, 8

   ~~1. Do~~   ~~5. Not Mentioned~~
   ~~2. Do~~   ~~6. Don't Do~~
   ~~3. Don't Do~~   ~~7. Don't Do~~
   ~~4. Do~~   ~~8. Not Mentioned~~

EXERCISE 6

1. not to eat
2. to arrive
3. to sleep
4. not to exercise
5. not to use
6. to put

EXERCISE 7

Answers will vary.

EXERCISE 8

Answers may vary slightly.

His parents told him (OR said) not to stay up after 10:00, but it's 11:30 and he's not in bed.

His parents told him (OR said) not to drink cola, but he drank some.

His parents told him (OR said) to drink some milk, and he did.

His parents told him (OR said) to have some cake, and he did.

His parents told him (OR said) to save some cake for them, but he and his friends ate almost the whole cake.

His parents told him (OR said) to take the garbage out, but he didn't.

His parents told him (OR said) to wash the dishes, and he did.

His parents told him (OR said) to put the dishes away, but he didn't.

His parents told him (OR said) to let the cat in, and he did.

His parents told him (OR said) to lock the back door, but the door is open.

His parents told him (OR said) to do his homework, but he didn't.

His parents told him (OR said) not to watch any horror movies, but he did.

His parents told him (OR said) not to invite his friends over that night, but he did.

EXERCISE 9

Answers will vary.

UNIT 28 (pages 445–459)

AFTER YOU READ

A. 1. c **2.** b **3.** a **4.** c **5.** a **6.** b
B. Items checked: 2

EXERCISE 1

Underlined items

Don: So, how did the interview go?

Melissa: It was very strange.

Don: What happened?

Melissa: Well, it started off OK. He asked me <u>how much experience I'd had</u>, and I told him I'd been a public relations officer for 10 years. Let's see . . . He also asked <u>what I would change about my current job</u>. That was a little tricky.

Don: What did you say?

Melissa: Well, I didn't want to say anything negative, so I told him that I was ready to take on a lot more responsibility.

Don: Good. What else did he ask?

Melissa: Oh, you know, the regular things. He asked <u>what my greatest success had been</u>, and <u>how much money I was making</u>.

Don: Sounds like a normal interview to me. What was so strange about it?

Melissa: Well, at one point, he just stopped talking for a long time. Then he asked me all these questions that weren't even related to the job. I mean, *none* of them were appropriate.

Don: Like what?

Melissa: He asked me <u>if I'd cleaned out my car recently</u>.

Don: You're kidding.

Melissa: No, I'm not. Then he asked me <u>why my employer didn't want me to stay</u>.

Don: That's crazy. I hope you told him that you hadn't been fired.

Melissa: Of course. In fact, I told him I'd never even gotten a negative evaluation. Oh, and then he asked me <u>if I was good enough to work for his company</u>.

Don: What did you tell him?

Melissa: I told him that with my skills and experience I was one of the best in my field.

Don: That was a great answer. It sounds like you handled yourself very well.

Melissa: Thanks. But now I'm asking myself <u>if I really want this job</u>.

Don: Take your time. This job is a potential opportunity for you. Don't make any quick decisions.

Direct questions checked

1, 2, 4, 5, 7, 9

EXERCISE 2

2. She asked (him) when the interview was.

3. She asked (him) where the company was.

4. She asked (him) if he needed directions.

5. She asked (him) how long it takes (OR took) to get there.

6. She asked (him) if he was going to drive.

7. She asked (him) who was going to interview him.

8. She asked (him) when they would let him know.

EXERCISE 3

Answers may vary slightly.

2. Ms. Stollins asked (Jaime OR him) what kind of experience he had.
3. Jaime asked (her OR Ms. Stollins) if (OR whether) there was opportunity for promotion.
4. Ms. Stollins asked (him OR Jaime) if (OR whether) he was interviewing with other companies.
5. Jaime asked (her OR Ms. Stollins) what his responsibilities would be.
6. Jaime asked (her OR Ms. Stollins) how job performance was rewarded.
7. Ms. Stollins asked (him OR Jaime) what his starting salary at his last job had been.
8. Ms. Stollins asked (him OR Jaime) if (OR whether) he had gotten along well with his last employer.
9. Jaime asked (her OR Ms. Stollins) when the job starts.
10. Ms. Stollins asked (him OR Jaime) why he had applied for this position.
11. Jaime asked (her OR Ms. Stollins) if (OR whether) they had had any major layoffs in the past few years.

EXERCISE 4

This morning I interviewed Carlos Lopez for the administrative assistant position. Since this job requires a lot of contact with the public, I did some stress questioning. I asked Mr. Lopez why ~~couldn't he~~ *he couldn't* work under pressure. I also asked him why his supervisor disliked him. Finally, I inquired when he would quit the job with our company~~?~~.

Mr. Lopez kept his poise throughout the interview. He answered all my questions calmly, and he had some excellent questions of his own. He asked ^X if we expected changes in the job. ^X He also wanted to know how often ~~do we perform~~ *we perform* OR *we performed* employee evaluations. I was quite impressed when he asked why ~~did I decide~~ *I decided* to join this company.

Mr. Lopez is an excellent candidate for the job, and I believe he will handle the responsibilities well. At the end of the interview, Mr. Lopez inquired when we could let him know our decision~~?~~. I asked him ~~if whether~~ *if* OR *whether* he was considering another job, and he said he was. I think we should act quickly in order not to lose this excellent potential employee.

EXERCISE 5

A. Items checked:

OK to Ask
Reason for leaving job
Reason for seeking position
Skills
Job performance

Not OK to Ask
Age
National origin
Height or weight
Marital status
Information about spouse
Arrest record
Financial situation

Illegal questions
2. Are you married?
3. What nationality are you?
4. What does your husband do?
5. Do you owe anyone any money?
6. Have you ever been arrested?
7. How tall are you?

B. 2. He asked her if she was married.
3. He asked her what nationality she was.
4. He asked her what her husband did.
5. He asked her if she (OR they) owed anyone any money.
6. He asked her if she had ever been arrested.
7. He asked her how tall she was.

EXERCISE 6

B. 1. A: So, did the interview go OK? ↗
　　B: I think so. The interviewer asked me if she could call my old employer. ↘
2. A: Did you say yes?
　　B: Of course. And she also wanted to know whether I could start next month. ↘
3. A: Sounds good. Did you ask any questions? ↗
　　B: Yes. I asked her if she liked working there. ↘
4. A: Great question. So, does she like working there? ↗
　　B: She said Yes. But was she telling the truth? ↗
5. A: Never mind. Just ask yourself if you want the job. ↘
　　B: I don't know. Can we talk about something else? ↗
6. A: Sure. I forgot to ask you if you wanted to eat out tonight. ↘
　　B: Sounds good. Do you want to try that new Japanese restaurant. ↗

EXERCISES 7–10

Answers will vary.

UNIT 29 (pages 461–476)

AFTER YOU READ

A. 1. d **2.** c **3.** f **4.** b **5.** a **6.** e

B. 1. the United States
  2. why
  3. the server
  4. a smaller
  5. often not logical
  6. a travel website

EXERCISE 1

you've ever avoided a situation just because you
   didn't know <u>how much to tip</u>.
you've ever realized (too late) that you were
   supposed to offer a tip.
you've ever given a huge tip and then wondered <u>if a</u>
   <u>tip was necessary at all</u>.
you've ever needed to know <u>how to calculate the</u>
   <u>right tip instantly</u>.
you're new to the United States and you're not sure
   <u>who you should tip here</u>.
you'd like to learn <u>how tipping properly can get you</u>
   <u>the best service for your money</u>.
What readers are saying . . .
"Essential, reliable information—I can't imagine <u>how</u>
<u>I got along without it</u>."
   —*Chris Sarton, Minneapolis, Minnesota*
"Take *Tips* along if you want a stress-free vacation."
   —*Midori Otaka, Osaka, Japan*
"I took my fiancée to dinner at Deux Saisons and
knew exactly <u>how to tip everyone</u>!"
   —*S. Prasad, San Francisco, California*
"You need this book—whether you stay in hostels or
five-star hotels."
   —*Cuno Pumpin, Bern, Switzerland*
*Send for the ultimate guide to tipping and answer all
your tipping questions.*
   Yes! I want to learn <u>who to tip</u>, <u>when to tip</u>,
and <u>how much to tip</u>. Please send me additional
information on *Tips on Tipping*. I understand that
the book will be $4.95 plus $2.00 postage and
handling for each copy. (New York residents:
Add sales tax.) Contact Martin Unlimited, Inc. at
dmifdmif@yahoo.com.

EXERCISE 2

  2. how I can tell if (OR whether) the tip is included
   in the bill?
  3. if (OR whether) restaurant servers accept tips
   now?

  4. why this happened?
  5. if (OR whether) I should offer them a tip or not
   OR whether to offer them a tip or not
  6. who accepts a tip and who doesn't
  7. if (OR whether) it's the custom to tip the airport
   and train porters?

EXERCISE 3

  2. how much we are supposed to tip the taxi
   driver?
  3. how we are going to choose.
  4. how much a bus tour costs?
  5. what they put in the sauce.
  6. where the Forum is?
  7. how much the subway costs?
  8. how far you're going.
  9. if (OR whether) they have tour buses that go
   there.
 10. we could rent a car and drive there?

EXERCISE 4

  2. how to get
  3. when (OR what time) to leave
  4. where to go
  5. how to figure out
  6. who to invite

EXERCISE 5

   if
   I wonder ‸you can help clarify some tipping
                    to do
situations for me. I never know what ~~doing~~ at the
hairdresser's. I don't know if I should tip the person
                       .
who washes my hair? What about the person who
cuts it, and the person who colors it? And what
                  ?
happens if the person is the owner‸Do you know
if OR *whether*
~~do~~ I still need to tip him or her? That doesn't seem
logical. (And often I'm not even sure who ✗ the
                  is
owner!) Then I never know how much to tip or
          ‸ *I should*
where ~~should I~~ leave the tip? Do I leave it on the
counter or in the person's hands? What if somebody's
hands are wet or have hair color on them? Can I
just put the tip in his or her pocket? It all seems so
complicated! I can't imagine how ✗✗ customers
             . OR !
figure all this out? What's the custom? I really need
to find out what to do—and FAST! My hair is getting
very long and dirty. Please help!

EXERCISE 6

A. 2. True

   3. False. He wants to know where to leave the tip.

   4. True

   5. True

   6. False. She wants to know where to leave the tip for the person who washes her hair.

   7. True

   8. False. He and his friends just ordered a pizza.

B. 2. a   **5.** b   **7.** a

   3. b   **6.** b   **8.** a

   4. a

EXERCISE 7

Falling intonation: 1, 4, 7
Rising intonation: 2, 3, 5, 6

EXERCISES 8–12

Answers will vary.

PART X   From Grammar to Writing
(pages 478–480)

1

   In September 2012, I purchased a computer from your company. After the one-year warranty expired, I bought an extended service contract every year. I always received a renewal notice in the mail that told me <u>that my policy was going to expire in a few weeks</u>. This year, however, I did not receive the notice, and, as a result, I missed the deadline.

   Upon realizing this mistake, I immediately called your company and asked <u>if I could renew the service contract</u>. The representative said, "<u>It's too late, Miss</u>."

He said that <u>if I wanted to extend my contract, they would have to send someone to my home to inspect my computer</u>. He also told me <u>I would have to pay $160 for this visit</u>. He said <u>that my only other option was to ship my computer back to the company for inspection</u>. I told him <u>that neither of these options was acceptable</u>.

   When I asked him <u>why I hadn't been notified that my contract was going to</u> expire, he said, "<u>We don't send notices out anymore</u>." I said <u>that I wanted to make a complaint</u>. He said, "<u>Don't complain to me. I don't even park the cars of the people who make these decisions</u>."

   I think <u>that your representatives should be more polite when speaking to customers</u>. I also think <u>that your customers should have been told that they would no longer receive renewal notices in the mail</u>. That way, I would not have missed the deadline. I would, therefore, greatly appreciate it if I could have my service contract renewed without having to go through the inconvenience and expense of having my computer inspected.

   Thank you for your attention.

2

   2. direct

   3. inside

   4. indirect

   5. direct

   6. word *that* . . . statement

   7. direct

3–6

Answers will vary.

Single-User License Agreement

THESE TERMS APPLY TO ALL LICENSED SOFTWARE ON THE DISK EXCEPT THAT THE TERMS FOR USE OF ANY SHAREWARE OR FREEWARE ON THE DISKETTES ARE AS SET FORTH IN THE ELECTRONIC LICENSE LOCATED ON THE DISK:

1. **GRANT OF LICENSE AND OWNERSHIP:** The enclosed computer programs ("Software") are licensed, not sold, to you by Pearson Education, Inc. ("We" or the "Company") and in consideration of your payment of the license fee, which is part of the price you paid, and your agreement to these terms. We reserve any rights not granted to you. You own only the disk(s) but we and/or our licensors own the Software itself. This license allows you to use and display your copy of the Software on a single computer (i.e., with a single CPU) at a single location, so long as you comply with the terms of this Agreement. You may make one copy for back up, or transfer your copy to another CPU, provided that the Software is usable on only one computer.

2. **RESTRICTIONS:** You may not transfer or distribute the Software or documentation to anyone else. Except for backup, you may not copy the documentation or the Software. You may not network the Software or otherwise use it on more than one computer or computer terminal at the same time. You may not reverse engineer, disassemble, decompile, modify, adapt, translate, or create derivative works based on the Software or the Documentation. You may be held legally responsible for any copying or copyright infringement which is caused by your failure to abide by the terms of these restrictions.

3. **TERMINATION:** This license is effective until terminated. This license will terminate automatically without notice from the Company if you fail to comply with any provisions or limitations of this license. Upon termination, you shall destroy the Documentation and all copies of the Software. All provisions of this Agreement as to limitation and disclaimer of warranties, limitation of liability, remedies or damages, and our ownership rights shall survive termination.

4. **LIMITED WARRANTY AND DISCLAIMER OF WARRANTY:** Company warrants that for a period of 30 days from the date you purchase this Software, the Software, when properly installed and used in accordance with the Documentation, will operate in substantial conformity with the description of the Software set forth in the Documentation, and that for a period of 30 days the disk(s) on which the Software is delivered shall be free from defects in materials and workmanship under normal use. The Company does not warrant that the Software will meet your requirements or that the operation of the Software will be uninterrupted or error-free. Your only remedy and the Company's only obligation under these limited warranties is, at the Company's option, return of the disk for a refund of any amounts paid for it by you or replacement of the disk. THIS LIMITED WARRANTY IS THE ONLY WARRANTY PROVIDED BY THE COMPANY AND ITS LICENSORS, AND THE COMPANY AND ITS LICENSORS DISCLAIM ALL OTHER WARRANTIES, EXPRESS OR IMPLIED, INCLUDING WITHOUT LIMITATION, THE IMPLIED WARRANTIES OF MERCHANTABILITY AND FITNESS FOR A PARTICULAR PURPOSE. THE COMPANY DOES NOT WARRANT, GUARANTEE OR MAKE ANY REPRESENTATION REGARDING THE ACCURACY, RELIABILITY, CURRENTNESS, USE, OR RESULTS OF USE, OF THE SOFTWARE.

5. **LIMITATION OF REMEDIES AND DAMAGES:** IN NO EVENT, SHALL THE COMPANY OR ITS EMPLOYEES, AGENTS, LICENSORS, OR CONTRACTORS BE LIABLE FOR ANY INCIDENTAL, INDIRECT, SPECIAL, OR CONSEQUENTIAL DAMAGES ARISING OUT OF OR IN CONNECTION WITH THIS LICENSE OR THE SOFTWARE, INCLUDING FOR LOSS OF USE, LOSS OF DATA, LOSS OF INCOME OR PROFIT, OR OTHER LOSSES, SUSTAINED AS A RESULT OF INJURY TO ANY PERSON, OR LOSS OF OR DAMAGE TO PROPERTY, OR CLAIMS OF THIRD PARTIES, EVEN IF THE COMPANY OR AN AUTHORIZED REPRESENTATIVE OF THE COMPANY HAS BEEN ADVISED OF THE POSSIBILITY OF SUCH DAMAGES. IN NO EVENT SHALL THE LIABILITY OF THE COMPANY FOR DAMAGES WITH RESPECT TO THE SOFTWARE EXCEED THE AMOUNTS ACTUALLY PAID BY YOU, IF ANY, FOR THE SOFTWARE OR THE ACCOMPANYING TEXTBOOK. BECAUSE SOME JURISDICTIONS DO NOT ALLOW THE LIMITATION OF LIABILITY IN CERTAIN CIRCUMSTANCES, THE ABOVE LIMITATIONS MAY NOT ALWAYS APPLY TO YOU.

6. **GENERAL:** This agreement shall be construed in accordance with the laws of the United States of America and the State of New York, applicable to contracts made in New York, and shall benefit the Company, its affiliates and assignees. This agreement is the complete and exclusive statement of the agreement between you and the Company and supersedes all proposals or prior agreements, oral, or written, and any other communications between you and the Company or any representative of the Company relating to the subject matter of this agreement. If you are a U.S. government user, this Software is licensed with "restricted rights" as set forth in subparagraphs (a)-(d) of the Commercial Computer-Restricted Rights clause at FAR 52.227-19 or in subparagraphs (c)(1)(ii) of the Rights in Technical Data and Computer Software clause at DFARS 252.227-7013, and similar clauses, as applicable. Should you have any questions concerning this agreement or if you wish to contact the Company for any reason, please contact in writing: Customer Service, Pearson Education, Inc., 10 Bank Street, White Plains, NY 10606.

System Requirements

WINDOWS®	MACINTOSH®	BOTH
• Windows XP/Vista/7	• Mac OS X (10.4 & 10.5)	• 256 MB RAM minimum (512+ MB recommended)
• Intel Pentium processor 1GHz or higher	• PowerPC & Intel processor 1GHz or higher	• Monitor resolution of 1024 x 768 or higher
• Internet Explorer® 7.0 or higher OR Firefox® 2.0 or higher	• Safari® 2.0 or higher OR Firefox® 2.0 or higher	• Sound card and speakers or headphones
		• 500 MB hard disk space
		• 10X CD-ROM drive or higher
		• Adobe Flash 8 plug-in or higher
		• Internet Connection: DSL, Cable/Broadband, T1, or other high-speed connection
		• Microsoft® PowerPoint Viewer

Installation Instructions

WINDOWS®

- Insert the CD-ROM into the CD-ROM drive of your computer. On most computers, the program will begin automatically.

If the program does not begin automatically:

- Open "My Computer."
- Right-click on the CD-ROM icon.
- Click on Open.
- Double-click on the "Start" file. Leave the CD-ROM in the computer while using the program.

MACINTOSH®

- Insert the CD-ROM into the CD-ROM drive of your computer.
- Double-click on the CD-ROM icon on your desktop.
- Double click on the "Start" file. Leave the CD-ROM in the computer while using the program.

Note: The original CD-ROM must be in the CD-ROM drive when you use the program.

TECHNICAL SUPPORT

For Technical Product Support, please visit our support website at www.PearsonLongmanSupport.com. You can search our **Knowledgebase** for frequently asked questions, instantly **Chat** with an available support representative, or **Submit a Ticket/Request** for assistance.